Overripe Economy

Overripe Economy

American Capitalism and the Crisis of Democracy

Alan Nasser

First published 2018 by Pluto Press
345 Archway Road, London N6 5AA

www.plutobooks.com

British Library Cataloguing in Publication Data
A catalogue record for this book is available from the British Library

ISBN   978 0 7453 3794 4   Hardback
ISBN   978 0 7453 3793 7   Paperback
ISBN   978 1 7868 0293 4   PDF eBook
ISBN   978 1 7868 0295 8   Kindle eBook
ISBN   978 1 7868 0294 1   EPUB eBook

This book is printed on paper suitable for recycling and made from fully managed
and sustained forest sources. Logging, pulping and manufacturing processes are
expected to conform to the environmental standards of the country of origin.

Typeset by Stanford DTP Services, Northampton, England

Simultaneously printed in the United Kingdom and United States of America

If I should write a book for you
That brought me fame and fortune too
That book would be
Like my heart and me
Dedicated to you

Dedicated To You
(Sammy Cahn, Saul Chaplin and Hy Zarat), ASCAP

for

Julia Ann and Lydia WanGui

sine quibus non

Contents

Acknowledgements

Without the substantial sacrifices my parents, George Nasser and Freda Monsour Nasser, took on, I would not have had the first-rate education – which, in the U.S., only money can buy – that provided me with the training and resources, both political-economic and philosophical, to write this book. My gratitude to George and Freda is boundless.

One's intellectual development typically features key transition periods. Extensive interchange with John Beversluis, Julia Garnett, Hugh Lacey, Richard Nasser, Lydia Nasser and Charles Nisbet were instrumental over the course of these evolutions. During my 31 years on the Faculty of The Evergreen State College, my teaching colleagues and friends Jeanne Hahn, Peta Henderson, Charles Nisbet and Tom Rainey contributed to a substantial broadening and deepening of my social-scientific understandings. My former students and dear friends Adam Hilton, Thomas Herndon, Genevieve LeBaron, James Parisot and Ellis Scharfenaker have been sources of encouragement, affection and intellectual stimulation and challenge. They have become what every teacher wants of his finest students, their teacher's teacher.

Radhika Desai offered helpful comments on Chapters 1 through 5, and Julia Garnett provided detailed suggestions on the organization of Chapters 6 and 7.

I almost certainly would not have begun this project had my daughter Lydia not imposed a starting time for the writing I had talked about, but not begun, for years. She made me promise to begin the book "on Monday, not one day later." One doesn't break promises to one's daughter; on Monday the book was under way.

David Shulman at Pluto was the Platonic Form made flesh of every author's dream editor. He was exceptionally solicitous in the face of unmet deadlines, and his patience, encouragement and attunement to the kind of concision and clarity a book of this kind requires has substantially benefited the reader. Alethea Doran identified errors and inconsistencies and supplied reformulations that have significantly improved my telling of the story.

The political-economic cosmology that informs this book was developed over many years of teaching and writing in political economy and in philosophy. My thinking on these matters owes much to James Crotty,

Robert Heilbroner, John Maynard Keynes, James Livingston, Alasdair MacIntyre, Harry Magdoff, Karl Marx, Martin Sklar and Paul Sweezy.

The Evergreen State College provided me full access to its resources, and to the many outside sources the Library was able to obtain, without which this book could not have been written. I am especially grateful to Michiko Francis, Marla German and Mindy Muzatko at the Library for their unstinting efforts.

It is common for authors to acknowledge great intellectual debts and yet to insist that any flaws the reader encounters be attributed only to the author. But some of the responsibility for such defects as might blight this book must surely be borne in part by those to whom I am indebted …

Introduction

> We have now grown used to the idea that most ordinary or natural growth processes (the growth of organisms, or populations of organisms or, for example, of cities) is not merely limited, but self-limited, i.e. is slowed down or eventually brought to a standstill as a *consequence of the act of growth itself*. For one reason or another, but always for some reason, organisms cannot grow indefinitely, just as beyond a certain level of size or density a population defeats its own capacity for further growth.
>
> Sir Peter Medawar, *The Hope of Progress*, p.121

Eighty-eight years ago American capitalism, soon to be followed by the rest of the global system, underwent what was to date capitalism's greatest historic crisis and transformation. In September 2008 the system underwent its second crisis and transfiguration, whose origins, nature and possible futures this book aims to illuminate by means of a historical narrative beginning with the nineteenth-century period of industrialization. We live now in a world quite different from the more-or-less social-democratic settlement put into place in all the developed capitalist countries after the Second World War. The roughly 25 years following the war have been called the Great Boom or the Golden Age. This was the only period in the history of the American republic without a severe economic downturn; it provided most white Americans with the highest standard of living in world history. The current period of slow growth or stagnation in the productive economy has visited austerity on working people. The working class has been subjected to declining living standards, record and growing inequality, the disappearance of secure full-time employment, the emergence of part-time, no-benefit contingent work as the largest growing type of job, an economy addicted to debt, and a repressive and militarized State.

Austerity did not fall from the blue. The main aims of this book are twofold: to provide an account of the rise and the fall of the halcyon days and of the emergence of financialized austerity capitalism, and to identify the most desirable and feasible future alternative to what I argue would otherwise be permanent austerity and State repression. I argue that the historical dynamics discussed in this book point to two alternative futures for American capitalism: either ongoing repressive austerity for working people, or a society constituted by a shift from private to public investment, a much-shortened work week, and a vast increase in household income, enabled in large part, as was the case during the Second New Deal, by large-scale government employment. (The "New Deal" refers to Franklin Roosevelt's policies during the Great Depression creating government-funded programs to generate employment. This was a radical moment, since U.S. economic philosophy held that only the private sector should allocate resources and distribute income, by means of impersonal and allegedly apolitical market forces.) This alternative is not merely a "better idea." I contend that the present historical conjuncture, properly diagnosed, points to its own prescription: a democratic socialist polity as successor to a capitalism that has, like living organisms, exhausted its potential for non-predatory growth. Capitalism's life can be prolonged only at the expense of democracy and of material and psychological security. Thus, the course of capitalist development itself points to the feasibility and desirability of democratic socialism.

THE INEFFECTIVE RESPONSE TO THE CURRENT CRISIS

Mainstream economists have put forward putative remedies for the current stagnation-cum-austerity. None of them has worked. Barack Obama initiated an anemic fiscal stimulus, and the Federal Reserve Bank implemented a program of "quantitative easing" (QE). Because neoliberal elites had long repudiated the legacies of the New Deal and the Great Society (ND/GS), monetary policy, enormous injections of cheap money, has become the elixir of elite choice. (The "Great Society" was the last of the New Deal programs, introduced by President Lyndon Johnson, allegedly intended to address the elimination of poverty in the United States.) But despite massive purchases of financial assets and the lowering of interest rates to zero and even below, there has been no revival in the real economy. QE, however, spurred a stock-market boom which has helped make the very richest richer than ever. Nor has monetary policy significantly reduced financial speculation. What economically insecure households need is not more debt, an implicit aim of current policy, but secure employment, higher incomes and more expansive public services.

THE ORIGIN OF THIS BOOK

This book is a development and a correction of a 1976 article of mine anticipating some of the key features of the emerging Age of Austerity, entitled

"The Twilight of Capitalism: Contours of the Emerging Epoch" (Nasser, 1976). The article described the repeated business complaints in the 1960s and 1970s that labor had gained too much power relative to capital, and that working people must learn to do with considerably less than they enjoyed during the Golden Age. The article discussed the imminent end of rising wages, the coming of slower growth than we had witnessed since the end of the war, and the apparent addiction both of the economy as a whole and of households to rising levels of debt relative to income. So far so good. But the title of the article implied that a severe crisis would spell the end of capitalism. That was a non sequitur from such truth as the article contained. No economic crisis, however severe, could spell "the end of capitalism." Only a politically educated working class, actively organized, could bring about a transition to a post-capitalist future. Without working-class rad-icalization, sustained economic debilitation will be accompanied by a settlement which is in evidence as I write: anti-democratic movements and a political economy resembling, but not yet equivalent to, that of fascism. Capitalism, in the absence of effective resistance, might go on forever; *democratic* capitalism cannot. If democracy is indispensable, capitalism must be dispensable.

My major aim is to provide a historical narrative that both describes the origin and course of the present ongoing crisis and points to the limited alternatives history puts before us. Mature (in a sense to be sketched on pages 7 and 8 and further elaborated over the course of this book) industrial capitalism morphs into neoliberal financialized capitalism, whose features place the alternatives of socialism or barbarism on the historical agenda. If effective popular resistance fails to materialize, we face a future of secular stagnation whose character is already in evidence: bubble-driven slow growth punctuated by recurrent crises, great and growing inequality, high levels of under- and unemployment, persistent austerity for the working majority and a resulting state of social dislocation eliciting from the elite a repressive, police-state response. If organized resistance does take shape, it must call for a reorganization of the political economy along the lines described by Marx and by Keynes in *Economic Possibilities For Our Grandchildren* (Keynes, 1972: 321–32). Keynes failed to see that his radical proposal was incompatible with capitalist political and economic social relations. Thoroughgoing democracy, political *and* economic, not capitalism, is what a well-served working class needs.

CAPITALISM'S TWO HISTORICAL SIGNATURE INCARNATIONS: FREE-MARKET AND SOCIAL DEMOCRATIC

Capitalism everywhere has, at any given stage of development, featured either a more-or-less laissez-faire economy, with virtually no union power, a politically and economically weak working class with stagnant or declining wages, and virtually non-existent or declining government social spending (from the beginning to 1932, and from 1975 to the present), or a more-or-less social-democratic, "welfare state" economy, with relatively strong organized labor, rising wages and sufficient government spending to supplement the private wage such that a decent standard of living was possible for most white Americans (1949–73). I say "possible" because the private wage rising in step with productivity gains combined with government support was insufficient to maintain the touted American middle-class standard of living during its only apparent manifestations, the 1920s and the "Golden Age" of 1949–73. Required in addition were substantial infusions of unsustainable debt in order to bring about the appearance of "middle-class prosperity" in both periods. The chronic insufficiency of U.S. wages, under both laissez-faire and welfare-state economies, to provide U.S. workers with acceptable living standards and full employment, and the consequent addiction of the economy to household, corporate and government debt, is central to the argument that follows.

So-called prosperity periods have characterized a very small fraction of American history, namely the "roaring twenties" of 1922–29 and the postwar ND/GS period of 1949–73, a total of 33 years. The first of these periods came to an ignominious end because of both a structural economic configuration making for a powerful tendency to breakdown and the weakness of unorganized labor (see Chapter 3). The second period, the Golden Age, came to an end because of structural instabilities in oligopoly capitalism and, of equal importance, because of the profit-threatening militancy of the working class during these years. *The New Deal/Great Society years from 1934 to 1973, a time, as we shall see, of extraordinary labor militancy, was the only period in U.S. history to feature downward redistribution of income from the richest one percent to the rest, due in large part to these massive labor actions.* Elites were of course well aware that the continuation of this trend could result in the growth of working-class economic and political power, an outcome incompatible with capitalist hegemony and thus with capitalism itself. They called for an economic arrangement more in accord with the laissez-faire configuration of the 1920s, what came to be

4

known as neoliberalism. The lesson is clear: working-class security enables workers' militancy and transfers income and economic and political power from capitalists to workers. American business responded to this threat with a capitalist "counter-revolution" culminating in what former IMF Chief Economist Simon Johnson has described as a "quiet coup" of finance capital aimed at gaining control of the State. I elaborate on this in Chapters 6 and 7. As this book will show, the current capitalist command of the American State is the result of repeated efforts, since the early days of the republic, by the capitalist class to gain control of the State. Economic elites have long understood that the hegemony of the capitalist class is possible only if the business class has full command of the State.

THE LONG-TERM HISTORICAL ORIGINS OF
THE POST-SOCIAL-DEMOCRATIC SETTLEMENT

Thus was ushered in a stage of capitalist development characterized by finance capital's virtual privatization of the State, with its concomitant slow real-economy growth or secular stagnation, striking and growing inequality, working-class austerity and debt peonage, and recurring over-investment and/or underconsumption crises. Elites' realistic anticipation that the sustained austerity attending the demolition of the ND/GS political economy would result in large-scale social dislocation has prompted the militarization of the State, i.e. a police state prepared to effect the mass repression required to contain active social discontent, whether organized or chaotic.

The argument of this book is developed by tracing the genealogy of the emergence of financialized austerity capitalism from nineteenth-century U.S. industrialization to the present. I argue that financialized capitalism and its ideology, neoliberalism, are the outcome of structural tendencies inherent in capitalism's developmental process, working-class militancy and a series of 13 historic interventions, by one of the two defining classes of the system (or an agent, e.g. the State, acting on its behalf), in response to perceived crisis. Interventions such as the New Deal are in response to structural crises, such as the Great Depression. Other interventions, such as the 1947 Taft–Hartley Act, are responses to non-structural, agency-centered crises, in this case the massive postwar labor actions of 1946, seen by elites to have followed from New Deal policy. Each of these intercessions was initiated by the ruling class in response to widespread labor militancy. The New Deal was a great concession to white workers; Taft–Hartley was indicative of anti-New-Deal ruling-class interventions to come. The labor actions of 1930–34, Occupy, and the Bernie Sanders movement were interventions initiated largely by working people. Thus, the notion of *crisis* I employ includes, but is not confined to, structurally induced severe economic downturns, recessions or depressions. Through the series of crises and interventions we witness the interplay of structure and agency that culminated in the current regime of financialized austerity and its ideological counterpart, neoliberalism. These interventions and the crises that precipitated them are listed in the table at the end of this Introduction.

THE PERIODIZATION OF THE BOOK'S HISTORICAL GENEALOGY

The historical narrative this book tells requires, as do all histories, periodization. My own demarcations include most of what is generally considered essential for grasping the trajectory of U.S. political-economic history, plus some neglected markers indispensable both to that history and to my central arguments. Crucial to the narrative is the development of what I call "framework stimulants," i.e. technologies and inventions (the steam engine, the railroad and the automobile) and projects (the building of the military–industrial complex, suburbanization) whose linkages to a broad range of industries provide a sweep of demand on a national scope such as to sustain extended periods of economic growth. Without such far-reaching stimulants, the economy cannot sustain healthy growth rates sufficient to maintain full employment and high wages. We shall see that such stimuli required massive quantities of investment capital before the digital age. Thereafter, such innovations as emerged were IT-informed and required significantly smaller investment outlays. As the distinguished economist Robert J. Gordon has in effect argued, in a landmark study of the future of American growth, we have arrived at the era of framework-stimulant saturation (Gordon, 2016). This accounts for both the current difficulties of maintaining sustained economic growth and employment and the likelihood of a future of endless stagnation, slow, bubble-driven growth, declining living standards, greater inequality and police-state politics.

Chapter 1 deals with the years 1865–1907, the period of heavy capital accumulation, America's industrial revolution, during which the nation built up its basic industrial infrastructure; and the subsequent years up to 1920, including the long recession of 1907–14, the First World War and the explosion of labor militancy after the war. During industrialization the fastest-growing sector of the labor force was producing capital goods, the means of production. The capital-goods sector was both labor-attracting and investment-capital-attracting, and *the accumulation process was consequently investment driven*, specifically by investment in capital goods put to use mainly in the railroad, mining and steel industries. (The mass production of consumer goods was not possible when the process of installing the means of producing such goods was still under way.) During most of the period of industrialization, the introduction of improved, more efficient or productive capital goods was a costly endeavor. New equipment was more expensive than the equipment it replaced. But, as one expects under capitalism, the production of the means of production inexorably became more efficient, i.e. productive, producing more and more equipment per worker. Thereupon, the cost of producing the means of production, and therefore the cost of the means of production themselves, began to decline. As a result, between 1911 and 1920 the cost of new, more efficient capital goods had become lower than the cost of replacing existing equipment. Accordingly, the capital-goods sector began to displace both labor and (investment) capital. During the 1920s the consumer-goods sector did the same.

Thus began the secular decline of net investment, i.e. of the money outlays required to replace existing equipment with improved means of production, as the driver of economic activity. Both the capital- and consumer-goods sectors became, by the 1920s, both *capital- and labor-displacing* as the cost of producing improved means of production continued its long-term decline. At the same time, consumption came to displace investment as the primary driver of economic activity. This transition from investment to consumption as the engine of accumulation follows from *the principal criterion of economic maturity: the long-term atrophy of net investment.*

Yet both economic and political elites persisted in regarding investment as the prime mover of production and employment. I follow the historian Martin Sklar (Sklar, 1992) in designating the period characterized by both the ongoing decline of net investment and the displacement of labor, first from the production of capital goods and thereafter from the production of consumer goods, as the period of "disaccumulation." I argue that the persistence of disaccumulation and its consequences both contributes to the delegitimization of capitalism and points to the contours of a post-capitalist, genuinely democratic social order.

Industrialization also featured fratricidal competition by persistent price cutting, a recipe for corporate bankruptcy. The entire period evidenced severe recession or depression almost as frequently as economic upswings. Chapter 1 describes businessmen's successful efforts to create a State regulatory apparatus to save capitalists from themselves. This is only the first important example of a major theme of this book, that capitalists require increasing control of the State in order to maintain their economically and politically superordinate position.

Chapter 2 surveys the salient features of capital–labor relations and attempts by workers to enhance their power through unions during the period from the beginning of industrialization through the first two decades of the twentieth century. Because every major enhancement and protection of workers' interests has historically been the result of strikes, this chapter looks at the ceaselessness of labor's militancy during this period and the persistent violence visited upon workers in return, by both private and government forces, frequently working in collaboration. Capital–labor relations have been far more violent in the United States than in any other developed country. With both organized and unorganized resistance to persistent austerity bound to increase in the U.S., it behooves the subordinate classes to learn the history of the measures that capital is prepared to take to enforce austerity. The current militarization of the U.S. police should be warning enough.

Chapter 3 deals with the 1920s, the period marking the accomplishment of basic industrialization. After the steep postwar depression of 1920–22, the economy embarked upon its first sustained period of growth after industrialization, 1923–9, during which time *consumption replaced investment as the driving force of economic growth and employment*, with the production of consumer goods, especially durable goods like automobiles, ranges, refrigerators, radios and phonographs supplanting capital goods as the economy's largest category of output. In fact, from 1922 to 1926, the decade's period of fastest growth and capital accumulation, *net* investment was zero. Here we find a singular criterion of economic maturity, the secular expulsion of capital from production. Labor too was continuously displaced from manufacturing, the most rapidly growing industry, to the services. A surplus population of unemployed and underemployed formed and grew. The underlying cause of all this is evident: production and productivity soared while wages remained stagnant over the decade. National income therefore concentrated among the wealthiest. The majority of the population was on or below the poverty line and the high consumption of the "roaring twenties" was enabled only by growing and unsustainable debt. Unemployment grew markedly and inequality reached its twentieth-century then-high in 1928. Not coincidentally, the following year saw a financial crisis initiating the Great Depression of the 1930s. The similarity of this scenario to the development of post-Golden-Age neoliberalism is unmistakable. 2007 was the

8

second year of peak inequality since 1928, and it too was followed in one year by a financial crash and a real-economy steep downturn.

The 1920s were in many ways a model of an industrially mature capitalist economy. The organization of the economy during that decade set the stage for the longest depression in the history of the republic.* This provides the historically first clue as to the course economic development must take if the working majority is to be spared the depredations of austerity and its attendants, declining physical and mental health and a loss of faith in democracy, indicated principally by the tendency to authoritarian rule in response to the social dislocation accompanying long-term immiseration. With the atrophy of net investment, we must see a shift of the social surplus from private to public investment and to social and household consumption.

The most fundamental driver of economic activity is the most fundamental source of the economy's tendency to crisis. During industrialization the economy was driven by private investment, and the serial economic downturns of the period were, as is shown in Chapter 1, a manifestation of overinvestment and overproduction. Once the economy becomes industrially ripe and consumption becomes the driving force of production, the basic weakness and source of crisis becomes the paucity of household consumption demand, i.e. low wages, and an insufficiency of *public* investment. These contentions will be further discussed in subsequent chapters.

Chapter 4 addresses the Great Depression, the natural outcome of the structural and class contradictions of the 1920s, and reveals the profound fiscal conservatism of Franklin Roosevelt, a legacy he bequeathed to the postwar Democratic party. The severity of the Depression was not sufficient to motivate Roosevelt to initiate the Second New Deal. It was the massive strike actions of the mid-1930s and the fear of revolution that swayed the president. It is almost universally believed that the postwar order evidenced the triumph of the economic teachings of John Maynard Keynes. Social democracy and the "welfare state" have been construed as applied Keynesian economic theory. This chapter begins the refutation of this common and far-reaching error. The budget-balancing Roosevelt rejected Keynes's principal exhortations that higher wages and a policy of permanent public investment and employment are essential to sustained prosperity and full employment. It was therefore not political-economic

---

* The 1930s marked the longest *cyclical depression* in American history. It featured two severe downturns sandwiching the expansion of 1933–37. The downturn lasting from October 1873 to March 1879, at 65 months, was the longest-lasting *contraction*.

Keynesianism that ended the Depression but military Keynesianism in the form of the Second World War.

The chapter concludes with a discussion of the relevance of Keynesian theory to the question of secular stagnation. We shall see that Keynes anticipated the long-term atrophy of net investment in the development of mature capitalism, a key strand in the thread of the argument of this book.

An appendix to Chapter 4, Appendix B, is therefore devoted entirely to the political economy of the real Keynes. His critique of the neoclassical orthodoxy is outlined and his genuine position, disregarded by the mainstream and their textbooks, is laid out. Keynes was an "institutional socialist," far more radical than orthodoxy would have us believe. He never used the term "fiscal policy" and he famously described monetary policy in the context of severe economic crisis as tantamount to "pushing on a string." Keynes advocated an unemployment rate of no more than 1 percent, permanent and large-scale government employment during economic contractions *and* expansions, higher wages, a much-reduced work week and abundant leisure time to develop our manifold intellectual and aesthetic capacities. And he explicitly acknowledged what later political economists would call the "atrophy of net investment," i.e. the tendency for capitalist development to require ever-smaller (measured in dollars) additional investment outlays. I discuss the withering of net investment in Appendix A. The extended historical analysis of this book points to Keynes's prescriptions as essential components of the alternative to long-term austerity, if working people's interests are to be paramount.

Chapter 5 describes and explains the rise and fall of the Golden Age or Great Boom, an unprecedentedly sustained period of relative prosperity. The postwar attempts to roll back the achievements of the New Deal, the assault on labor unions and the grand mobilization of business in the mid-1970s to undo the American "welfare state" were responses to the great labor actions of the 1930s and of postwar labor militancy. The success of business and government attempts to unravel the New Deal/ Great Society settlement were facilitated by three seminal developments, namely deindustrialization, which has been accomplished in all the developed capitalist countries, financialization and the Reaganization of the Democratic Party, effected decisively by Bill Clinton and sustained by Barack Obama, which is discussed at the beginning of Chapter 6. I argue that these assaults on the working population were motivated primarily by the downward redistribution of income effected during the ND/GS settlement through sustained labor actions, especially strikes. I illustrate this in an analysis of the wage-push profit squeeze evidenced in the three longest cyclical expansions of the Golden Age.

In Chapters 6 and 7 I bring the historical and political-economic analyses of the first five chapters together in a discussion of the persistence of financial-credit bubbles and secular stagnation, the decline of net investment, the cheapening of capital goods, the long-term expulsion of labor from both the productive and service sectors accelerated by automation and robotization (made possible by the digitalization of innovation), the formation of a precariat (a sporadically employed, low-wage, no-benefits working population) and the growth, in response to elite concerns over social dislocation and disruption caused by the foregoing developments, of a police state in America. Secular stagnation, bubble-driven slow growth, declining living standards and growing inequality are shown to be, under the entrenched conditions listed above, abiding features of mature, overripe capitalism.

I show that this dire picture is in fact the default condition of industrialized capitalism. Recall that in its entire history the United States has exhibited "prosperity" for only 33 years, and this was possible only by means of spreading unsustainable debt. Any gains working people may be able to achieve for themselves will be brutally resisted, as the historical narrative shows, by the most powerful ruling class in history. What the working class must aim for, I argue, is a people's democracy, both economic and political, marked by social ownership and control of the means of production, a very comfortable living wage, a very short work week and the election of political representatives by, for example, instant runoff voting. This is, I argue, the only foreseeable alternative to increasingly depressed living standards and slow growth following from serial credit bubbles and their subsequent real-economy crises.

In the Conclusion I suggest that only organized working-class resistance with clear democratic socialist goals, and some working-class formal organization, which may or may not be a political party, can overcome ruling-class resistance to democracy and establish an egalitarian socialist democracy. I tentatively discuss the prospects and preconditions for such an outcome.

An Inventory of Historic Interventions and the Crises that Precipitated Them	
Crises	*Interventions*
Broadly 1870–1900: A quarter-century of fratricidal price competition, overproduction, overinvestment and serial bankruptcies.	The first (late nineteenth to early twentieth centuries): J.P. Morgan's pressure on industrial capital to consolidate.
Late 1880s–1906: Recurring competition, especially from industry newcomers.	The second (1899–1907): The capitalist push for government regulation of business. This was the first major attempt to enlist the State in the service of capital.
The 1929 financial crash and its real-economy fallout, including falling wages, soaring unemployment and plunging investment.	The third (1933–34): The "First New Deal."
1933–34: The impotence of the First New Deal.	The fourth: The labor actions of 1934–35.
1933–34: Business's perception that Roosevelt's social programs were turning the State into the executive committee of the working class and that Roosevelt was about to expand New Deal programs.	The fifth (1934): The plot to replace, by means of a military coup, the Roosevelt administration with a regime based on Mussolini's.
The massive labor actions of 1934, which were perceived by Roosevelt possibly to portend the large-scale radicalization of the working class.	The sixth (1935–36): The "Second New Deal."
The historic labor actions of 1946.	The seventh: The passage of the Taft–Hartley Act of 1947, with the intention of eviscerating the 1935 Wagner Act and rolling back the power of organized labor.
Roughly 1967–74: The petering out of the exceptional one-time stimulants that made possible the Golden Age, the reemergence of international competition and U.S. business's subsequent loss of both domestic and overseas market share in many manufacturing industries.	The eighth (roughly 1968 onwards): Deindustrialization.

An Inventory of Historic Interventions and the Crises that Precipitated Them

Crises	Interventions
1946 onwards: Labor activism during the Great Boom, which brought about a wage-push profit squeeze and the correlative 40-year downward redistribution of income beginning in 1935 – the only such redistribution in American history.	The ninth (1972 onwards): Business's organized counteroffensive against the New Deal and Great Society settlement.
1976 onwards: The Democratic Party's postwar New Deal/Great Society legacy perceived by the party leadership as out of synch with the emerging anti-New-Deal, anti-Great-Society neoliberal consensus.	The tenth (1996–2001): Bill Clinton's Reaganization of the Democratic party, overtly turning both establishment political parties into parties of business.
The meltdown of September 2008.	The eleventh (2008 onwards): The State bailout, i.e. recapitalization, of insolvent big banks. Homeowners who suffered under the crisis got virtually nothing. This culminated capital's efforts to gain complete control of the State.
2008 onwards: The bailout and the State's indifference to the well-being of the working population in times of hardship not seen since the Great Depression.	The twelfth (September 17, 2011): Occupy. A popular reaction to the bailout. This development led to widespread awareness of America's historic inequality.
1975 to the present day: The decline in living standards and job opportunities since the end of the Golden Age and the capitulation of the Democratic Party to neoliberal policy.	The thirteenth (2015 onwards): The Bernie Sanders movement.

I

The Nineteenth Century: Framework Stimulants, Destructive Competition and the Making of Oligopoly Capitalism

Relatively long-term sustained capitalist growth has required major innovations. The most significant of these are of a singular kind, *framework stimulants*: distinctive types of creation which *facilitate and stimulate sustained economic growth by providing an economically fecund configuration within which a broad, nationwide surge of investment, production and employment is made possible.* I adapt here Paul Baran and Paul Sweezy's notion of "epoch-making innovations" and Edward Nell's concept of "transformative innovations" (Baran and Sweezy, 1966; Nell, 1988, 2005). These promote overall economic growth in their capacity as *large-scale national projects* "which create vast investment outlets in addition to the capital which they directly absorb" (Baran and Sweezy, 1966: 219).

In this chapter I discuss the two major framework stimulants of the U.S. period of basic industrialization, the steam engine and the railroad, and the general-purpose technologies of the Second Industrial Revolution (roughly 1870–1900) whose large-scale impact on production was not as immediate as were the steam engine and the railroad, and which did not exhibit as immediately and directly some of the key contradictions of industrializing capitalism, mainly overinvestment or excess capacity, and overproduction. I give special attention to the railroad, the innovation most directly implicated in early industrialization and in fact the biggest industry in both the country and the world at the time. We shall see how the railroad is a paradigm case of the destructive tendency of capitalist competition to generate overinvestment and thereby to bring about serial business failures. Private capital by itself was unable to expunge this destabilizing feature of the system and had to call upon an extra-market agent, namely the State, to intervene in order to impose upon business a regulation that business, left to its own devices, could not successfully sustain.

THE FIRST INDUSTRIAL REVOLUTION'S FRAMEWORK STIMULANTS: THE STEAM ENGINE AND THE RAILROAD

Two framework innovations created the initial conditions for mass production and mass distribution: the steam engine first opened the door to mass production by overcoming geographical restrictions on the location of business enterprises; the railroad enabled these enterprises to distribute their output to a national market. Between them, these framework innovations removed the principal initial obstacles to American industrialization. The steam engine ended the original reliance of human societies on human and animal energy, a severe limitation to the possibilities of production and growth. Since then, reliance on inanimate forms of power has been a hallmark of capitalism. The use of water power was an important precursor of the steam engine in this respect. Water powered the nation's earliest textile mills in New England. As U.S. industrialization proceeded apace, the demand for power correspondingly increased, and the inefficiency as well as the geographical limits that the waterwheel placed on industrial location became fetters on the development of increasingly energy-intensive production. Moreover, industrialization was creating competing uses for water in the cities and towns growing up around the new factories. The demand for drinking water and sanitation underscored the restrictions on capitalist growth imposed by direct dependence on nature as the animating source of the production process (Atack and Passell, 1994: 197–201). What the dynamism of capitalist production and distribution required were increasingly efficient energy sources free from the limitations of geography.

The water turbine provided the spectacular spike in energy efficiency essential to the growth of industrializing capitalism. The limited number of sources of water power meant that the spread of industry required reliance upon steam for power (Atack, 1979). By the mid-nineteenth century, regions of the country where waterpower sites were more limited, such as the Midwest, the plains and the southeastern seaboard, were in the process of industrialization, and it was steam that made this possible. By the 1860s steam accounted for most of the total power generated in the U.S. In sum, by overcoming the site-specificity of water as a source of power, steam power created a framework within which great surges of capitalist activity on a transcontinental scale were made possible.

Framework stimulants can be "transformative" and can revolutionize not only the means of production but also entire ways of life (Nell, 1988, 2005). The steam engine facilitated the establishment of towns and cities and the location of economic activity in places where it was not hitherto possible. These processes required, in turn, major migrations and shifts in population. As local ethnic and religious populations relocated and mixed, parochiality was reduced and an embryonic national-identity consciousness began to form. Economic activity reliant on water flows for energy was constrained by the seasons and was thus unsuitable for capitalist production. By the latter half of the nineteenth century, the steam engine made *year-round work habits* possible for the first time in the U.S. A huge burst of productive potential was thus released.

The development of the national railroad network engendered political and economic crises, the responses to which brought about major reconfigurations of the economic system. Much of this chapter will illustrate precisely how the railroads both created severe crises and laid the groundwork for a transition to a more advanced stage of the development of industrially mature capitalism. (See the Introduction for a general characterization of industrial maturity.) Let us look first at the framework features of the railroad.

The railroad was the most growth-inducing application of the steam engine. In every industrializing country, the railroad has been the most powerful single initiator of sustained take-off into industrial growth. The groundwork was put in place in the U.S. between 1830 and 1860. The national market was greatly widened before mid-century by the railroads' lowering of transportation costs, facilitating the delivery of new products into new geographical areas. Towns and cities multiplied across the nation. Supplementing this enormous boost to domestic investment and consumption, the railroads hastened and cheapened the transportation of finished goods to coastal areas, encouraging further investment in export-oriented lines of production. That the predominant role of the railroad was its framework functions is reflected in the fact that before the mid-nineteenth century freight revenues, associated with the distribution of output, exceeded those from passengers (and have done so every year since then) (Atack and Passell, 1994: 429).

In response to these general growth-stimulating developments, core industries such as steel, iron, stone and lumber were launched into high gear. By the early 1880s ninety percent of the steel industry's total output was sold to the railroads. Industrialization involves the building of an infrastructure of basic and increasingly efficient capital goods. No less typical of industrial development is the proliferation of consumer goods industries. Increasingly advanced capital equipment enabled mass production of a limited but growing number of such items. Railroads provided the means of mass distribution of these goods by linking the states into a national market. The prospect of emerging mass markets gave further impetus to manufacturers to extend the mass production of consumption goods.

Thus, railroads made available for the first time to a growing transcontinental market the nation's first mass-produced basic consumer goods such as soap, baking powder, breakfast cereals, canned soups, cigarettes, cigars, matches, hats, ready-made clothes, carpets, shoes, brooms, telephones, light bulbs, electric lamps and more.

The railroad industry could not have performed its framework functions within the context of the private economy alone. Government was an indispensable enabler of railway expansion. Here we find what is merely the first historic illustration of a pattern that will be a leitmotif of this book, *the politicized nature of the accumulation process*. U.S. capitalism's developmental dynamic is periodically interrupted by crises precipitating either direct class intervention or the enlistment, by either the propertied or the working class, of state power in order to address crisis on terms beneficial to the class in question. Capital accumulation will be seen to become a progressively political process. In 1996 Robert Heilbroner and William Milberg wrote that "capitalism is today a social order at bay before forces that require containment or channeling by strong government policy" (Heilbroner and Milberg, 1996: 123).

The spread of the railroad would not have been possible without the system of federal grants which transferred 250 million square miles of public land to the railroad barons – Leland Stanford, Jay Gould and Collis P. Huntington, among others. Publicly owned land was given, free of charge (with qualification: U.S. troops were required to be transported for free, and mail was to be carried at rates fixed by Congress, not the market) to the railroad companies. In the nineteenth century the State had generally been regarded by the population as decisively dominated by business, effectively privatized. This did not appear to change until the popular movements of the 1930s, discussed in Chapter 4.

COMPETITION AND CRISIS

The story told in mainstream economic textbooks about the workings and merits of competitive capitalism is a remarkable ideological production. The market is alleged to require no human intervention because it is held to be a self-regulated system, almost instantaneously correcting outcomes that are out of accord with the desires of economic agents. The benefits of the market system must be brought about *apolitically*, without the exercise of political agency aimed at bringing about social goods. The dynamics alleged to bring about this felicitous outcome constitute the core of Microeconomics 101. On this account, sustained recession or depression are impossible. This secularization of Divine Providence was nowhere to be found in the real world of capitalist self-interested competition.

Nor does this orthodox vision accord with the period of nineteenth-century U.S. industrialization, which saw unbridled profit-seeking competition with virtually no oversight or regulation by either private individuals or the State. Leading elites and influential commentators soon came to question and finally to reject the received wisdom. The very first business elites soon recognized, as we shall see on pages 23–5, that the story of the self-regulating crisis-immune market was a fairy tale.

The development of the railroad industry illustrates vividly how the orthodox narrative misrepresents the tendencies endogenous to capitalist competition. Even the most observant capitalists and business commentators were stricken at the irrationality of single-handed cutthroat competition. They sought to bring an end to unbridled price-cutting, urged concerted collusive action in the pursuit of profit, and advocated government regulation of economic activity. What we shall see in the case of the railroads is true of every stage in the development of American capitalism, that *few class agents have in fact wanted the free market or its political counterpart, the liberal, hands-off State.*

Free-market outcomes have been continuously resisted by those under its aegis, including capitalists. Alfred E. Kahn, chairman of Jimmy Carter's Council on Wage and Price Stability, put it this way in testimony before the Joint Economic Committee, U.S. Congress, December 6, 1978: "The fact is that most people in this country don't like the way a truly competitive economy operates, and have found ways of protecting themselves against it." Developments in the railroad and steel industries illustrate the persistent tendency of economic agents to intervene in order to obviate disastrous market outcomes. From the late 1870s to the present, businessmen and workers have sought to minimize the influence of the market on the generation of profits and wages.

The late nineteenth century exhibited a prolonged crisis of competitive capitalism. When the economy returned to peacetime conditions after the Civil War (1861–65), its performance was highly troublesome through the remainder of the century. Economists have referred to the "Great Depression of 1873–1896" (Capie and Wood, 1997: 148–9; Fels, 1949: 69–73). The period featured three long contractions. The first and longest in U.S. history, from 1873 to 1879 (referred to by some economists as the "Long Depression"), lasted 65 months and surpassed the plunges of 1882–85, 1893–97 and 1929–33. In the 396 months between 1867 and 1900, the economy expanded during 199 months and was in either recession or depression during 197 months (DuBoff, 1989: 41–2). Chronic over-production and serial bankruptcies blighted the economy from 1870 to the late 1890s. How can it be that a century featuring an unprecedented growth of industrial output, urbanization, railroadization and the formation of the greatest business enterprises in the world was simultaneously a period of persistent crisis?

Prominent scholars have argued that the "dynamism" of the economy during this period belies the claim of crisis. In *The Making of Global Capitalism: The Political Economy of American Empire,* Leo Panitch and Sam Gindin make light of "misleading American business notions of surplus capital" and write, in a section headed "The Dynamic Economy," that "The huge strength and expansive dynamism of the U.S. economy was momentarily obscured by an economic crisis that began in 1893." The 1873–79 depression, the longest downturn in American history, receives no attention, and the deep and protracted depression of 1893–98 is described as a "recession," a negligible blip in a period of spectacular growth (Panitch and Gindin, 2013: 27–9). In fact, the last 30 years of the nineteenth century evidenced both unparalleled growth and deep-rooted and prolonged insta-bility. "Expansive dynamism" is compatible with overexpansion, as is an investment boom with overinvestment. We shall see that the latter lay at the heart of the century's economic turbulence. As the economic historian Richard DuBoff put it, "The paradox of the last third of the nineteenth century is that it was a Golden Age – the heyday of private enterprise if ever there was one – and yet a period of profound instability and anxiety" (DuBoff, 1989: 41).

The unprecedented growth of output, the object of Panitch and Gindin's enthusiasm, is entirely compatible with declining growth rates, profit rates and productivity – sources of deep disruption unmentioned by those writers. Capitalists are concerned not merely with increasing the absolute size of overall output but also with *selling it at remunerative prices and profit rates.* Capital was wildly successful on the former front, but encountered recurring obstacles on the latter, due to the destabilizing effects of unregulated competition. Hence the retardation of annual growth *rates* of GNP from 1870 to 1900. The downshift was evident in key indicators: the growth of per capita GNP, of GNP per worker and of labor productivity all declined over the period (Livingston, 1987: 72–3, 74). Prices too fell about 30 percent between 1873 and 1896 under the pressure of the cutthroat competition unleashed by the widening of the national market and the rapid rate of technological innovation. In many cases revenues fell faster than costs, giving further impetus to competitive price cutting. Commodity price levels trended downward from the late 1870s through the late 1890s (United States Bureau of the Census, 1975: 200–1, 208–9). The result was downward pressure on profits (DuBoff, 1989: 47; Livingston, 1987: 70). On top of all this, during the final two decades of the century a class of skilled workers successfully resisted the wage reductions that capitalists sought in order to counteract price, profit and productivity declines, and thereby secured wage levels that cut into profits (Livingston, 1987: 79–82).

At the core of nineteenth-century economic instability were two factors inherent in the process of basic industrialization. The first was unbridled competition when massive investments in fixed capital were at stake. The neoclassical theory of competition takes little or no account of the costs associated with large fixed investments. Fixed costs (or sunk costs) are those that remain constant irrespective of whether the firm is doing well. They include the repayment of borrowed capital, the cost of administrative staff and the rent of land. Unlike the payment of wages, which fall when workers are fired or laid off, the payments for fixed expenditures constitute a steady drain of companies' resources when revenues decline because competition has driven down prices, or when market share contracts. A second factor endogenous to basic industrialization is a skilled, well-paid segment of the labor force capable of driving up wages at the expense of profits.

A systematic effort would be made to eliminate both cutthroat competition and the resistance of skilled workers to wage reductions and management control of production. Over the course of the final three decades of the century, captains of industry and finance would come to recognize the first factor as a major contributor to the turbulence of the period and both factors as serious threats to their class interests. Insight would lead to action. Class interests would come to trump received laissez-faire ideology. Businessmen took unprecedented steps to eliminate fratricidal competition when huge fixed investments were at stake. No less importantly, they would come to defeat both the skilled workers' unions, whose members' high and rigid wages aggravated the consequences for capital of declining growth rates, profit rates and productivity, and the workers themselves, by mechanizing production as a means of rendering their skill and the economic power implicit in it decreasingly relevant to the process of production.

The result of this capitalist intervention would be the emergence of the dominant form of twentieth-century capitalism, variously labeled organized, regulated, monopoly or oligopoly capitalism. In the process, big business acquired the social, political and cultural cachet that made it a permanent and dominant feature of American life, and the capitalist class acquired a class consciousness which it would come to refine and adapt when faced with crises to come. These formative developments were an outgrowth of the stormy trajectory of the building of the U.S. railroad network.

RAILROADS, CRISES OF OVERINVESTMENT AND OVERPRODUCTION AND THE FORGING OF CAPITALIST CLASS CONSCIOUSNESS

The railroad was the most significant offshoot of the steam engine, with respect to both its impact on the demand for the output of other key industries such as steel and its predominant contribution to the growth of GDP during the period 1860–1900. The U.S. transcontinental link was completed as early as 1869, and by the end of the century the country had the most extensive transportation system in the world. The railroads were the fastest-growing and biggest industry not only in America but in the world. During the second half of the nineteenth century the building of the transnational U.S. railroad system absorbed more investment capital than all manufacturing industries combined and accounted for more than half of total U.S. investment (Chandler, 1965). If railroads were emblematic of the new economy, they were also representative of the kind of crisis endemic to competitive, industrializing capitalism.

The Great Depression of 1873–79 both registered the destructive tendencies of what the textbooks call "perfect competition" and ushered in the initial stage of mature corporate capitalism. A major factor precipitating the contraction was investors' realization that their railroad assets were overvalued (White, 2012). In 1876, two-fifths of all railroad bonds were in default. By 1879, 65 lines were bankrupt. Much of the stock was dumped, the market collapsed and a 65-month depression ensued, lasting from October 1873 through March 1879. Profits plunged, leading to mass layoffs, skyrocketing unemployment, a fall in wages from 20 to 40 percent and an alarmingly low level of consumer demand (DuBoff, 1989: 47, 191). Prior to the depression, giant enterprises like railroads and steel, as well as smaller-scale manufacturers of consumer goods such as cigarettes, canned soup, breakfast cereals and photographic film, had engaged in serial overinvestment frenzies in order to reap the rewards of new technologies and capture larger shares of rapidly expanding markets. The basis of these chronic instabilities was unbridled competition.

These businesses believed in the benefits of unrestricted competition, with businessmen investing and price-cutting when innovation and new markets promised a leg up. In the real world, capitalists found to their dismay that their competitors did the same, ultimately flooding the market and depressing prices. Prices were in secular decline and revenues fell faster than costs from the onset of the depression of 1873 through 1896. Capitalists soon learned two key lessons: that their larger mutual interest to prosper and survive required that competition be managed by cooperative means, and that this could not be achieved without political intervention in the form of federal government regulation.

Cutthroat competition and overinvestment in rail lines was the single most powerful deflationary force precipitating the depression of 1873–79. As Keynes famously observed, "Two pyramids, two masses for the dead, are twice as good as one; but not so two railways from London to York. ... [I]t is likely that the illusions of the boom cause particular types of capital assets to be produced in excessive abundance" (Keynes, 1964: 131). The enormity of the initial investment in equipment and infrastructure makes a multiplicity of competitors cost-inefficient. For the railroad barons, however, the owl of Minerva had not yet spread its wings, and the received ideology of perfect competition encouraged what the barons themselves would soon recognize as self-destructive business contestation.

As the nation's railroad networks spread, the proliferation of competing (in reality, redundant) routes vying for limited passengers and freight became common. The initial competitive weapon was price-cutting, and the effect of price wars was to drive prices down to a point at which fixed costs could not be covered. This was a pervasive feature of railroad expansion. The extensive losses that the roads suffered left half of them either bankrupt or in receivership by the close of the century.

The burden of fixed-capital costs weighed heavily on American capitalism from the early years of industrialization. Capitalists spoke openly about the relation between fixed costs, the hazards of price competition and the desirability of consolidation during each of the three severe cyclical contractions (October 1873 to March 1879; March 1882 to May 1885; January 1893 to June 1897) of the last three decades of the century (Vatter, 1975: 189). But it was the tumultuous history of railroad expansion which made the issue paramount in the minds of businessmen and commentators. Railroads invested heavily in fixed-capital, heavy durable goods, which, unlike other inputs such as raw materials or utilities, are not used up in a single cycle of production and may be held for many years before recouping their cost. During this time, moreover, these "sunk costs" remain the same in every cycle or year of production even if production or sales are low. By the 1880s, the cost of fixed capital had come to average two-thirds of total costs (Chandler, 1977: 134). Under cutthroat competition, sunk costs magnified the risks of capitalist production. The *Commercial and Financial Chronicle* commented that "[After a businessman] has invested his money, he will not be able to withdraw it without loss. This plant ... must be maintained in operation, even though the returns do not pay interest or fully cover maintenance charges. It then becomes a life and death struggle for him to maintain his position in the trade. He will compete all the more actively while prices are below cost" (cited in Perelman, 1996: 72). *The nineteenth-century capitalist was repeatedly forced to lower his prices to the point where he was unable to cover his sizeable fixed costs.* Since fixed costs could only be expected to rise, the magnification of gluts into more and more severe and destructive crises could not be avoided unless something was done to regulate competition.

And that something had to be done collectively. Individually, each capitalist, fearful of missing market opportunities, invested in freight cars simply to ensure that he had the capacity to move freight when demand expanded. However, individual rationalities amounted to collective irrationality when all railroads saddled themselves with empty boxcars. Total excess capacity among the duplicated lines was substantial. Since the empty cars represented costs which must be covered, e.g. creditors who must be paid, the owners were under structural pressure to reduce rates. Reduced rates would increase freight volumes for one carrier only if other carriers failed to adopt the same strategy – an unrealistic assumption in any competitive market. The results included prices being driven below costs, and revenues below payment obligations. Bankruptcy or receivership usually followed.

The theory of self-adjusting markets was incapable of handling this structural problem. Experience of it did, however, have lessons for major business figures, editors and popular historians of the time, who had become keen to the hazards of overproduction. The widely read economist David Wells wrote, in what was probably the most cited book of the period 1890–1910, that "there may be... an amount of production in excess of demand at remunerative prices; or, what is substantially the same thing, an excess of capacity for production" (cited in Livingston, 1987: 75). Arthur Hadley, president of the American Economic Association (1898–99) and of Yale University (1899–1921), argued that the structure of modern industry made this outcome inevitable. Corporate and civic leaders were forming an understanding of capitalist dynamics as endogenously generating crises of overproduction well before these ideas were put forward by Hobson and Lenin (Livingston, 1987: 560–2, 563).

Charles Conant (an American journalist, author and recognized expert on banking and finance), Arthur Hadley and Charles Francis Adams Jr. (a descendant of two presidents, a president of the Union Pacific Railroad from 1884 to 1890 and a railroad regulator) saw the economically precarious structure of the railroad industry as *paradigmatic of the economy as a whole*. These men anticipated the outline of a coherent theory of twentieth-century corporate oligopoly capitalism. Adams began with the problems of the railroad industry, and noted that, because the received economic theory obstructed their identification, "The teachings of political economy were at fault" (cited in Perelman, 2006: 82). The textbook claim that competition generates maximal outcomes for capitalists plainly contradicted the facts. Destructive competition had to be mitigated, and this could be done only by collusive combination and by administering prices upward. Hadley argued that:

> The traditions of political economy ... notwithstanding, there are functions of modern life, the number of which is also continuously increasing, which necessarily partake in their essence of the character of monopolies ... Now it is found that, whenever this characteristic exists, the effect of competition is not to regulate cost or equalize production, but under a greater or less degree of friction to bring about combination and a closer monopoly. This law is inevitable. It knows no exceptions ... in those [other] lines of industry which involve large capital, under concentrated management, the old theory of free competition is as untenable as it was in the case of railroads. (Cited in Perelman, 1996: 70, 71)

Hadley noted that the spread of manufacturing was tending to make fixed investment a growing feature of industry as a whole. These intractable problems eventually led industrialists to realize, as we shall see, that *both a coordinated go-slow policy regarding output and collusion to maintain a common price level would be necessary to circumvent the contradictions of unbridled competition. This strategy would become a permanent feature of modern oligopoly capitalism.*

The steel magnate Andrew Carnegie was slow to learn the lesson. In spite of the steel industry suffering the same destructive effects of price competition as the railroads, technological innovation raced ahead, with ill effects for both the steel magnates and some of the nation's largest banks. Carnegie was an innovator par excellence, introducing more efficient technologies with uncommon frequency. The effect was to devalue his competitors' capital, precipitating bankruptcies across the industry. The Cornell economist Jeremiah Jencks reflected on this painful history in 1900: "No sooner has the capitalist fairly adopted one improved machine, than it must be thrown away for a still later and better invention, which must be purchased at a dear cost, if the manufacturer would not see himself eclipsed by his rival" (Livingston, 1986: 30; Perelman, 1996: 63, 2006: 75). Consolidation was to be the solution.

THE FIRST INTERVENTION: CONSOLIDATION AS THE ANTIDOTE TO OVERINVESTMENT AND OVERPRODUCTION

The epidemic of bankruptcies in big steel and railroad companies threatened finance capitalists like J.P. Morgan, who repeatedly urged Carnegie to slow down his innovations and to join with his competitors in collusive agreements to allocate markets and mitigate price competition. Carnegie ignored Morgan's imprecations and persisted in what he regarded as an eminently profitable strategy. Morgan used his financial clout to persuade Carnegie to sell his interests. He was now able to effect the consolidation he had in vain urged upon Carnegie. The enormous influence of the banker Morgan on the development of industrial capital during this period reflects the predominance of finance capital over industrial capital during industrialization (Kotz, 1978: 23–40). Industrial firms had not yet matured to the point at which they could finance investment from retained earnings. *Once industrial firms gained that capacity in the 1920s, investment-led accumulation yielded to consumption-led growth and the characteristic cause of economic crisis became underconsumption* (see Chapter 3).

The firm put together by Morgan in 1901, The United States Steel Company, was the first billion-dollar company in American history. Consisting of Carnegie Steel and its eight largest competitors, it encompassed every facet of steel production from ore beds to finishing plants. Morgan repeatedly urged his industrial brothers-in-accumulation to consolidate for the sake of their collective interests. It is hardly surprising that, like labor, capital understood the necessity of class solidarity. In urging industrial capitalists to form the capitalist equivalent of labor unions, "America's most famous financier was a sworn foe of free markets" (Chernow, 2010: 54).

Morgan's efforts were unstinting but only partially successful. In the 1880s he offered lucrative incentives to the railroads, designed to induce agreement among individual capitalists, not to cut rates. But the intense individualism of capitalists doomed Morgan's efforts to failure. One firm would count on the others abiding by their commitment and would break ranks in order to reap a windfall. Once this happened, all capitalists were back in the game of destructive competition. Morgan came to realize that merger was the only effective way to ensure that collusive agreements would not be broken. Once the independent legal and business identity of some competitors was done away with, the practice of breaking promises had lost its necessary background condition.

THE ESTABLISHMENT OF OLIGOPOLY CAPITALISM

Here was the beginning of a new era. The 1890s generated the realization that effective consolidation was not possible unless enforced by an agent with the power to do away with the independence of individual competitors by bringing them under the aegis of a single firm. Morgan was the first major capitalist figure to have put this realization to work on a grand scale. "I like a little competition," he reportedly remarked, "but I like combination better" (Heilbroner and Singer, 1994: 206).
Consolidation in the face of destructive competition became a continuous process of industrial concentration and centralization, which culminated in the emergence of full-blown oligopoly capitalism at the end of the century (Chandler, 1967: 76–80, 1977: 287–344). We shall see in the next chapter that an additional reason for capitalist consolidation was, as the vice president of National City Bank put it, "to meet organization with organization," that is, to defeat organized skilled workers by organizing their employers (Chandler, 1967: 86). The shorter-term outcome of consolidation was the formation of oligopoly capitalism. Consolidation became a cross-indus-trial development, so that major industries, as we shall see on pp. 27, 30, 68–9, came to be dominated by a few giant firms controlling a substantial percentage of the industries' total market. The process was protracted, and it was not until the 1920s that it became finally solidified (see Chapter 3).

CONSOLIDATION AND CENTRALIZATION IN THE NINETEENTH CENTURY: THE ABIDING CONTRADICTIONS OF INVESTMENT-LED GROWTH AND THE PERSISTENCE OF DESTABILIZING COMPETITION

Capitalists designed a number of strategies to overcome the economic and legal obstacles to effective consolidation. The trust was the first type of consolidation designed for this purpose, and John D. Rockefeller's Standard Oil Trust, founded in 1863, was the first major form of such consolidation. Many other mergers were effected during this period. Each of these con-solidations enabled the firm to effect a go-slow output policy and set a floor under prices. The oligopolistic form of corporate organization thus enabled firms to circumvent the three principal problems that had hitherto led to the kind of severe economic contraction endemic to nineteenth-century invest-ment-driven competition: overproduction, falling prices and insufficiently effective cartels.

Rockefeller's pioneering gambit established a precedent for some of the nation's largest businesses. In the 1880s eight such trusts were formed. These were Standard Oil, American Cotton Oil, National Linseed, National Lead, Distillers Corporation, American Sugar Refining, American Cattle Trust and National Cordage Association. Each one operated nationwide and commanded hitherto-unheard-of economic power. The market share which these behemoths had captured over the course of the 1880s staggered observers. Note that *these agglomerations are associated with consump-tion goods, anticipating the relative decline of the growth of investment-goods industries and the corresponding growth of consumption-centered production.* The full flowering of this tendency would become evident in the 1920s – the subject of Chapter 3.

In parallel with the formation of trusts and the wave of mergers, the normal dynamics of *internal* corporate growth also made it possible to limit competition. By virtue of technological advantage, sheer size, expanding markets and dynamic business leadership, some firms grew faster than others and thereby gained a competitive edge. The uncommonly large size of these firms enabled them to exploit the economies of large-scale production, chief of which was to greatly lower unit costs. The late 1870s and 1880s saw many new firms oligopolizing or monopolizing their industries without the benefit of combination. Many of these companies remain household names in the U.S. to this day: American Telephone and Telegraph (1885), Campbell Soup (1881), Coca Cola (1886), Diamond Match (1881), H.J. Heinz (1880), National Cash Register (1882), Proctor and Gamble (1879), Remington (1886), Swift (1878) and Westinghouse (1884), among others. Again, *these newly emerging firms belong not to the capital-goods sector but to the sphere of consumption.*

From the 1880s to the late 1890s the American business landscape was transformed. Giant concentrations of wealth and power were now everywhere. The dynamics of competition had changed. No longer did competition function to prevent any single firm from dominating its market. Competition now functioned to bestow upon the biggest and most productive firms an ever-larger share of the market. Most of the small businesses that had been created since 1823 were no more. These changes also transformed the nature of work. The typical worker was now the employee of a giant enterprise. Wage labor, as the historian Alan Trachtenberg shows in a classic study of the Gilded Age (the late nineteenth-century period of economic boom and widespread corruption after the Civil War), was no longer the imagined nightmare of independent artisans but the typical lot of American workers (Trachtenberg, 2007: 38–48, 52–60, 62–9, 70–100). The older American conception of the individual as producer was giving way to a commercialized notion of the individual as wage-laboring consumer.

The wrenching of Americans from the moorings of traditional republican values, including the independence of the worker, his/her control of the pace of work and, most importantly, the equal division of property, was experienced as an assault, and the response of workers and farmers was correspondingly ridden with conflict. The Haymarket insurrection and the strikes at Homestead and at Pullman were only the most visible of the strikes and lockouts of the period. The popular resistance to corporatization linked disproportionate corporate wealth and power to the grand size associated with concentration. Popular pressure was sufficiently intense to impel Congress to pass the Sherman Antitrust Act of 1890, which declared that "every contract, combination in form of trust or otherwise, or conspiracy in restraint of trade … is hereby declared to be illegal" and that "every person who shall monopolize or attempt to monopolize or combine or conspire with any other person to monopolize any part of trade or commerce … shall be deemed guilty of a misdemeanor."

How was it possible that the Sherman Act could be passed, without a murmur of dissent, by a Congress whose Senate was called at the time "The Millionaires Club"? The lawmakers knew that the law's actual clout would depend upon judicial interpretation, and the American judiciary had historically ruled in accord with the interests of capital. Combination had become an entrenched practice by this time, and the judiciary recognized its centrality to industrial development. The task of the industrialists was clear, namely to find new legal devices through which to continue to combine companies in a manner consistent with the (vague) constraints of the Sherman Act.

The courts were in fact enabled to interpret the Act in such a way as to facilitate further consolidation. A firm could organize a "holding company" in order to exercise the kind of control over the companies whose stock it had come to hold. This was the functional equivalent of "trustification" under unified management. What was forbidden was collusion by independent firms. But nothing in the courts' interpretation ruled out activities of unified combinations, integrated holding companies formed by the legal union of previously separate businesses (DuBoff, 1989: 49, 79). In sum, sheer scale enabled the same market power as that enjoyed by trusts and cartels. That the Sherman Act did not proscribe oversize operations accounts for its long-term irrelevance to the unobstructed advance of oligopoly capitalism.

This ingenious maneuver encouraged the transition from concentration (when individual capitals grow such that the amount of capital under the control of each increases) to merger (when hitherto independent capitals combine, further concentrating the distribution of existing capital) as a means of centralization. Leading business figures wanted to duplicate in their own industries the design of companies like Standard Oil and American Sugar Refining. Accordingly, the 1890s witnessed the onset of one of the most extensive waves of mergers in U.S. history, lasting from 1894 to 1904 (DuBoff, 1989: 57–61). Horizontal integration represented the first major phase of the movement of owners to control an ever-larger part of the output of many major and different industries. This phase, spanning the years 1879–93, combined industries that produced the standard staples of consumption. Thanks to railroad expansion, these relatively small firms in the consumer-goods industries experienced an unprecedented increase in the demand for their products. The resulting new investment in expanded facilities tended to bring about, as we have seen, excess capacity and repeated rounds of overproduction. As prices dropped below production costs, a great many firms sought to protect themselves from insolvency by combining horizontally into larger operations. In the starch, sugar, salt, biscuit, kerosene, glucose, whiskey, leather, glove and rubber-boot industries, firms combined horizontally into larger units.

During the wave's cresting period, from 1898 to 1902, more than 2,653 large firms disappeared by absorption into new, consolidated enterprises (Nelson, 1959: 37). The steep depression of 1893–97 accelerated the explosion of large-scale enterprise. It was precipitated by a marked slowdown in railroad construction and the bankruptcy of several large firms and investment houses. The failure of the railroads devastated industries dependent on them. By the summer of 1893, 32 steel companies went bankrupt (Falkner, 1959: 145). Most of the affected firms had taken on huge fixed debts, which we saw earlier to have been a major factor in turning price wars into debt-insolvency crises. Historical memory faded under the urgency of the times, and the contradictory logic of capital con-strained businessmen to re-enact the fratricidal scenario. Another price war ensued as businessmen sought to raise revenues in order to pay off their creditors. But a depression was no time to make money, and many companies folded and looked for buyers. Larger companies with resources were able to snatch up the failing outfits at desperation prices, incorporat-ing them into big single firms. A good number of the failed companies had been on a course of rapid expansion, and most of them, in steel, petroleum, meat packing and paper, were saddled with large stocks of fixed capital (Porter, 2006: 86). Excess capacity once again loomed as a reminder of industrializing capital's chronic penchant for overinvestment (Lamoreaux, 1985: 50–86, 187–9).

Ten years of continuous merger activity transformed the structure of U.S. industry with extraordinary rapidity. In 1865 no single company dominated any market or industry. By 1904 one or two giant enterprises, typically formed by merger, produced more than half the output in 78 different industries. The size of firms grew astronomically. In 1865 no firm was worth $10 million. Not even in 1896 were there a dozen firms worth that much. But only eight years later, after the merger wave had run its course, there were 300 such firms, altogether owning $20 billion (Heilbroner and Singer, 1994: 209). This was more than 40 percent of the nation's total industrial wealth.

By 1910, many of the nation's best-known and most influential corpora-tions had been created through integration, including Standard Oil, Gulf, Texaco, U.S. Steel, Anaconda Copper, Goodyear, U.S. Rubber, General Electric and Westinghouse (both formed through one of Morgan's con-solidation schemes), Nabisco, United Fruit, Swift and Co., Armour, Du Pont, American Harvester, Singer and Eastman Kodak, among others (Porter, 2006: 86). All had predominance in their respective markets, and most dealt in consumer goods. The basic structure of twentieth-century American capitalism was thus shaped in the first decade of the century. The process of increasingly centralizing and integrating firms in the same industry exhibits in embryonic form *the conscious class intercession into the workings of the economy that the development of capitalism will reveal to be not anomalous but increasingly necessary.*

Nineteenth-century law forbade price fixing. But that was irrelevant to "price leadership," the principal means of administering prices under the new order. The big companies had developed much-improved means of cost accounting, enabling not only a reasonably accurate measure of their own present and expected costs but also a reliable estimate of their competitors' costs. Outright concerted price fixing was therefore unnecessary. The largest firm was expected to establish the going price and the other large firms would follow its lead. A standard industry price was thus set. The players' tacit agreement to maintain this price eliminated the risks of old-time price competition and greatly improved the likelihood of remunerative investment. Declining demand no longer necessarily meant price reductions.

Firms came to practice "target pricing," whereby the firm targets the rate of profit required to cover costs and meet investors' expectations, sizes up its sales prospects, and proceeds to set the appropriate price (Blair, 1974). The oligopolized economy thus came to exhibit a price structure quite different from the deflationary trend of the nineteenth century. Over the course of the twentieth century, prices were, in the argot of the business press, "downwardly sticky." The price trend was upward, even during downturns, when what declined was the rate of growth of price increases. But what is stabilizing under one macroeconomic settlement can be destabilizing in another. We shall see in Chapter 3 that price rigidity in the face of soaring production and productivity and relatively stagnant wages in the 1920s was one of the key factors laying the groundwork for the Great Depression of the 1930s.

As we have seen, the stabilization of prices and the tacit collusion enabled by industrial consolidation did not mean the end of competition altogether, nor did it guarantee the market share of even the leading firms formed by merger. Thus, while oligopolization proceeded apace, the degree of centralization was insufficient to rule out disruptive price competition. Sufficient competition from newcomers remained to render many of the giants susceptible to failure. Only about half of the large enterprises formed by combination between the late 1880s and 1906 were successful (Heilbroner and Singer, 1994: 210; Lasch, 1972: 89; DuBoff, 1989: 74). The newcomers were able to operate at lower levels of production, were burdened with less excess capacity and enjoyed greater pricing flexibility than the established behemoths. This contributed to the persistence of excess capacity among the giants and intensified the temptation of smaller firms to price-compete in an oligopolized industry structure that strongly discouraged it. The larger companies had an interest in abiding by collusive agreements for the sake of stabilizing the industry as a whole. The smaller newcomers lacked the macroeconomic consciousness generated by consolidation and were inclined to play by the old rules. Their price-cutting cost U.S. Steel one-third of the market share it had enjoyed in 1902. The practice of price leadership was not yet so firmly established as to offset the pressure on individual firms to seek advantage by any means necessary. Price wars continued until the First World War. It would take a far greater degree of oligopolization, finally established in the 1920s, to reduce the rate of failure of giant firms and to establish more firmly the price leadership of the survivors. And, most importantly, the liabilities of investment-led growth, especially the contradiction between the enormous magnitude of sunk/fixed costs and the revenue-reducing effects of price competition, had to be overcome. This contradiction was inherent in the buildup of the nation's stock of basic capital goods. It was overcome with the accomplishment of industrialization. The driving force of accumulation then shifted from investment to consumption during the "roaring twenties." Only then, with basic industrialization accomplished and the now-central consumer-goods industries accomplishing a remarkable degree of centralization, as we shall see in Chapter 3, would disruptive domestic price competition come to an end.

THE SECOND INTERVENTION: REGULATION

All the private methods of eliminating competition had failed to effect the stable market environment sought by the consolidators. When consolidation and price leadership failed to produce stability, businessmen concluded that not only did capitalism preclude *automatic* market self-regulation but it also resisted any *private* efforts to render the system sufficiently dependable to enable investors to expect profits with the desired confidence. The only alternative was *government* regulation.

The rhetoric of the business community since the New Deal has been replete with ritual denunciations of government regulation of the private economy. The bulk of these tirades are aimed at government intervention intended to protect working people from the vicissitudes of the market. However, when the interests of capital are jeopardized, business does not hesitate to seek government succor. In the period of industrialization, prominent businessmen evidenced no hesitation about government intervention to regulate and stabilize an economy otherwise insufficiently responsive to the needs of capital. In effect, these captains of industry recognized chronic recessions and depressions, with their retarding effects on the growth of output, productivity and profits, as a *political* problem demanding a political solution. Thus was born what the historian Gabriel Kolko has called "political capitalism," namely business-elite support for the "utilization of political outlets to attain conditions of stability, predictability, and security – to attain rationalization – in the economy" (Kolko, 1967: 3).

Speaking of the persistence of destructive cutthroat competition, Andrew Carnegie wrote: "it always comes back to me that Government control, and that alone, will properly solve the problem" (cited in Kolko, 1967: 173, 321). Business leaders were clear that it was *federal* government regulation they were after. State and local laws were disparate; local protection could not fend off competitors from other states. Production for a national market required the uniformity that only federal authority could produce. Between 1899 and 1907 a consensus was formed among large-corporate capitalists, trade unionists and small producers in support of legislation establishing federal regulation of reasonable restraints of trade.

A new relationship was established between the capitalist class and the State, a "capital–government accord" if you will. In an important study of the origins of railroad regulation, Gabriel Kolko pointed out that:

> When these efforts [of private business to cooperate in rate setting] failed, as they inevitably did, the railroad men turned to political solutions to [stabilize] their increasingly chaotic industry. They advocated measures designed to bring under control those railroads within their own ranks that refused to conform to voluntary compacts. ... [F]rom the beginning of the 20th century until at least the initiation of World War I, the railroad industry resorted primarily to political alternatives and gave up the abortive efforts to put its own house in order by relying on voluntary cooperation. ... Insofar as the railroad men did think about the larger theoretical implications of centralized federal regulation, they rejected ... the entire notion of laissez-faire [and] most railroad leaders increasingly relied on a Hamiltonian conception of the national government. (Kolko, 1965: 3–5)

"Regulatory capture," the domination of the regulatory agencies by executives of the firms supposed to be regulated, was built into the regulatory regime from the start, and would persist through the aftermath of the crisis of 2008, when representatives of the banking industry were the principal drafters of the Dodd–Frank regulations purportedly aimed at constraining the most dangerous speculative activities of the biggest banks. Regulation in the first decade of the twentieth century was openly welcomed by the regulated interests in nearly every case. As Upton Sinclair said in 1906 of the meat industry, which he is given credit for having tamed, "the federal inspection of meat was historically established at the packers' request. ... It is maintained and paid for by the people of the United States for the benefit of the packers" (cited in Kolko, 1967: 103, 314). As had been the case earlier in steel, small newcomers represented a competitive threat to the big packers. The imposition of uniform standards was expected by the latter to level the playing field. Representing the large Chicago packers, Thomas E. Wilson publicly announced: "We are now and have always been in favor of the extension of the inspection." (cited in Kolko, 1967: 105, 314). J. Ogden Armour, the biggest Chicago meat-packing magnate, skewered by Upton Sinclair in *The Jungle*, explained why the largest packers supported the Meat Inspection Act of 1905: "No packer can do an interstate or export business without Government inspection" (cited in Lasch, 1972: 90). It had become crystal clear to the majority of the biggest businessmen that capital accumulation required political intervention.

That the accumulation process is in need of what we shall see is increasing political direction makes it necessary, from the capitalist viewpoint, that the political process be directed by big capital. President Woodrow Wilson, who anachronistically wanted to restore competition by breaking up monopolies, wrote presciently that "If monopoly persists monopoly will always sit at the helm of government. I do not expect monopoly to restrain itself. If there are men in this country big enough to own the government of the United States, they are going to own it" (cited in Hofstadter, 1960: 231).

2

Working-Class Resistance, the State-Supported Capitalist Response, the Mechanization of Industry and the Defeat of Organized Labor

Industrialization begins by relying on skills developed by artisans over centuries. Soon, however, it appropriates these skills, incorporating them, usually in a degraded form, into machines, thereby reducing the need for workers' labor in a given line of production. Skilled artisans were thus turned into wage workers or proletarians, enhancing the productivity of labor and conferring upon management greater control of the workplace. The much-touted increase in efficiency is only part of the story. During the 1880s and 1890s, industrialists came to feel that an essential part of the solution to the problem of overproduction and the deflation of prices and profits was to reduce wages by increasing mechanization and thereby reducing workers' control at the point of production. This attack on wages, skills and workers' control over their work naturally intensified the recalcitrance workers had shown to mechanization since the 1860s. In this chapter I illustrate both the extent to which workers resisted proletarianization and its technological counterpart, mechanization, and the intense force with which both businessmen and their government minions met workers' recalcitrance to the new labor regime from the late nineteenth century through the end of the First World War.

The latter part of the nineteenth century was marked by continuing economic turbulence and political elites' unwavering hostility to labor. It is acknowledged by historians of every stripe that presidents Hayes, Garfield, Arthur, Cleveland, Harrison and McKinley "obeyed the will of the industrialists with reliable servility" (Bromwich, 2015: 56). The first two decades of the twentieth century featured the entrenchment of corporate behemoths, a seven-year recession, a world war and some of the most intense labor actions and anti-labor retaliation in American history. These precedents are worth heeding in the current period of continuing economic crisis, escalating police brutality in the U.S. and elsewhere, and increasing State disregard of constitutional rights.

THE EARLY AMERICAN SENSE OF FREEDOM AND EQUALITY

Workers' opposition to what industrialization required of them sprang from an established conception, deeply ingrained among nineteenth-century Americans, of what it was that gave dignity to their work. Long-standing conceptions of freedom and independence were key motivators of revolutionary struggle and also informed a deeply rooted American (colonial or post-colonial) aversion to wage labor (Huston, 1993: 2002). To Benjamin Trumbull, historian of the state of Connecticut and influential public spokesman, for instance, maintaining republicanism required that property be kept "as equally divided among the inhabitants as possible, and not to suffer a few persons to amass all the riches and wealth of a country" (Huston, 1993: 1079). To workers, inequality of property meant material dependence of the many on the wealthy few and the corresponding asymmetrical power relation threatening workers' highly valued autonomy that went along with independence.

Such republicanism was rooted in the Jeffersonian tradition, according to which economic independence was a necessary condition of freedom (Hardt, 2007). Wage labor fails to satisfy this condition. No one can be free if his ability to support himself depends on his finding an employer who finds it profitable to hire his labor. In this case the worker's material security will depend on the caprice of his employer. Jefferson saw this kind of dependence as a species of inequality incompatible with freedom. In his original draft of the constitution of the state of Virginia, he entered provisions bestowing 50 acres of land to those who did not already own at least that much land. Land was the principal means of production in those times, and Jefferson attempted to create conditions under which no one would have to turn over a portion of his production, the fruits of his labor, to an owner in exchange for access to the one resource to which everyone must have a ticket in order to live. (A key irony here is that Jefferson and many others took the natural subjects of these rights to be white, adult males. While Jefferson spoke against slavery, he was among the last to free his slaves when the time came. The emancipation of slaves would require a political struggle of its own.)

Jeffersonian republicanism was held by most Americans, especially during the period following independence, to be the political bulwark par excellence of a free people and to require an equitable, if not necessarily an equal, distribution of wealth. The common use of the phrase "the fruits of labor" in nineteenth-century political rhetoric was a vital conceptual bequest of the revolution and was used consistently in discussions of the distribution of property. This was a popular version of the labor theory of property, expressed tersely in 1768 by Samuel Adams: "[I]t is acknowledged to be an unalterable law in nature, that a man should have the free use and sole disposal of the fruit of his honest industry, subject to no controul [sic]." Not surprisingly, this was understood by American artisans, craftsmen and farmers to be incompatible with wage labor, whose fruits accrued to the employer. The lawyer and legislator John Dickenson, in his *Letters From a Farmer in Pennsylvania*, was explicit: "[A]s long as the *products* of our *labor*, and the *rewards* of our *care*, can properly be called *our own*, so long will it be worth one's while to be *industrious* and *frugal*" (Huston, 1993: 1082). The prevalence of this conception of "honest work" explains nineteenth-century American workers' persistent resistance to proletarianization. As business historian James Oliver Robertson puts it, "workers were gradually becoming aware that they were not in business for themselves and had interests opposed to those of their employers" (Robertson, 1985: 153).

PROLETARIANIZATION, WORKERS' RESISTANCE AND PRIVATE–PUBLIC REPRESSION

When workers found themselves with no choice but to seek an employer who found it profitable to hire them, they demanded wages sufficient to compensate for the degradation to which they ruefully submitted. From the 1870s into the twentieth century, low wages or attempts at wage cuts ignited many bitter strikes against the railroads. In 1877, railroad workers launched a general strike against wage cuts, affecting all the major Eastern lines and resulting in riots in Baltimore, Chicago and St. Louis, and violent confrontations with federal troops enlisted to protect the owners in Martinsburg, West Virginia and in Pittsburgh. In St. Louis a self-styled Committee of Public Safety "authorized" the creation of a private army with orders to "shoot to kill" strikers and their supporters (Roediger, 1985–6: 214). The Bureau of Labor Statistics determined that in the 1880s 9,668 strikes and lockouts occurred; in 1886 alone, 143 strikes and 140 lockouts involved more than 610,000 workers. In that same year the Southwest railroad strike engaged about a quarter of a million workers in the Midwest and the South. In 1892 the great strike at the Homestead Steel plant was prompted by Carnegie's attempts to cut wages to offset declining steel prices. The 1894 Pullman strike involved workers in more than half the states of the union (Dubofsky, 1996: 40; Bromwich, 2015: 56). From the period of industrialization through the first two decades of the twentieth century the nation exhibited a proliferation of strike actions in a range of industries and an increasingly organized and militant working class. Strikes became more planned and less spontaneous, indicative of the growing role of unions as wageworkers' major line of defense against employers' exactions (Dubofsky, 1996: 40).

Businessmen watched with great alarm as labor militancy persisted from the 1870s into the twentieth century. During the Progressive era (1900–16) employers were increasingly inclined to resort to both private and state violence to defeat strikes. Carnegie hired gun-slinging Pinkerton detectives to defeat strikers at Homestead. During 1910–11 U.S. Steel had workers beaten, evicted from their homes and "killed miners at the rate of one for every five days they were on strike" (Wiebe, 1995: 182). The results were not merely a victory for U.S. Steel, where unionism was ended at the Homestead plant, but for the entire industry, where the twelve-hour work day and the seven-day work week quickly became the norm. These were not isolated cases; the use of privately organized bullies was common in labor disputes during the formative years of corporate capitalism. We shall see in Chapter 4 that re-awakened labor militancy during the Great Depression was again met with private-*cum*-government violence against militant workers.

Often neglected is the full array of *government* modes of repression of striking workers increasingly in evidence from the 1870s through the Great Depression. During this period we see the bold outline of class war waged by business and by federal and local governments against organized working people. This very broad offensive took many forms, from violence to the denial of workers' democratic rights to further reductions of workers' control over their work through deskilling and mechanization. On the whole these offensives, especially intense between 1900 and 1919, were successful in disabling unions and generally weakening the economic and political power of workers.

Two historians of American politics describe the uniquely State-backed class blitz this way:

> From approximately 1873 ... until 1937 ... American labor suffered governmental repression that was probably as severe or more severe than that suffered by any labor movement by any other Western indus-

trialized democracy ... The great bulk of violence leading to deaths and injuries was initiated by business and government and the great majority of casualties in labor disputes were suffered by workers. (Goldstein, 1978: 3)

In the early twentieth century, state coercion and violence against strikers was substantially greater in the United States than in other industrial nations. (Forbath, 1991: 105)

Just as business and government had worked together to regulate business under the instigation of capital, so did federal and local government act in concert with capital to reduce the social, political and economic power of labor in this period of acute class struggle. The government assault intensified in the late nineteenth century and continued into the twentieth. Between 1886 and 1894, armed government forces participated in "the most intense (and probably the most violent) counteroffensive ever waged against any country's organized workers" (Wilentz, 1984: 15). The poor were frequently denied fundamental rights by legislatures. Under pressure from agricultural and industrial capital, North Carolina re-wrote state constitutional provisions and election laws which burdened both black and white workers with regressive taxes and often deprived them of their vote.

THE MILITARIZATION OF REPRESSION

Especially noteworthy is that private-cum-public repression of labor activism led to *military* action against labor. Corporations resorted to espionage to gather information about union activities from private detectives paid to infiltrate the unions. In Idaho, mine owners called upon the state government and the army to repress a growing union movement. In the 1894 Chicago Pullman strike, *private* power enlisted *public* sources of repression: the railroads set the schedules for the Army's deployment and withdrawal of strike-breaking troops (Cooper, 1980: 127). The Pennsylvania State Police formed cavalry who drove their horses into gatherings of unionists. In many states the National Guard, sheriff's deputies and state police functioned as an infantry enjoined by private employers physically to assault union leaders and fire into groups of strikers, leaving more than a few dead or wounded. Publicly funded military sources were armed with ordnance purchased by private corporations for use against strikers. Many of the armories in industrial cities today were constructed alongside likely strike sites, and both state police and other government-armed forces inflicted casualties among strikers and demonstrators which were officially recorded as legitimate battle casualties. In many cases, women and children were killed or wounded. When workers retaliated they were prosecuted (Dubofsky, 1996: 122). American historians would do well to describe this as the Second Civil War, this time waged by the State against the country's own workers.

When similar tactics were undertaken in 1912 at the behest of West Virginia mine owners, the governor declared a "state of war" as miners were arrested and tried by military commissions. The governor's words laid bare what had become standard practice across the nation, and unwittingly underscored the unconstitutional nature of capital's game plan in the class war. States have no constitutional power to declare a "state of war." What had become common was the imposition of *martial law*, detention and trial before a military court, the widespread suspension of civilian law in the service of class interests. These were not episodic misbehaviors. From 1877 to 1910 armed troops crushed over 500 strikes across the nation (Licht, 1995: 193). When workers at the Bethlehem Steel plant in New York struck in 1910, state police forced their way into the homes of foreigners and compelled them to work in the plant as involuntary scabs. Between 1892 and 1916 the New York National Guard were deployed to put down 19 strikes (Ray, 1995: 407). It is a measure of capitalist alarm at working-class militancy that it was only against unionized workers that government cavalry was used.

In the period under discussion, there was no Constitutional or otherwise political legitimacy permitting the State to perform paramilitary functions in response to non-revolutionary domestic discord. Under U.S. Code 12406, the president may call the National Guard to federal service if the nation is under attack from a foreign enemy, or if there is a rebellion against the authority of the U.S. government, i.e. a revolution (Legal Information Institute, no date). In the above cases, there was no threat of revolution, and it was local authority, e.g. the state governor, not the president, who called upon the National Guard to suppress strikes.

We have seen the use of company goons and private "police" agencies such as the Pinkertons employed to suppress workers' militancy. Private capital needs State support to protect both its economic and its political interests. We have reviewed private capital's inability to impose upon itself the discipline required to mitigate the tendency of unbridled competition to generate overproduction crises and serial bankruptcies. The political counterpart is reflected in private capital's inability by itself to impose upon labor the restraint and compliance needed to maintain profits. Thus we see the increasing intervention of federal and local political agents in the service of private capital's attempts to crush a growing labor movement. It appears that everything required to enable the unobstructed accumulation of capital calls for politicization, the enlisting of government participation in the project of expanding production and profits. Thus, the accumulation process cannot and in fact has not proceeded by means of purely economic dynamics alone.

MECHANIZATION, THE DE-SKILLING OF THE PROLETARIANIZED LABOR FORCE AND THE ASSAULT ON SKILLED LABOR

"It would be quite possible," wrote Karl Marx, "to write quite a history of the inventions, made since 1830, for the sole purpose of supplying capital with weapons against the revolts of the working class" (Marx, 1961: I, 436). Marx, among other historians and economists, saw Richard Roberts' invention of the self-acting mule as early as 1825 as a watershed in the history of mechanization (Rosenberg, 1969: 13). Manchester cotton manufacturers faced strikes by highly skilled and independent mule-spinners. They commissioned Roberts to develop a labor-saving device that would help rid them of the bothersome workers. The received conception of mechanization as solely a means of raising the productivity of labor misses the historic political role of the machine in reducing the power of skilled labor in the production process and over the owning class. Indeed, in nineteenth-century England it was widely held, by observers ideologically far apart, that strikes were a major inducement to technological innovation (Rosenberg, 1969: 12). The U.S. was no different. In a study of the labor-, capital- and materials-saving biases of technological change in the U.S. from 1850 to 1919, the economic historians Louis P. Cain and Donald G. Paterson showed that "[t]he biases are overwhelmingly labor-saving" (Cain and Paterson, 1986). The labor-displacing function of technological progress has continued to this day. As *The Economist* recently put it, "[P]roductivity growth has always meant cutting down on labor" (Whadcock, 2014). What the mainstream consistently overlooks is that technological progress enables the same or more output to be produced with ever-fewer workers. It takes the worker less and less time to produce the value of her wage. This creates the possibility of a significantly shorter work week with higher wages. I shall examine this issue in greater detail in Chapters 4, 5 and 7.

By the end of the nineteenth century the remaining skilled workers had become the most powerful segment of the growing proletariat and were seen by capital as a major obstacle to reducing or eliminating excess capacity and bolstering chronically threatened profit rates (Livingston, 1987: 75–87). Reducing the skill level of the labor force became a corporate priority. Technological innovation, supplemented by private and State violence, was to be the principal means.

During the culminating years of U.S. industrialization, between 1865 and 1920, mechanization transformed the skill requirements of the production process. Mental and manual labor were redistributed. A measure of manual skill was retained by the worker, while knowledge was relocated from the worker to the machine and the engineers who designed it. This did not pass without resistance. Workers fought to maintain the indivisibility of mental and manual labor by means of work rules that had grown organically out of trade and artisanal traditions and become drawn up in union contracts and enforced by strikes. But corporate and State force were to defeat the tradesmen. The separation of mind and hand was initially evident in the iron and steel industry and spread rapidly to other lines of production. Highly skilled mechanics' skills were transferred to the machine, which reduced the number of skilled workers needed and gradually turned those remaining into either Smithian detail laborers, repeatedly performing a simple low-skill task, or tenders of the machine. A machinist described the new arrangement to a Senate committee in 1883: "The machinery instead of the man is the brains" (Livingston, 1987: 79). The business historian Glenn Porter describes the historical interdependence of mechanization, the assault on skilled labor, strikes and class conflict thus:

> The spread of the division of labor and of mechanization led to ... "de-skilling," or the building of production skills into machines ... to undermine the reliance on skilled workers. In industry after industry ... mechanization brought discontent among the existing workforce, resistance by the elite skilled workers, labor unrest, and strikes ... The transformation of some skilled work into a more dehumanizing experience, with workers subjected to boring repetitive tasks, was a part of industrialization itself. The introduction of de-skilling also brought the beginnings of a long struggle over who would control shop-floor working conditions, the skilled workers or the bosses ... [T]he new technologies that propelled so many of the early big businesses ... made workers feel like insignificant cogs in giant, impersonal wheels. (Porter, 2006: 105, 106)

Workers and bosses had long been aware that the high labor costs and skilled workers' control of conditions at the point of production obstructed capital's efforts to reverse retarded growth rates and sluggish and unstable profits under circumstances of chronic overproduction. That skilled labor tended to be unionized further aggravated the "labor problem," facilitating as it did labor's recalcitrance to speedup and the accelerated pace of mechanization. It was not until the latter part of the 1890s that capital was able to initiate its defeat of craft unionism and reverse the shift in the distribution of income from profits to skilled workers' wages that had begun at the end of the depression of the 1870s and persisted until around 1894. Overproduction, declining prices, flatlined or declining productivity and rigid wages spelled a redistribution of income from profits to wages. Rendering rigid wages more (downwardly) flexible would not only contribute to protecting profits from the depressing effects of excess capacity and falling prices but also address the most challenging cost problems facing capital in the final two decades of the century. Let us look more closely at the conditions effecting the wage-push profit squeeze of the late nineteenth century. (The second profit squeeze, which took place during the Golden Age, is discussed in Chapter 6.)

THE FIRST WAGE-PUSH PROFIT SQUEEZE

Overproduction affected profits adversely by exerting downward pressure on prices. In the first stages of the history of the overproduction problem, during industrialization, firms were not yet able to adopt a collusive go-slow policy regarding output, restricting supply and keeping a floor beneath prices. Decades before administered prices had become possible, capitalists saw wage-cutting and union-busting as the only supply-side options for keeping profits up in the face of retarded revenue growth. The vice-chairman of the Chicago Conference on Trusts spelled out the logic of the problem concisely: "A large part of the friction that has existed between capital and labor, causing strikes, lockouts and riots, was the result, in part, of overproduction. The product was unloaded at a loss, the owners tried to compensate themselves by cutting the wages of their workmen" (cited in Livingston, 1987: 83). The treasurer of the Lowell Manufacturing Company was terse: "When profits disappear wages must fall" (ibid.).

It was not until the early 1880s that the resistance of labor to the intense work demands of employers took on crisis dimensions in the form of a burst of strike activity. Nineteenth-century shop-floor arrangements up to that time are difficult for us to imagine. Workers had a significant degree of control over work conditions and the pace of work. Worker control over conditions at the point of production in large industrial enterprises is unheard of in our times and seems incompatible with labor's dependence on capital as employer. But in fact deeply established tradition enforced workers' power in the nineteenth century on the shop floor – the subjugation of labor at the point of production was not accomplished by capitalists overnight. Mechanization as such does not entail total subordination of the worker to the machine. Early machines did not have the character of the assembly line. Skilled workers were able to set work rules, control the pace of production and delay the introduction of new labor-saving technologies. From the perspective of capital, workers' control of the rate of output was an obstacle to the productivity increases necessary to offset the constant downward pressure on profit rates caused by excessive competition and newcomers to the industry. The success of skilled workers' strikes during the 1880s in consolidating their control of work conditions was facilitated by support they could count on from small proprietors, local office-holders, editors and clergymen (Livingston, 1987: 80–1). The social and market power of big business had not yet achieved the legitimacy that it was finally to attain in the 1920s. The flip side of pervasive social resentment of the trusts was a degree of sympathy for workers' resistance not seen again until the 1930s.

Perhaps the most significant consequence of skilled labor's power in the 1880s and early 1890s was its impact on the distribution of income. Two factors contributed to the increase in wages during this period. The irreplaceability of skilled laborers and their membership of strong unions enabled these workers not merely to protect but sometimes to increase their wages when sluggish or declining sales revenues would otherwise have driven them down (Livingston, 1987: 76). And the price deflation of the period had the effect of raising real wages even when the nominal wage remained constant (ibid.: 78). At the same time, productivity in manufacturing from 1884 to 1894 flatlined or barely increased even as real wages rose at a rate of five to six times faster than productivity (ibid.: 77, 78). The result was that the distribution of income shifted from capital to labor (ibid.: 85–6; Licht, 1995: 161). Charles Conant expressed the concerns of many big businessmen:

> Those laborers who continue to earn their customary wages are benefitted materially in a period of low prices, because of the greatly increased purchasing power of their earnings. An industrial enterprise which continues to operate without profit or at a loss during a depression

44

... transfers all its benefits, therefore, to the wage earners, and their wealth is enhanced at the expense of the owners of inherited or accumulated capital. (Cited in Livingston, 1986: 75)

This was a redistribution between two groups that had since 1820 already enjoyed a disproportionately large share of national income. Owners of capital and skilled craftsmen commanded a share that typically kept up with overall economic growth, while common labor's rewards lagged significantly behind (DuBoff, 1989: 24, 189). Between the mid-1880s and the mid-1890s skilled labor's growing share ate into capital's shrinking share. The driving forces behind the share shift were rigid or rising wages, worker control of the workplace and declining productivity. The next time we would see anything like this was to be the wage-push profit squeeze of the Golden Age (see Chapter 6).

The declining rate of output per unit of labor input was not due to technological retardation; between the 1870s and the 1880s capital endowment per worker doubled. Between 1884 and 1894 worker resistance to creeping mechanization led to an increase in the number of strikes sparked by struggles over control of the workplace (Livingston, 1987: 80; Edwards, 1981: 84–114). Workers' struggles to control the pace of machine production heightened in the face of intensified efforts of managers to speed up the labor process. Owners and their managers recognized this as a deliberate slowdown aimed at preserving worker control of the labor process. *The introduction of labor-saving machinery was thus not primarily motivated by considerations of technological efficiency but rather by class-power issues around control of the production process.* To be sure, machines were known to be sometimes more efficient than *unionized* workers. Frequently enough, the efficiency advantage was available only when the machine replaced organized workers. Non-union labor could be driven by employers at a pace more efficient than both machines and organized labor. This was of course a pace workers would not choose voluntarily.

The U.S. Commissioner of Labor found that cutting leather for footwear, among other manufacturing tasks, was done by hand by non-unionized workers in roughly half the time it took by machine (Livingston, 1987: 85–6). Thus, it was not labor-saving machinery in itself that enabled more efficient economies of scale. What made the higher-productivity difference was who controlled machine production. The transfer of craft knowledge to the machine was an attempt by owners to disable worker control by the development of capital equipment that would overcome union attempts to limit the use of machinery. Workers sought to restrict the use of machines in order to preserve what grounded labor's control over work conditions: the indissolubility of skill and knowledge. The defeat of the skilled workers made it possible to hire a new workforce, semi-skilled workers who would learn how to operate one machine but not how to set it up, repair and maintain it, or operate similar equipment.

What the new semi-skilled labor force lacked was generalized knowledge. This had the intended effects: to reduce workers' control of production and their bargaining power, and to remove the greatest cost-related threat to profits. At the same time, time-and-motion specialists Frederick Winslow Taylor and Frank Gilbreth were enabling owners, through their foremen, to simplify and speed up the labor process, replacing "useless" movements with more efficient ones (Braverman, 1974: 85–138; Edwards, 1979: 97–104). The result was that by 1893 three closely related developments were in place that would persist through 1919 and whose most important effects were to reduce labor costs and increase productivity: the labor-displacing mechanization of the production process, the homogenization of the workforce and the waning control of workers over production. The most immediate effect of these developments was the reversal of the shift of national income from owners to skilled labor. After 1895, real wages declined and capital's share of total income grew (Livingston, 1987: 82 ff.). Charles R. Flint, a founder of U.S. Rubber Co. and a major advocate of corporate consolidation, argued that the major advantage of industrial centralization was that it was only the "consolidated enterprise" that could provide the great amounts of capital required to supply the desired labor-de-skilling and labor-displacing machinery (Livingston, 1987: 85). Here was yet another, later, advantage of "morganization," the centralization or consolidation of a number of firms into a very large one.

One of the historical lessons learned thus far is that consolidated action is a *sine qua non* of class advantage. The experience of nineteenth-century skilled workers teaches us that struggles for control over the pace and conditions of work goes to the heart of workers' interests. Yet this is one of the issues deemed off the page in the typical union contract. A revitalized union movement would up the negotiable ante by demands for increased worker control (Wolff, 2012). Any respectable employer will resist this demand, especially in these times of loose labor markets and desperate workers, which employers know make it harder for workers to put forward demands as radical as these. But the advantage to employers of hard times can be trumped by further consolidation, this time among different unions. Swedish unions after the Second World War had all their contracts brought up for negotiation at the same time. If one union struck, they all struck. The greater the extent of organization among workers, the more the Sweden-type synchronized work stoppage comes to resemble a general strike – the most powerful of all of labor's class weapons.

THE MECHANICAL COUNTERPART OF PROLETARIANIZATION: THE ASSEMBLY LINE

The next major innovation in the organization of work under capitalism might have resulted in far greater unionization, but for the fact that the most grueling, productive and fastest-growing sector of production, manufacturing, was both the principal innovating sector and conspicuously *unorganized* when manufacturing reached its height during the 1920s. The few sectors that were left organized during this decade were craft, not industrial, sectors.

The development of de-skilling and labor-displacing machinery set the stage for the introduction of the most significant reorganization of the labor process in the history of modern capitalism. The de-skilling of the labor force, the reduction of its power at the point of production, the boosting of its productivity and the creation of a mass market for the most growth-enhancing consumer durable good, the automobile, which was to become the main driving force behind the explosion of production, profits and productivity during the 1920s, were accomplished by means of one monumental innovation, the assembly line. Developed by Ford in 1913, the assembly line should not be understood as a purely, or even predominantly, technological innovation. Embryonic continuous materials-handling systems had been tried earlier, and their physical organization was not qualitatively different from the defining features of the assembly line. In fact, Ford introduced not one single mechanical invention or discovery; the mechanisms he used were well known (Drucker, 1949: 19).

What was new was the mode of human organization required by the assembly line. The line embedded in machinery the principles of scientific management introduced by the time-motion studies of Frederick Taylor. *Standardization and simplification or atomization* were the operative concepts. In production, only one Ford model was produced, the Model T, which came in one color, black. The production of standardized parts made it economical to use machines designed to do only one simplified operation, with unprecedented efficiency. Reflecting on the history of this trend, the Hoover Committee's study *Recent Economic Changes in the*

*United States** wrote of "standardization" as a "national policy of simplification …. A basic principle in quantity production is that every element of the product shall be, as nearly as possible, exactly like every other similar element or part." In the "interchangeable system of manufacturing … the refinement of transfer of skill, as illustrated in modern tools, is astonishing" (Hoover, 1929: 89–90). The *transfer of skill from worker to machine* or, in our times, frequently to robots, will be seen in coming chapters to be *a permanent feature of capitalist development.* Along with rising productivity, *the inexorable displacement of labor from production in what we shall see is an age of secular stagnation can mean one of two things: either long-term austerity and its concomitants of widening inequality, increasing austerity and working-class debt peonage, or a much-shortened work week, a great increase in leisure time, high wages and greater provision of public services. This is the conclusion towards which the narrative of this book points.*

Single-purpose machines enabled standardization at the level of the labor process. Machine operators required limited training, with each worker assigned only a few simple operations on parts that passed before him on the line. Taylor's time-motion studies forced workers to perform their tasks as quickly as possible, with a minimum of motion. The result of this transformation of the production process was that the final assembly time for a Model T was reduced from 12.5 man-hours in 1913 to less than 2 man-hours one year later. By 1925 Ford's workers were turning out over 9,000 cars a day, one every 10 seconds (Dubofsky et al., 1978: 160). And the price of the Model T had been reduced from $850 in 1908 to below $300.

Ford's assembly line created the standard that was soon to define work and production all across the economy's most productive and technologically dynamic sector, manufacturing. Key features of assembly-line production were later to become permanent features of much of capitalist production as a whole, with later adaptations enabling the transfer (application) of some of the most important of these features to a broad range of service occupations (see Chapter 7).

The assembly line's impact on the workers was devastating. The pace of work was hugely increased. In place of foremen setting the pace of production, the assembly line itself determined how fast work was to be done. (Charlie Chaplin toured Ford's largest facility at River Rouge, Michigan, and captured the dehumanizing effect on the worker

---

* Toward the end of the 1920s President Hoover assembled an impressive array of major economists to produce a comprehensive study of every principal feature of the economy of the United States during the1920s. *Recent Economic Changes* is an indispensable source, impressively detailed, informative and relatively non-ideological.

of assembly-line work in his popular 1936 film *Modern Times*.) Worker resistance to Ford's methods was immediate. Assembly-line production only intensified a pattern of worker recalcitrance begun decades before the introduction of the system. Just about every sector of American industry was plagued by high turnover, especially by semi- and unskilled workers. Upward mobility was rare, workers had no grounds for close ties to their employers, and their relations to the despised foremen were bitter. Workers left without notice for better opportunities elsewhere or just for extended time off. Absenteeism at Ford's Highland Park plant stood at a daily rate of 10 percent of the total workforce. Quit rates were so high that Ford had to hire 52,000 workers to maintain a workforce of 13,600 (Beynon, 1973; Meyer, 1981). Adding to Ford's woes was the headway the Industrial Workers of the World (IWW) and other unions were making in his plants. Ford's costs rose significantly as he was forced to meet union demands and to hire and train new workers. Something had to be done.

In 1914 Ford announced an astonishing concession. He reduced work hours at his plants from 9 hours to 8, and increased the wage to $5 a day, double the prevailing wage rate in Detroit. We commonly read that Ford raised wages "so that his workers could afford his product." Not so. Ford raised wages in order to attract *and retain* employees (Braverman, 1974: 149–50). That Ford felt the need to double wage rates is a measure of the intensity of workers' resistance to the heightened exploitation of labor embedded in the modern factory, the prototypical form of work organization of mature capitalism. The organization of factory work is reproduced today in offices, call centers and many types of workplace outside the industrial sector.

The assembly line was only the first major instance of modern mechanization. We shall see in subsequent chapters that it is an ongoing feature of capitalist development. Mechanization has resulted in the secular expulsion of both labor *and capital* from both production and the services. The "expulsion of capital" comes about as the ongoing cheapening of capital goods that is partially constitutive of "disaccumulation," which will be further elaborated in Chapter 3 and Appendix A. The declining price of the means of production is reflected in new forms after the "digital revolution" and contributes to sustained austerity and chronic job insecurity.

THE END OF THE RAILROAD AGE, THE FIRST WORLD WAR AND THE RESURGENCE OF LABOR'S MILITANCY

By the end of the nineteenth century the industrializing economy's growth was tempered as railroad investment exhibited a marked slowdown in the

1890s and plunged sharply during the depression of 1893–97. With the conclusion in 1902 of the merger wave, overall growth picked up and railroad investment evidenced a weak revival. It was not until the bankers' panic of 1907 and its aftermath that railroad investment dropped sharply and remained permanently at post-maturity levels (Bruner and Carr, 2007). Railroads had absorbed almost half of all private investment between 1880 and 1900, and accounted for a great deal of economic activity in a host of related industries. The railroad slowdown therefore constituted a huge drag on macroeconomic performance, as we should expect from the exhaustion of a framework stimulus. As Paul Baran and Paul Sweezy put it, "the new pattern of economic geography and the new composition of national product which the railroad brought into being had become pretty well stabilized by 1907 [when] the greatest external stimulus in capitalist history lost its tremendous force" (Baran and Sweezy, 1966: 227). The result was an unusually long eight-year slump that lasted until the outbreak of the First World War.

The extended slowdown of 1907–15 was the result of two developments: the exhaustion of the stimulative powers of America's first transformative innovation, the railroad, and the excesses associated with a high level of financial innovation. By 1907, investment banks' role in financing railroad expansion had created a vast securities market that led to the emergence of a new source of investment capital, life insurance companies. With $20 billion of life insurance in force by 1900, the executives responsible for investing these funds became major stock-market speculators, spurred in large part by shriveled investment opportunities in railroads. Investors found ways to blur the line between personal and company investments, profiting at their policyholders' expense. Muckraking journalists and populist politicians publicized these scams and instigated government regulations prohibiting certain forms of life insurance and threatening further restrictions on other forms of financial activity (Clews, 1908: 799; Bruner and Carr, 2007: ix–xii, 65–70). *This was the first of three major financial crises triggered by investment capital turning to speculation in response to insufficient remunerative opportunities in the productive economy.* The second such crisis was the Great Depression; the third was the secular stagnation that began in 1975, culminating in the meltdown of September 2008.

The effect on the stock market was chilling. Share prices fell precipitously in October 1907, setting off a series of bank runs. In conjunction with the virtual cessation of net investment in railroads, a seven-year slowdown ensued. The pattern would be repeated in 1929 and 2007–08, and reveals a paradigmatic feature of advanced capitalism's tendency to crisis: the correlative problems of, first, overinvestment during the stage of industrialization, after which deficient consumption demand after 1920 led to a shift of the investable surplus from production to finance. Financial growth in conjunction with stagnation in production leads to financial crisis, with devastating blowback effects on the real or productive economy.

The First World War provided an exogenous stimulus that revived production and employment and initiated a four-year period of renewed economic growth. The war raised government deficit spending to historic levels and the demand for U.S. exports soared. With Europe's resources diverted to war production, countries that had imported goods from Europe shifted their demand to U.S. exports, including steel, copper, rubber and petroleum. Europe itself bought from America products it wasn't producing while it was fighting. The financial sector too benefited from European wartime desperation. American banks lent money to America's European allies. Much of that money returned to the United States as purchases of food, raw materials and manufactured goods. Additional export opportunities opened for U.S. producers, as Latin American markets dominated by European countries turned to American exporters. The impact of these changes on the economy was restorative. By late 1917 manufacturing output increased by 40 percent and mining by over 30 percent, while GNP was 20 percent above its 1914 level. War and government deficit spending had rescued the economy from a protracted slowdown. Sixteen years later, deficit spending and war would again prove to be effective antidotes to severe economic slowdown.

At the same time, the war had created conditions for a renewal of unprecedented labor militancy. Capital's response would figure importantly in creating a much-weakened labor force in the 1920s, a factor indispensable to understanding how that decade laid the groundwork for the Great Depression. The war presented employers with a historic problem and workers with a rare opportunity: a shortage of labor. The influx of European immigrants was sharply curtailed by the war, just as the demand for U.S. labor in factories, mines and fields was surging. Workers seized at their enhanced bargaining power by demanding higher wages, switching jobs, joining unions, forming new unions and, most conspicuously, going on strike on a grand scale (American Social History Project, 1992: 227–31). The acute labor shortage during the First World War had almost doubled the percentage of unionized workers by 1918, and the nation witnessed a major outbreak of strikes, with an almost continuous series of confrontations occurring from 1914 to 1919. Between April 1917, when Congress declared war, and October 1917, 3,000 strikes occurred, including 407 in the strategic mining industries. From 1917 through 1920 over one million workers struck annually. The nation had never before seen this proportion of the labor force on strike. That the abstraction called "the economy" was doing well, with finance capital and export industries awash in profits, was no comfort to workers, who overwhelmingly opposed U.S. entry into the war and saw war lending as diverting national income away from wages, which were at the same time declining in real terms due to a sharp rise in prices spurred by European wartime demand.

Never before had employers experienced such a threat to their interests. Every sector of the economy evidenced industrial conflict. From munitions plants to corset factories and laundries, workers walked off the job. Copper miners, longshoremen, machinists, grain harvesters, loggers, packinghouse workers and telephone operators struck vital war industries (Dubofsky, 1996: 132). Demands were bold and sympathy strikes were common. Workers demanded an eight-hour day, increased benefits, union recognition and closed-shop status. Because fired workers were hard to replace, firms with highly profitable war orders ceded to higher wage demands rather than face work stoppages.

These prolonged labor struggles were all the more impressive for having been waged against the armed resistance of private and state power. The government-girded class violence we have seen visited upon striking workers during the last three decades of the nineteenth century was redoubled in the first two decades of the twentieth. At the turn of the century, the American Federation of Labor had organized about 10 percent of the labor force. Both private and public power were deployed against the strikers. In 1914, as the nation was preparing for war, "the [New York] state police made frequent use of the mounted baton-swinging charge through strike crowds" (Ray, 1995: 417). In a 1916 strike at Westinghouse, three strikers were killed by troops. Three years later the nation experienced one of the most strike-torn years in its history.

In 1919 one-fifth of America's workers, four million, went on strike. Workers felt strengthened by the vast wartime increase in union membership, which they believed would enable them to garner a larger and fairer share of the surge in revenues the war had brought to business. The need for a better day for American workers was underscored by the erosion of real income resulting from the sharp postwar inflation (American Social History Project, 1992: 258–64). Early in the year a general strike in Seattle began with the heavily unionized city's 35,000 shipyard workers, who struck when a government panel refused wage increases above what the union had won before the war had ended. Within two weeks, 25,000 other workers struck for wage increases and in sympathy for the shipyard workers. The city's work came to an almost complete halt as 110 local unions took part in the shutdown and Seattle was largely run by a General Strike Committee, which

> set up twenty-one community kitchens to feed strikers and other residents, issued special permits to allow milk delivery for children and laundry service for hospitals, established collective butcher shops and laundries. The General Strike Committee exuberantly declared that working people were "learning to manage" the local economy. (American Social History Project, 1992: 260)

The country had never seen this kind of militancy and solidarity across such a broad range of industries. In New York, 50,000 men's clothing workers struck and won a 44-hour work week. In New England 120,000 textile workers walked off the job for a fair wage, and female telephone operators struck and won higher wages from the Post Office. 400,000 coal miners defied a federal court injunction and refused to work until they won a 14 percent wage increase. Shortly afterwards The Boston police struck when 19 police officers were suspended because the policemen's organization had chosen to affiliate with the American Federation of Labor (AFL).

Business and political leaders were especially troubled by the scope and success of the labor actions and the radical nature of some of the unions' demands and actions. Capital feared that the Bolshevik revolution and the recent growing strength of an uncommonly radical British Labour Party had set in motion historical tendencies which had spread to traditionally individualistic American workers. The United Mine Workers had demanded the withdrawal of U.S. Marines sent to the Soviet Union to topple the Reds and restore White rule. West-coast longshoremen refused to load guns being sent to the Marines and private groups bent on defeating the Bolsheviks. Business decided that the traditional terror tactics so frequently deployed in the past against workers needed again to be brought to bear on the increasingly militant workers.

The test case would be what turned out to be the most significant strike of 1919. Since its birth at the turn of the century, U.S. Steel, the largest corporation in the world, had succeeded in keeping the industry almost entirely non-unionized. Strengthened by the extraordinary wartime demand for steel and encouraged by the ongoing strike wave, the AFL began a campaign to organize the steel industry. After successful organizing drives in Chicago the union began recruiting in the industry's heartland, the Pittsburgh region. The companies were unyielding in their refusal to negotiate, and proceeded to fire countless union organizers. In September the unions struck, 30,000 workers walked off the job, and the entire industry was crippled.

THE BUSINESS COUNTERATTACK AND THE DEFEAT
OF ORGANIZED LABOR

The companies retaliated with a vengeance, initiating the most bitter class confrontation of the early twentieth century. With the cooperation of public officials, strikers and their supporters were subjected to violent retaliation. U.S. Steel deputized 25,000 persons, who arrested hundreds of strikers on fabricated charges and killed twenty. Strikers in many cities were beaten by companies' private militias and state troopers, and shot or driven from town. The elite response to these struggles is a major factor in accounting for the weakness of labor in the 1920s and in generating the great inequality, overproduction and underconsumption of that decade, the first period of U.S. economic maturity.

The companies were saddled with a major challenge, to legitimize to the public their widely publicized resort to violence. Many observers held the firms in contempt, since it had been a major news story that they had rejected the president's recommendation that they meet with the unions. The companies decided that the conflict had to be redescribed as other than a conflict with labor over issues of labor's fair share. With the support of the press and the political establishment, business represented the conflict as a patriotic corporate response to the threat of an attempted revolution (Gengarelly, 1996; Murray, 1964). During the war, concerns about "loyalty" were created in an effort to detain or deport workers perceived as radical, irrespective of their participation in labor actions. In 1917 the Phelps Dodge copper company led the industry in the Loyalty League of America, the industry's own private paramilitary organization charged with rooting out radicals, with priority given, in the words of the organization's constitution, to the "extermination" of the IWW, then organizing in metal-mining regions. The ruling class – the class in whose interests State power is predominantly exercised – was permitted to exercise powers of violence constitutionally restricted to government.

Contrary to Max Weber's dictum that the State is the only institution in modern society having a monopoly on the legitimate use of violence, private business was permitted to exercise what was in effect State power by adopting violent means to repress workers forming unions. Corporate officials frequently became officers of military associations (Weinberg, 2003: 180–4). In these struggles State militias, municipal police forces and the federal courts were marshaled against strikers. The principal rhetorical strategy in this mobilization was to label strikers as radicals bent on subverting domestic tranquility. In 1919, red-hunting Attorney General Mitchell Palmer initiated the "Palmer Raids," intended to purge the labor movement of allegedly subversive elements. Workers were arrested and beaten, and some, including the noted anarchist Emma Goldman, were deported to the Soviet Union. The largest of the raids took place in early 1920, when more than 6,000 alleged Communists were arrested, many without warrants and not permitted to contact lawyers, in 33 cities across the country.

Remarkably, this nationally coordinated anti-labor putsch was insufficient to avert increased militancy or substantially reduce the size of the organized labor force. In 1920, more than 5 million workers were union members, more than double the number of the prewar organized labor force. In spite of this, organized labor was greatly weakened during the 1920s. Unions persisted in limiting membership according to ethnicity, gender and racial criteria. These same divisions were exploited by employers in their attempts to capitalize on tensions within the working class. The emergence of the AFL as the nation's dominant union organization at the close of the nineteenth century meant that unionism in the U.S. typically meant craft unions. Thus, only those workers still commanding irreplaceable skills and employed by smaller firms, like printers and building tradesmen, still belonged to effective unions, which in fact grew in size and power through the 1920s. But the new and more rapidly growing mass production industries in manufacturing, employing workers in clear need of union representation, remained outside the orbit of unionization. As the labor historian David Montgomery noted, "by the end of the depression of 1920–2, American workers' militancy had been deflated, trade unionism largely excluded from larger corporate enterprises, and the left wing of the workers' movement isolated from effective mass influence" (Cited in Porter, 2006: 121).

In the meantime, during the first decade of the twentieth century, corporate capitalism had become established in America. The giant industrial corporation had become the dominant armature of the U.S. economy. The contradiction-laden structural dynamics of this system of production and distribution would become evident over the course of the 1920s and 1930s.

3
The 1920s: The Dynamics
of Mature Industrial Capitalism

There once was a man from Wales
Whose performance his boss mostly hails
One day he got canned
For lack of demand
His supply far outnumbered his sales

Tom Osenton, *The Death of Demand* (2004), p.xxi

By the 1920s the U.S. economy had developed its basic industrial infrastructure on the foundation of mass production without self-destructive
competition, mass consumption and giant corporations in manufacturing,
mining, banking, insurance, transportation and regulated public utilities. It
had, in other words, achieved what we call industrial maturity and, having
done so, had become the very model of a modern major capitalist economy.
Its overall organization between 1922 and 1929 exhibited every signal
feature of a mature capitalist economy, with the corresponding tendencies
to underconsumption, overinvestment and ever-increasing centralization
of capital that figure prominently in generating the kind of crisis to which
such an economic formation is structurally subject. This chapter discusses
the unfolding of these tendencies. We shall return to them in Chapter 7
in order to consider the close similarity of the post-Golden-Age period –
from 1974 to the present – to the 1920s and 1930s.

The years 1923–29 serve in this book as the model of the mechanisms
of capitalist growth under laissez-faire conditions, and will be seen to
throw light on the neoliberal period from 1974 to the present. In 1920–22
the economy suffered a short but steep slump, made the more severe for
having been postponed by the spike in government deficit spending and
the export boom of the two years following the First World War. By 1922
the economy was in recovery and 1923 was the first of four years of the
decade's most robust growth. The years 1929–40 represent the type of
crisis to which such an economy is always liable, and the kind of political

intervention that may mitigate or reverse the dire consequences of crisis. The 1930s also represent, in inchoate form, the kind of politicization and socialization of the growth process that this book argues is required in order to avert crisis.

Implicit in the maturity-to-Depression scenario is a transformation of the accumulation process: a transformation which ought to have, but did not, correspondingly transform the way we think about growth under capitalism. It has been axiomatic to both orthodox and heterodox analyses of the current crisis that private investment is the Let There Be Light of capital accumulation and overall economic growth. This book challenges that assumption. In fact, *net investment has been a declining factor in production, profit and employment since the 1920s* (Sklar, 1992; Livingston, 1994: 3–118; Vatter, 1975: 333–7; Vatter, 1982; Vatter and Walker, 1990: 6–22; Walker and Vatter, 1997: 235–54; Creamer, 1954: 5; Cochran, 1957: 25; Block, 1984: 68, 70; Gordon, 1955: 291; Murad, 1954: 242–3; Lorant, 1975: 50). *After the 1920s its place was taken by consumption.* The production of capital goods waned as the production of consumer goods waxed. As one important study of U.S. capitalism in the twentieth century put it:

Throughout the decade [the 1920s], the national economy shifted away from the production of heavy capital goods and toward the manufacture of household durables and soft consumer items. Having built its economic infrastructure and a strong foundation of heavy industry in the years between the end of the Civil War and the end of World War I, the United States economy in the 1920s inaugurated what Walt W. Rostow characterized as the "age of high mass consumption" … In the course of building a substantial base of heavy industry, the great firms … had to adjust their resources to a dominant consumer market … to produce goods and sell them to myriad millions of individual consumers rather than to a handful of familiar manufacturers who traditionally purchased a standard line of capital goods … Dupont branched out from the production of munitions to the manufacture of chemicals and synthetics … General Electric and Westinghouse added mass-produced household appliances to their basic line of industrial generators and dynamos. (Dubofsky et al., 1978: 160, 168)

Public and private consumption have now been the major drivers of capitalist growth for almost one hundred years. Yet both economic theory and policy have proceeded on the axiom that private investment remains the *fons et origo* of capitalist development. We pay a high price for this misconception.

It leads to political and economic policies that reproduce underconsumption, overaccumulation and sluggish growth at best; depression at worst. Such mature investment-driven capitalism also exacerbates inequality. I illustrate why this is so by examining the growth process of the 1920s.

There were a number of weak spots in the otherwise dynamic economy of that decade: textile production lagged and coal suffered from competition with rapidly spreading electrification. Vestiges of hazardous competition persisted through the 1920s, mostly among small family businesses. Falling prices and incomes, along with waves of bankruptcies and foreclosures, hit agriculture the hardest, because agriculture was one of the very few major industries in which concentration and centralization of capital did not proceed apace. Competition among small farmers battered them on the revenue side with falling prices and incomes resulting from chronic overproduction, and on the cost side by the need to purchase expensive machinery. The new productivity-enhancing machinery and inputs such as chemical fertilizers that became available were on the one hand expensive and on the other caused per-acre yields to skyrocket. It is a vivid illustration of the spectacular growth of agricultural productivity that, despite the withdrawal of 13 million acres of farmland from cultivation during the decade, output rose at an unprecedented rate and overproduction never abated.

But the challenge that a mature U.S. capitalism posed to American society came primarily from the most dynamic sector of the decade, manufacturing. And this challenge was far greater than that of the slow growth rates, overinvestment and serial bankruptcies characteristic of the years 1863–99. The response to those problems had brought about a new oligopolized capitalism that was creating new problems of its own. The unparalleled growth of production, productivity and profits of the 1920s only generated the old problems of underconsumption, overaccumulation, stagnation and speculative excess on a much greater scale. Let us look first at the principal drivers of growth in the second Gilded Age, 1922–29.

FRAMEWORK STIMULUS: THE AUTOMOBILE INDUSTRY

The First World War stimulated the production of weapons, ammunition, uniforms and airplanes. The momentum generated by this stimulus lasted two years after the war ended. A sharp deflationary recession set in during 1920–21, as output fell when the war ended. But the downturn ended as the capacity added during the war was put to use by a historic boom in the steadily increasing output of automobiles and other durable goods, business plant and residential housing.

As argued in Chapter 1, sustained growth on a national scale under capitalism requires the kind of large-scale national project that provides framework stimulation. We have seen how the railroads and their associated stimulants grew the entire economy and brought about broad transformations in Americans' way of life. The automobile was to perform a comparable function in the 1920s. As Robert A. Gordon put it in a classic study of U.S. economic growth through the early 1970s, "The most important stimulus to investment and to the expansion of total output in the 1920s was the automobile" (Gordon, 1974: 28).

The automobile industry accounted for a significant portion of the nation's total investment and consumption expenditures. Automobile output rose by a spectacular 255 percent from 1919 to 1929. Motor-vehicle production, including trucks, trebled during the decade (Soule, 1947: 147; Fabricant, 1940: 97, 110). By 1929, 23 million passenger cars were on the road and one in six Americans owned an automobile (Walton and Ruckoff, 1990: 456). At the end of the decade the auto industry accounted for 12.7 percent of the value of all manufacturing output, employed 7.1 percent of manufacturing wage earners and paid 8.7 percent of all industrial wages (Atack and Passell, 1994: 578). The dramatic increase in automobile production created new demand for plant and equipment across the industrial sector through backward linkages to steel, rubber, plate glass and petroleum. The production of automobiles and trucks absorbed 15 percent of steel production and 80 percent of rubber production, and stimulated the purchase of larger quantities of gasoline, rubber, plate glass, chrome, nickel and lead than any other industry (Soule, 1947: 164–5). Nor was the industry's economic impact confined to the U.S.: the auto industry drew on resources all over the world. The vast rubber plantations of the East Indies, and Henry Ford's Fordlandia, the largest rubber plantation in the world, in Brazil's Amazon rainforest, were developed largely to meet the American demand for tire rubber.

The railroad and the automobile as framework stimulants also brought about the proliferation of a range of related industries which attracted investment and, in their initial stages, created a plethora of new jobs. Hundreds of manufacturers turned out gadgets to decorate, clean and improve the performance of automobiles. Tourism began to flourish in the 1920s. Filling stations, roadside stands, billboards, motels and other businesses catering to the motoring public cropped up across the nation. The broadening of the scope of vehicular transit heightened the need for surfaced rural and municipal roads between and within towns and cities. They were supplemented by federally supported highways connecting the principal population centers. Thus was triggered the most gigantic road-building program in history: from 387,000 miles of paved road in 1921 to 662,000 in 1929. By 1929, federal, state and local governments had spent more than $2 billion, about 2 percent of GNP, twice what they had spent a decade before, on the construction and maintenance of these roads (Atack and Passell, 1994: 578). The newly available roadways further stimulated demand for both automobiles and trucks, while the public sector also expanded as bureaucracies were required to administer the licensing, ownership and registration of motor vehicles and the establishment of traffic courts.

The motor car continued the geographical and demographic transformations that had begun with the spread of the railroads. The entire auto-related complex further encouraged the growth of urban centers initially spurred by the spread of the rails. Whole cities and neighboring towns grew up around automobile production. Detroit went from a population of 285,000 in 1900 to 1.5 million in 1930. Flint, Michigan, where General Motors had numerous plants, increased in population twelvefold during the decade (American Social History Project, 1992: 278). Tourists' and vacationers' desires to visit, and sometimes to relocate to, unfamiliar parts of the nation quickened the multiplication of towns and cities from New England to southern California. The migration of population from the inner cities, which was first stimulated by the streetcar, took off and was sped up by the auto and suburbanization, which would expand even more after the Second World War. The now-familiar activity of commuting to work began in this period. The individual mobility provided by the automobile, and the popularity of the radio (with its nationally recognized celebrities), the national prominence of major sports figures like Babe Ruth, and the movie industry, functioned to undermine geographical, cultural and ethnic parochialism. A distinctively American mass consciousness was in the making.

Like the railroads, the automobile industry mobilized resources nationwide and created during the 1920s a period of growth with fewer contractions than in any decade in the nineteenth century. The relative prosperity and optimism of the decade obscured the devastating structural vulnerabilities that lurked beneath the surface, vulnerabilities that were to teach grim lessons about the sustainability of any form of non-social-democratic capitalism. (The unsustainability of capitalism combined with the Keynesian social safety net will be the subject of Chapters 6 and 7.) The specific kind of output that gave the decade its dynamism, and the relations between

production, productivity, profits and wages, explains the manner in which
the 1920s set the stage for the Great Depression to come, and exposes the
key weakness of the kind of free-market capitalism the decade epitomized.

PRODUCTION AND PRODUCTIVITY IN THE 1920S

The political-economic settlement that laid the groundwork for eventual
crisis was the unbalanced relation of the surge in productivity, profits and
production to wages. The developments which defined the 1920s as both
a paradigm of unregulated, pre-Keynesian capitalism and a stage-setter for
the Great Depression were as follows. Productivity and profits soared while
production also grew, albeit much slower, and prices and wages remained
relatively constant. The inevitable result was that income gains accrued disproportionately to profits. The result was record inequality. This brought
about – in the context of continuing investment outlays, overproduction,
excess capacity, and the saturation of key markets in consumer durables,
construction and housing – the final resort to financial speculation as the
most promising target for profits.

The outstanding economic accomplishments of the 1920s were the
extraordinary productivity increases of American industry and the mass
production and consumption of consumer durable goods (most of which
were first introduced during that decade). A crucial background condition
for the decade's historic increase in the production of consumer durable
goods was the electrification of the nation, which had begun slowly earlier
in the century but greatly accelerated during the 1920s. By 1919, 55 percent
of the power in manufacturing was provided by electricity. By 1929 this had
increased to 82 percent (American Social History Project, 1992: 577–8).
Just as the steam engine had increased the geographical mobility of capital,
electrification increased the mobility and efficiency of machinery in the
factory. In the nineteenth century, machines and material had been located
only where belts and shafts could most easily reach them. The introduction of the fractional horsepower electric motor effected an increase of
efficiency without technological innovation. The electric motor made it
possible to locate machinery just about anywhere in the factory, enabling
the reduction of both the space between stages of the production process
and the time required to produce a given quantity of output with existing
equipment. The same setup made the application of Taylorist time-motion
discipline far easier. The automobile industry, electric machine power and
the many technological innovations introduced during the decade were the

greatest contributors to the burst of production and productivity definitive of the 1920s.

I have noted that it was consumption that drove the economy of the 1920s. The durable goods most responsible for the length of the boom required homes equipped with electrical power. Households purchased ranges, radios, vacuum cleaners, toasters, washing machines, sewing machines, telephones, phonographs, furniture and fans. There was a veritable explosion in the output of these products, the likes of which were hardly imaginable a decade earlier. From the end of the 1920–22 downturn to 1929, the national income (production, output or GNP) in 1929 dollars grew by 40 percent (Arndt, 1972: 15; Wilson, 1941: 117). Manufacturing was the most dynamic element of total income and economic growth during the decade. Between 1919 and 1929, total manufacturing output grew by 64 percent (Fabricant, 1940: 61). Between 1922 and 1926, before the saturation of these markets became evident, the production of durable goods increased by 51 percent, while the production of nondurable and semidurable goods increased by only 14 percent. The combined production of agriculture, manufacturing, mining and construction increased by 34 percent from 1922 to 1929, a considerable lag behind far more impressive productivity leaps (Hoover, 1933, I: 232).

Durable goods among all consumer goods have a special significance for economic growth, profits and employment, and not merely because they are among the highest-ticket items. More than 80 percent of the increase in GNP between 1919 and 1929 was accounted for by the purchase of consumer goods (Gordon, 1974: 23–4). While durable goods were the largest component of all consumer purchases, the demand for them was the most volatile. When purchasers had need to save or reduce spending for any reason, they postponed purchases of durable goods before they reduced their consumption of food. As we shall see, in 1927 the rate of growth of consumers' expenditures declined for the first time since 1921. At that point underconsumption and excess capacity began to appear in those industries producing consumer durables.

We have discussed both the decade's remarkable expansion of production and some productivity gains not requiring technological innovation. Let us look next at the even more impressive productivity gains achieved by technological advance. Increases in output per unit of labor input were greatest in manufacturing, the most capital-intensive sector of the economy. The use of more efficient machinery enables a given number of workers to produce more output in a given amount of time. In industry as a whole, productivity increased by 43 percent from 1919 to 1929 (Radice and Hugh-Jones, 1936:

43). Over that same period, productivity per hour worked rose about 70 percent in manufacturing (Gordon, 1974: 29), and 98 percent in automobiles (Livingston, 1994: 108), at that time the greatest such increase in the nation's history (Hoover, 1929: xv). "The first effect of an increase in efficiency is to reduce unit labor costs" (Soule, 1947: 122) and to make possible, as we have seen in Chapter 1, the displacement of labor. The means of production were also made cheaper and thus net investment was lowered.

New glass machines reduced labor time 97 percent in the production of electric bulbs; the productivity of labor in lamp assembly plants was multiplied four- and fivefold in the decade. Cigar machines reduced labor between 50 and 60 percent; a warp-tying machine in textiles dispensed with 10 or 15 workers for each machine; new machines in clothing shops reduced pressing labor between 50 and 60 percent; in mixing mills of automobile tire plants labor per unit was reduced about one half by the Banbury mixer; a new method of making inner tubes increased output per man about four times. (Soule, 1947: 129; see also Jerome, 1934: 368–9)

The application in these and other industries of some of the cost-reducing methods pioneered by Henry Ford was an important element in the efficiency achievements of American industry as a whole, and, not incidentally, a major factor constituting the automobile as a transformative stimulant. The incentive for other industries to emulate as far as possible Ford's methods was obvious; productivity in Ford's plants increased by an unprecedented 98 percent during the decade. Standardization – one Model T, one toaster, one range or washing machine was just like another – became ubiquitous in just about all industries. The use of single-purpose machines made it possible to combine hitherto separate operations and required operators of only limited training.

Perhaps the most efficient of Ford's innovations which was also adaptable across industries was the assembly line, discussed in Chapter 2. No longer was it necessary to hand-carry parts between work stations. Now gravity slides, rollways and conveyor belts moved the parts in less time and with fewer workers. And, of course, the speed of the line was controlled by management. The virtual nonexistence of unions in the 1920s made this kind of superexploitation possible and of course kept wages from rising in step with productivity gains. We shall see that the failure of wages to keep up with increases in productivity is a chronic and destabilizing condition of capitalist economies organized mainly along free-market lines and without strong unions. The widening of the productivity–wage gap in the 1920s became a major structural cause of the Great Depression of the 1930s. The dramatically widening productivity–wage gap beginning in the 1974 correspondingly contributed to the debacle of September 2008.

Advances in efficiency are typically discussed in connection with the production of consumer goods. But U.S. industry has also featured from its beginnings *rising productivity in the capital-goods sector*. The significance of this feature of capital accumulation cannot be overstated. It is a crucial contributor to two developments which are among the most significant for an adequate grasp of some of the most destabilizing features of both laissez-faire and neoliberal capitalism. These are the secular stagnation which has afflicted the U.S. (and most of the other advanced capitalist countries) since the mid-1970s, widening inequality, the ongoing obsolescence of middle-skill, routine labor in post-Golden-Age capitalism (to be discussed in Chapter 7), and the secular atrophy of net investment, to be discussed later in this chapter – perhaps the major source of the persistence of secular stagnation, which this book argues will afflict the U.S. economy in the absence of major structural transformation.

The very rapid introduction of innovations during this period increased productivity in the production of capital goods and depressed costs. Productivity increases in the consumer-goods industry are typically called "labor-saving." In the capital-goods industry they are both labor- *and capital-saving*, i.e. they reduce the exchange value of the means of production. Over time, the production of capital goods requires less labor as they become more efficiently produced *and cheaper*. James Livingston describes a number of such improvements in capital goods during the 1920s. The continuous thermal cracking of crude oil replaced straight-run distillation in petroleum refining. The process

almost quadrupled the yield of gasoline per barrel of crude yet had cut refinery construction costs in half; capital inputs per unit of refined output declined accordingly, by 12.3 percent between 1910 and 1930. Similar patterns hold in other capital-intensive industries. In iron and steel ... there was no increase in the value of fixed capital or in the number of wage earners, ca. 1919–29, but output rose 40 percent because productivity per man-hour increased 63 percent for the decade. In motor vehicle and parts manufacturing ... the largest American industry of 1925, the value of fixed capital declined after 1926 ... while productivity per man-hour kept rising. (Livingston, 1994: 108; also 334, note 43 for further sources)

Mining and construction also benefited from capital- and labor-saving innovations. Mechanized loading devices reduced labor in bituminous coal mining by 25–50 percent and finishing labor on cement highways was reduced by 40–60 percent by the introduction of finishing machines. On both roads and sidewalks, mechanical pavers replaced the traditional dump-and-wheelbarrow method (Jerome, 1934: 367; Soule, 1947: 129).

THE ADVANCE OF PRODUCTIVITY AND THE ONGOING
EXPULSION OF LABOR AND CAPITAL FROM PRODUCTION:
THE ERA OF DISACCUMULATION

What this amounted to was a great reduction in the labor required to produce output of both consumer and capital goods. During industrialization, the fastest-growing and largest sector of the labor force was producing the means of production. With the accomplishment of basic industrialization, this trend ended. After 1919 the proportion of workers producing capital goods began to contract (Livingston, 2011: 189). The years 1914 to 1929 saw a net displacement of labor from the capital-goods industries to consumer-goods production and services. In all the industrialized countries, the number of workers in capital-goods industries steadily decreased over the 1920s (Corey, 1934: 291–2; Livingston, 2011: 189). Railroads, mining, manufacturing and construction "were the industrial sites on which most new jobs – that is, most of the increase in the demand for labor – had been created since the 1840s" (Livingston, 1994: 107). These same industries saw during the 1920s a net displacement of one million workers (ibid.). In manufacturing, the 1920s featured the expulsion of 300,000 workers from capital-goods production, a reduction of 10 percent. Workers producing consumer goods were reduced by 138,000, or 2 percent (ibid.: 193–216, esp. 197; 291–3). Thus, the 1920s saw the beginning of the tendency of mature industrial capitalism to expunge labor from the production of both capital and consumer goods. A comparison of the relative capital-intensity of the consumer- and capital-goods industries reveals that between 1922 and 1928 capital increased by 44 percent in the consumer-goods sector, but by only 32 percent in the capital-goods sector. Sales of consumer goods increased by 73 percent (Epstein, 1934: 182). Here is another indication of the decline of private investment as a driver of economic growth.

This marks a secular tendency. In a mature capitalist economy, capital-goods production becomes much more efficient and requires less labor, and thus makes capital goods cheaper. In this sense, mature capitalism tends to expel both labor and capital from production. Following the historian Martin Sklar, I refer to this tendency, and its implications for our understanding of investment, growth and employment under mature capitalism, as "disaccumulation" (Sklar, 1992: 153–60). Sklar states it this way:

> At the point where there is no such increased employment of labor-power in the production and operation of the means of production, that is, where the production and operation of the means of production results in expanding production of goods without the expansion of such employment of labor-power, capital accumulation has entered the process of transformation to disaccumulation. In other words, disaccumulation means that the expansion of goods-production capacity proceeds as a function of the sustained decline of required, and possible, labor-time employment in goods production … [T]he period of the passage from the accumulation phase of capitalist industrialization of goods-production, to the disaccumulation phase, coincides with the partial and progressing extrication of human labor from the immediate goods-production process. This is as true of agriculture as it is of industrial manufacturing. (Sklar, 1992: 155)

Sklar's analysis of the productivity-enhancing and labor-displacing function of the accumulation process beginning with the ripening of industrialization implicitly points to the historic function of capital to shorten the work week, i.e. *to reduce necessary labor time without compromising rising wages.* The disaccumulation of the 1920s went along with an unparalleled burst of production, productivity, consumer spending and profits. The radio, newspapers and popular magazines hailed the advent of "a new economy" and a "New Era," which many described as an historic period of "abundance" (Walton and Ruckoff, 1990: 470; Soule, 1947: 281). The contradictions simmering beneath the surface of the boom soon asserted themselves, however, in the debacle of the 1930s. The Great Boom of 1949–73 would also be followed by a comparable period of burgeoning austerity.

WAGES, PRODUCTION, PRICES AND PROFITS IN THE 1920S

The mechanics of 1920s free-market structural instability can be seen in the relation of wages, production, prices and profits to the remarkable productivity surges discussed above. George Soule pinpointed the key constellation of forces:

The first effect of an increase in efficiency is to reduce unit labor costs. The gain may be retained by the employer as a larger margin of profit. It may also be utilized either to pay higher wages or to reduce selling prices or to do both at once. Increase of wages serves to enlarge the purchasing power of the wage earners, while reduction of prices naturally augments the purchasing power of all consumers. Thus the manufacturer may, through larger volume of sales, gain more in aggregate profits than he loses by cutting his widened profit margin. If output and sales do not increase or do not increase rapidly enough, gains in productivity are likely to result in reduced employment. (Soule, 1947: 122)

In fact, as the Hoover Commission reported, "The spurt in output per worker between 1920 and 1930 was not accompanied ... by an equally rapid increase in the actual production and consumption of goods" (Hoover, 1933, I: 284). Nor did the productivity burst issue in comparably higher wages. If productivity gains are not passed along as higher wages or lower prices (or both) encouraging the purchase of greater output, then declining consumption expenditures, unemployment, growing inequality, excess capacity, retarded growth and recession or depression are likely to result. Output did not increase in step with productivity, nor did wages rise or prices fall sufficiently to circumvent the underconsumption problems with which some of Franklin Roosevelt's most influential advisors were concerned during the Great Depression. Let us look in turn at output, prices and wages.

Productivity gains in every sector of the economy exceeded increases in output. The most robust growth stretch of the decade occurred from 1923 to 1926, between the 1920–33 recession and the latter year's market saturation, which began to retard growth in manufacturing and construction. Over this boom period the capital stock did not increase at all in money value; *net investment was zero* (see pp. 6, 67, 82, 239, 240).

Ironically, the virtual elimination of cutthroat price competition, one of the major factors in the instability of the industrializing period of 1870–1900, created a price settlement that contributed to a very different species of structural instability characteristic of oligopoly capitalism. The "price level ... was remarkably stable" during the decade (Soule, 1947: 281, 285). Because of "administered pricing", stimulating sales by reducing prices was ruled out. The centralization of capital brought about by nineteenth-century mergers made price stabilization possible and necessary. The "downward stickiness" of prices in the 1920s was reinforced by another major merger movement indirectly encouraged by the Harding and Coolidge administrations' dedication to the principle that business should be free to grow without government interference. Thus was a major stimulus to consumption ruled out.

THE ONGOING CONCENTRATION AND CENTRALIZATION OF PRODUCTION AND DISTRIBUTION

Business became even more consolidated in the 1920s than in earlier decades. Secretary of Commerce Herbert Hoover allowed competing firms to form "trade associations," which would permit them to standardize tools and share technical information and, no less importantly, to administer prices more effectively. The earlier development of "political capitalism" with its price-stabilizing regulatory agencies was adapted to allow political authorities actively to promote corporate growth by further encouraging the centralization of capital. *The formation, stabilization and perpetuation of oligopoly capitalism was due as much to active political intervention as to any lawlike dynamics of capitalist growth.*

Over the course of the decade, banking, manufacturing, retailing, electronics, iron and steel, automobiles and mining all came to be controlled by large conglomerates, thereby making competitive price reductions less likely still. The chief field for mergers in the 1920s was the electric light and power industry. Finance capital was able to increase its size and power, through a surge in centralization, in the face of declining corporate dependence on external financing. Large banks either swallowed smaller ones or established branch banks that took away the former's business. Banking capital doubled, while the number of banks declined: by 1929 1 percent of all financial institutions conducted 46 percent of the nation's banking business. Retail merchandising, upon which most of the nation's growth had come to depend, passed from the domain of the small shopkeeper to that of giant corporations. Typically four to eight companies sold to 80 percent of the industry's market, and none pursued aggressive price-cutting in pursuit of market share. Centralization of capital proceeded most rapidly in chain stores, drugs and toiletries, drug manufacturers, retail chain stores, tobacco, meat packing, automobiles, coffee, toothpaste, and advertising (DuBoff, 1989: 78–81).

While the names have changed – we now find Safeway, Costco, Walgreen's, Walmart, Home Depot and, most significantly, Amazon – the system of nationally outposted giant retailers has remained in place since it congealed in the 1920s. With the emergence of financialized capitalism in a consumption-driven economy, the twenty-first century has seen two intensifications of the tendency for business to concentrate and centralize, in banking and retailing or distribution. Since the near-meltdown of 2008, the six largest banks control 67 percent of all U.S. banking assets, up from 2002, when the top ten banks controlled 55 percent of assets. In retailing, Amazon threatens to dominate the market in countless product lines: virtually anything can be purchased through Amazon. The internet has greatly accelerated the centralization of distribution.

Between 1919 and 1930, 8,000 businesses disappeared. Perhaps the most detailed study of industrial concentration in the 1920s is Berle and Means' *The Modern Corporation and Private Property*. The authors found that by 1930, the 200 largest non-financial corporations in the U.S. owned nearly half of all non-banking corporate wealth; more than 300,000 smaller companies owned the other half (Berle and Means, 1939: 29). The assets of these 200 giants increased by 85 percent during the 1920s. Since size is a major determinant of corporate growth, the behemoths were growing much faster than the smaller firms (ibid.: 33–5, 40–1). The U.S. economy has since remained oligopolized and consumption-driven.

The cost of living did fall slightly, by 10–15 percent, due in no small part to falling food prices. But price reductions across the economy were sporadic and minimal and not such as to bring about a fall in the overall price level comparable to the fall in the costs of production. We have seen that falling prices could have contributed to a proportionate distribution of the surplus between profits and wages. The Hoover Commission recognized the downward stickiness imparted to prices by oligopoly and the contribution this arrangement made to what we shall see is a fundamental affliction of mature industrial capitalism: "[T]he period since 1920 was featured by the organization of a multitude of informal price controls and trade associations ... [T]he effect of these measures of private regulation was ... to sustain some prices at excessively high levels, to encourage the abnormal expansion of productive plant equipment and hence to aggravate the existing instabilities in the system" (Hoover, 1933, I: 250). While the "price level ... was remarkably stable" during the decade, and "real wages did not rise so rapidly as increases in per capita output would have permitted" (Soule, 1947: 281, 283), profits tripled between 1920 and 1929 (Heilbroner and Milberg, 1998: 102). *A key factor in setting the stage for the Depression to come was that gains in productivity were not distributed between capital and labor such as to preclude imbalances between productive potential and purchasing power.*

If output and sales were not to be stimulated by falling prices, the remaining alternative was to raise wages. The immense power of business interests in the private and public spheres and the weakness of organized labor ruled this option out. Employers continued the use of anti-union tactics developed before the First World War – union members or organizers were harassed or fired. The judicial arm of the State contributed to employers' repression. Repeated court injunctions forbade such practices as picketing, secondary boycotts and even the feeding of strikers by unions. Only skilled workers employed by smaller firms, building tradesmen and printers belonged to effective unions, which grew in size and power even during the twenties – but they largely abandoned political militancy and fought for economic gains within the system. Their victories did not affect the working class as a whole. The number of union members fell from a high of over 5 million in 1920 to less than 3.5 million by 1929. The unions' sins of omission in effect aided the assault of capital and the state. Because American Federation of Labor (AFL) unions took no interest in organizing mass-production workers, organized labor remained excluded from most basic industries. The nation's most powerful union in 1919, the United Mine Workers of America, was by 1929 bankrupt and impotent. The paralysis of the labor movement contributed greatly to workers' inability to gain their share of productivity increases in the form of wage gains.

Money wages thus failed to increase between 1923 and 1929 (United States Bureau of the Census, 1975: 170; Soule, 1947: 127; Corey, 1934: 78). "[T]he dollars received changed little in their purchasing value throughout the period [1923–29]" (Soule, 1947: 127). *Rigid prices and wages in the face of soaring productivity guarantees a shift of national income to corporate profits.* From 1922 to 1929, dividends paid grew by slightly over 100 percent. The owners of large corporations were the greatest beneficiaries of the decade's productivity gains (Soule, 1947: 123). The failure of wages to rise and prices to fall even as profits rose at historic rates rendered the economy highly liable to the twin crises of underconsumption and overaccumulation. Slower growth, unemployment, underutilized productive capacity, uninvestable profits and gross inequality became increasingly evident after 1925.

The tendency of prices not to fall and of wages not to rise in response to productivity increases became an abiding feature of liberal and neoliberal oligopoly capitalism.

EXCESS CAPACITY, UNDERCONSUMPTION, ADVERTISING, CREDIT AND THE BIRTH OF AMERICAN CONSUMERISM

The nineteenth-century elite consensus to eliminate fratricidal price-cutting was key to putting an end to excessive capital formation. Prices were indeed stabilized by the 1920s. But this did not avert the reappearance of overpro-duction. It merely *relocated excess capacity from the production of producers' or capital goods to the production of consumer goods*. When capital formation drives the economy, overproduction takes place in the capital-goods sector. Once industrialization has been accomplished and the economy comes to be driven by consumption expenditures, excess of capital appears primarily in the consumer-goods sector. High levels of investment in the production of consumer durables, soaring productivity and profits, and relatively stagnant wages combined to create overinvestment and underconsumption. Financial publications registered alarm from the middle of the decade at accumulating idle capacity. We find frequent reference to "the superabun-dance of capital which seeks incessantly some place in which it may earn a reasonable return for its use ... [O]ur production is obviously greater than our power to absorb it" (cited in Corey, 1934: 160). A company founded in 1919 to manufacture household appliances and which had by 1923 captured one-quarter of its market reported that its "production facilities were expanded to a capacity sufficient to produce two-thirds of the annual requirements of the industry. This overcapacity is now a burden on the business ... More and more markets are being saturated by our methods of mass production, and as many of these show signs of becoming limited markets, the tendency toward declining income is broadening to include many well-known and wealthy corporations" (Corey, 1934: 161). In response, the 1920s evidenced the first-ever continuous barrage of adver-tising and salesmanship in U.S. history.

Expanding capacity combined with deficient purchasing power, lower production costs and advertising were mutually reinforcing. The former conjunction was necessary to avoid losing share of what were thought to be perpetually expanding markets, and advertising continuously sought to stimulate the desire to buy. No amount of advertising was enough. The president of the Business Bourse wrote in 1928 that "American business has gone 'salesmanship mad' in the last ten years ... A great horde of salesman is overrunning the country ... The number of commodities on the market and the number of salesmen representing them is now enormous ... And the amazing thing is that with all this enormous effort we can sell only 65 percent of the products that American factories can make" (George Frederick, 1928: 19–20). In a word, between 1922 and 1929 capital accu-mulation had far outstripped the growth of effective consumer demand (Mills, 1932: 280). The level of effective demand required by the new consumption-driven economy would not emerge from the workings of the "free market." It was the function of advertising, as the Hoover Commission put it, "to break down consumer resistance; to create consumer acceptance; to create consumer demand" (Hoover, 1933, II: 873).

Advertisements were everywhere. Promotional campaigns were conducted through newspapers, mailings and magazines; in movie theaters, barber shops and chain stores; on billboards, and, for the first time, on the radio. Cigarettes were peddled to women as "torches of freedom." But sales promotion was deemed insufficient fully to utilize the economy's vast productive potential. Supplementing the effort to stimulate purchases was the effort to instill new motivations to buy by speeding up the *rate* of purchase. A major industry publication outlined the strategy manufacturers had employed since mid-decade: "I refer to a principle which ... I name *progressive obsolescence* ... buying goods not to wear out, but to trade in or discard after a short time when new or more attractive goods or models come out ... The one salvation of American industry, which has a capacity for producing 80 percent or 100 percent more goods than are now consumed, is to foster the progressive obsolescence principle, which means buying for up-to-dateness, efficiency and style, buying for change, whim, fancy ... We must either use the fruits of our marvellous factories in this highly efficient 'power' age, or slow them down or shut them down" (Frederick, 1928: 19–20).

Here we witness the formation of a new cultural and commercial phenomenon, the making of consumption into a way of life. Consumption has always been with us; consumer*ism* was a product of the 1920s. Thrift, saving and deferred consumption were virtues appropriate to the investment-driven building of capitalism's industrial infrastructure. With industrialization accomplished, these virtues become vices. As consumption replaced new investment as the principal driver of growth and employment, consumerism became the ethos appropriate to a mature economy.

But how was the consumer-durables boom of 1922–1926 possible when wages barely rose even as production and productivity soared? The buying spree was sustained by turning saving, spending less than one earned, into its opposite – credit purchases, spending more than one earned. *Demand out of wage income alone would be insufficient to purchase what the economy was capable of turning out.* Rising standards of living could not be maintained in the face of stagnant wages without the ability of consumers to mortgage future income. The 1920s were the first instance of what was to become an abiding feature of American capitalism, the need for large-scale credit financing to sustain levels of consumption required to stave off economic retardation.

"The most spectacular and the most novel development in the field of credit was the growth after 1920 of a variety of forms of consumers' borrowing ... the amount of such credit was tremendously expanded, both absolutely and relatively, during the past decade" (Hoover, 1933, I: 256). The proportion of total retail sales financed by credit increased from 10 percent in 1910 to 15 percent in 1927 to 50 percent in 1929 (ibid.). A prime reason General Motors pulled ahead of Ford in car sales was that it enabled credit purchases through the General Motors Acceptance Corporation (GMAC). Credit was even used to buy clothes. Young single working women often went into debt to keep up with the latest styles (American Social History Project, 1992: 275). By 1929, sales on installment approached $7 billion (ibid.: 862). Many more people bought these goods than would have done so had they had to save the total price in cash before making the purchases. *Credit disguised low wages, as it would again in the period 1973–2008.* During the Golden Age, 1949–73, the ratio of household debt to disposable income steadily rose, and really took off after the mid-1970s, when the median wage began its secular decline (See Chapter 6).

In their landmark study of the industrial town Muncie, Indiana, in the years 1924–25, Robert and Helen Lynd note the pervasiveness of credit in the everyday lives of working people there: "Today Middletown lives by a credit economy that is available in some form to nearly every family in the community. The rise and spread of the dollar-down-and-not-so-much-per plan extends credit for virtually everything – homes, $200 over-stuffed living-room suites, electric washing machines, automobiles, fur coats, diamond rings – to persons of whom frequently little is known as to their intention or ability to pay" (Lynd and Lynd, 1959: 46).

A 1930 report on consumer credit sponsored by the Twentieth Century Fund linked the expansion of installment credit in the 1920s to the parallel expansion of consumer-durables industries. The study, *Financing the Consumer*, reflected the transition, central to the thesis of this book, from an economy primarily driven by capital accumulation to one whose dynamism would be henceforth driven by consumption. "The working masses of the world's population ... who streamed into factories and shops in the morning and out again at night ... have been thought of in the past primarily as *producers*. Today they are being visualized more as *consumers*: as business men or women in their own right" (cited in Livingston, 1994: 109–11). The study construed consumers as "going concerns" deserving of the "extension of reasonable credits" which in an earlier period had financed industrial development through *investment* in capital goods (ibid.: 109). "If markets are to be maintained [the "working masses"] must be able to buy more and more goods. But they can do this only if they are solvent, going concerns, with a constantly growing excess of net income from which further purchases can be made" (ibid.). This essential condition for avoiding severe economic downturns can be met only if two requirements are satisfied: the demand for consumer durables must be kept high; and current wages must be supplemented by credit, the license to spend future income. Advertising was to boost the demand for durable goods. The "growing excess of net income" would not come from rising wages but from an increasing debt burden. This line of reasoning acknowledges the need for greater purchasing power to sustain an economy that is driven by consumption, even as it rejects higher wages as the most effective means to increase consumption. We shall see below that households' credit binge was in large part due to the fact that *during the 1920s over 70 percent of working-class households earned income at or below the federally established poverty line.*

INEQUALITY AND THE FAUX "MIDDLE CLASS" OF THE 1920S

The 1920s and the Golden Age have been represented as the two periods in American history when the working class was able to achieve middle-class status. Political scientists and economists of the Golden Age/Great Boom period assured Americans that, contrary to the forecast of Karl Marx, the United States was not a class society, polarized into an immiserated working class and a wealthy ruling class. In fact, the working class of the 1920s was indeed impoverished, but their condition was disguised by growing debt. Let us look at the economic situation of working people as measured by their earned income.

By 1929, 71 percent of American families earned incomes of under $2,500 a year, the level that the Bureau of Labor Statistics considered minimal to maintain an adequate standard of living for a family of four (Leven et al., 1934: 55; Dubofsky et al., 1978: 163). 60 percent earned less than $2,000 per year, the amount determined by the Bureau of Labor Statistics "sufficient to supply only basic necessities" (Leven et al., 1934: 56). 50 percent earned less than $1,700 and more than 20 percent earned less than $1,000 (ibid.: 54–7).

These income statistics show that the oft-touted claim that the 1920s saw America's first prosperous middle class is entirely spurious. A true middle-class standard of living is experienced by those whose wage is more than is minimally sufficient to maintain a just and comfortable standard of living. The income of 71 percent of Americans in the 1920s was below this level. Most Americans were officially poor, yet able to enjoy a standard of living featuring the enjoyment of an unprecedented quantity of newly available consumer durable goods. This was made possible by households taking on an *unsustainable* amount of debt. The ratio of household debt to household income rose steadily through the 1920s. In 1923, 1924, 1926, 1927 and 1928, the ratios stood at, respectively, 13, 18, 22, 25 and 31 percent (International Monetary Fund, 2012). The fact that most working-class households were in penury during these years was disguised by the supplementing of poverty-level wages with *mounting* debt. That debt was unsustainable because incomes were stagnant during the decade. When the limits of household debt accumulation were reached, at around 1926, the especially rapid rise in the production of durable goods could not be and was not maintained. By 1929 there was a troubling decline in investment and in the demand for types of durable goods most responsible for the post-1921 growth surge. The production of automobiles and tires, residential construction and even agricultural production declined sharply. These telling declines accelerated more sharply still as the Depression commenced in 1930–31. The decline in the crucial consumer durable goods sector, the principal source of the decade's boom, was particularly harsh (Gordon, 1955: 44). Spending on these goods had fallen 20 percent by 1930 (Fearon, 1979: 34). In parallel with these developments, excess capacity became evident, productive investment was discouraged, and corporate profits shifted to financial speculation. Household debt, then, constituted a bubble bound to burst, creating the conditions for the crash of 1929. We shall see in Chapter 6 that the same thing occurred in the postwar years beginning in 1945, i.e. immediately after the end of the war. In both cases, severe economic decline ensued.

STAGNATION TENDENCIES IN THE 1920S

From 1921 to 1929 the number of registered cars on the road continuously increased, from 9.3 million to 23.1 million. The *rate* of increase was another story. It had reached its peak early on, in 1923, at 24 percent. Thereafter the rate of growth of the industry dropped steadily, to 5 percent in 1927, when automobile output decreased by 22 percent. In 1928 and 1929, spurred by then-soaring stock-market prices, the industry's growth rate took a slight rise, but failed to match any previous annual rate (Fearon, 1979: 286). The auto market had become saturated, the inexorable fate of every new industry. The same logic applies to efforts to augment sales by extending credit. The time would surely come when all the households inclined to utilize installment plans were saddled with all the debt they could carry. The auto companies failed to see the relative growth of replacement demand as a limit to the industry's banner growth rates. Replacement sales grew from 21 percent in 1923 to 59 percent in 1927. Yet output was churned out as if there were no tomorrow. This scenario was portentous. Given the framework character of the automobile industry, any reduction in its sales revenues and profits would surely contribute to a sharp decline in the rate of growth of the economy as a whole.

The same dynamic was at work in housing. From the beginning of the recovery from the 1920–22 recession, the construction of new houses increased every year until 1926. Thereafter the rate of growth began a slowdown that reduced residential construction by one-third by 1929, leaving a considerable inventory of unsold and unsellable houses on the market (Bolch et al., 1971: 259–83). Stationary wages meant there was an upper limit to the market for new houses, which would be met as the number of households who could afford houses at the existing price level dwindled. It is not as if there was no need among many households for more and better housing. "There was still an actual need for better housing in large quantities, but this need could not be converted into market demand unless either the number of those who could afford the housing was increased by sufficient enlargement of income, or the prices of the new housing could be materially decreased. Neither of these developments occurred" (Soule, 1947: 288).

Limited expansion was a feature of both manufacturing and construction, and bode ill for the prospects of sustained prosperity. As *Recent Social Trends** reported, "it is doubtful whether [the] expansion of production and markets can continue indefinitely in the basic industries or in manufacturing industry as a whole. If not, the further advance of productivity may be accompanied by an aggregate displacement of labor instead of the mere reduction in unit labor requirements which in the past has usually been followed by an absolute expansion of employment" (Hoover, 1933, I: 311). As the economic historian H.W. Arndt put it, "investment opportunities in some of the new industries had passed their peak" (Arndt, 1972: 16). *The limits of investment were, unlike during the period of industrialization, a function of the limits to consumption imposed by low wages.* The remedy for industrial saturation and impending economic slowdown in a consumption-driven,

---

* In 1929 Herbert Hoover assembled a Research Committee on Social Trends to provide a factual portrait of American society, a sociological counterpart to *Recent Economic Changes*. This study was the result.

stagnant-wage economy was, as Soule had observed, either to raise wages or lower prices (Soule, 1947: 287, also 284). We have seen why neither alternative was taken.

Soule's observation points to the critical role of class power in determining outcomes in situations such as these. Under the economic-structural settlement in place by the 1920s, elementary economic theory teaches that declining prices and/or rising wages will stimulate growth. But whether either or both of these alternatives will be effected, of course, cannot be settled by theoretical analysis alone. The situation that emerged in the 1920s illustrates clearly the failure of technocratic approaches to policy and economic problem-solving. The contradictions implicit in rising production, productivity and profits, and stable prices and wages, reached a critical mass in the 1920s. The alternative strategies for coming to grips with the crisis were not acceptable to all stakeholders. Declining prices are favorable to labor but portend disaster for capital. Rising wages are always desired by labor, but constitute rising costs to capital, and are on that account quite rationally resisted. As Marx observed, when right is pitted against right, only power settles the issue. *In a consumption-driven mature capitalist economy, the operative condition of sustained economic health, including full employment, is wages rising in tandem with productivity. The level of employment and workers' degree of material security will depend increasingly on the class power of working people.*

GALLOPING DISACCUMULATION: THE LONG-TERM EXPULSION OF LABOR FROM PRODUCTION, DE-SKILLING AND TECHNOLOGICAL UNEMPLOYMENT

The labor-displacing function of 1920s productivity advances broke historic precedent. "During the decade preceding 1930 the trend of actual employment in manufacturing industry was downward for the first time in our history" (Hoover, 1933, I: 312). "There have been prosperous periods in the past ... but none so far as the committee can learn which has shown such a striking increase in productivity per man-hour" (Hoover, 1929: xv). In the most dynamic and productive sector of the economy, the workers needed were a declining percentage of the total working population (Hoover, 1933, I: 311). By 1926 the relevant literature featured much discussion of "'technological unemployment' resulting from the introduction of new machinery and processes ... [T]he time has come to devote continuing attention not only to the problems of cyclical unemployment but also to [the] problem of 'technological' unemployment if we are to forestall hardship and uncertainty in the lives of the workers … This is a serious aspect of the problem of unemployment" (Hoover, 1929: xvii).

We have seen that the displacement of labor by machines is integral to industrialization as such. The Hoover Committee acknowledged that "technological unemployment is nothing new. It is as old as the present industrial system and is inherent in this system" (ibid.: 92). From the beginnings of industrialization, technological advances have made the production of both capital goods and consumer goods increasingly labor-saving. *The permanent imperative to reduce the costs of production thus results in increasingly capital-intensive production. That is, capital equipment tends increasingly to substitute for labor.* The accumulation process as a whole tends to reduce the largest single component of total costs, labor. In the process, the productivity of both capital and labor is greatly increased. *The declining ratios (in money terms) of both capital and labor to output points to the decreasing importance of net investment in accumulating capital and, therefore, of profit in financing new investment.*

Ford, Taylor and Gilbreth had pioneered the process of linking the enhanced productivity of both labor and machines to the deskilling of the remaining labor force. The result was to transfer whatever control skilled workers managed to retain over the labor process to management, and to shorten the training time for workers, thereby lowering the price of their labor. Marx had observed in a much-quoted passage that industrial mechanization had turned the worker into an "appendage of the machine." The point was regarded by the members of the Hoover Committee as uncontroversial. Here is what the Committee reported in the chapter titled "Industry," under the heading *Basic Principles*: "Transfer of tools and its effects … is inherent in the use of tools of every kind. Whenever the tool is improved, less skill is required upon the part of the operator to produce a given result … [The] Industrial Revolution … carried transfer of skill to such a degree as to make the worker an adjunct to the tool, whereas formerly the tool was an adjunct to the skill of the worker. Modern industry differs from handicraft primarily in this particular" (Hoover, 1929: 86). During the 1920s a greater percentage of the workforce was engaged in this type of work than at any time in the nation's history. The work regimen in manufacturing was experienced as a step backward by labor. During the First World War, the 50–54 hour work week in manufacturing had been reduced to 48 hours. During the 1920s unorganized workers were made to surrender a considerable part of those gains, when the proportion of workers on a 48-hour schedule declined and those working as many as 54 hours increased (Wolman, 1938: 7).

The overall employment picture in the 1920s was not encouraging. During the steep recession beginning the decade, unemployment (among non-farm workers) hit 19.5 percent in 1921 and 11.4 percent in 1922. In 1924 it rose from 4.1 to 8.3 percent, fell to 2.9 percent in 1926 and was back up to 6.9 percent in 1928 (Dubofsky et al., 1978: 163). Manufacturing employed no more workers in 1929 than it had in 1919. And the growth in earnings of those who remained employed slowed down over the decade. Net additions to the active labor force were in sectors less productive than manufacturing. Almost all increases in employment during the decade were in trade, service, finance and construction (Gordon, 1974: 27). These additions, however, did not offset the displacement of labor in manufacturing, where capital- and labor-saving innovation proceeded at a more rapid rate. Wesley Mitchell reported, in his Review of the findings of *Recent Economic Changes 1–2*, included at the end of the two-volume book, that "Adopting a new occupation, however, does not guarantee getting a new job. The surplus workers from our farms and factories who hunted for fresh openings increased unemployment in other fields ... [T]he supply of new jobs has not been equal to the number of new workers plus the old workers displaced. Hence there has been a net increase in unemployment, between 1920 and 1927, which exceeds 650,000 people" (Hoover, 1929: 878). The trend, clearly in evidence in the 1920s, for these industries to be labor-displacing as greater output was turned out continued through the postwar period. The tendency of the most productive industries to employ a declining percentage of the total labor force means that an increasing percentage of all workers will be employed in lower-productivity, and therefore lower-paying, occupations. It follows that the rate of wage growth in the aggregate will slow down over time.

INEQUALITY, SURPLUS CAPITAL AND SPECULATION: EMBRYONIC FINANCIALIZATION

Soaring productivity and profits combined with stagnant wages is a formula for gross inequality. In 1919, the percentage shares of total income received by the top 1 percent and the top 5 percent stood, respectively, at 12.2 percent and 24.3 percent; in 1923 the shares had risen to 13.1 percent and 27.1 percent, and by 1929 to 18.9 and 33.5 percent (United States Bureau of the Census, 1975: series G341; Heilbroner and Milberg, 1998: 103; Garraty,

1971: 825; Dubofsky et al., 1978: 162–3). According to the Brookings Institution, in 1929 "o.1 percent of the families at the top received practically as much as 42 percent of families at the bottom of the scale" (Leven et al., 1934: 56). All of the increases in real income in the 1920s went to upper-income groups and most of the rest merely held firm or lost ground (Holt, 1977: 277–89). The 1920s evidenced the greatest inequality of the century up to that point. 1928 was the century's peak year of inequality. 1929 saw the stock-market crash followed by the Great Depression. (It is worth mentioning that the second-peak-inequality year since that time was 2007, followed by the debacle of 2008.)

We have seen the most fundamental reason for 1920s inequality: "Productive capacity raced ahead of buying power. Too large a share of the profits went into too few pockets" (Garraty, 1971: 825). Government policy contributed to the maldistribution. Tax rates for the rich were lowered substantially in the 1920s, encouraging investors to shift their wealth into assets yielding taxable income and to report income that went unreported previously. The same pattern would become evident in the post-Golden-Age period, when a continuing wage–productivity gap would begin and households would respond to the accompanying decline in their standard of living, as they did in the 1920s, by taking on *increasing* quantities of *unsustainable* debt (see Chapter 6).

An increasing percentage of income arising from production was distributed to those who could not possibly spend all of it in consumption purchases. That portion of income that is not spent is, by definition, saved. For both corporations and wealthy households, the growing accumulation of savings represents an increasing pressure to invest. How were large corporations and wealthy households to invest the huge funds they had accumulated? The excess capacity and saturation of the major growth markets that had formed during the decade, and the paucity of household purchasing power relative to productive capacity made further investment in production otiose. Soule describes the recourse taken by capital:

toward the end of [the decade] large amounts of cash remained in the hands of the big manufacturing and public-utility corporations that they did not distribute either in dividends or by means of new investment … the large corporations accumulated even more cash than they needed for their own uses, with the result that interest-bearing time deposits grew to large proportions. This money eventually spilled over into stock speculation. … [T]he surplus funds of large business corporations were now being lent directly to speculators … A curious commentary on the state of the American economy at the time is the fact that *business could make less money by using its surplus funds in production than it could by lending the money to purchasers of stocks, the value of which was supposed to be determined by the profit on that production.* (Soule, 1947: 284, 280; emphasis added).

The foregoing settlement imparts to the economy features that come to constitute not only key elements of the pre-Keynesian economy of the 1920s but also defining components of the post-Keynesian period of neoliberalism. This is no surprise, since neoliberalism rejects Keynesian social spending and in effect calls for a return to the relatively laissez-faire economy of the 1920s. Let us examine two salient features of this arrangement: the tendency for investment to shift from production to finance and the creation of a debt-dependent impoverished working class. I begin with the growth of finance, which began early in the 1920s and virtually exploded in the latter half of the decade.

Financial activity had begun a bull run as early as 1923. During the period 1921–25 speculation in land in Alabama, California and Florida burgeoned; just about all of these ventures ended in lost investments. From 1923 through 1929 there were steady and great increases in the prices of common stock, the number of shares traded and the issuance of corporate securities. The state of the productive economy made no difference to these trends. In fact the recession year of 1927 saw one of the two biggest annual increases of the decade in paper values. During the last two years of the decade earnings and dividends paid by corporations rose, but stock prices rose even faster. Thus, price/earnings (PE) ratios were unusually high, a clear indication that earnings were not driving the market. At this point speculative mania had reached such a level that high P/E ratios were no more of a deterrent to investors than they were in the U.S. in the late 1990s – speculators could see the market "going nowhere but up." The principal speculative activities were stock-market speculation and business building of commercial structures in the cities, resulting in many barely occupied structures, quite like the commercial overbuilding in the U.S. in the late 1990s and early 2000s (Steiner, 1934: 884).

Financialization had appeared in embryonic form. Investment opportunities in production had been saturated in an industrialized, mature economy. But the shift to a public and private consumption-based economy was not effected. Under these conditions, we discover *the tendency of an industrially overripe capitalist economy to detach finance from the fortunes of the productive economy*. It had become possible for finance to flourish – for a time – even as the real economy languished. Non-financial corporations had for some years accumulated surpluses so sizeable that they were able to finance their investments from retained earnings, with more left over than they knew what to do with. Industrial corporations had never before experienced this degree of independence from the banks. They could now resuscitate profit prospects by aping the banks themselves; they would earn interest on loans to speculators. As for the banks, with the corporate demand for commercial loans in decline, they were now free to extend a large volume of collateral loans to speculators (Soule, 1947: 279). During the years 1925–27 the security loans of the member banks of the Federal Reserve increased by 40 percent and their investments by 20 percent, while their commercial loans increased by only 12 percent (Steiner, 1934: 883). In the later years of the decade both financial and non-financial companies were fanning the flames of speculation. Speculative mania was by no means restricted to large corporations and banks. Many truck drivers, barbers, janitors, butlers and ditch diggers had a portion of their earnings in the stock market and were making money on their money. By 1925 stock prices were soaring at hitherto unheard-of rates. And you didn't have to have a lot of money to make a lot of money. Brokers encouraged investors to buy on margin. Shades of the 1990s: here was history anticipating itself.

INVESTMENT AND EMPLOYMENT IN MATURE CAPITALISM:
THE DISPLACEMENT OF CAPITAL AND LABOR FROM
PRODUCTION AND WAGE-DRIVEN DEMAND

We have seen that the transition from industrializing to consumerism capitalism featured the decline of investment in capital goods, i.e. the decline in the production of the means of production. By the 1920s both less capital and less labor was required in the capital-goods sector. The same came to be true in the consumer-goods sector. It is of greatest interest that during the years when the bulk of the decade's capital goods were created, from 1923 to 1926 (the year when excess capacity, declining rates of sale and market saturation in autos and residential construction were first evident), capital in the producer-goods sector remained unchanged. *No net investment took place during those years* (Epstein, 1934: 182; Coontz, 1965: 148). The unprecedented and relatively sustained prosperity of the 1920s consisted primarily in a boom in the consumer-goods sector. With basic industrialization accomplished, the economy was to be driven by consumption expenditures, *wage-driven demand*. In the current period, wage-driven demand remains the key to stable growth and full employment (Stockhammer and Onaran, 2012).

The prominent New Dealer Rexford Tugwell described the shift from investment to consumption in 1933:

> Our economic course has carried us from the era of economic *development* to an era which confronts us with the necessity for economic *maintenance*. In this period of maintenance there is no scarcity of production. There is, in fact, a present capacity for more production than is consumable, at least under a system which shortens purchasing power while it is lengthening the capacity to produce ... *More and more conspicuous is the dependence of our economic existence upon the purchasing power of the consumer – upon wages, that is.* (Tugwell, 1933: 323–4; emphasis added)

Tugwell identified a major turning point in the development of modern capitalism. The "scarcity of production" which once made it technically impossible to provide a healthy standard of living for all had been overcome. (We shall see in Chapter 5 that Keynes construed this "development" as the solving of "the economic problem" and the end of "scarcity.") With the basic system now set up, the task at hand was to attend to its "maintenance," to provide for all workers the level of wages necessary to put the economy's capacity to produce goods and services to use. The *principal* motive for production would no longer be the need to develop society's productive powers but rather the goal of raising the standard of living of the working population, whose (higher) wages had been deferred since the inception of the republic for the sake of capital accumulation. With production no longer society's overriding task, the order of the epoch was to raise the wages and consumption of the working majority. The "maintenance" of capitalism, its preservation and sustenance, would now require a permanent policy of high wages.

4

The 1930s and the Great Depression

The economic dynamics of 1920s U.S. capitalism serve as an exemplar of mature industrial capitalism. Not only do they account for the Great Depression, but they do so exhaustively. That is to say, the factors precipitating the Great Depression in America were entirely internal to the United States. Nothing comparable can be said of the origins of the Depression in other developed capitalist countries. Great Britain's internal economic conditions were dependent on her foreign trade, which helped soften the impact; not so the United States. The nation had a sizeable export surplus that was maintained throughout the Great Depression. The U.S. had been, since the First World War, a net international creditor, ran a continuous favorable trade balance throughout the 1920s and, thanks to war and continuing political uncertainty after it in Europe, held about 28 percent of the world's stock of gold. No other capitalist country enjoyed this complete relative absence of external sources of economic instability (Arndt, 1972: 18).

An accurate account of the Depression will both shape our understanding of the New Deal as a political intervention and reveal the severe limitations of any form of capitalist social democracy. The Great Depression, like the current one, was no mere business-cyclical downturn. Not only did the business cycle operate during it, it was, in fact, made up of three distinct phases, two depressions sandwiching an expansion. The first contraction, the longest and most severe, ran from August 1929 to March 1933, a total of 43 months. The second began in May 1937 and ended in June 1938, a total of 13 months. The economic upturn between them, lasting 49 months, was based on the New Deal's greatest intervention. It is important to note that while that expansion was one of the longest in U.S. history, neither of the contractions were the longest (the longest contraction having been from October 1873 to March 1879, lasting 65 months).

Why, then, do we call this period the Great Depression? Certainly one reason is its severity. Long as the upturn of 1933–37 may have been, even at its peak, the investment, level of output and national income levels preceding the stock-market debacle of 1929 were not restored. Moreover, the Depression impacted the national consciousness deeply. For one thing, it followed a decade during which capitalist apologists repeatedly declared the end of scarcity, the advent of abundance and the conquest of poverty. For another, in its severity, it manifested the peculiar characteristics of capitalist crises. Pre-capitalist economic crises were usually characterized by shortages, whether of labor or food, caused by natural disasters. Capitalist crises, by contrast, tend to be crises of "too much." Bafflingly, without any insufficiency of the requisites of economic activity, production is severely cut back and human misery mounts. As John Kenneth Galbraith put it:

> In 1929 the labor force was not tired; it could have continued to produce indefinitely at the best 1929 rate. The capital plant of the country was not depleted. In the preceding years of prosperity, plant had been renewed and improved … Raw materials were ample for the current rate of production. Entrepreneurs were never more eupeptic. (Galbraith, 1954: 178)

However, the term 'The Great Depression' is also appropriate because it reflected *secular stagnation*, a chronic malady of capitalism's maturity.

We have seen that the 1920s featured an economic configuration preset for crisis. As a model of the structure of mature capitalism, the 1920s suggest that chronic stagnation is the normal state of industrialized capitalism. While this analysis was proposed and defended by prominent New Dealers, the most influential economic thinkers of the time construed the downturn on the orthodox model of a business-cycle downturn. There was no empirical or theoretical comprehension of the possibility that the demand curve under mature capitalism could be shifting inexorably to the left, with insufficient demand at any *remunerative* price.

It is noteworthy that in our own times many prominent mainstream economists have expressed apprehensions that recent developments in American capitalism, and perhaps of world capitalism, portend a prolonged period of secular stagnation: slow growth and declining living standards, with no return to the growth or employment rates of the Golden Age (Krugman, 2013a,b,c; Summers, 2013a; Gordon, Robert J., 2012, 2016; Piketty, 2014). I anticipated a defense of that thesis in Chapter 3, and shall flesh out the analysis as the argument of this book unfolds.

The effectiveness of the framework that powered the dynamism of the 1920s was exhausted. Overcapacity had been building up in virtually all consumer durable lines since 1926, and the abnormally high levels of investment of 1928–29 increased it to alarming levels. Expectations were already weakening and, with the October 29, 1929 stock-market crash they sank to rock bottom (Gordon, 1974: 70). On "Black Tuesday" the market had opened at an average share price of $299 and within a few hours fell 23 percent to $230. Bankers recoiled, making capital unavailable, and the demand for both ordinary consumer durables and luxury goods plummeted, taking investment with it (Gordon, 1974: 66–70; Galbraith, 1954: 177–8, 191–3). The Great Depression was under way.

By 1932 more than 32,000 businesses would go bankrupt. National output fell by 50 percent (Wilson, 1941: 159). Unemployment soared, reaching its peak of 24.9 percent of the labor force in 1933. Between 1929 and 1933 consumption declined by more than 20 percent and fixed investment by more than 70 percent (Magdoff and Sweezy, 1987: 53). A thousand homes per day were being foreclosed, not including the half-million farm foreclosures. In the era before deposit insurance, bank collapses went viral as savers flocked to withdraw their savings at the merest hint that their bank might be insolvent. 20 percent of U.S. banks, at least 5,000, would fail. As Keynes remarked in 1931, "The slump in trade and employment and the business losses which are being incurred are as bad as the worst which have ever occurred in the modern history of the world" (Keynes, [1931] 1972: 135). It was not until 1954 that the stock market recovered its pre-crash numbers.

In what follows, I discuss the Great Depression as the inevitable outcome of conditions established during the 1920s, conditions which are paradigmatic of capitalism *as such*, i.e. without colonies, unions, a negative trade position or significant government involvement, none of which are part of any model of the essential capitalist dynamic. I prescind from America's international relations, having shown in the previous chapter that the domestic settlement achieved in the 1920s, the default arrangement of the system as represented in the standard models, was sufficient to bring about the Depression. I go on to detail Franklin Roosevelt's response to the Depression and John Maynard Keynes's reservations about the president's policies.

I especially emphasize Roosevelt's fiscal conservatism. Two of the New Deal's most impressive achievements, the Works Progress Administration and the Social Security Act, are discussed with an eye towards revealing the serious limitations imposed upon these legislations to this day by the hovering imperative of fiscal conservatism or "sound finance." There are important lessons here regarding current American economic policy, whose overriding guiding principle is fiscal conservatism, as it is expressed in the quasi-pathological obsession with "the deficit." Finally, I uncover the implications of the Depression, and especially of Keynes's critiques of Roosevelt's policy, for this book's central contentions regarding declining net investment and persistent secular stagnation.

HERBERT HOOVER'S RESPONSE

Contrary to the prevailing myth, president Herbert Hoover did not respond to the Depression as a thoroughgoing fiscal conservative. His approach was eclectic, combining fiscal activism, "sound finance" policies and a commitment to administered pricing through voluntary cartelization between big corporations, lest the sharp price declines following the 1929 crash turn into a deflationary freefall. Hoover's belief in the inexorability of recovery made it possible for him to contend that government spending was a mere aid to the inevitable upturn. Indeed, well before Keynes's work became widely known, it was appreciated, even by conservatives like Hoover, that government spending was an effective counter-cyclical tool. During 1931–32, federal spending on public works was more than double what it had been during the 1920s. Such spending turned the federal government surplus in 1930 into a deficit of $616 million the following year. It increased more than fourfold in 1932 (Wilson, 1941: 160 ff.). But such reflation was more than offset by a large reduction of public-works spending by cities, states and counties, characteristic of severe downturns, much as Barack Obama's timid stimulus plan after September 2008 was severely limited by state and local economic contraction thanks to balanced-budget legislation.

None of this sat well with the financial sector, a reflection of their aversion to encouraging public expectation that workers' needs might be met through democratic policy rather than the market. Unlike the 1920s, when many of the largest firms were able to finance their activities out of retained earnings, the Depression restored the banks to prominence as providers of capital. The "confidence of the financial community" thus carried a great deal of weight with Hoover, who was under unremitting pressure from bankers to return to his roots in the principles of a balanced budget and fiscal austerity (Blyth, 2002: 51–6).

Hoover finally caved in under the banks' pressure and in 1931 increased taxes to shrink or eliminate the deficit. The effect was predictable: deflation intensified and counteracted whatever price-stabilization effects voluntary cartelization might have had. The administration seemed confused and rudderless, and Hoover's image was dealt another blow by newsreel and newspaper coverage of his cruel and violent treatment in 1932 of the veterans participating in the Bonus Army March (see page 91) on Washington. Hoover's analysis remained within the bounds of modified orthodoxy described above. He consistently refused to provide unemployment relief at the federal level. Hoover was unwilling to use State power in the service of workers in trouble, to apply the notion of "political capitalism" to the unemployment crisis the way State support of regulatory agencies had employed political capitalism on behalf of threats to business interests. The popular response to Hoover's inactivity was reflected less than one month later in the massive defeat suffered by Republicans in congressional elections. They lost fifty-two seats in the House and eight in the Senate.

The now-unpopular Hoover was defeated in the 1932 election and Franklin Roosevelt was brought to office, setting the stage for the first grand experiment in massive government social spending in American history, the New Deal. The political economy of the New Deal was shaped by two key factors: the interweaving of the structural constraints and imperatives of secular stagnation, and the class struggle between a working class whose hopes of endless prosperity had been dashed by a Depression that government appeared unwilling or unable to address and a capitalist class anxious about government action changing the balance of power which, until then, had retained a pronounced tilt in its favor. We begin with the working-class end of this struggle as it began during the Hoover administration.

POPULAR DISSENT OVERCOMES THE
POLITICAL APATHY OF THE 1920S

The Depression wakened the U.S. working population from the political slumber into which the 1920s, with its ethos of consumerism, had cast it. This ethos had been built by the linking of consumption to the core American value of freedom, which had long been thought of as central to what it means to be an American. Solidarity had never been as highly placed among American values as "freedom" had been. The preeminent symbol of freedom in the 1920s was, unsurprisingly, also the preeminent consumable, the automobile. In this culture built on working-class defeat and the equation of liberty and consumption, equality and solidarity had no place. Nor did political resistance.

The politically comatose citizenry of the 1920s was insightfully profiled by Robert and Helen Lynd in their classic study of the social climate of the industrial city Muncie, Indiana, in 1924–25. *Middletown*: *A Study in Modern American Culture* compared Americans' beliefs and practices at home, at work, in child-raising and in cultural and community activities in the 1920s with how they had lived in the 1880s. Their detailed investigations revealed that what Americans called "getting a living," acquiring money in order to live and to purchase consumption goods, was the single most influential factor in shaping the activities and attitudes of "Middletowners." "The money medium of exchange and the cluster of activities associated with its acquisition drastically condition the other activities of the people" (Lynd and Lynd, 1959: 21).

The society of the Lynds' studies was also polarized: the working and business classes lived in different neighborhoods, attended different churches, drove different cars (Fords or Buicks) and belonged to different clubs. They were not only polarized at work but also in the way they spent leisure time, though in one respect they were at one: for both, the primary concern was acquiring money. "For both working and business class no other accompaniment of getting a living approaches in importance the money received for their work" (ibid.: 80). The Lynds portrayed the rising centrality of consumption vividly by showing in detail how the rise of large-scale advertising, popular magazines, movies, radio, and other channels of cultural diffusion caused Middletowners, and, by implication, all Americans, to seek fulfillment in multiplying occasions for consumption.

The working-class culture of earlier times was a fading memory: Labor Day had largely lost its significance; unions neither organized the major social functions nor enjoyed the favor of the working class. However, this was not because workers had no problems. In fact, most workers did not vote in the elections of 1922, because they felt powerless in both local and national affairs and, despite the purported good life newly accessible in the twenties, looked to the future with as much apprehension as hope. Muncie's businessmen, by contrast, felt differently. They reveled in their predominant political and economic power and were confident that the future belonged to them.

This ethos did not endure with the arrival of the Great Depression, not least because two features of the 1920s made working-class apathy of the decade less deeply rooted than it seemed at the time. The "new prosperity" may have been heady but it was also short-lived. And memories of more active social and political engagement may have been dulled but were not entirely expunged. The blow to the decade's optimism and the sudden severity of the meltdown began to awaken working people.

The first instances of mass resistance in 1930 came in response to the surge in unemployment. The first participants were the unemployed and farmers (American Social History Project, 1992: 338–45). More than 3,800 workers at General Motors' Flint plant struck over wage cuts, but the fear of job loss led most workers to avoid job actions. Existing community networks were mobilized by the Communist Party on March 6, 1930, declared International Unemployment Day by the organizers. Street protests, rent strikes and anti-eviction struggles motivated 50,000 protesters in Boston and in Chicago, and 100,000 in Detroit. The South too saw organized dissent. In Alabama the Communist Party organized the Sharecroppers Union (SCU), composed almost exclusively of blacks. Many protesters called, for the first time on a large scale, for a national program of unemployment insurance.

The violent government and corporate repression of workers in the nineteenth and early twentieth centuries, discussed in previous chapters, made a comeback during these 1930s protests. In New York City hundreds of police clubbed and jailed protesters. In Alabama landowners backed by local sheriff's forces raided SCU offices and exchanged fire with SCU members. And that was only the beginning.

THE BEGINNINGS OF BUSINESS MOBILIZATION

The decline of business activity and the series of mounting protests of the first years of the decade led many leading American businessmen, preeminently Gerald Swope of General Electric, to propose large-scale recovery programs with the full participation of private interests. Such cooperation between business and government had a long American pedigree. They had partnered in 1917 and 1918 in the War Industries Board (WIB), which had regulated American production during the First World War. If such coordination and planning was uncontroversial in war, the argument went, the Depression was a similar national emergency. Collaboration between business and government to prevent strikes, one of the goals of the WIB, and to legitimize administering prices as a measure against deflation, were deemed necessary. However, such thinking represented only a minority, and while this proposal did the rounds in both political parties, neither raised it in the 1932 presidential election campaign.

THE 1932 PRESIDENTIAL ELECTION

During the campaign Roosevelt not only did not repudiate Hoover's policies but also attacked them from the right for failing to balance the federal budget (Leuchtenburg, 1963: 3; Schlesinger, 1957). Roosevelt would remain at heart a fiscal conservative throughout his presidency. Nor did he use his campaign to lend support to the multiple labor actions and demonstrations of the time. The largest demonstration to date in the nation's capital took place in January 1932, when the Catholic priest James Cox led "Cox's Army" of the unemployed to the Capitol demanding legislation on behalf of the jobless. Once again, private and public means of violence were used against the demonstrators. Four demonstrators were killed and sixty jailed as Ford's security forces fired revolvers and local police used machine guns. During the campaign Roosevelt made no reference to these events, nor did he express support for the demonstrators' demands.

The most famous instance of resistance to Depression conditions was the summer Bonus Army March, from all over America to the Capitol, of First World War veterans, not long after New York Governor Roosevelt had recommended cutting veterans' benefits in order to balance the budget. Congress had passed a bill after the First World War pledging that a bonus be paid in small increments, beginning in 1924, to veterans of the war. As the Depression gathered steam with no signs of recovery, the marchers, who had grown to 20,000 by summer, demanded that the full bonus be paid immediately. After the marchers had been camped outside the Capitol building for two weeks, Hoover sent troops commanded by General Douglas MacArthur and then-Major Dwight Eisenhower to evict the veterans. The vets were assaulted with tear gas and billy clubs by cavalry troops, tanks and soldiers, who began the eviction by setting fire to the vets' tents. MacArthur boasted that he had saved the country from revolution, and Hoover characterized the marchers as "Communists and persons with criminal records" (Mitchell, 1947: 110).

The public responded with revulsion. Roosevelt's advisors urged him to seize the day and support the veterans in order to bolster his chances for nomination. Roosevelt did not favor the bonus and rejected the advice. In fact, as president he would support the Economy Act of 1933, which cut veterans' benefits and reduced the salaries of federal employees. In 1932 he was attuned to the palpable public disapproval of Hoover and increasingly confident of his party's nomination. But he was unaware of both the depth of the economy's malaise and the intensity of popular disillusion. In August, American Federation of Labor president William Green warned that if the political managers did not "get at the fundamentals in an orderly, constructive way, we shall be swept aside by a tide of revolt" (American Social History Project, 1992: 345). It would take a while before Roosevelt would appreciate the extent of popular disaffection. He was elected in a landslide in November and inaugurated in March 1933. The stage was now set for the third major political intervention in response to crisis, the (first) New Deal.

THE THIRD INTERVENTION:
THE FIRST NEW DEAL AND ITS LIMITATIONS

The New Deal was slow to compose itself, not least because Roosevelt was no New Dealer himself when elected. Instead, he responded to problems as they came up, in a largely ad hoc fashion. But some New Dealers close to Roosevelt were underconsumptionists – Harry Hopkins, Henry Wallace, Frank Murphy, Phil LaFollette – and they were among those who influenced Roosevelt to set aside or temporarily suspend his fiscal conservatism in some of the Second New Deal's more progressive policies (Rosenof, 1975: 39–42).

ROOSEVELT'S LIMITATIONS AS A NEW DEALER

Five months after Roosevelt's inauguration the economy would plunge to its lowest point of the decade, with unemployment at 24.9 percent. (This figure counted government workers as unemployed, since their employment was a function of the Depression. Without them, the unemployment figure would stand at over 17 percent.) Responding to record unemployment and the continued debilitation of the financial sector, Roosevelt declared a national "bank holiday," during which banks were closed to prevent mass runs on savings accounts, and proposed legislation enabling the government to lend to failing banks and reorganize failed ones. Once the banks were shored up, the task of balancing the budget, which remained fundamental for Roosevelt throughout, could be undertaken in a stabilized environment. Not only did Roosevelt lower federal salaries and reduce veterans' benefits in pursuit of balanced budgets, but so antediluvian did his economic thinking remain that he urged people to save rather than spend their incomes as wages fell. In 1932 the federal government's expenditures were still about half of what state and local governments spent.

The newly elected president was indeed convinced that some dramatically new initiative was called for, but an effective policy escaped him, due largely to his dogged adherence to the doctrine of sound finance. As the depth of the Depression impressed itself on the new president, there was much rhetoric about "cooperation" and social solidarity at the individual, private level, and about "experimental" activism, but the need for large-scale government action in support of working people remained off Roosevelt's agenda. The president's advisors, on the other hand, were alert to the need for drastic action. Adolf Berle wrote in 1932 that "we may have anything on our hands from a recovery to a revolution. The chance is about even either way" (cited in Levine, 1988: 67). Roosevelt's more intimate advisors, such as Harry Hopkins, Henry Wallace and Marriner Eccles, along with many prominent and influential New Dealers such as Robert Wagner, Robert La Follette, Fiorello La Guardia and Burton Wheeler, all embraced the underconsumption/overinvestment analysis of the cause of both the persistent downturn and of the subsequent deep popular discontent. Eccles, Roosevelt's Federal Reserve chairman from 1934 to 1945 (and until 1948), stated the dominant view of Roosevelt's most progressive advisors in his 1951 memoirs, *Beckoning Frontiers*:

> *As mass production has to be accompanied by mass consumption, mass consumption, in turn, implies a distribution of wealth — not of existing wealth, but of wealth as it is currently produced — to provide men with buying power equal to the amount of goods and services offered by the nation's economic machinery.* Instead of achieving that kind of distribution, a giant suction pump had by 1929–30 drawn into a few hands an increasing portion of currently produced wealth. This served them as capital accumulations. But by taking purchasing power out of the hands of mass consumers, the savers denied to themselves the kind of effective demand for their products that would justify a reinvestment of their capital accumulations in new plants ... [A]s in a poker game where the chips were concentrated in fewer and fewer hands, the other fellows could stay in the game only by borrowing. When their credit ran out, the game stopped. That is what happened to us in the twenties. (Eccles, 1951: 76; emphasis in original)

The analysis was not uncommon among prominent Democrats. Shortly after Roosevelt's inauguration, Senator Hugo L. Black argued that "Labor has been underpaid and capital overpaid. This is one of the chief contributing causes of the present depression. We need a return of purchasing power. You cannot starve men employed in industry and depend upon them to purchase" (cited in Mitchell, 1947: 234).

The implications of this analysis are indispensable for a proper grasp of the severe limitations of the New Deal as a response to secular stagnation, the malaise specific to mature, disaccumulating capitalism. An economic configuration of rigid prices (a normal feature of oligopoly capitalism), soaring productivity and unorganized labor earning stagnant wages *must* place increases in national income "in fewer and fewer hands" and "[take] purchasing power out of the hands of mass consumers." With the rate of investment far lower than during industrialization, the growth of output, employment and wages depends on high levels of *consumption* demand. History demanded that the New Deal reorganize the economy so as to minimize the role of further *net* private investment as the principal guarantor of economic stability, full employment and a good living wage, and also increase the role of government investment and orientate government policy towards providing the mass of consumers with the means of a good life by effecting a bold redistribution of income from accumulators to workers. But Roosevelt mostly remained deaf to history's demands.

We shall see on p. 119 and in Appendix B that Keynes understood the need of the hour to include both the socialization and planning of investment and, for the first time in the history of capitalism, a significant reduction of the work week. By failing to re-evaluate mature capitalism *as a system* and by adhering religiously to the doctrine of sound finance or fiscal restraint ("responsibility") as the hallmark of a properly non-intrusive public sector, the New Deal not only fell far short of what was desirable at the time but also set precedents that would, ironically, buttress key features of neoliberalism. With these considerations in mind, let us look at the New Deal as it shifts into high gear.

THE MAKING OF THE FIRST NEW DEAL

Under pressure from the likes of Hopkins and Eccles, Roosevelt acted on his two principal but vague early convictions, that restrictions on banking activity were necessary and that it was urgent to come up with some policy for boosting workers' purchasing power without full-throttle government planning. Along these lines he implemented in 1933 the Banking Act, the Agricultural Adjustment Act (AAA) and its industrial counterpart, the National Recovery Administration (NRA).

The Banking Act, also known as the Glass–Steagall Banking Act, was not Roosevelt's initiative, having been conceived and urged upon him by its congressional sponsors, Senator Carter Glass (Democrat) of Virginia, and Representative Henry B. Steagall (Democrat) of Alabama. The Act divided banks accepting deposits from the public from banks investing on Wall Street. The sponsors wished to curb the kind of speculative activity instrumental in the precipitation of the 1929 crash. The limitations the Act placed on commercial banks' ability to trade in securities was one of the most effective achievements of the New Deal. Without it, the kind of financial speculation that led to 1929 would surely have recurred. The Act also established the Federal Deposit Insurance Corporation (FDIC), which insured savings accounts, regulated the stock market by (among other measures) setting margin requirements, and regulated banking by establishing reserve requirements. After the FDIC began operating, bank failures almost entirely disappeared. The repeal of Glass–Steagall under Bill Clinton in 1999, and the lifting of the most effective FDIC restrictions, as part of the neoliberal project of doing away with as much of the legacy of the New Deal as elites could get away with, was to have predictable and devastating consequences.

The AAA and NRA were in tune with the anti-deflationary policy of administered pricing. The AAA declared a state of "agricultural emergency" and sought agricultural price stability by the same means – restricting output – employed by industrialists earlier in the century. Farmers were urged to plow under millions of acres of cotton and to slaughter 10 million piglets so as to reduce overproduction and thereby raise farm incomes. However, by taking land out of cultivation, this also dispossessed many sharecroppers and added to the ranks of the jobless. The project of destroying cotton crops while millions were without adequate clothing, swelling the number of unemployed and wiping out sources of food in the midst of widespread hunger, struck many Americans as preposterous (Badger, 1989: 163). Public anger swelled.

Because the American executive has always had discretion to violate established practice in situations deemed critical, Roosevelt would have found support among the public, many of his advisors and more than a few congressional figures for a government-subsidized plan to distribute those surpluses to workers in need. But the fear that a government plan allocating essential resources outside the market mechanism would set a "socialist" precedent limited the horizons of the president.

The National Industrial Recovery Act (NIRA), administered by the NRA, was the industrial counterpart to the AAA. It was designed to establish voluntary "codes" regulating "fair" administered prices and to combat unemployment. NIRA's regulatory codes were based on industrial self-regulation. Predictably, prices and profits still rose faster than wages and unemployment continued to rise (Mitchell, 1947: 275). The NRA became known in popular parlance as the "National Run-Around" (Brecher, 1972: 177).

Roosevelt's antipathy to direct federal provision of jobs resulted in imposing on the states an unbearable fiscal burden. The Public Works

Administration (PWA) of June 1933 was aimed at building or repairing bridges, roads, schools, airports, dams, ports and other public works. But PWA's actual disbursements nowhere near matched the budgeted amount, since the PWA required local governments to come up with the majority of a project's total funding. The PWA's net employment effect was negligible. Other smaller initiatives met with similar fates. In 1932, the Civilian Conservation Corps (CCC) was created to construct recreational facilities and maintain public lands. The CCC had no net effect on the continuing contraction and rising unemployment. The May 1933 Federal Emergency Relief Act (FERA), like the PWA, was also limited by how much money the already-hobbled states could raise. U.S. elites' congenital anti-federalism remains to this day a permanent obstacle to overcoming sustained downturns like the current slow-motion depression.

The failure of these programs led Harry Hopkins to persuade Roosevelt to set aside his ideological aversion to direct federal employment and to establish an agency to provide not "relief" but *employment* to the jobless. Recipients would be federal employees like postal workers and workers in government offices. In November 1933, the Civil Works Administration (CWA) was created and funded through NIRA to the tune of $400 million. This explicitly temporary program allowed four million Americans to build or maintain roads, schools, parks, public buildings, docks and rural outhouses. However, Roosevelt feared that the CWA would set a precedent, a permanent expectation that government would provide citizens with the means of earning a living when the market would not. The president did not want the CWA to "become a habit with the country" (Rauchway, 2008a: 66; Leuchtenberg, 1963: 122). He ended the CWA less than five months after it was created. Roosevelt failed to understand that the intractability of the Depression lay in the structure of the mature capitalist economy, whose rigid wage and price levels, and spectacular productive power and profitability, made vast inequality, excess capacity, underconsumption and joblessness inevitable without major and permanent public provision of employment. No wonder the economy was back to square one.

The fatal flaw of the New Deal was that it did not grasp mature capitalism's need for a permanent program of government job creation that operated not only during economic contractions *but also during expansions* (see Appendix B). Under the settlement established in the 1920s, it was imperative, as I have argued in the previous chapter, to shift the surplus from private investment to private and public consumption. None of the means of achieving this end – progressive income taxes, the socialization of investment, large-scale government employment and the acknowledgement of labor's right to consolidate and organize as capital had done – was acceptable to the captains of industry and finance. *A great historical lesson of the Great Depression was that it foretold, in veiled and distorted form, what overripe capitalism requires if it is to do justice to its workers: a shift from private to public investment and consumption and massive government employment.* These transformations, as we shall see, are not possible under capitalism. Indeed, during the Depression, when these measures were enacted, the U.S. economy achieved substantial innovations and productivity gains close to those of the Golden Age. And it featured the steepest economic expansion in the nation's history (Field, 2012).

THE NATIONAL INDUSTRIAL RECOVERY ACT
BIRTHS A NEW LABOR MILITANCY

Only a major increase in popular pressure could bring about a change in policy. Until late 1933, unions had remained cautious out of fear of job losses. The number of strikes had fallen from 1929 to 1933. But as workers lost more and more – 1920s-style benefits like paid vacations, good-attendance bonuses and subsidization of home mortgages were disappearing – and as their wages and working conditions worsened with layoffs, hour reductions, pay cuts and speedups, they eventually turned to collective action. If labor action was going to change anything in this context, it needed a legal framework that would not merely permit but also encourage organized action by labor of a kind not seen since the last three decades of the nineteenth century and during the First World War. The NIRA contained just such a provision.

Business leaders railed against the NIRA. Their ire was focused on section 7a, which declared that "employees shall have the right to organize and bargain collectively through representatives of their own choosing … free from the interference, restraint, or coercion of employers." Section 7a also allowed organizers to portray joining a union as a patriotic contribution to national recovery, directly repudiating the 1920s denunciation of unions as "un-American." As of June 1933 workers would have the kind of power that until then had been refused them by both business and government. Historic labor repression was to end. Companies could not force workers to join company unions, nor could they count on government assistance in union-busting. *To businessmen, government now appeared to have shifted its class allegiance.* The president was empowered to set an upper limit on working hours and a minimum limit on wages. The June 1933 Act put American labor relations on new ground.

In February 1933 a United Mine Workers of America member had complained that "there is no sign of organization … you could not organize a baseball team." The day after Roosevelt signed NIRA, 80 percent of Ohio miners had signed union cards (American Social History Project, 1992: 356). Less than three months later a series of wildcat strikes forced the owners to accept NIRA codes that business-led committees had initially been able to skirt. Wages were raised and standardized across different geographical regions, child labor was prohibited and the 8-hour day and 5-day week were established. NIRA codes were still in the making and reborn union power now enabled workers to contribute to refashioning the codes in labor's interests. The two largest garment unions, the Amalgamated Clothing Workers Union and the International Ladies' Garment Workers Union successfully struck in order to increase their input to the code-writing process. Greatly increased membership and wage gains followed (ibid.: 357). Gains such as this, even when enabled by labor-friendly legislation, are *never* secured without labor militancy including strikes and other forms of disruption.

KEYNES'S INTERCESSION

In England, John Maynard Keynes was wrestling with the problems posed by the Depression and drafting his *General Theory of Employment, Interest and Money*. Observing U.S. developments from afar, he noted both the novelty and the limitations of Roosevelt's policies and even wrote to the president in December 1933 urging him to undertake large, permanent programs offering employment during economic contractions and expansions.* Keynes plaintively wondered "whether the order of different urgencies is rightly understood, whether there is a confusion of aim, and whether some of the advice you get is not crack-brained and queer" (p.1). The basic issue, Keynes insisted, is "Recovery," whose object is "to increase the national output and put more men to work" (p.1). An increase in output depends on "the amount of purchasing power … which is expected to come on the market" (p.2). There are, Keynes points out, three factors operating to raise purchasing power and output: increased consumer spending out of current income, increased investment by capitalists, and "public authority … called in aid to create additional current incomes through the expenditure of borrowed or printed money" (p.2).

---

* The letter can be found in its entirety at https://tinyurl.com/ybjnrdk6

Since the vast majority of consumers are workers, he reasoned, increased expenditure on that front is impossible on the required scale during a period of high unemployment and low wages. Business investment will eventually kick in, but only "*after* the tide has been turned by the expenditures of public authority" (p.2). *A compelling argument for increased State expenditure is implicit in that observation.* Recovery is supposed to consist in a revival of investment by capitalists. However, investment by any individual capitalist in the context of a severe downturn would be irrational. Each capitalist will defer investment until there is evidence of recovery, i.e. evidence that *other* capitalists had undertaken productive outlays. A structural contradiction is thus in place. If each investor refrains from investment until all the others invest, no capitalist will invest. Each will die waiting for the others to come through. In the absence of a *political* impetus to the system, the depression promised to be endless. Recovery in the context of deep and sustained economic downturn is possible only if *a force outside the private market* gets the ball rolling. Once the State has "put more men to work," Keynes wrote, "the tide has been turned." Hence Keynes's conviction that only government expenditures on a grand scale can breathe life back into a depressed economy. He suggested as an example "the rehabilitation of the physical condition of the railroads" (p.4).

No crisis, even in capitalism, is merely economic. Keynes had witnessed the rise of revolutionary movements in response to the protracted inability of capitalism to meet the needs of working people. He had written about both the Bolshevik revolution and the tendency of austerity to spawn revolt from the Right. Keynes was antipathetic to both fascist and worker rule, and feared revolutionary consequences should the New Deal fail. "If you fail," he wrote to Roosevelt, "rational change will be gravely prejudiced throughout the world, leaving orthodoxy and revolution to fight it out" (p.1). The *political* stakes were high, as they must be under conditions of protracted capitalist austerity. They are no less high as I write. In Appendix B I discuss Keynes's specific analyses and proposals, including his insistence that unemployment was no mere temporary problem, nor could it be addressed within a policy framework based on the need for a balanced budget.

THE FOURTH INTERVENTION: FED-UP LABOR RESURGENT

Keynes's early warning was ignored by Roosevelt and the worker upheaval that had alarmed Keynes resumed, on stilts. By 1934 the union movement was burgeoning and strikes became more frequent. In February 1934, 4,000

Toledo auto parts workers struck Auto-Lite, which then hired scabs to do the work. In response, 10,000 workers and their supporters blockaded the plant to prevent the strike breakers from leaving. The dishonorable American tradition of labor repression again kicked in. The company's own forces joined local police and National Guard units, using gunfire, tear gas and water hoses, to disperse the activists. Many protesters were injured and two killed (Smith, 2006: 107-9). In the end, the union was recognized, the minimum wage increased and the then-current wage raised by 5 percent. That same month 5,000 Minneapolis Teamsters, truck drivers and warehouse workers walked off their jobs. Again, strikers and local police exchanged fire. In a second strike five months later, two strikers were killed (Lichtenstein, 2013: 32–3; American Social History Project, 1992: 362–3). These were the circumstances under which the labor victories that would prompt the Second New Deal were to be won. Historically, major gains for labor have never been brought about without militancy, including strikes and attacks on non-bodily property such as the overturning of police cars, the breaking of (e.g. corporate) windows and paint balls, among other breaches of ceremonial etiquette (Piven and Cloward, 1978; Burns, 2011, 2014; Meckfessel, 2016).

In May 1934 the greatest labor action in U.S. history to date began with 14,000 San Francisco longshoremen striking for union recognition, higher pay, a shorter work week and exclusive union control of the hiring halls. Waterfront truckers and sailors also stopped work in sympathy. The patience of workers had worn thin and labor activism spread up and down the West Coast. From Seattle to San Diego, 25,000 maritime workers walked out. After two months of intense struggle the employers' private forces shot and killed two strikers and scabs were brought in. Workers' outrage grew, and by July, San Francisco workers called for a general strike that paralyzed the city by spreading from the waterfront and quickly enlisting 127,000 workers, including almost all port and city workers (Mitchell, 1947: 276).

Sympathy strikers from construction workers and bartenders to enter-tainers brought the total number of participants to about 130,000, extending the shutdown to Berkeley and Oakland. The NRA administrator, General Hugh S. Johnson, commanded a force composed of 9,000 police and militiamen to suppress the insurrection with the boilerplate accusation that the leaders of the "mob" were communists, a charge this time not without merit. The undaunted dock workers wanted to continue to press for more generous benefits, but the more conservative union leadership called the strike off when it had become clear that the companies were prepared to concede recognition of the union, pay increases and a 30-hour work week.

Some labor actions failed, but business leaders remained on guard. What troubled them was the fact of labor militancy itself, government's apparent support of labor's right to organize, and labor unions' earlier successes. It seemed natural to capital that government be dominated by business interests as it always had been, and that the function of legislation is to assert and reinforce the subordination of labor to capital. The New Deal appeared to upset that defining arrangement of social relations under capitalism and to portend an era fundamentally hostile to the interests of property. American capitalists feared that the "foundations of civilization" were crumbling. Certainly the State was slipping from their hands and something had to be done.

Business leaders retained memory of precedent. In past labor disputes, the recourse to private and State violence was, as we have seen in Chapter 2, greater in the U.S. than in any other industrial country. Violence and preparations for violence, particularly private violence, against workers persisted through the 1930s. Strikes and sit-downs were met with State force in support of employers; troops were called out in at least 16 states. Most of the largest employers in the country resisted worker militancy by means of industrial espionage and the overt use of force backed by an astonishingly large private arsenal and troops/armies. What was frequent in the twenties – union officers working as detectives in the paid service of the employer – became ubiquitous during the Depression. The labor historian Clinch Calkins wrote that such industrial espionage in the 1930s was at its peak when worker-friendly legislation or tight labor markets led workers to "feel confidence in their strength" (Calkins, 1937: 22).

There was extensive industrial spying and the deployment of a massive corporate arsenal and armed force against union members and supporters. From 1933 to 1936 major corporations had spent almost $9.5 million on spies, strikebreakers and munitions (United States Congress, Senate Report, 1937a: 23). Chrysler, General Motors, Firestone, Kellogg, the RCA Corporation, Montgomery Ward, Standard Oil, Campbell Soup, Bethlehem Steel, Frigidaire and Statler Hotels, among many others, employed spies in every one of their unions and almost all of their workplaces. Employers also turned to the purchase of tear gas, machine guns and other weapons to suppress strikes and union-organizing. The companies which made greatest use of these weapons were in the automobile, steel, shipping and mining industries, where workers had shown the greatest militancy. Indeed, mining and steel companies created their own private police forces responsible only to the companies themselves. The independent detective agencies and the companies' private police shared an interest in boosting the demand for their services by prolonging strikes and instigating violence (United States Congress, Senate Report, 1937b: 1619). The companies' private police appeared to be the most aggressive in the use of violence against union members and organizers. Should tendencies comparable to Occupy, the antiwar movement and the Bernie Sanders campaign develop in response to persistent austerity in the U.S., history tells us what we must be prepared to confront.

The La Follette Committee identified businesses supplying large companies with weapons such as sickening gas especially designed for use in labor disputes. *More than two thirds of the tear gas purchased by corporations was bought when unions were struggling for recognition.* La Follette found that as much tear-gas equipment was sold to corporations as was sold to law-enforcement bodies. The Senate Committee reported that The Republic Steel Corporation was not only the largest purchaser of tear and sickening gas in the nation but it also had "more ... gas equipment than has been purchased by any other corporation, or by any law-enforcement body, local, State, or Federal, in the country. It has loosed its guards, thus armed, to shoot down citizens on the streets and highways" (cited in Mitchell, 1947: 282–3).

Throughout the period the "Red Scare" was widely deployed against unions. The bogey of communism, and of its late-twentieth-century successor, terrorism, has throughout modern American history offered private and State power carte blanche to visit surveillance and violence upon unions and Left activists. Though some have characterized the postwar New Deal/Great Society settlement as a "capital–labor accord," and though the New Dealers of the 1930s were fond of terming the administration's reforms as representing a "partnership" between capital and labor, as labor historian Jerold Auerbach has written, "The La Follette Committee did not warn of the imminence of class warfare, it documented its existence" (Auerbach, 1966: 152).

THE FIFTH INTERVENTION: THE PLOT TO OVERTHROW ROOSEVELT

During the New Deal, class warfare took an astonishing turn. A class putsch was in the making, with the aim of capturing the State apparatus by replacing the Roosevelt administration with a regime modeled on Mussolini's in Italy.

The Depression, though deepest in the U.S., spread like a virus across much of the world, creating the conditions for the rise, in the developed capitalist countries, of far-Right populist movements. In an important study of the legacy of the New Deal and the Great Depression, Ira Katznelson observes that "[T]he country's leaders were keenly aware that threats to liberal democracy were proliferating in a way that was without precedent … [T]here were plenty of dangers at home and a continuing atrophy for liberal democracy abroad" (Katznelson, 2013: 38–9).

Fascist tendencies were either in place or growing in Germany, Italy, Spain, Japan and elsewhere. As the Depression endured, by the end of the decade only France, Britain, the Netherlands and Scandinavia had eluded the anti-democratic wave sweeping across Europe. In the U.S. racism was manifest in full force, imperial expansion was in the works, and the anti-Semitic Rightist populism of Father Coughlin was heard regularly on the radio. "[A]nd there was a good deal of anti-civil liberties counterpunching by Congress, the courts and the executive branch. American democracy may not have risked the same apocalyptic fate as the Weimar Republic. Nevertheless, there was a real set of pitfalls" (Katznelson, 2013: 39). But "pitfalls" grossly understates the power of fascist tendencies in the U.S. in this period. Katznelson's otherwise illuminating work makes no mention of the business plot to overthrow Roosevelt.

What we know of this comes from the findings of the 1934 special congressional committee appointed to conduct an investigation of the planned coup. At the time, the shocking results of the investigation were only patchily reported, and it soon faded from public memory as Roosevelt hushed it up and consigned the Committee Report to the National Archives.

On the domestic front, business felt betrayed by deficit spending, business regulation, the administration's social programs and the president's apparent encouragement of organized labor actions and the strikes they encouraged. On the international front, Roosevelt's initiatives only confirmed businessmen's conviction that the president was a Red in capitalist clothing. In 1933 Roosevelt had granted diplomatic recognition to the Soviet Union. Washington's official stance until then had been to support the return to power of the White Russians. Roosevelt exchanged embassies with the Soviets. (His change of heart was no doubt prompted by his anticipation of a U.S.–Soviet alliance against German and Italian looming aggression.) Nor did it comfort industry and finance that about 63 percent of the nation's 1,139 newspapers supported Roosevelt's overture, largely on the grounds that it would open a very large export market (Denton, 2012: 193). Roosevelt went on to enlist the Soviet Union as an ally in the event of German aggression, and shortly thereafter announced, as part of his "Good Neighbor" policy, that Washington would cease sending troops to Latin America to protect what were in fact vast private investments there. If "business confidence" was a key condition of investment, recovery efforts could be expected to fail. And they did.

Businessmen's horror at what they considered Roosevelt's socialism engendered the conviction that only a fascist-style government could enforce the kind of economic "discipline" that needed to be imposed on the working class, and restore their own confidence and profits. Italy was perceived as the more promising model. Business leaders there had financed Mussolini's ascendancy, effected a bloodless coup, made the king of Italy into a powerless figurehead and established a corporate-military state relatively immune to the ravages of the global depression (United States Congress, 1934: 21).

In November, as the congressional committee discovered, about 24 of the foremost members of the economic elite hatched a generously funded plot to effect a fascist coup. The plotters represented prominent families – Rockefeller, Mellon, Bush, Pew – and enterprises like Morgan, Dupont, Remington, General Motors Corporation, Swift, Sun Oil, Anaconda, Bethlehem and Goodyear, along with the owners of Bird's Eye, Maxwell House and Heinz. They had planned to assemble a private army of half a million men, composed largely of unemployed veterans, which would constitute the armed force behind the coup and defeat any resistance to it. The economic elite would provide whatever else was required to sustain the new government (Archer, 2007). The aim was not to topple Roosevelt, who was to remain as a figurehead, but to put real executive power in the hands of a business–military coalition (not unlike the business–military junta later assembled by President Trump). "Presidential" decisions were to be made by a key member of the new cabinet.

Capitalists sought to capture the State itself, which it perceived as a greater threat to its dominance than the Depression and the Second New Deal. What the coup plotters had in common with the four previous interventions was that they too were responding to a perceived need to address perceived crisis conditions. The success of the late-nineteenth-century drive – "morganization" – to consolidate industry and avert destructive competition was spearheaded by big capital. The early-twentieth-century attempt to stabilize business and address the persistence of price competition through government regulation was also led by corporate interests. But now businessmen were convinced that private initiative alone was insufficient. Government had to be enlisted to accomplish what business alone was powerless to bring about. The apprehensions of businessmen were not unfounded. We shall see that the State functions set in place by the New Deal and expanded under the Great Society did indeed notably enhance the power of the working class and in fact effected a steady and growing downward distribution of national income from the 1930s to the early 1970s, the only such downward distribution in American history (Picketty And Saez, 2006: 200–5). *Beginning with the New Deal and extending through the Golden Age, capital learned a lesson it would finally apply consciously and persistently from the mid-1970s and on: capturing State power for capital must be a deliberate and sustained political project.*

The fly in this ointment lay in the coup plotters' choice of agent. They chose General Smedley Butler to lead the veterans' army. This Medal of Honor recipient and Marine Major General was to force Roosevelt to resign because of bad health while retaining him as a figurehead (Denton, 2012: 195). According to the plotters' representative in contact with Butler, the country needed "a man on a white horse ... a dictator who would come galloping in" in order to "save the capitalistic system" (United States Congress, 1934: 21). James Van Zandt, the national commander of the Veterans of Foreign Wars, revealed that he had been invited by "agents of Wall Street" to participate in an operation to overthrow the Roosevelt administration (Weber, 2007: 201). The plotters hoped that widespread working-class discouragement at the persistence of the Great Depression would have sufficiently disenchanted the masses with Roosevelt's policies to make the coup an easy ride.

However, Butler turned out to have been the wrong choice. In one of the most consequential ironies of American history, before his retirement from the Marine Corps, having won every medal conferred by the U.S. government, by 1931 Butler had come to recognize the imperialist character of the operations he had led. In an August 1931 speech to an American Legion convention he reported that "I spent 33 years [in the Marines] ... most of my time being a high-class muscle man for Big Business, for Wall Street and the bankers. In short, I was a racketeer, a gangster for capitalism" (cited in Archer, 2007: 118). He named the business interests behind interventions he had commanded in "half a dozen Central American republics" and in Haiti, the Dominican Republic, Cuba, Mexico and China.

It was Butler who thwarted the plotters. Appalled by the plot, Butler exposed it to the press, which sat on the story lest the public, already sour on big business, be moved to action far more threatening than strikes. This enabled Roosevelt to nip the plan in the bud. Butler testified about the planned coup before unpublicized hearings of the House Committee on Un-American Activities in November 1934. Some of the testimony is available in a 1934 government report (House of Representatives, 1934).

Butler's fuller reflections on corporate control of U.S. foreign policy can be found in his booklet *War Is a Racket* (Butler, 1935).

That the leading echelons of America's capitalist elite looked with approval upon politics in Japan, Italy and Germany and sought to replicate fascist government at home was one of the most stunning developments in the history of the republic, and something every American needed to know. There was, after all, no reason to think that the scotching of the plot erased the fascist instincts of the ruling class. But Roosevelt was himself a member of the very class that moved against him. He had no interest in publicizing a plot that might constitute a public-relations victory for anti-capitalist tendencies. He therefore refused to expose the plotters, and sought no punitive measures against them. In the end, class solidarity carried the day for Roosevelt. The congressional committee cooperated by refusing to reveal the names of many of the key plotters. Thus, *fascist tendencies gestating deep within the culture of the U.S. ruling class were effectively left to develop unopposed by mass political mobilization.* The current forging of the infrastructure of a police state in the U.S., and the dismantling of some of America's most powerful constitutional protections in the context of the most severe economic crisis since the Great Depression, should come as no surprise.

THE SIXTH INTERVENTION: THE "SECOND NEW DEAL"
AND ITS PARADIGMATIC ACHIEVEMENTS

Even as investment, output and employment plunged to their nadir just months after Roosevelt assumed office, major developments during his first year set the stage for the steepest cyclical expansion in U.S. history. Between late 1933 and 1937, real GDP grew by 12 percent and nominal GDP by 14 percent. A combination of increased unionization and higher wages, along with projects such as the Triborough Bridge complex and the Tennessee Valley Authority, got the expansion under way. What accounted for the duration of the upswing were larger-scale New Deal projects spurred by labor activism and the uncommonly radical wave of congressmen who were newly elected to Congress.

The tumultuous labor actions of 1934 in which labor tested the rights offered them under NIRA Section 7a forced the administration and Congress to launch what has come to be called the "Second New Deal" of 1935–36. In July 1935, Roosevelt established the Works Progress Administration (WPA), which replaced the Federal Emergency Relief Act (FERA). It was historic because it aimed, in the words of Roosevelt's Executive Order 7034, "to move from the relief rolls to work ... the maximum number of people in the shortest time possible," and to do so entirely with federal funds and under federal administration. The WPA was thus the first explicit acknowledgement that the federal government needed to expand employment to end the Depression. It employed Americans to work on highways, airports, schools, libraries, sewage plants, hospitals, electrification, conservation and housing, among others.

The National Labor Board (NLB) had been set up under the National Recovery Administration (NRA) to "supervise labor relations." The toothlessness of the Board had motivated the West Coast strikes. After it was declared unconstitutional by the Supreme Court in 1935 and abolished, wages fell, work hours were lengthened and unemployment increased (Mitchell, 1947: 258). In July 1934 Roosevelt had abolished the NLB and set up in its place the National Labor Relations Board (NLRB), which succeeded in doing away with company unions as approved instruments for collective bargaining, but still fell far short of labor's expectations.

Shortly after the NLB was declared unconstitutional, Senator Robert F. Wagner, a vociferous underconsumptionist, sought to strengthen the collective bargaining provisions of Section 7a by effecting the passage of the National Labor Relations Act (NLRA), commonly known as the Wagner Act. The bill focused on two factors, the need to empower workers to drive wages upward and the threat of further labor insurgency if labor's bargaining power was not fortified. One representative warned of the consequences of failing to pass the NLRA: "You have seen strikes in Toledo, you have seen San Francisco, and you have seen some of the Southern textile strikes ... but you have not yet seen the gates of hell opened, and that is what is going to happen from now on [if NLRA is not passed]" (cited in Goldfield, 1989: 1253).

Roosevelt refused to give the proposed legislation his strong approval and he remained aloof until it was clear that Congress was about to pass the Act. The NLRA was passed in July 1935, and marked the first time the federal government guaranteed without qualification workers' right to organize and bargain collectively. Correspondingly, companies were prohibited from forcing workers to join a company union and from interfering with union-organizing. Nor could they harass or fire activists for attempting to organize workers, and they were forbidden to refuse to participate in collective bargaining with unions.

Labor was finally able to exploit, through legislation, organized power, which capital had had the good sense to achieve through government regulation late in the nineteenth century. Organization enables gains unavailable to those who act as individuals. The rewards in question are returns to the organized group, and to the individual via membership of that group. The organization may be informal, e.g. industrialists who have agreed among themselves out of self-interest not to engage in price competition; or formal, like the American Medical Association or the United Auto Workers. In a capitalist society businesspersons possess, in addition to the power conferred by organization, structurally determined power by virtue of their ownership of society's productive and financial resources. Such power is enabled and guaranteed by the State. Labor is deeply disadvantaged and subordinated without its own form of organization backed by State power. The union was, and one hopes could once again be, such a form. It can constrain the power of capital and strengthen the power of workers.

Business resistance to the NLRA was intense. When a group of steel companies' Chicago workers struck for union recognition, the companies, armed with millions of dollars' worth of arms, ammunition and gases, enlisted the local police and National Guard to join their own forces to assault picket lines and vandalize strikers' homes. Eighteen workers were killed. Though the NLRA proscribed this sort of private–public violent suppression of labor struggles, Roosevelt seemed indifferent. In response to the Chicago massacre, Roosevelt declared "A plague on both your houses." Fifty-eight prominent lawyers representing the ultra-conservative American Liberty League sought to have the traditionally conservative Supreme Court declare the Wagner Act unconstitutional (Preis, 1972: 70). The NLRA was upheld. Workers and union leaders were satisfied that NLRA acted for the most part in their interests.

It wasn't elite non-profits working hand-in-hand with the Democrats that won the gains of the New Deal. Quite the opposite. It was bottom-up solidarity between different groups of workers, across different industries, employed and unemployed, and, crucially, working independently of the Democrats, that allowed strikes against individual employers to blossom into the three citywide general strikes of the era and to win massive, costly concessions from the 1 percent. Capitalists did not take these losses sitting down. Very soon after the passage of the Wagner Act, business launched a new and successful blow against the very core of the legislation, workers' right to strike. The right to strike was in the crosshairs of the Supreme Court's 1938 decision in National Labor Relations Board vs. Mackay Radio & Telegraph Company (Kohler and Getman, 2006). Mackay and the business community in general understood that the right to strike depended for its efficacy on limits to the companies' ability to access substitute workers. The decision in favor of Mackay permitted companies permanently to replace striking workers. *The impact of the right to strike included in the Wagner Act was severely reduced within three years of its passage.* In 1947 the Taft–Hartley Act would deal the Wagner Act another severe blow in response to the massive worker militancy of 1946.

The Wagner Act and its legacy transformed the social base of the Democratic Party, which had been a minority party for more than 25 years. The resulting image of the party has stuck to this day, in spite of the party's leadership having discarded, under Bill Clinton, the New Deal legacy. Democrats' support in the period 1949–76 of organized labor and increasing government social programs rendered the public susceptible to the Democrats' widely propagated notion that they represent the "party of the working man" while the Republicans are "the party of Big Business." Although by the 1990s the Democrats had repudiated the legacy of the New Deal, most of its members have failed to grasp this, a fact which, as we shall see, bodes ill for the prospects of democracy in America.

SOCIAL SECURITY AND THE WORKS PROGRESS ADMINISTRATION: MAJOR CASUALTIES OF ROOSEVELT'S FISCAL CONSERVATISM

Under the prodding of his most progressive advisors, and fearful of another burst of labor insurgency, Roosevelt sought to advance new programs to alleviate workers' temporary or permanent loss of income from unemployment, old age and disability. He appointed a cabinet-level Committee on Economic Security (CES), whose efforts eventuated in the Social Security Act (SSA) of August 1935, which Roosevelt considered the "crowning jewel" of his administration, the centerpiece of the United States' commitment to public social provision. But it was not unmarked by Roosevelt's fiscal conservatism.

While the SSA provided for federal old-age benefits, most of its provisions consisted in grants to states for old-age assistance, unemployment compensation plans, aid to dependent children, maternal and child welfare, aid to the blind and maintaining public health services. By far the most consequential feature of the Act was the way it was financed. Social Security was to be a "contributory" system supported by taxes levied on employees and employers. *Roosevelt insisted that the program's financing should reflect actuarial principles and resemble as closely as possible a system of private insurance.* Old-age "assistance" or "relief" was stigmatized by the president, and the program, he insisted in November 1934, could not be allowed "to become a dole through the mingling of insurance and relief" (Roosevelt, 1934).

The SSA was not merely the nation's grandest scheme to date to provide essential material security otherwise unavailable to Americans through the private market. It also set the mold for the profoundly conservative political-economic values and assumptions which would frame all subsequent political struggles around social policy and provision. None of the New Deal's policy innovations embraced unreservedly the legitimacy of federal efforts, national in scope, to ameliorate social dependency. Outside the contributory insurance scheme, federal grants to the states were matching grants, requiring substantial contributions from the hard-pressed states as a condition of federal assistance for aid to the elderly, the blind and dependent children, all of whom were categorized as a sub-class of the unemployed. As with unemployment insurance, states were left responsible for setting benefit levels and standards of eligibility. In order to discourage enthusiasm for a national plan of unemployment insurance, employers were permitted to deduct what they paid their state governments from what they owed the federal government (Rauchway, 2008a: 101). The law thus provided an incentive for states to prefer their own unemployment insurance programs to a national, federally funded plan. By the same token it guaranteed that benefits from state to state would differ, sometimes greatly.

It is clear from Roosevelt's 1935 State of the Union Address that his unwillingness to support a system comparable to what had been established earlier in a number of European states, a federal nationwide and universal system of social protection, was due in large part to his inability to put aside the balanced-budget imperative. The 1935 address advised the public of Roosevelt's forthcoming program of social insurance and his "new and greatly enlarged plan" for "emergency public works," the Works Progress Administration, and alerted the public to his forthcoming program of social insurance. Referring to "those unable … to maintain themselves independently," Roosevelt noted that "Such people, in the days before the great depression, were cared for by local effort – by states, by counties, by towns, by cities, by churches, and by private welfare agencies. It is my thought that in the future they must be cared for as they were before … [C]ommon sense tells us that the wealth necessary for this task exists and still exists in the local community, and the dictates of sound administration require that this responsibility be in the first instance a local one" (Schlesinger and Israel, 1966, 3: 2811). This was as unambiguous a commitment as one could imagine to American anti-federalism. Roosevelt's picture of local communities awash, in the midst of a deep depression, in wealth sufficient to meet the needs of the handicapped and the ill was fanciful in the extreme, based on little other than his dogma that the federal budget must be balanced.

Roosevelt's plan for an unparalleled public works program too was based in large part on his aversion to "giving people something for nothing," but the dramatic labor actions finally convinced him that large-scale public employment was the only means to "putting people back to work" (ibid.). Most Americans considered public relief a stigma, a sign of dependence that diminished personal liberty and a license to others to judge one as lazy or incompetent. Elites and their government disparaged relief as encouraging social expectations of government assistance and as an alternative to workers' dependence on the employer for their livelihood. The aristocrat Roosevelt shared the disdain for relief characteristic of his class. In the 1935 Address he declared that

> [D]ependence upon relief indices a spiritual disintegration fundamentally destructive of the national fiber. To dole out relief in this way is to administer a narcotic, a subtle destroyer of the human spirit. It is inimical to the dictates of a sound policy. It is in violation of the traditions of America. Work must be found for able-bodied but destitute workers. The federal government must and shall quit this business of relief. (ibid.: 2814–15)

In the same passage the president revealed a more fundamental rationale for the rejection of public assistance, that it is inconsistent with "sound [fiscal] policy." Roosevelt's obsession with budget-balancing explains the basic contours of his preferred version of Social Security and the sharp curtailment of New Deal programs precipitating the recession of 1937–38.

Roosevelt's commitment to "sound finance" placed severe limits on the New Deal's ability to design policies that would transform American capitalism into an advanced social democracy. The president's repeated use of "emergency" in the Address – "new program of emergency public employment," "emergency public projects" – suggests that the WPA was confronting a temporary malfunction, not the chronic symptoms of contradictions inherent in the basic organization of a mature capitalist economy.

As for the WPA, "The main idea was that employment on public projects, as distinguished from acceptance of doles, would preserve the workers' precious self-respect, conserve skills, and utilize vast resources for the creation of wealth" (Mitchell, 1947: 319). According to the 1935 Executive

Order No.7034, WPA was charged with "the honest, efficient, speedy, and coordinated execution of that program … to move from the relief rolls to work … the maximum number of persons in the shortest time possible." As we saw earlier, Keynes's alternative position was that capitalism required a permanent public works project that would operate during economic contractions *and* expansions. This was not the idea behind the WPA conceived as a temporary emergency effort. But the WPA succeeded in undertaking precisely those tasks Keynes argued were always needed, at any point in the business cycle. Under the program, workers built bridges, hospitals, public parks, schools, playgrounds and airports. It employed architects, artists, musicians and writers. Troupes of actors were paid to perform Shakespeare in towns and cities across the country.

Roosevelt's deficit phobia would also infect his Social Security program. The CES appointed by the president to draft plans for social insurance sent Roosevelt a report calling for universal coverage for the elderly, financed partly by contributions from the elderly and partly from the Treasury's general revenues. Gradually the Treasury's contribution would grow to cover most or all pension payments. The Committee also recommended universal health insurance, on the traditional Americans grounds that a citizen could not be truly "independent" if his ability to function were threatened by health issues. The powerful American Medical Association strongly opposed this provision, and Roosevelt rejected universal provisions for the elderly on the grounds that they were "the same old dole under another name" (cited in Rauchway, 2008a: 98). Roosevelt wanted a plan with no traces of "relief," understood as any form of government contribution to Americans' welfare unrelated to their work contribution. It was essential for the president that the program's financing not draw on the Treasury. It had to be "self-financing," i.e. paid for by the co-parties of the work relation, employee and employer. Each would pay, out of its income, a tax which would be placed into a fund from which the worker would draw upon retirement.

Roosevelt's essentially regressive plan could not possibly be universal and equitable in scope. Contributions as a percentage of income imposed a heavier burden on low-income workers. A bold new government program of social insurance had been announced in the throes of a severe depression. The public, the press and many of Roosevelt's most sophisticated advisors were in agreement that Roosevelt's version of Social Security was undesirable because its regressive character flew in the face of the conspicuous fact of gross income inequality. Hardly discussed, however, was the racist character of the legislation. Social Security excluded from coverage about half the workers in the American economy. Among the excluded groups were agricultural and domestic workers – a large percentage of whom were African–Americans.

The landslide election of 1934 brought to Washington many Democrats, a few third-party candidates and secular stagnationists elected on promises to fight for redistribution. The new Congress was in fact far more radical than the president, framing the main problem in class terms: the "channels of surplus investment" and the "idle" and "sterile" savings of the rich were seen as the depleted resources of the working class. The quoted terms were common parlance in Congress and in some of the most prestigious magazines, such as *The Nation* and *The New Republic* (Leff, 1983: 364).

The nation's leading social-insurance authorities were among the redistributionists. Abraham Epstein repudiated Roosevelt's plan as "a system of compulsory payments by the poor for the impoverished" that relieved "the well-to-do from their share of the social burden" (Epstein, 1936: 782). Prominent New Dealers such as Harry Hopkins, Robert Wagner, Paul Douglas, Henry Wallace, Robert La Follette, Gardiner Means and Fiorello La Guardia espoused the underconsumptionist account of the cause of the Great Depression. In their eyes the account followed from the fact of gross inequality. It is no surprise that *none of the popular financing alternatives for Social Security envisioned payroll tax contributions*. The ideology of fiscal conservatism had not taken root among the general population. A payroll tax was a wage tax, and who would support reducing wages in depression times? A progressive tax or an entirely federally funded program to fund Social Security would perform what so many of Roosevelt's advisors took to be the cardinal task of the day, to redistribute income downwards.

One of the administration's responses to the charge of the unfairness of the wage tax was to remind his advisors and the general public that employers too would be required to contribute to the program through taxes. Mainstream economists of the time dismissed the argument, and for good reason. If the employer was required to pay a tax based on the worker's wage, which would return to the worker in the form of old-age insurance, then that tax was equivalent to a wage increase. The rational response of capitalist employers would be either to offer lower wages to offset the employer tax, or to raise prices, or both. In a press conference Roosevelt himself confessed that he understood this: "[O]bviously in 9,999 cases out of 10,000" the employer share of payroll taxes "will be passed on in the cost of goods sold" (Leff, 1983: 380–1). They were right. It is now generally accepted that the employer Social Security tax is offset by a reduced real-wage level.

Roosevelt insisted that workers' benefits should "be a result of their own efforts and foresightedness." Otherwise, the virtues of individual thrift and self-reliance would be diminished. Roosevelt reiterated his philosophy two years after the SSA was passed: "[A]s regards social insurance of all kinds, If I have anything to say about it, it will always be contributed, both on the part of the employer and the employee, on a sound actuarial basis. It means no money out of the Treasury" (Leff, 1983: 368, 370, 373). The president's partial privatization of Social Security functioned historically to make any future claim on general revenues, e.g. for grants to the states to administer unemployment compensation plans, for aid to dependent children, for maternal and child welfare or for maintaining public health services, appear remote and out of synch with American traditions.

Roosevelt's repeated characterization of social insurance as an "earned right" is an oxymoron. States confer rights in accordance with the *kind of society* the State wishes to uphold. One needn't *earn* the politically constituted entitlement to the material requisites of a satisfying and fulfilling life. One's level of income is irrelevant to one's claim to material security.

No capitalist regime would contribute to the forging, on a permanent basis, of the *kind of society* for which considerations such as these carry overriding weight. One of the leading policy-guiding axioms currently precluding public provision of social benefits in capitalist societies is the same doctrine that guided Roosevelt's design for Social Security, the doctrine of sound finance. The antipathy to government deficit spending would again come to the fore under neoliberalism, when it would become simultaneously the overriding argument against addressing working-class needs in times of crisis and a major tool in the construction of the post-democratic age of austerity under financialized capitalism.

THE END OF THE RECOVERY AND THE TRIUMPH OF "SOUND FINANCE"

The WPA and other smaller stimulus measures provided sufficient momentum to the economy that a sharp upturn began in late 1933 and lasted until the slump of late 1937. By summer of that year industrial production had recovered from about half the 1929 level in 1933 to within 5 percent of that level (Economic Intelligence Service, 1938: 136). This was one of the two longest cyclical expansions in the nation's history (Hansen, 1941: 83). But between 1929 and 1937 the labor force had grown from 48 million to 53 million and industrial productivity had grown at a rate faster than the

Golden Age average. Thus, even if production had been restored to the level of 1929, the economy of the richest and most productive country in the world would have made no progress at all (Arndt, 1972: 60–1). 1929 saw 3 million unemployed; in 1937 the figure was 8 million. The economy fell short of full employment by about 5 million. Keynes's charge that the Roosevelt administration had overestimated the success of the recovery was confirmed.

The recovery of 1933–37 exhibited the fastest growth rates of the twentieth century. At the peak of the expansion, industrial output and national income had returned to 1929 levels and purchases of new autos surpassed 1929 sales (Livingston, 2009: 39). New auto sales were fuelled by consumer spending. *The consumer demand that drove this exceptional recovery was enabled by public, not private, investment.* It is not investment as such that capitalist development renders increasingly otiose, but (net) *private* investment. Public investment as the predominant form of investment is both required to avert chronic bubbles-cum-stagnation and not possible under capitalism. Even so, government investment during the New Deal was not the direct cause of the recovery of 1933–37. To think otherwise is to focus only on the employment-generating nature of New Deal programs. Overlooked is the fact that employment growth is economically significant only by virtue of providing income or spending power to workers, whose consumption expenditures constitute the main incentive to increased production and sustained, rather than mere "emergency," employment. The direct cause of the recovery was the increase in consumption demand in an economy whose vitality was no longer dependent on private investment demand but on the purchases, principally of durable goods, of working-class households. As H.W. Arndt put it:

Whereas in the past cyclical recoveries had generally been initiated by a rising demand for capital goods in response to renewed business confidence and new investment opportunities, and had only consequentially led to increased consumers' income and demand for consumption goods, the recovery of 1933–7 seems to have been based on rising demand for consumers' goods. (Arndt, 1972: 62; Livingston, 2009: 40)

This rise in consumers' demand did not require new, net investment; replacement and maintenance expenditures were sufficient to the task (Arndt, 1972: 64). While "it was the Government's 'net contributions' to consumers' purchasing power which were directly responsible for the rise in consumers' demand," (ibid.: 63) the New Deal took no steps to ensure the permanence of adequate consumer demand or household income. Roosevelt took his policies to be temporary urgencies to be terminated once their "jump-start" aims had been accomplished. He impatiently anticipated the time when he could reduce deficit spending and return to the principles of sound finance. Things began looking encouraging to the president in 1937. From fiscal year 1936 to fiscal year 1937, total government expenditures dropped and the deficit fell, while federal tax receipts increased (*Statistical Abstract of the United States 1938*, 1939: 171–3).

As early as January 1937, Roosevelt was planning retrenchment (*The New York Times*, "President Plans 600,000 WPA Cut," January 26, 1937, cited in Rauchway, 2008a). In January 1938 the president announced with relief that the increase in government income meant that New Deal deficits – meaning New Deal programs – must be reduced to 0.1 percent of GDP and that taxes would be increased to fund the Social Security program. So eager was the president to bring the budget closer to balance that he could overlook the sharp declines in employment that had begun in September 1937. The president had felt forced by circumstance to accept policy to which he was otherwise opposed, direct federal employment. The improved fiscal picture provided Roosevelt with the opportunity to cut WPA jobs and other income-generating programs. Keynes promptly wrote to the president, shortly after his announcement, that it was an "error of optimism to act as if recovery were assured when it had only just begun." The president should invest, Keynes urged, more heavily in public works lest another disaster ensue (Barber, 1996: 108–112; Brinkley, 1996: 82–5, 94–7).

The president paid no heed. New Deal spending fell and unemployment rose (Renshaw, 1999: 343–4). The economy plunged into another, somewhat shorter and shallower, depression. The new contraction was doubly discouraging, causing public confidence in the New Deal to diminish and business to feel threatened by the radical claim that it had been shown to be unable to deliver on its promise to bring about economic renewal once government had withdrawn.

Federal Reserve Chairman Eccles urged renewed government spending and Roosevelt increased WPA and Agricultural Adjustment Act (AAA) spending, but not by very much. His eggs were in another basket: "The president banked heavily on new military expenditures" (Mitchell, 1947: 45). Roosevelt saw the growing aggression of Mussolini, Hitler and Tojo in Africa, Europe and East Asia as calling for a re-evaluation of American neutrality. Public opinion polls in 1938 and 1939 found the public disapproving of the military spending as excessive in the light of intensified economic hardship at home. The 1937 cyclical peak did not after all end the Depression. In that year workers were still pressing for what they deserved but had not yet gained. 1937 saw a massive sit-down strike at the General Motors plant in Flint, Michigan. That the strike enjoyed broad public support is a measure of the public's awareness that the recovery did not mean that the Depression was over. In a surprise move, the Governor called out the National Guard to protect the strikers from possible violent resistance by General Motors.

Observing all this from Cambridge, UK, Keynes wrote another letter to Roosevelt on February 1, 1938* politely urging the president to redouble the efforts that had produced the 1937–38 upswing:

> the present recession is partly due to an "error of optimism" which led to an over-estimation of future demand ... The recovery was mainly due to the following factors: ... the establishment of easy short-term money; ... the creation of an adequate system of relief for the unemployed; ... public works and other investments aided by Government funds or guarantees; ... investment in the instrumental goods required to supply the increased demand for consumption goods; ... the momentum of the recovery [was] thus initiated. (pp. 1–2)

But the recovery nonetheless came to an end. What accounted for the resumption of the Depression, and how could that outcome have been prevented?

The remedy would have been to resume government spending as before. Keynes insisted that the problem rested with current policy, which not only must not be retrenched, as Roosevelt had done, but must be amplified. More-of-the-same is not enough. Of the above-mentioned stimulants that had produced the 1937–1938 upswing, the most important were government investment in public works and similar projects and in the production of consumer goods, but they were not large enough. *The momentum of recovery resulting from the initial stimulus is not self-sustaining.* "recovery ... requires for its continuance, not merely the maintenance of recovery, but always *further* recovery. Thus it always flatters the early stages and steps from under just when support is most needed. It was largely, I think, a failure to allow for this which caused the 'error of optimism' last year" (p. 3, emphasis added).

---

* The text of the letter can be found at https://tinyurl.com/y9u9x6yw

Keynes makes it clear that *increasing* spending on public works is the linchpin of sustained recovery. If spending is not increased, the economy's "forward movement" will reverse itself. Thus, forward movement must also be what Keynes called "upward movement" (p.3), creating a higher level of demand, not merely sustaining the existing level. Output and income must increase together over time. This means that investment spending too must increase. The nature of capitalism is that demand requires not merely to be maintained but to be increased, and that requires increased investment. The upshot is that government must be permanently involved in support of effective demand, and since the precondition of demand is the availability of jobs, government must become a permanent provider of employment.

In his letter to Roosevelt, Keynes recommends "increased investment in durable goods such as housing, public utilities and transport ... in the United States at the present time the opportunities, indeed the necessity, for such developments were unexampled" (p.3). Keynes expressed his disappointment at the Roosevelt administration's indifference to these priorities. "Take housing. When I was with you three and a half years ago the necessity for effective new measures was evident ... But what happened? Next to nothing" (p.4).

He went on to make the case for investment in public housing as, in effect, an ideal framework stimulant for a more buoyant and sustained recovery.

Housing is by far the best aid to recovery because of the large and continuing scale of potential demand; because of the wide geographical distribution of this demand; and because the sources of its finance are largely independent of the Stock Exchanges. I should advise putting most of your eggs in this basket, *caring* about this more than about anything, and making absolutely sure that they are being hatched without delay. (p.4; emphasis in original)

Roosevelt apparently did not "care" enough to launch such a program. To this day the U.S. has one of the poorest records on public housing of all the developed capitalist countries. Perhaps Roosevelt's and future administrations were aware of intimations of socialism implicit in Keynes's urgings: "There are few more proper objects for such than working class houses. If a direct subsidy is required to get a move on (we gave our subsidies *through* the local authorities), it should be given without delay or hesitation" (p.4).

As if to add insult to injury, Keynes implores Roosevelt to nationalize the utilities, have the State plan heavy investments, encourage collective bargaining, set a minimum wage and limit the hours of work:

Personally I think there is a great deal to be said for the ownership of all the utilities by publicly owned boards ... If I was in your place, I should buy out the utilities at fair prices in every district where the situation was ripe for doing so, and announce that the ultimate ideal was to make this policy nation-wide ... a policy of *competing* plants with losses all round is a ramshackle notion. ... Nationalize [the railroads] if the time is ripe ... I accept the view that durable investment must come increasingly under state direction ... I regard the growth of collective bargaining as essential. I approve minimum wage and hours regulation. (pp.5, 6, 8)

Summing up his policy recommendations, Keynes declares that "A convincing policy, whatever its details may be, for promoting large-scale [government] investment under the above heads is an urgent necessity... Far too much precious time has passed" (pp.6–7). There will be resistance, Keynes acknowledges, to these measures. Capital will greet all these recommendations with great alarm. Keynes's instructions to Roosevelt on the proper handling of businessmen is wonderfully clever, close to Oscar Wilde at his best:

Business men have a different set of delusions from politicians; and need, therefore, different handling ... You could do anything you liked with them, if you would treat them (even the big ones), not as wolves and tigers, but as domestic animals by nature, even though they have been badly brought up and not trained as you would wish. It is a mistake to think that they are more *immoral* than politicians. If you work them into the surly, obstinate, terrified mood, of which domestic animals, wrongly handled, are so capable, the nation's burdens will not get carried to market. (p.7)

The notion that big capital can be cajoled to acquiesce in the socialization of some of the nation's biggest private investments strikes us as naïve. In Keynes's day capital had nothing resembling the virtually complete hegemony over public policy that finance capital enjoys today. But about this Keynes was right: capitalists are not more immoral than politicians. The need to enlarge profits under conditions of international competition does not permit moral restraint, any more than those sitting around a Monopoly board should throw the game out of empathy with the losers. The rules and objects of the game are such that moral considerations have no application. Not so with politicians, who are supposed to legislate in the interests of the population as a whole. Protecting the citizenry from the vagaries of the market is a moral and political imperative. This is why picketing the banks, as some did after the September 2008 debacle, betrays a failure to grasp the source of economic power. In themselves, the banks are powerless. Such powers as they have are *legislated*, all of them. Banks will do what they do, Capital (sic) Hill willing. Political economy is first political.

Roosevelt could not have been expected to embrace Keynes's counsel. The resumed spending, niggardly as it was, brought about a minor rebound, but the overall contraction was not ended until the U.S. mobilized for entry into the Second World War. The economy's recalcitrance to sustained recovery was due to the post-industrialization architecture, identified earlier, exhibited in the 1920s.

WAS THE DEPRESSION THE RESULT OF OVERINVESTMENT OR UNDERCONSUMPTION?

Commentators have described the 1929 downturn as either an overinvestment or an underconsumption crisis. A prima facie case can be made for either or both. Key markets had become saturated and excess capacity was conspicuous. Wages barely moved over the decade, so households had to resort to debt in order to finance rising consumption expenditure.

It is true that capacity expansion in the most dynamic industries of the 1920s could not be sustained without limit. In this sense the excess capacity in durable-goods industries reached its limit for much the same reasons that excess capacity in railroads and steel reached their limits during the nineteenth century. In the latter case basic capital-goods industries were just getting off the ground. But the very notion of industrialization implies a limit or terminus. An industrializing economy becomes industrialized, at which point private investment must slow down. In a rationally planned economy, investment would be made to taper off and the surplus shifted to wages and consumer-goods industries, but in a profit-driven economy in which present optimism or competitive pressure (or both) determines future production, overinvestment in inevitable. During the 1920s consumer-goods industries were just getting off the ground on a mass scale. Robert A. Gordon claimed that consumption could not have continued to increase at the same rate as investment in consumer-goods production was increasing *while consumer durable-goods industries were being built from scratch (just as were capital-goods industries in the nineteenth century)* (Gordon, 1974: 71). Indeed. But why could consumption not increase at the same rate as the means of producing consumer goods were increasing?

One possible reason why consumption could not grow as fast as investment in consumer-goods production is that consumption at a given level of economic development has an in-effect-natural limit in the absence of a sustained effort, such as described in the previous chapter, to raise it artificially through an intense advertisement and credit drive. The notion that consumption becomes normally sated is not eccentric. It was, as we shall see, a key assumption of Keynes in his argument for shorter work hours and the predominance of public investment in *Economic Possibilities For Our Grandchildren*. It is a notion held also by those who understand much of modern desire under capitalism to be fabricated. The distinguished American economist Joseph Stiglitz comments on the consumerism we have seen to have originated in the 1920s: "[W]e can think of ourselves as learning how to 'consume' ... [F]irms have been as inventive in creating new demands as they have been in creating new products ... [W]e are 'taught' to consume by others, especially by firms" (Pecchi and Piga, 2010: 57). We shall see in Appendix B that Keynes believed that the rational desire for consumables was and should be limited, and that this conviction was essential to his conception of the greater possibilities for humankind that capitalism has made possible for the first time in history.

The most compelling reason behind Gordon's claim that consumption in the 1920s could not have risen as rapidly as investment can be found in the historical analysis presented so far in this book. I have argued that *an economic downturn is brought about by the retardation of whatever it is that primarily drives capitalist growth in the period in question.* Nineteenth-century growth was driven by investment demand, which proved to be recurrently excessive. Nineteenth-century crises are accordingly theorized as overinvestment crises. After industrial maturation, economic growth is propelled, as it surely was in the 1920s, by consumption demand. *Recall that in the most dynamic period of capital expansion during the 1920s, 1923–26, there was no net addition to the capital stock* (see Chapter 3, pp. 67, 82). Since it was effective household demand that was the driver of the economy in the twenties, the decade's limits on wage increases constituted at the same time a limitation on that species of demand that had become necessary and sufficient for growth and employment. Spending power was buoyed by debt, but wage limits set debt limits, and consumer demand was correspondingly curtailed. The outcome was crisis. I conclude, contrary to Gordon, that the Great Depression was an underconsumption crisis.

SYSTEMIC PROBLEMS AND SECULAR STAGNATION

In his December 1938 presidential address to the American Economic Association, Alvin Hansen argued that the U.S. had reached economic maturity (Hansen, 1939: 1-15). Population growth had decelerated dramatically, continental expansion had reached its limit, and there had been no major demand-stimulating technological innovation since the automobile. Hansen did not consider overseas expansion as an offsetting factor, but in the meantime history has shown that America's extensive overseas economic presence has not averted the current underconsumption crisis and the consequent financialization of the economy. Nor could inventions like the railroad and the automobile be counted on to materialize into perpetuity. Economic stagnation was on the permanent agenda unless government investment and employment took up the slack. Hansen's position was virtually identical to the argument that Keynes had put forward a year earlier in the important but rarely referenced Galton Lecture delivered before the Eugenics Society in 1937 (Keynes, [1937] 1973: 124-33).

In that presentation Keynes revealed more explicitly than he had in *The General Theory* his historical approach to the analysis of capitalist dynamics. He understood the nineteenth century to have been the high point of capital accumulation in the United States. Referring to the period 1860–1913, he observed that "[T]he demand for new capital has come from two sources, each of about equal strength: a little less than half of it to meet the demands of a growing population; a little more than half of it to meet the demands of inventions and improvements which increase output per head and permit a higher standard of life" (ibid.: 130).

Population growth "increases proportionately the demand for capital" (ibid.: 126) and had slowed down dramatically since the period in question. This tended to reduce the demand for capital. Since significant population growth functions, like a framework stimulant, to boost aggregate demand, its slowing down will reduce the rate of capital accumulation in the absence of an effective replacement. Productivity-enhancing "inventions and improvements" too will cease to increase the demand for new capital. This occurs not because technological advance is retarded or diminished, but rather because innovation can now proceed with less investment than was required during the period of basic capital formation. "Many modern inventions are directed towards finding ways of *reducing the amount of capital investment necessary to produce a given result*" (ibid.: 127; emphasis added). With more efficient means of producing more efficient means of production, new investments tend to cost less. Net investment atrophies.

These developments permit – but, as we shall see in the next chapter, do not necessitate – "a gradual evolution in our attitude towards accumulation" so that we are able "to maintain the liberties and independence of our present system, whilst its more signal faults gradually suffer euthanasia as the diminishing importance of capital accumulation and the rewards attaching to it fall into their proper position in the social scheme" (ibid.: 132-3). But the vices of "our present system" will not disappear in the absence of substantial changes in pervasive features of the current settlement. We shall be "absolutely dependent for the maintenance of prosperity and civil peace on policies of increasing consumption by a more equal distribution of incomes. ... If capitalist society rejects a more equal distribution of incomes ... then a chronic tendency towards the under-employment of resources must in the end sap and destroy that form of society" (ibid.: 132).

Thus, greater equality and higher wages are necessary to avert secular stagnation, whose most epochal effect is to "destroy" capitalism. These decidedly radical claims look nothing like what typically passes for Keynesianism. Keynes's thinking is grossly misrepresented in both popular and scholarly sources. Keynes is in effect an institutional socialist. Appendix B presents a more detailed discussion of both the main features of Keynes's theory and his final policy recommendations, most of which would be put to use by economic planners in a socialist democracy.

5

The Rise and Fall of the Golden Age

THE GOLDEN AGE AS HEIR TO THE NEW DEAL
AND THE GREAT SOCIETY

After the Depression and during the great expansion of the Golden Age or Great Boom, we witnessed the unexpected and unprecedented: *the wealthiest 1 percent's share of national income continued to fall by an increasing percentage each decade during the '30s, '40s, '50s, '60s and early '70s* (Piketty and Saez, 2006: 200–5). The postwar redistribution was the result of New Deal and Great Society social legislation, and the power of labor unions. In the period 1935–73, wage increases were typically led by gains in the unionized industrial sector, and spread thereafter to most other workers. The result was the only 40-year period (1935–75) of downward distribution in the history of the republic, reflected most explicitly in the wage-push profit squeeze, discussed on pp. 148–53, which characterized economic expansions during the Great Boom. A powerful motive was provided capital to begin an organized offensive to reverse the achievements of the New Deal and Great Society and reverse the balance of class power.

WOULD NEW DEAL VICTORIES REMAIN PERMANENT?

If the war ended the Depression and brought about full employment, many Americans wondered what would happen after the war, when 12 million job-seeking veterans would return home. Would the Depression resume or would New Deal policies be restored? By 1945 the administration had in fact dissolved some of the largest New Deal programs. Capitalist uneasiness with "welfare state" policies persisted throughout the postwar period and was expressed in legislation intended to undo the New Deal's most labor-friendly measures. The notion that the postwar period saw a "capital–labor" accord will be shown to be a myth. In fact, postwar developments were to provide early portents of later elite attempts to undo the New Deal settlement.

Against this background American labor felt that it had to consolidate New Deal gains during wartime. Most trade unionists were wary of the administration's new alliance with business leaders and feared that government's assault on labor during the Red Scare after the First World War would resurface during the new war. These apprehensions were prescient. Ongoing labor activism was called for, even in wartime. Labor militancy was essential in sustaining and expanding New Deal programs and creating the unprecedented Golden Age.

LABOR STRUGGLES TO SECURE AND EXPAND NEW DEAL GAINS

As defense production got under way, the Congress of Industrial Organizations (CIO) unions launched a series of strikes from June 1940 through the end of 1941, during which the American Federation of Labor (AFL) and CIO both enrolled 1.5 million new members. In response, government resorted to tactics we have seen employed earlier in situations of labor militancy. Patriotic – more properly, nationalist – feelings were exploited to portray strikes during wartime as subversive of the war effort, even though labor had in fact fully supported it. Roosevelt resurrected anti-communist rhetoric to tame labor. The administration and the United Auto Workers leadership combined to declare the strike a communist-led initiative in opposition to the war itself. Roosevelt sent in 2,500 active-duty troops to break a strike at North American Aviation in California. This was but one instance of cooperation between the federal government and union leaders to curtail labor's freedom during the war (American Social History Project, 1992: 435).

The mass support for labor's gains during the New Deal of 1933–37 made it unfeasible for business and government leaders to attempt, as they had in 1919–20, to do away with trade unionism altogether. Washington attempted in 1945 to extend the wartime "no strike" pledge, a first effort to nullify the Wagner Act. The response of workers was a national wave of strikes. Just as the Wagner Act had solidified labor's power in the mid-1930s, nothing less than new legislation would now be required to weaken it. Thus, it was the 1947 Taft–Hartley Act that would undercut the Wagner Act. The firm determination of business and political elites to defeat labor was prompted by the historically unparalleled labor militancy of the immediate postwar years.

From September through November 1945, 647,000 petroleum, coal mining and lumber workers, machinists and teamsters went on strike. In January 1946, workers upped the ante: 1,474,000 electrical workers, meatpackers and steelworkers struck. In spring, 350,000 miners went out, with the full support of rail workers. The potential unavailability of coal and rail transportation threatened to shut the whole country down. The year ended with a bang: a 54-hour December general strike in Oakland, California. Striking workers controlled traffic in the downtown center of the city. Anyone could leave but entry was permitted only to those with union membership cards (Finamore, 2009). This wave of protests, walkouts and other job actions easily matched in number and scope the landmark strikes of 1919 and 1934, and climaxed in a series of well-organized general strikes that shut down key industrial cities across the country, from Rochester, New York to Houston, Texas and Oakland, California (American Social History Project, 1992: 473). In two years the labor movement had signed up more workers than at any time in its history; by the end of 1946, 40 percent of the labor force was unionized.

The strikes of 1946 brought historic but limited gains for labor. Unions appeared to be recognized as a permanent feature of the postwar landscape and, unlike the situation after the First World War, no major company refused to negotiate with the union representing its employees. But business succeeded in convincing Congress, the president and the courts that in return for the unprecedented rights unions gave workers, postwar contracts must include a "management rights" clause. Firms were thus empowered to claim virtually unlimited rights to determine production standards and to curb the authority of local union officials and shop stewards. The Taft–Hartley Act of 1947 would, we shall see, further increase firms' power over their workers.

The strike actions featured two demands intended to establish a precedent for the postwar order: wage increases and price ceilings to protect wage gains. But corporations continued to administer prices through target pricing in order to prevent price competition and offset wage gains. Here was a clear instance of the limitations of the Wagner Act, which did nothing to prevent these kinds of strategy as instruments of capitalist class power. And because Wagner did nothing to control prices, the most damning defect in the legislation was its severe limitation of workers' ability to achieve real wage gains without incurring mounting debt. *The ongoing cumulative increase in household debt during this period laid the groundwork for the bursting of the credit bubble in 2008.*

In this way the stage was set for an eventual repetition of the scenario of the 1920s. Rising household debt had at that time functioned to maintain purchasing power sufficient to avert economic contraction. Why then did not the postwar period devolve into a repetition of the excess capacity/

underconsumption crisis of the 1920s and 1930s? In fact it did, but this time the crisis was delayed by a cumulative infusion of credit into the economy (see pp. 131–2, 136–7). When the crisis arrived in 2007–08, it took a form appropriate to the peculiar conditions of the increasingly financialized and debt-bloated postwar period.

On the supply side, a good share of corporate profits took the form not of productive investment but of outlays intended to bolster the mentality of ever-growing consumption. *During the entire postwar period capital consumption exceeded net investment* (Livingston, 2011: 219). The resulting surfeit of profits that might have gone into investment flowed instead to advertisement, public relations, market research, artificial product differentiation, expense account entertaining, the multiplication of sales outlets, extravagant office buildings, and the employment of countless business law firms.

THE PERSISTENCE OF THE 1920S STAGNATIONIST SETTLEMENT

It is said that the Second World War ended the Great Depression, but in fact the ghost of the Depression haunted the postwar era. As John Kenneth Galbraith put it: "The Great Depression of the thirties never came to an end. It merely disappeared in the great mobilization of the forties" (Galbraith, 1956: 69). The war addressed none of the factors making the economy liable to catastrophic downturn; the stagnationist configuration of the 1920s remained in place after the war. American capitalism had become industrially fleshed out or mature, its major industries oligopolized, and dramatic gains in production and productivity had become a fixed feature of the economic landscape. Oligopoly pricing policy precluded price declines, and employers would have mitigated wage gains in the absence of organized labor's success in achieving real wage gains when productivity increased. But these gains were insufficient to maintain then-current living standards without cumulative resorts to credit. Keynes had pointed to the disproportionate flow of profits toward investment rather than wages prior to the Depression (Keynes, 1930: 192–5). After both the First and Second World Wars capitalists proceeded as if the economy were still in the business of industrialization: investment was still regarded as the prime mover of production and employment. The shift from investment to consumption had not occurred. The conditions of an underconsumption crisis remained firmly in place.

Do organized labor and debt-supplemented wages explain why the economy did not sink back into depression once the war was over? Yes and no. Labor's militancy and consumer debt were two of nine factors making possible the Golden Age. A number of framework innovations and their functional equivalents, and the lack of effective international economic competition, placed the U.S. in a uniquely advantaged position within the global capitalist order and succeeded in staving off, for about a quarter of a century, a renewed outbreak of growing unemployment and declining living standards.

With the exception of the power of organized labor and mounting debt, each of the other conditions making for the long American boom was necessarily temporary. When the effectiveness of all but one (mounting debt) of the sources of sustained economic growth became spent, roughly between 1965 and 1975, the foundations of the Golden Age were undermined. The power of organized labor was dependent for its long-term efficacy upon a supportive State. Neoliberalism, originating in a well-organized business counteroffensive against the New Deal and the Great Society, spelled an end to such qualified support as the State had offered labor. Business interests set out to restore, in effect, the economic settlement of the 1920s. The putsch of capital was not in vain. Its success would initiate the Age of Austerity.

THE FOUNDATIONS OF THE U.S. GOLDEN AGE

How did the Golden Age come about, and why did it end? The answer lies in a unique set of nine factors contributing to the sustained economic growth and relative prosperity of the Golden Age.

1. The least enduring of these factors was the pent-up purchasing power built up during the war. Wartime strikes kept wages substantially higher than Depression levels. Conversion from civilian to military production meant that goods were limited and rationed. Workers had accumulated sizeable savings, some of which they spent after the war when consumption restrictions were lifted. By its nature, this source of economic expansion was temporary.
2. A far more durable stimulus was the regeneration of the decisive framework innovation of the 1920s, the now-rapidly-growing automobile industry. The automobilization of American society generated massive production and employment across the nation, stimulating the demand for surfaced roads between and within cities, new federally supported highways spanning the entire country, steel, rubber, glass, chrome, oil, gasoline stations, repair shops and more. The travel

industry, with its hotels and motels, was given a hefty boost by the growth of automobile ownership. Equipment, resources and labor were mobilized from coast to coast in the service of what was in effect a national project. Without this development, the wave of postwar suburbanization would not have been possible.

3. The suburbanization of America took off at breakneck speed soon after the war. This revved up the demand for automobiles, housing, road construction, shopping malls, schools, hospitals, libraries, restaurants and workplaces of all kinds. Just about all the requirements of urban life were reproduced in the suburbs, smaller in scale than the great cities, but much greater in number. Suburbanization, like automobilization, constituted a national project marshaling economic resources in a world-class economic growth surge (Jackson, 1987).

4. The nation's unique standing among the advanced capitalist countries allowed it to initiate an international framework stimulus in the form of the Marshall Plan. Much of Europe's industrial infrastructure was in ruins after the war, while America's plant and equipment remained intact and technologically advanced. During the Great Boom the U.S. enjoyed global economic hegemony, as its principal challengers, Europe and Japan, had not yet come forward as formidable competitors. Profits that might otherwise have been shared among global competitors accrued disproportionately to U.S. capital.

America contributed greatly to the effective reindustrialization of Europe, supplying a continent's worth of productive equipment to both victors and vanquished. The Plan had the twofold aim of restoring Western Europe's industrial prowess and shoring it up against communism. It was a great success. In the same process the stage was set for the emergence of renewed international competition, which would contribute to the decline of U.S. economic supremacy and the undoing of the Golden Age.

5. The economic successes of the Soviet Union, the strength of Communist parties in Europe and the appeal of socialism to newly liberated post-colonial states, advances of the Communist Party USA during the Depression and the fear that militant labor could take a "communist turn" led president Truman to initiate the most colossal domestic and global military machine in human history, the military–industrial complex. This "military Keynesianism" required a vast recruitment of personnel, the endless production of increasingly advanced means of warfare enlisting every sector of the industrial economy, the employment of large numbers of engineers and scientists, and of course

the peppering of both the nation and the globe with hundreds of costly – more than 700 overseas to date – military bases. All of this stimulated production and employment on a broadening scale from the early 1950s to the mid-1960s (Dunn, 2014: 99).

6. Organized labor achieved a degree of power hitherto unknown in the U.S. At least one-third of the private workforce was organized by the early 1950s, sufficient for the first time in American history to raise wages at roughly the same rate as increases in productivity. The ability of unions to drive wages upward benefited the entire working class. Significant wage increases across the board during the Golden Age were always spearheaded by gains in the organized sectors. All employers were thus under competitive pressure to offer wages comparable to union wages. Without these wage gains, the framework innovations would not have been sufficient to bring about the sustained expansion definitive of the Golden Age. Rising wage demand increased production, and profits. But prices were not to fall under oligopoly capitalism. Wage increases were insufficient, as we shall see, in the absence of mounting debt, to avoid a recapitulation of the scenario of the 1920s and 1930s. In both the postwar period and the 1920s the key issue was underconsumption, for the economy was during both periods driven by consumption demand, not investment. During the postwar period every cyclical expansion was driven by consumption, typically purchases of homes and durable goods.

   Thus, very much is at stake in keeping the domestic wage level high. Only organized *and militant* workers can accomplish this. Union density is not enough; the strike option must be kept alive. Every substantial gain for labor in the nation's history was achieved only after strike actions (Burns, 2011, 2014). Capital needs always to reduce costs, chiefly labor costs. This ongoing organized pressure to depress wages can be successfully resisted only by organized counterpressure. During both the Great Depression and the most prosperous postwar years, labor unionized and exercised its strike option. Never in U.S. history have workers fared better than during the Golden Age. The fate of the working class depends in part on *militant* labor unions.

7. The postwar period saw the first historic acceptance – reluctant acceptance, we shall see – by elites of significant government programs and transfer payments functioning to raise the level of spending power of the working class, such as unemployment insurance, food stamps, retirement and disability insurance (Social Security), Medicare, Medicaid and Aid to Families with Dependent Children. All these

"welfare state" measures supplemented the employment wage and played a large part in countering the abiding tendency for household purchasing power to be insufficient to maintain production and employment at non-recession levels. But these measures were insufficient to sustain growth and employment. Cumulative private and public debt growth was a necessary condition of Golden Age prosperity.

It is of paramount importance that the federal government ran a fiscal deficit every year during the entire postwar period, with three exceptions: 1960, 1969 and the Bill Clinton surplus of 1997–2001 (Cogan, 1993; Weisenthal, 2012). The most prosperous years for American workers were 1950–73, during which time the deficit gradually increased. Ongoing deficits, Keynes had taught us, were essential to maintain production and employment above severe recession or depression levels. *Substantial* deficits would be necessary to prevent or overcome protracted slowdowns or severe downturns. Accordingly, after the end of the Golden Age, deficits more than doubled during the economically stagnant 1980s and 1990s.

8. During the Golden Age, rising wages were a necessary, but not a sufficient, condition of the increase in purchasing power necessary to produce such a period of economic expansion. It is a measure of just how high wages must be in order fully to avert mass unemployment and growing inequality that increasing injections of household or consumer debt were required to provide the requisite purchasing power. This constitutes further evidence of the persistence of the 1920s stagnationist settlement after the war.

Averting another underconsumption crisis was accomplished by initiating a bubble in consumption, encouraging households to augment their buying power by taking on increasing burdens of debt. Debt is traded for purchasing power and becomes a new source of income. It renders liquid otherwise illiquid assets (Watkins, 2009: 471). Future income is a potential and illiquid asset – made actual and liquid by credit cards, which enable the spending of currently nonexistent income. Home-equity loans turn one's home into an ATM machine, enabling consumers to turn illiquid wealth into consumer purchases and payments of rising healthcare and education bills.

Debt is the postwar settlement's response to underconsumption, which I have argued is the central source of stagnation, inequality and declining living standards in post-industrialization capitalism. In 1946 the ratio of household debt to disposable income stood at about 24 percent. By 1950 it had risen to 38 percent, by 1955 to 53 percent, by 1960 to 62 percent, and by 1965 to 72 percent. The ratio fluctuated from 1966 to 1978, but the stagnation of real wages which began in 1974 pressured households further to increase their debt burden in order to maintain existing living standards, just as they had done during the 1920s, pushing the ratio of debt to disposable income to 77 percent by 1979. By the mid-1980s, with neoliberalism in full swing and wages continuing to stagnate, this ratio began a steady ascent, from 80 percent in 1985 to 88 percent in 1990 to 95 percent in 1995 to over 100 percent in 2000 to 138 percent in 2007 (Federal Reserve System, 2011, Table B.100; Duncan, 2012: 90; *Business Week*, 1974b: 45, 94–6). When the housing bubble first showed signs of leakage in 2006, the percentage of total household debt consisting of mortgage debt rose from 68 to 76 percent (Bradford, 2010: 18–23). As debt rose relative to workers' income, households' margin of security against insolvency began to erode. The ratio of personal saving to disposable income under neoliberalism began a steady decline, falling from 11 percent in 1983 to 2.3 percent in 1999 (Council of Economic Advisors, 2000).

It is clear that some of the strongest roots of the current crisis go back to the immediate postwar period. During the Golden Age the tendency to underconsumption was in operation, was exercised, but was not realized in the form of crisis because it was counteracted by the factors identified above.*

Mirabile dictu, these eight broad stimulants were still insufficient to bring about a 24-year period of uninterrupted economic growth and relative prosperity. For "prosperity" signifies above all that more working-class households than ever before experienced an unprecedented degree of material security. Unthinkable as it seems today, from the late 1940s to the late 1960s the most salient manifestation of economic security was that a household's standard of living was measured by the income of one "bread-winner," typically an adult male. Dad's (debt-supplemented) income was sufficient to feed, clothe and shelter the family, pay medical bills, own an automobile, send the kids to college and save for retirement. This was the condition of much of the fabled American *white* "middle class." Talk of

---

* The distinction between the *exercise* and the *realization* of a tendency is implicit in much scientific theory. The tendency of falling bodies near the surface of the earth to fall at the same, constant rate of acceleration is always exercised by falling bodies, but it is unrealized in observation because of the effects of counteracting forces. The law of falling bodies is not falsified because falling bodies do not conform to the law. Rather, offsetting forces prevent the realization of an exercised natural tendency.

the touted postwar U.S. middle class tacitly presupposes that the heralded benefits of middle-class membership were purchased with the private wage alone as the reward for hard work. This was certainly not the case in the 1920s, when the wage alone left more than 70 percent of households at or barely above the official poverty line (see Chapter 3, pp. 74–5). The postwar debt picture, as we have seen, suggests that the same was the case during the Golden Age. In the absence of substantial debt supplements to household income, most Americans would not have enjoyed the American "middle-class standard of living."

But neither the Golden Age nor its middle class would have come into existence by the normal operations of the private economy alone. *As during the Great Depression, private consumption had to be substantially enabled – not merely supplemented – by public spending.*

9. Thus the final key factor was the Servicemen's Readjustment Act of 1944, the "GI Bill," comparable to a latter-day Works Progress Administration (WPA). It was a major boost to household demand. Among the factors prompting both chambers of Congress unanimously to fund the GI Bill were fears of a repetition, after the war, of the previous postwar strikes and a revival of the Bonus Army March protests of 1932 by millions of returning veterans whose employment prospects were not promising. Elite foreboding was not unfounded. 1946, we recall, turned out to be the second most strike-ridden year in U.S. history.

Elites were apprehensive that the entry of millions of men and women into the labor force might renew mass unemployment and resume the Great Depression. Postwar America was increasingly industrial, as manufacturing soon replaced agriculture as the largest single-occupational category. But manufacturing, like agriculture, was essentially a labor-displacing industry. The need for innovative legislation was clear (Bennett, 1999).

This challenge required a new New Deal strategy addressing the fundamental economic problem, the chronic deficiency of effective demand or purchasing power built into the mature macroeconomic structure. The administration was convinced that these objectives could be achieved by social legislation that would lock in its effects for generations to come (Altschuler and Blumin, 2009). The GI Bill would accomplish this goal.

The impact of this legislation on education, job training and housing was enormous. After the war millions of veterans flocked to colleges and universities across the country. The Bill allowed students to attend schools like Harvard and it prompted the appearance of hundreds of private colleges and bolstered enrollment in both public and private schools. Very much unlike today, young adults had reason to be hopeful about their and their children's future. And they knew that they owed much of that optimism to government's commitment to their well-being. From 1945 to 1956 the GI Bill provided more than 8 million veterans with full post-secondary tuition support and supplements to live on, as well as tuition and book expenses for more than half the nation's college students, and on-job training and farm training. 40 percent of those who had enrolled in college under the GI Bill would not otherwise have done so. These benefits extended well beyond the direct beneficiaries, whose increased income and occupational and employment opportunities were passed on to their children.

Funds were made available for starting small businesses, and low-interest loans were offered for homes. In 1947 about 40 percent of all housing starts were funded by the Bill's loan guarantees. The facilitation of home ownership was a major factor in initiating postwar suburbanization. The GI Bill was a necessary condition for the emergence of the postwar middle class. In 1950 the income gap between social classes was as low as it has ever been in America. The Bill boosted the spending power of working-class households, as credit injections had done.

The Works Progress Administration (WPA) and the GI Bill together provide a paradigm for our times. Each demonstrates that *public spending on a large scale is necessary to sustain economic growth and employment, and provide working people with adequate purchasing power and more than a minimally acceptable standard of living.* In these times, a national commitment to government programs combining the goals of the WPA and the GI Bill is, we shall see, necessary not merely to revive production and employment but also to avert a future of persistent austerity, gross inequality and repressive government. The GI Bill underscored what is most needed in a mature capitalist economy prone to secular stagnation: ongoing government investment, bolstering both public and private consumption. But this was not to be.

THE GREAT SOCIETY:

A FURTHER RESPONSE TO PERSISTENT POVERTY

New Deal advances notwithstanding, poverty was far more widespread during the Great Boom than we were led to believe, and largely invisible to the majority of Americans (Harrington, 1962). Pressure from below led Lyndon Johnson to attempt to extend New Deal policies not only to the economic insecurities arising from unemployment, retirement and disability, but also to the general problem of poverty itself (Johnson, 1964).

But Great Society programs were blighted by the same anti-federalism that limited Franklin Roosevelt's New Deal measures. The War on Poverty was organized at the state and the local level and was supported and directed by state and local efforts. When the Great Society expanded Social Security's Aid to Dependent Children (ADC) to Aid to Families with Dependent Children (AFDC), the expanded program's federally decentralized implementation retained uneven standards of eligibility, coverage and benefits from state to state. The inevitable result was that the program offered the smallest benefits to the poorest people in the poorest states (Skocpol, 1995: 14). After the Great Society, the last of the New-Deal-inspired American social programs, welfare programs remain separate both from national economic management and from non-means-tested programs benefiting employed citizens (ibid.: 15).

During the Johnson administration both leading Democratic and Republican policymakers, and a good portion of the public, regarded "welfare," in contrast to Social Security, Medicare and Medicaid, as comprising giveaways to the indolent. AFDC became the embodiment of this sentiment. Unemployed mothers became objects of suspicion and such benefits as they received were resented by many low-wage workers who had experienced the employment insecurity of deindustrialization and the withering of the New Deal/Great Society settlement. When Ronald Reagan would later promise a full-bore neoliberalism, his goal was based on two promises, to balance the federal budget and to do away with "welfare." His main targets were the social programs of the Great Society, principally AFDC. In this endeavor he failed. Just as only a Republican with unimpeachable anti-communist credentials, like Richard Nixon, could establish official recognition and normal diplomatic relations with "Red China," so it was that only a Democrat could keep Reagan's promises. That Democrat was Bill Clinton, who did away with AFDC, "welfare as we know it." By finally disengaging the Democratic Party from the policies of the New Deal and the Great Society he reconstituted the character of the postwar Democratic Party. I shall discuss Clinton's landmark contribution on pp. 159–62.

THE DUSK OF THE GOLDEN AGE:

THE WITHERING OF THE GOLDEN AGE'S STIMULANTS

Between the late 1960s and the mid-1970s the framework stimulants had become exhausted. The stock of savings built up during the war was soon spent. Because of the sharp drop in (war) production after 1945, with no corresponding rapid shift to the production of consumers' goods, prices of consumption goods rose sharply (Keyserling, 1948: 347). Wartime savings were used up and the real purchasing power of average disposable income declined by nearly 8 percent from January 1946 to December 1947 (Council of Economic Advisors, 1948: 2, 17). The household response was to become a leitmotif of the U.S. postwar economy, as it had become in the 1920s: consumer credit began its secular growth immediately after the war as a supplement to low wages and a niggardly social safety net. Outstanding consumer credit grew by about 30 percent, from $10.2 billion at the end of 1946 to $13.3 by the end of 1947 (ibid.: 20).

By the late 1960s the automobile industry showed clear signs of saturation, as replacement demand became the most rapidly increasing portion of total demand (Rothschild, 1973: 73, 229–30; Nell, 1988: 167). At the same time the restoration of the European and Japanese economies generated vigorous international competition, especially in manufacturing markets, absent from the Golden Age of U.S. global economic hegemony. The result was comparable to the nineteenth-century pattern of robust national competition, but this time on an international scale: prices were driven down faster than the costs of production, and profit rates fell (Brenner, 2006: 101–2). With the end of U.S. global economic hegemony, a major source of Golden-Age expansion was ended. By the mid-1960s the basic infrastructure of the military–industrial complex was in place and military spending was no longer the largest single share of the federal budget. The unprecedented downward income distribution of income unique to the New Deal/Great Society (ND/GS) years motivated elites to launch a retrenchment of Keynesian redistributive policy. This depressed the social wage of working households, exacerbated underconsumption and did away with the exceptional growth rates of the Golden Age. The rate of growth of the suburbs declined at about the same time. The GI Bill has been revised regularly since the end of the war, and each revision has raised eligibility requirements and lowered assistance (Mettler, 2007; Humes 2006).

The secular decline of the median wage since 1974 and the slowdown of Golden-Age growth rates intensified the pressure on working households as well as on financial and non-financial corporations and state, local and federal government to take on additional debt. From the mid-1960s, the beginning of the end of the Golden Age, to 2005, just before the housing bubble began to deflate, total debt has grown faster than the economy (Federal Reserve System, 2006: Tables L1 and L2; Magdoff and Yates, 2009: 75). When debt grows faster than GDP, debt has a diminishing impact on economic growth: it takes increasing amounts of debt to generate an additional dollar of GDP. In the 1970s an additional dollar of debt increased GDP by about 60 cents. By the early 2000s the same amount of debt generated about 20 cents of GDP (Foster and Magdoff, 2009: 48–9). And mortgage debt, which stood at 46 percent of GDP in the 1990s, had climbed to 73 percent in 2008, the year of the Great Meltdown. Both the economy as a whole and, most importantly for our purposes, American working households had during the entire postwar period become *addicted* to debt in order to maintain middle-class living standards. This is indispensable to our understanding of the decline of the Golden Age and of the origins of the financial crisis of September 2008. We shall see in the following chapter how this figured as the principal factor precipitating the financial meltdown of 2008. It is a supreme irony that of all the stimulants that enabled the Great Boom, the only one that survived and grew was what would prove to be the most potentially toxic stimulant, debt.

The Golden Age's sustained economic growth and historically high living standards were unique in American history and were a felicitous accident, the result of a confluence of nine forces, described earlier in this chapter, of which all but two – union strength and mounting debt – were inherently temporary. When these forces had spent their collective potential, the system would revert to its default position of stagnation. In the U.S., the average annual rate of increase of real GDP was 3.8 percent from 1950 to 1973. From 1973 to the end of the dot.com boom, 1997, the figure had dropped to 2.5 percent (*Economic Report of the President* 1985: 243; 1992: 300; 1999: 328; also cited in Albritton et al., 2002: 94). For the UK, Germany, France, Italy and Japan, the respective Golden Age figures are 3.0, 6.0, 5.0, 5.6 and 9.2; the 1973–97 figures are 1.8, 2.1, 2.1, 2.4 and 3.3 (Maddison, 1995: 83).

After the framework stimulants had run their course and ND/GS policies had come under attack, the economy began to revert to what I have argued is its normal, free-market position. Stagnation became increasingly evident. Wages stagnated or declined for a quarter-century and then began to decline more rapidly after the turn of the millennium. As we have seen, production grew, but at a slower rate than during the Golden Age. Not only had production slowed down, but private and public investment had also declined. Equipment per worker grew at an average annual rate of 3.3 percent between 1947 and 1973, but fell to 1.9 percent between 1974 and 1990. In the public economy, non-military capital per worker fell from an average annual growth rate of 1.7 percent in the former period to 0.09 percent in the latter. The growth rate of the sale of manufactured goods (measured in constant 1982 dollars) fell from 4.1 percent to 1.7 percent, a 59 percent decline (Peterson, 1994: 185, 192).

The three most salient features of the Golden Age – rising wages, the closest approximation to material equality ever witnessed in the U.S., and an uncommonly high growth rate – were no more. Inequality comparable to the 1920s emerged and worsened, and life became harder and riskier for most workers (Hacker, 2006). In fact, the mid-1970s marked not merely the natural exhaustion of important framework stimuli but an organized effort by political and economic elites to reverse the tendencies of the Golden Age to redistribute income downward and to raise wages at the expense of profits. Elites anticipated, as early as the mid-1930s, that Keynesian policies would work against their fundamental interests.

THE SEVENTH INTERVENTION: THE TAFT–HARTLEY ACT

There is among many on the Left the quaint idea that the postwar period, until the emergence of neoliberalism, was blessed by a peace treaty between business and workers, a "capital–labor accord." But we saw in Chapter 4 that the Wagner Act encountered business resistance from the very beginning. Immediately after the war, business redoubled its efforts, through Congress, to undermine the provisions of the Wagner Act, which was thought to represent government's legitimization of union-led militancy. The first powerful postwar legislative attack on the legacy of the New Deal, the Taft–Hartley Act (The Labor-Management Relations Act) was a direct response to the labor militancy of 1945–46.

Disparaging the Wagner Act as unfairly targeting employers, Taft–Hartley sought to outlaw "unfair labor practices." It forbade wildcat strikes, sympathy or solidarity strikes, jurisdictional strikes, mass picketing and union political contributions. It required a 60-day "cooling off period" for strikes, authorized the president to impose an 80-day cooling-off period or injunction against labor stoppages that might affect the "national interest," authorized employers to petition the National Labor Relations Board (NLRB) for new representational elections when they estimated that a recognized union no longer commanded majority support, and required labor leaders to take an oath that they were not communists.

Two of the most far-reaching elements of Taft–Hartley were its exclusion of supervisors and foremen from coverage under labor law and its provision allowing states to pass laws banning the closed unionized shop. The open shop, granting every worker the *individual* "right to work," was on the table. Under these combined conditions, unions could no longer act as a unified social movement; each union was its own "interest group" protecting its own turf. Each of these elements introduced both the ideology and the practices of individualism into a union tradition which had during the 1930s developed a profound sense of worker solidarity and the means (albeit limited) for workers collectively to influence corporate workplace policy (Nasser, 2014). The assault on unions and the planting of the seeds of union decline began well before the unabashedly aggressive anti-labor policies of Reagan–Thatcher neoliberalism.

Taft–Hartley's ban on supervisory unionization and the corresponding changes in the interpretation of labor law conferred supervisory status on "game wardens, registered nurses, fast-food restaurant 'managers,' purchasing agents ... medical interns, paralegals, engineers ... and college professors at private schools" (Lichtenstein, 2013: 120). This kind of wholesale narrowing of the possibilities of organization among workers belies the notion that the postwar period featured a "capital–labor accord," according to which capital was open to unionization so long as employers were free to make investment decisions and control the workplace environment.

The three most far-reaching and enduring effects of Taft–Hartley were to deradicalize the union movement, to virtually outlaw inter-union solidarity and to confine the unions to the geographical areas in which they grew up. The non-union locations at the time, like the South and parts of the West, remain largely non-union to this day. *In prohibiting secondary boycotts or sympathy strikes, which had in 1934 played perhaps the major role in the progressive innovations of the Second New Deal, the political system was undercutting one of labor's most effective instruments of class solidarity and power outside the workplace.* A settlement was now in place that virtually guaranteed the decline of organized labor.

THE SECOND RED SCARE

Echoing the "Red Scare" following the 1919 strike wave, a second Red Scare followed soon after the war and did much to reduce the ranks of leftists in unions, government, teaching and other professions. In 1938 the House Un-American Activities Committee (HUAC) was formed as a "special" committee and charged with expunging communist elements from the Roosevelt administration. In 1945 it was made a "standing" or permanent committee. At the same time the Democratic president Truman was instrumental in the formation of the surreal Red-baiting that culminated in "McCarthyism." The Attorney General was authorized to compile a list of "subversive organizations," which in effect permitted surveillance of all public or private employees. The criteria of "subversion" were astonishingly broad: from membership of Communist or Socialist parties to reading liberal magazines such as *The Nation* or *The New Republic* to opposing racial segregation to owning books about post- or *pre*-Soviet Russia. The hysteria surpassed that of the 1920s Red Scare. Truman's attorney general declared that communists "are everywhere – in factories, offices, butcher stores, on street corners and private businesses. And each carries in himself the death of our society" (Chafe, 2009: 146). Senator Joseph McCarthy's Permanent Subcommittee on Investigations, the inquisitions of the HUAC and the attorney general's investigations sought principally to expel from government liberals and radicals like Alger Hiss and Julius and Ethel Rosenberg, to hound perceived left-wingers out of Hollywood, to drive Left lawyers and teachers from their professions and, most importantly, to expunge radicals from unions and workplaces.

That the labor movement participated in the Truman–McCarthy campaign was a major factor in rendering unions politically weak and highly vulnerable to the anti-union practices accompanying neoliberalism. In 1949 the Congress of Industrial Organizations (CIO) prohibited any member of the Communist Party from holding union office. By the end of 1950, the CIO had thrown out 20 percent of its membership, 250,000 workers, on charges of "anti-Americanism" and communist "affiliation." (Nicholson, 2004: 254, cited in Smith, 2006: 190). It is most telling that none of this has prevented the rank-and-file from remaining well to the left of their alleged representatives in the union leadership. In the majority of major labor disputes the membership has been prepared to hold out and strike against the wishes of the aristocracy of labor.

THE EIGHTH INTERVENTION: DEINDUSTRIALIZATION

The U.S. contribution to the effective reindustrialization of Europe and Japan, motivated by the desire of elites to make the world economy the field of operation of U.S. capitalism, was, ironically, a major precipitant of the decline of the Golden Age and of U.S. economic hegemony. The resurgence of international competition changed the fortunes of Golden-Age business profits. Between 1965 and 1973, the profitability of manufacturing and private business as a whole declined dramatically, with the profit rate (the rate of return on capital stock) in the former declining by 41 percent and in the latter by 29 percent. It was not until 1982 that this trend bottomed out (Brenner, 2006: 101). With the major capitalist economic powers by the mid-1960s mature and growing on a level developmental field, the excess capacity and overproduction seen in railroads and steel in the nineteenth century re-emerged in a number of core industries, but this time on a global scale (Crotty, 2002a, b). Excess built-up capacity and overproduction had become unmistakable in one basic industry after another, including rubber, glass, steel, radio, television, shipbuilding, electrical equipment, machine tools, farm machinery and motor vehicles. Between 1970 and 1980 U.S. producers' domestic market share fell, and foreign producers' share rose significantly, in automobiles, footwear, consumer electronics, electrical components, industrial chemicals and machine tools (Bluestone and Harrison, 1982).

Especially striking was that the greatest decline in the U.S. share of both global and domestic markets was in some of the most profitable industries, such as autos and steel. Decreased demand for the output of these and other industries left "capacity overhang." The acceleration of these tendencies in the 1970s accounted for much of the stagnation component of the stag-flation of that decade. In response to the rise of international competition in markets for manufactured goods, U.S. companies' loss of both domestic and global market share, and the accompanying fall in their profit rates, industrial capital initiated an eighth intervention, deindustrialization, meant to restore the profitability enjoyed during the Golden Age and to undercut forces seen as responsible to the threatened decline of U.S. global economic supremacy. Not atypically, the threatening forces were identified as coming from labor. There ensued a wave of plant closings, job losses and community decline not seen since the Great Depression. That these were not cyclical phenomena but rather indications of deep-seated tendencies in the real economy was evident in their persistence during economic recoveries as well as recessions.

Capital shut down plants, shed domestic production and employment, and shipped production overseas as well as to non-union states in the U.S. South (Barnet and Muller, 1974). The phenomenon brought into common discourse the term "deindustrialization," a process of net domestic disinvestment and the first major postwar increase in capital mobility across state boundaries and geographical regions, e.g. from the Frost Belt to the Sun Belt to low-wage non-union locations in the U.S. and abroad, in an effort to restore declining profits by cutting labor costs. What were first known as "runaway shops" became a permanent feature of the economic landscape, as "outsourcing" and "offshoring" became some of capital's most effective means of boosting profits and disciplining labor in subsequent decades. *With revenues increasing at a slower rate after the mid-1970s, profit maximization became focused on cost-cutting. Since most non-labor costs are fixed, capital saw lower wages as the key to profit restoration. This remains a hallmark of neoliberal austerity capitalism.* The mobility of capital and the relative immobility of labor buttressed one of the first major corporate salvos against the power of unions and contributed to one of the first indications of the growth of income inequality that would become conspicuous by 1974. The Bureau of Labor Statistics issued a report showing that the relocation abroad of factories and jobs became a major factor in the growth of inequality from 1958 to 1970 (Henle, 1972).

All this resulted in higher unemployment rates in relocating industries during the 1970s. Total unemployment increased during the decade, and most workers who found new work suffered wage and benefit reductions. Industrial ghost towns like Youngstown, Ohio and Gary, Indiana proliferated. Thus began the decline of America as a world-class manufacturing center, and the creation of the "rust belt." By the late 1960s, manufacturing centers from Detroit to Pittsburgh to Chicago which once symbolized America's industrial supremacy had morphed into sprawling slums of decay marked by rising crime and unemployment, and the first traces of homelessness. The putsch against organized labor that has marked American history from its earliest times was given a major push by the reduction of manufacturing employment characteristic of deindustrialization. In this case it was capital's mobility – which, along with its relative organization, is one of its two principal trump cards against labor – that dealt a further blow to labor. This was one of capital's most coveted prizes in the game of globalization.

The political establishment did nothing to deter the mobility of capital. Once it became clear that government would not obstruct the freedom of capital to shift production and employment to low-wage areas, the mere threat by a company to relocate was highly effective in lowering business taxes, reducing social services, further weakening unions, keeping wages low and disciplining labor to acquiesce in speedup, longer work hours and employer noncompliance with workplace safety and health regulations. That labor enjoyed no comparable mobility further strengthened both capital's and the state managers' ability to pursue the politics of neoliberal austerity. The fulcrum of bargaining power was shifted to capital in what was to become the restoration of capital's social, economic and political power to the level of the 1920s. In sum, Taft–Hartley and the mere threat to move production and employment overseas were sufficient to deal a massive blow to American unions. Since the 1980s the share of American workers belonging to unions has fallen by half. Union membership had peaked in 1954 at 35 percent of all workers; in 2015 the unionization rate had fallen to 11.1 percent.

FINANCIALIZATION: THE FIRST STAGE

One of the major concomitants of deindustrialization has been the emergence, above the productive or real economy, of a distinct and separate economy, the "financial economy." This non-productive system threatens to wreak havoc from without on the real economy. But "financialization" indicates more than speculation centered exclusively in the financial sector. What, after all, has been financialized? In parallel with the financial sector's mounting speculative activities, non-financialized firms and households – the pillars of the real or productive economy – have been infused with financial activity and increasingly dependent on it. In the years leading up to the present crisis, General Motors' lending facility, General Motors Acceptance Corporation (GMAC), was GM's most profitable unit. "The company earned more profit from lending money to customers than in selling cars" (Solomon, 2012). General Electric too reaped greater profits from its financial-services activities than from its core real-economy business. Increasingly, firms in the real economy engage in activities that are concerned with making money in addition to those that make goods; an increasing portion of the typical large firm's portfolio consists of financial investments. And households have become dependent since the mid-1960s upon credit cards for consumption, thereby pledging extractive interest payments to the card-issuing banks.

A direct indication of this dynamic is shown in a comparison of the portfolio income, coming from financial investments, to the cash flow, generated by productive investments, of non-financial corporations (Krippner, 2005: 182–6; 2011: 27–57). Portfolio income comprises total earnings of non-financial corporations (NFCs) from interest, dividends and (realized) capital gains on investments. Cash flow consists of profits plus depreciation allowances. Portfolio income as a percentage of cash flow mirrors the relationship, for NFCs, of returns generated from financial activities to returns generated from productive activities. This ratio has increased dramatically in recent decades, so that *by 2000 financial assets accounted for more than 50 percent of the total assets of non-financial corporations* (Milberg and Winkler, 2010). This is what we should expect if surplus that could have made its way to private and/or public investment and higher wages is instead directed to financial outlets.

While financial and speculative activity have been a part of capitalism from the beginning, the more recent explosion of financial activity is a function of the waning of the framework stimulants, the atrophy of business fixed investment and the subsequent slower real-economy growth rates since the mid-1970s. Financialization filled the growth vacuum left by industrial stagnation. As *Business Week* put it, "Slow growth and today's rampant speculative binge are locked in some kind of symbiotic embrace." (*Business Week*, 1985).

The employment picture too from 1970 to 1980 pointed to the disproportionate growth of finance, prefiguring the growing distortions in the economy that would become evident to all 30 years later: over the decade manufacturing jobs would increase by a mere 200,000. Jobs in wholesale and retail, catering to people increasingly inclined to use credit to enhance their purchasing power, increased by 3.2 million. But most ominous was the 3.4 million increase in jobs in the financial and business services and the 1.6 million increase in jobs in the FIRE (finance, insurance and real estate) sector (Magdoff and Sweezy, 1987: 67). Thus there was a decreasing number of jobs in the *productive* sectors of the economy and an increasing number in the *extractive* financial sector.

The decline of both the framework stimulants and the labor movement were among the factors contributing to financialization, but the very success of the industrial economy during the Great Boom also tended to weaken profit opportunities for commercial banks and encourage the emergence of non-bank financial institutions. With large corporations increasingly able after the war to finance investment from retained earnings, banks came to play a perceptibly declining role in the monetary system (Corbett and Jenkinson, 1996, 1997). The trend was deep-seated: commercial banks now account for less than 20 percent of total credit-market debt in the United States. Over the last 40–50 years non-bank financial institutions such as investment banks, finance companies, mortgage companies, insurance companies and pension funds have proliferated and competed successfully with traditional banks in lending and in the provision of a variety of financial "products." Unlike in Europe, where banks still account for the bulk of corporate financing activity, most of the lending in the U.S. is now done by these relatively new institutions (*Economist*, 2012). The decline of demand for new loans from traditional banks pressured the banks to seek out, indeed to invent, new sources of profit (Dunn, 2014: 124).

The need of banks to originate new sources of financial activity would in the end deal a further blow to the productive economy. This was brought about by creating a debt-fuelled investment boom in novel and exotic financial instruments and a correlative debt-fuelled consumption boom in the productive economy, under conditions in which the explosion of financial activity did not reflect comparable strength in the productive economy. It was clear to many radical economists but to virtually no mainstream ideologues that exploding finance combined with stagnating production and declining wages foreshadowed crisis in the deceptively booming financial sector.

The 1970s and 1980s exhibited the first clear signs that the structure of the U.S. economy was undergoing major and troubling transformation. While profits in the financial sector had been growing faster than in industry since shortly after the war, in the early 1970s speculation in the form of futures trading began to grow much faster than production. Between 1977 and 1985 industrial production increased by 25 percent, while futures trading soared by 370 percent (Magdoff and Sweezy, 1987: 20–1). Financialized capitalism has been characterized by the making of money becoming increasingly unrelated to the making of widgets. This is best reflected in a comparison of the dollar value of GNP generated by the production and transportation of goods with the value of GNP imputed to financial activity. In 1950 the portion of GNP ascribed to the financial sector was 21 percent that of the goods-producing sector. By 1985 the figure had about doubled, to 40 percent (ibid.: 23). With respect to a key thesis of this book, that net productive investment tends to atrophy under mature capitalism, major shifts in investment are no less significant than changes in employment and production. The investment picture is most revealing.

THE CHANGING PATTERN OF INVESTMENT AND EMPLOYMENT
AND THE ONGOING EXPULSION OF LABOR FROM PRODUCTION

Of special significance is the change in investment associated with the FIRE sector's increasing share of GDP and employment. Let us look at the development of investment over the entire postwar period and into the mid-1980s, after financialization had already sunk roots. Magdoff and Sweezy examined the total U.S. fixed investment after the war, from the beginning of the Great Boom to the early years of the neoliberal period of financializing capitalism. Their analysis reveals the weakness, gradual decline and change in the composition of investment since 1945. *In each of the seven recessions between 1948 and 1980, investment in producers' durable goods declined significantly* and far exceeded consumption declines (Magdoff and Sweezy, 1987: 56). Moreover, after the postwar boom, investment gradually lost such stimulative power as it had wielded earlier. Average increases in gross investment got smaller in absolute terms annually after 1973, and the percentage change declined as well, from 72.7 percent to 38.2 percent from 1974–79 to 18.8 percent from 1980–82.

Especially striking about these slowdowns in the growth of investment are the factors accounting for such sluggish growth as did exist. From 1966 to 1979, just under half of the $27.3 billion increase in total investment in producers' durable goods was due to the $12.9 billion average annual increase in investment in hi-tech equipment and communications. *Thus, with the exhaustion of the unique and temporary stimulants of the Golden Age, we see a slowing down of the traditional industries that brought the economy to maturity – heavy industrial equipment, transportation equipment, construction and agricultural equipment – and the thriving of those industries requiring far less investment capital than did the basic industries associated with industrialization.* The eupeptic performance of the new industries was not, however, able to offset the slowing down of investment as a whole (Magdoff and Sweezy, 1987: 56).

That the decline and changing composition of investment foreshadowed newly entrenched features of post-industrially-mature capitalism is shown in the unique character of the impressive expansion of 1983–84, the first expansion following the severe Reagan recession (ibid.: 68–78). The largest component of business fixed investment during that expansion consisted in the purchase of producers' durable goods. The category of durable capital goods disaggregates into rising, stable and declining sectors. Changes in investment in these sectors between the 1979 and the 1984 peaks, immediately preceding and immediately following the Reagan recession, tell a prophetic story.

The stable sectors, electrical apparatus and miscellaneous products, represented about 15 percent of all investment in equipment. The declining sectors are those associated with the productive industrial economy: manufacturing machinery and equipment, transportation other than autos, and agricultural and construction machinery. Investment in these dropped by $12 billion over the period. It is noteworthy that at the peak of the 1983–84 expansion these sectors had not recovered to the 1979 peak. Here was a sharp divergence from traditional business-cycle recoveries, which had always featured heavy investment in plant and equipment in manufacturing, transportation and public utilities.

While the declining industrial sector fell sharply during the worst years of the recession and predictably picked up during the recovery, the rising sector advanced rapidly and unfalteringly during the entire period of

1979–83. Only two types of good account for the persistent advance of the rising sector: hi-tech products and autos for business. This category's impressive $36 billion rise over the period exceeded the $27 billion rise of investment in the entire category of producers' durable goods. The robust growth of investment in hi-tech equipment and business vehicles not only offset the drop in the declining sector but, most significantly, was also the exclusive reason for the strength of investment in equipment and machinery in this period (ibid.: 72).

These developments were accompanied by a change in both the distribution of profits and, as we have seen, financial profit's share of GDP. Intimations of the ascendancy of finance were evident almost immediately after the war. "Profits in the financial sector were already growing faster than in industry in the 1950s. By the early 1960s, the securitization of commercial banking (i.e. selling savings certificates rather than relying on deposits) and the enormous expansion of investment banking (including Morgan Stanley's creation of the first viable computer model for analyzing financial risk) were already in train" (Panitch and Gindin, 2009: 15). Because financial-market transactions have increased more rapidly than real production, financial profits have for decades come to account for an increasing share of total corporate profits (Stockhammer, 2010). In the U.S. the financial sector's share increased dramatically after the 1960s, from an average of 17.4 percent from 1960 to 1884, rising to 30 percent between 1985 and 2008. As the housing bubble took off after the dot.com burst, finance's share rose to above 40 percent by 2003 (Khatiwada, 2010). To be sure, finance's share has been volatile over this time; bubbles come and go, optimism waxes and wanes. After September 2008's housing debacle, finance's share plummeted to 10.2 percent. But by mid-2014 it had risen back up to over 27 percent (MacEwan, 2014). Volatility notwithstanding, what commands attention is the tendency in motion since 1960: the secular rise in the financial sector's share of corporate profits while outpacing the sluggish growth rate of GDP.

By the latter half of the 1990s financial profits skyrocketed, surpassing the growth of non-financial profits and outpacing much further still the laggardly growth rate of GDP (Foster and Magdoff, 2009: 123). It is now clear that the sectoral changes in investment and profits from the late 1970s to the mid-1980s anticipated what were to develop into the new financialized, extractive capitalism of the Age of Austerity.

The new technologies have been highly instrumental in accelerating the secular tendency of capitalism to render labor superfluous to production. The ability to squeeze more out of a shrinking labor force has been facilitated by digital advances. From marketing and coordinating the operations of a single firm's multinational activities to the use of automation and robots to reduce the number of workers needed to make profits, and using computers to monitor the movements and pace of workers, firms are able to increase productivity, reduce their payroll and exercise tighter control over the remaining employees.

Financial activities have not been exclusively speculative. They have been integral to the accumulation of productive capital, including receiving commercial paper (short-term unsecured loans to businesses) to pay wages and purchase supplies, lending idle funds to other firms and making commercial paper available to sell output, to name a few (Lapavitsas, 2013: 217). The effects of investment in hi-tech products at the expense of traditional machinery have become part of everyday life: ATMs replacing tellers, automatic scanners replacing supermarket checkers and online purchases of airline tickets replacing travel agents, among many others.

A major development behind the increased use of business computers is the vast proliferation of types of "financial products." Financial instruments from options, futures, commodities, foreign exchange, stocks and bonds to bets on Chile's inflation rate a year from now are handled by traders and brokers tied into national and international electronic networks. We shall see in Chapter 7 that innovation in both the capital-goods and the consumer-goods industries is retarded. New products in production have been replaced by new "products" in finance.

The above constitutes an introductory sketch of some of the most prominent features of a financialized economy. A fuller picture, including the implications of financialized capitalism for the operations and basic goals of firms, the financial situation of households, the entrenchment of austerity in secular stagnation and recurrent bubbles, and the decline of democracy are treated in the final chapter. In concluding my assessment of the decline of the Golden Age, I return to the class struggles which were cited by business in justification of the rejection of social democracy. These labor actions motivated the unmistakable assault on labor central to the transition to neoliberal financialized capitalism.

THE LONG BOOM, STRENGTHENED LABOR
AND THE WAGE-PUSH PROFIT SQUEEZE

The sustained economic expansion of the Golden Age enhanced the economic power of labor at the expense of capital by increasing the demand not only for real output but also for productive workers. Business is thereby threatened by the specter of full employment. As the supply of workers dwindles, labor's competitive bargaining power increases, workers become harder to control and profits are potentially threatened by wage increases that could cut into profits (Bowles et al., 1984: 98–121). This is precisely what happened. The 1960s and early 1970s marked the most militant labor actions since the historic strikes of 1946.

This period represented capital's nightmare: low unemployment and workers out of control in the streets and in the workplace. Urban rebellions of black workers were a throughline of the 1960s, with the five-day Detroit insurrection standing out as one of the most violent urban revolts of the twentieth century. Alongside this civil unrest were virtually continuous strikes beginning in 1965. Between 1967 and 1971 the average number of workers participating in strikes doubled. It is most revealing that this period also saw a continuous rise in working-class living standards. And 1965–69 was the closest the U.S. had ever come to near-full employment. The lesson was not lost on the business class: workers are hardest to control when they are most secure. Capital did not take this sitting down. As wages rose and labor markets tightened, firms attempted to tighten their grip on workers, by speedup, forced overtime, increased automation threatening job security and by negotiating, with the help of compliant union leaders, higher levels of output into union contracts. What business feared most was the blow to its economic hegemony entailed by an increasingly secure working class.

I noted at the start of this chapter the consistent and growing decline, during the ND/GS period, of the top 1 percent's share of national income. That the downward distribution was related to rising wages squeezing profits did not go unnoticed by business, establishment scholars and the media. Two prominent economists wrote that during the boom "A real wage boom resulted, which started a squeeze on profits even before 1973" (Bruno and Sachs, 1985: 7). William Nordhaus, a member of President Carter's Council of Economic Advisors, expressed a similar position in "The Falling Share of Profits" and in "The Worldwide Wage Explosion" (Okun and Perry, 1974; Nordhaus, 1972). Total wages and salaries stood at 72.2 percent of national income in 1965–66; by 1969 they had climbed to 76.3 percent. But corporate profits, which were 10.6 percent of national income in 1965–66, fell to 8.2 percent in 1969 (Ackerman and MacEwan, 1972: 10; *Fortune*, 1973: 184). An examination of the three longest business cycles of the Golden Age illustrates the wage-push profit squeeze.

A Federal Reserve Bank of St. Louis study showed that at the midpoint of the typical cyclical upturn during the Great Boom there is a pronounced decline in the ratio of profits to wages (Burger, 1973; also cited in Boddy and Crotty, 1975: 5). Business complained that a class struggle was taking place and labor was winning. In 1970 *The Wall Street Journal* reported that "Observers of the labor-management scene ... almost unanimously assert that the present situation is the worst within memory ... Morale in many operations is sagging badly, intentional work slowdowns are cropping up more frequently and absenteeism is soaring ... Men such as Mr. Burke at Otis [Elevator Company] contend the problem [of declining worker productivity] is so widespread it's their major headache at the moment" (cited in Brecher, 1972: 266–7). Two years later the *Journal*, in a front-page article commenting on the causes of the 1970–71 recession following the long expansion of the 1960s, noted that "Many manufacturing executives have openly complained in recent years that too much control had passed from management to labor. With sales lagging and competition mounting, they feel safer in attempting to restore what they call 'balance'" (January 26, 1972). After noting that total wages had risen and profits fallen from 1965 to 1969, *Fortune* lamented that "It appears that labor's share has moved into new high territory. Much depends on where it goes from here ... The biggest question is whether labor will go on claiming a larger share" (*Fortune*, May 1973). Arnold Weber, an administrator of Nixon's anti-inflationary wage and price freeze, testified to the efforts of business to pressure the administration to reverse the shift in power from management to labor: "Business had been leaning on [George P.] Schultz [Nixon's Secretary of Labor and later of Treasury] and [Paul] McCracken [chairman of Nixon's Council of Economic Advisors] to do something about the economy, especially wages. The idea of the freeze ... was to zap labor, and we did" (*Business Week*, 1974a). The *New York Times*'s chief economics reporter at the time, adumbrating what was to become a key feature of the austerity regime of financialized capitalism, wrote frankly of the political leadership's low-wage policy: "[T]he administration intends to reinforce its position by not shooting for so high a level of employment as to cause wage rates to race ahead of productivity gains ... Thus the administration itself is behaving like a profit-maximizer" (Silk, 1973). Successive administrations have similarly abandoned Golden-Age Keynesianism and with it any efforts to achieve full employment.

A major study of factor (i.e. capital's and labor's) shares during the three major Golden-Age business cycles demonstrates that profits were squeezed by labor's gains in the latter halves of these cycles' expansions (Boddy and Crotty, 1974, 1975). The authors examined cycles from third-quarter/54 to third-quarter/57, from second-quarter/58 to second-quarter/60, and from first-quarter/61 to fourth-quarter/69. The key question was: What happens to profits and wages over the course of the cyclical expansion leading up to the profit squeeze?

The movements of wages, productivity and prices account for cyclical changes in the income shares of capital and labor. The interrelated movements among wages, prices, productivity and profits both generate the profit squeeze and determine capital's response. In each of the longer expansions, wage rates increased dramatically in the latter half (midpoint to peak) of the expansion because sustained growth meant increased demand for labor as the supply for labor was decreasing. Marx argued that this predictable movement of wages would both squeeze profits and reduce the rate of profit (Marx, 1961, I: 620). The data indicate that he was right. The relation between costs and output prices is of course the crucial factor in the determination of profits (profits = revenues minus costs). Input costs are of two kinds, labor and non-labor. The latter comprise equipment and materials costs. In the second phase of the expansions, where wage increases squeezed profits, output prices rose faster than both (equipment and materials) non-labor input prices (Boddy and Crotty, 1974: 7–8; 1975: 5–7). Hence the profit squeeze was not caused by materials costs increasing faster than prices. It was the rising wages of labor that appropriated what would otherwise have been capital's larger slice. Since profits are squeezed, firms are not able to raise prices sufficiently to offset the profit squeeze.

Two contributing factors determine unit labor costs. The wage level is set in part by supply and demand in the labor market. No less important is the productivity of workers: the output they produce per unit of labor input. This is a function not only of the equipment workers handle but also of labor effort: how hard workers are willing to work. Boddy and Crotty noted a marked slowdown in productivity growth in the midpoint-to-peak stage of the expansion, when the profit squeeze occurs. A crucial factor in the declining rate of productivity increase is the unruly behavior of workers when labor markets are tight and labor's bargaining power and economic security are enhanced. This amounts to a boost to workers' class power: it is *the political dimension of the business cycle*. It is well known to employers that when workers feel economically secure and can easily switch jobs, they are far less easily controlled and do not work as hard as managers would like. The rates of strikes, industrial sabotage, quitting, tardiness and absences increased in times of Golden-Age economic security (Boddy and Crotty, 1975: 8; Brenner, 1999: 96; Bureau of Labor Statistics, 1973: Table 154). This should be expected to depress both productivity and the rate of profit. We shall see in Chapter 7 that the lesson was not lost on capital, which initiated in the mid-1970s an assault on labor undermining first the achievements of the Great Society (Carter and Reagan) and then the legacy of the New Deal (Bushes, and especially Clinton and Obama).

THE POLITICAL SIGNIFICANCE OF THE FULL-EMPLOYMENT PROFIT SQUEEZE

The wage-push profit squeeze theory is intended primarily to show that an even moderately social-democratic regime tends to enhance workers' power vis-à-vis capital such as to effect a transfer of income within the firm from capital to labor. A plethora of transfers from profits to wages in the context of a moderately social-democratic regime contributes to an explanation of Emmanuel Saez's demonstration of a national downward distribution from the 1 percent to the rest during the ND/GS years. The significance of the wage-push profit squeeze and its inherence wherever social democracy is found is reflected in Stephen Marglin's demonstration that "There was ... well before the oil shock, a general 'full-employment profit squeeze' throughout the OECD countries" (Marglin, 1990: 19; see also Glyn et al., 1990: 76–83). The profit-squeeze theory purports to identify perhaps the principal factor motivating capital to launch a vigorous and continuing pro-business and anti-labor campaign in the 1970s, to be discussed in the concluding section of this chapter. As such it is an important element in the explanation of the rise of neoliberal ideology and the pervasive austerity-inducing features of contemporary capitalist economic policy.

Capital responded to the profit squeeze by laying off workers en masse, precipitating a recession replenishing the reserve army of labor and defusing labor's power militantly to appropriate a larger share of the spoils it had produced. This is what class struggle looks like. *Business Week*, in its special issue on "The Debt Economy," spelled out the principal task facing capital in the transition from the Great Boom to the age of "normal" austerity:

[I]t will be a hard pill to swallow – the idea of doing with less so that big business can have more ... Nothing that this nation, or any other nation, has done in modern economic history compares in difficulty with the selling job that must now be done to make people accept the new reality. And there are grave doubts whether the job can be done at all. Historian Arnold Toynbee ... laments that democracy will be unable to cope with approaching economic problems – and that totalitarianism will take its place. (*Business Week*, 1974b)

The prescience of these remarks leaps out in these times of vanishing social spending, declining wages, lower living standards and the emergence in America of a police state. The seeds of the call for economic austerity were discernible in an influential call, in the "Powell memo" (see below) to the business community to tighten its political grip on the Washington.

THE NINTH INTERVENTION: THE POLITICAL COUNTERREVOLUTION OF CAPITAL, THE POWELL MEMO AND THE "QUIET COUP"

In 1972 the head of the powerful, conservative National Association of Manufacturers (NAM) was frank about the increasing recognition by business that its interests require its decisive control of the State: "[T]he thing that affects business most today is government. The interrelationship of business with business is no longer so important as the interrelationship of business with government" (cited in Hacker and Pierson, 2011: 116).

As David Vogel, a business-politics scholar, wrote: "From 1969 to 1972 virtually the entire American business community experienced a series of political setbacks without parallel in the postwar period" (Vogel, 1989: 59). Regulations, redistribution and labor militancy inspired capital to respond as a class. The business response to regulation shows that *power* is capital's priority. Regulation's bite is that it diminishes "management prerogatives." When government mandates seat belts and catalytic converters in the public interest, capital perceives this as a threat to its dominance. Regulations affect many firms and industries at once – by attempting to control capital *as a class. Business will not have its class power challenged by being told how to do business by a government responding to popular demands.*

Other threats to capital's power impelled business's new form of class mobilization. Business security was threatened by the relatively progressive postwar tax. "The *entire* benefit of the increased NFC profit rate from 1929 (17.5 percent) to 1959 (25.5 percent) was appropriated by the state through indirect business taxes and corporate profits taxes ... average profit rate in 1929 (11.7 percent) exceeded that of the 1950s (7.7 percent)" (Dumenil et al., 1992: 47–8; emphasis added). By 1970 it seemed that government had taken over the economy in the interests of working people. As James Livingston put it:

By 1970, public spending on health, social security, and education at home, combined with government spending on national security and economic development abroad, had made government at all levels the residual source of income for the majority of American citizens. In 1930 ... private investment was still 50 percent greater than all public spending; in 1970 public spending was 50 percent greater than all private investment. Between 1959 and 1999, transfer payments provided by the federal government were the fastest-growing component of all household income, rising by 10 percent per year; by 1999, these payments amounted to a fifth of all labor income. (Livingston, 2011: 58)

With the atrophy of net private investment, state and local governments were the fastest-growing job sources; by the 1960s about 20 percent of the labor force was directly employed by a government branch (ibid.). During the Golden Age, private employment grew at a rate of 1.57 percent, while government employment grew at 3.62 percent (Walker and Vatter, 1997: 80). At the same time, purchases at every government level grew faster (at 4.24 percent) than real GNP growth (3.67 percent) (ibid.). Accordingly, state and federal governments' net contribution to consumption expenditures had become "the single most important determinant of economic growth ... they provided the margin of consumer demand that smoothed the business cycles of the postwar boom" (Livingston, 2011: 58). These developments, so repugnant to business, exhibit the appearance within mature capitalism of some key features of a democratic socialist economy. *A mature industrialized economy – socialist or capitalist – must rely on increased household consumption and greater public spending to sustain production, employment and just living standards.* In a capitalist economy, this outcome leads to elite reaction and the attempt to return the political economy to its pre-welfare-state "normalcy."

Business's 1970s effort to mobilize was a coordinated political action aimed at control of the State apparatus, with a strategy of long-term class warfare. In 1971 future Supreme Court Justice Lewis Powell sent the memorandum "Attack on American Free Enterprise System" to the U.S. Chamber of Commerce (USCC), to mobilize industry to resist the ND/GS legacy. It reads like neoliberal instruction:

[T]he American economic system is under broad attack ... The overriding first need ... for businessmen ... may be *survival* ... of ... the free enterprise system ... Business must learn ... that political power is necessary; that such power must be assiduously cultivated; and ... used aggressively and with determination –.... Strength lies in organization, in careful long-range planning and implementation, in consistency of action over an indefinite period of years ... and in the political power available only through united action and national organizations. (Powell, 1971: 1, 3, 6)

Political scientists Jacob Hacker and Paul Pierson describe the ensuing counterattack of business as "a domestic version of Shock and Awe": "The number of corporations with public affairs offices in Washington grew from 100 in 1968 to over 500 in 1978. In 1971, only 175 firms had registered lobbyists in Washington, but by 1982, nearly 2,500 did. The number of corporate PACs [political action committees] increased from under 300 in 1976 to over 1,200 by the middle of 1980 ... the numbers reveal a dramatic rapid mobilization of business resources in the mid-1970s" (Hacker and Pierson, 2011: 118.) This period saw the birth of militant mega-organizations representing both big and small business. In 1972 the Business Roundtable was formed, its membership restricted to top corporate CEOs. By 1977 its membership included CEOs of 113 top Fortune 200 companies. The chairman of both the Roundtable and Exxon, Clifton Garvin, remarked "The Roundtable tries to work with whichever political party is in power ... the Roundtable works with every administration to the degree they let us" (ibid.: 121). The USCC and the National Federation of Independent Businesses doubled their membership, with the very effective USCC tripling its budget. During this period the corporate presence on Capitol Hill became ubiquitous. Not since the nineteenth century had the chambers of legislation seen such thoroughgoing corporatization.

The biggest organizations mimicked the strategies of their antago-nists – the public-interest groups pressing for regulation, and organized labor. Corporate groups organized mass campaigns by shareholders, local companies, employees, and retailers and suppliers. Washington was deluged with phone calls, petitions and letters pushing business interests. Elites soon surpassed both public-service organizations and organized labor in bottom-up organizing. *Organized militancy with clear political aims is the surest route to large-scale political-economic transformation.* Working-class organization is currently practically nonexistent, while capital is as con-solidated in its aims and as politically powerful as it was 125 years ago. As Warren Buffet, the world's third wealthiest person in 2015, put it, "There's class warfare, all right, but it's my class, the rich class, that's making war, and we're winning" (Stein, 2006).

Within ten years the corporate takeover was well established. In the 1980s corporate PACs paid five times as much money to congressional campaign-ers as they had in the 1970s. Mobilized capital's agenda was to undo policies and State priorities that had generated the redistribution and labor activism limiting capital's power and enhancing that of workers for almost five decades. These political-economic projects required ongoing bolstering by the State to be kept effective. Mobilized capital had to capture the State and render it inoperative for working-class purposes. This required the functional equivalent of a coup.

Simon Johnson, former Director of Research at the IMF, warned that a "silent coup," a "Wall Street takeover," "the re-emergence of a Wall Street financial oligarchy" had been effected in the bank bailout (Andrews, 2008; Johnson, 2009; Johnson and Kwak, 2011). But its agents were not the industrial interests Powell's triggering memo addressed. During the extended period of capitalist mobilization, capital had evolved. Finance was now the driver of a new kind of economic "growth" that did not include rising wages, production or employment. The term "jobless recovery" was born.

Finance had captured the State itself. Previously, a change in government, e.g. from the Eisenhower to the Kennedy administration, might mean a modest change in domestic policy within the context of an enduring "Keynesian" State. Finance capital has sought to change the fundamental priorities of the State, so that administrations, Democratic or Republican, would govern on behalf of the ruling financial oligarchy. Public policy is based on maintaining and expanding the value of financial assets, not productive assets. Manifestations included the 1980s Savings and Loans bailouts, the Long Term Capital Management bailout, government purchases of stock market securities, the shift from defined benefit pension plans to defined contribution plans run by private financial institutions and invested in the stock market, the repeal of legislation proscribing company buybacks, tax breaks for investors, the lowering of interest rates enabling unlucky speculators to borrow at attractive rates to regain their positions, the 2008 bailout, and the 2015 U.S. fiscal year budget – which reversed the bailout of the Pension Benefit Guarantee Corporation (government's pension-fund insurer) while promising to bail out Citibank and other big banks if they lost on their derivatives (Hudson, 2015b). The ND/GS settlement became what future president Barack Obama called "the old-time religion" (Obama, 2006: 31). Neoliberal ideology and financial-ized policy would capture policymakers of both major parties (see Chapter 6, pp. 159–62, on Clinton's Reaganization of the Democratic Party).

While neoliberal ideology asserts that the market alone should be counted on to deliver capitalism's material security, neoliberalism has required unparalleled State intervention. Business's organizing to make capital's priorities into the State's, through legislation to deregulate industry, lifting capital controls to render capital maximally mobile, and the bank bailout, made finance capital and a hyperactive State two sides of one coin. *Capitalism's ability to deliver the goods to either of its defining classes depends on class intervention advancing the class's hold on the State.* The persistence and expansion of neoliberal priorities from the Carter to the Trump administrations makes it clear that voting and electoral politics is irrelevant to the fundamental organization of the U.S. political economy. Class militancy makes the difference.

Society's transformation won't come from Democratic Party leadership, which was uniquely implicated in the advent of neoliberalism. Only Democratic Party liberals could have substantially lowered taxes on business, increased military spending and cut social spending (Carter); ended "welfare as we know it," run a budget surplus and repealed the Glass–Steagall Act (Clinton); and further committed Democrats to Reaganomics while dismissing New Deal liberalism as "the old-time religion" (Obama). Carter was the first Democratic neoliberal (Faux, 2012: 58–67), liberal on social issues but fiscally conservative. He deregulated banking and the airline, trucking and telecommunications industries, introducing competition that undermined firms' profits and led to declining wages and intensified anti-union efforts, arguing that the "free market" would prevent inflation acceleration (Nicholson, 2004: 318–19). As the liberal economist Jeff Faux put it, "[T]his … was the first in a series of episodes … in which Democratic presidents moved further to the right of Eisenhower and … Nixon" (Faux, 2012: 60). In an analysis of Reagan's 1981 Economic Recovery and Tax Act (ERTA), which greatly reduced corporate tax burdens, two prominent liberal political scientists averred that "*Both* parties were … in a determined struggle to show who could shower more benefits on those at the top" (Hacker and Pierson, 2011: 134; emphasis in original). The Republican Party represents reaction on stilts, while the Democrats have transformed themselves into the Party of well-educated and connected professionals who work in Silicon Valley, Wall Street, Hollywood, academia, medicine and government (Frank, 2016; Wray, 2017). Common allegiance to neoliberalism is what constitutes the two parties as a duopoly. Therefore, history has placed an entirely different kind of politics and society on our agenda.

6

The New Financialization: Debt, Investment and the Financialized Firm

A business firm grows and attains great strength, and afterwards perhaps stagnates and decays; and at the turning point there is a balancing or equilibrium of the forces of life and decay. And as we reach to the higher stages of our work we shall need ever more and more to think of economic forces as resembling those which make a young man grow in strength until he reaches his prime; after which he gradually becomes stiff and inactive, till at last he sinks to make room for other and more vigorous life.

Alfred Marshall, *Principles of Economics* (1961), Vol. I, p.323

Business's successful capture of the State brought about the transformation of the one institution that was perceived to legislate in the interests of the working population. It was the Democratic Party that spearheaded the New Deal and the Great Society, and it had come on that account to be known as "the party of the working man." The attempt by political, academic and economic elites to undo the political economy of the New Deal and Great Society (ND/GS) required capture of the postwar Democratic Party. Government policies furthering working-class interests were to be replaced by the extension of market relations, the withdrawal of the State's social-welfare functions, and the promotion of the ideology of "self-reliance." But if the new order was to represent a permanent resurgence of pre-Keynesian capitalism, it would have to be acceptable as a bipartisan consensus, and hence congenial to Democrats. In fact it was pre-Reagan Democrats who first led the fully fledged assault on postwar liberalism. Jimmy Carter got the ball rolling, Reagan ran with it and finally Bill Clinton made it the mantra of the Democratic Party.

THE STAGFLATION OF THE 1970S AND THE BEGINNINGS OF NEOLIBERALISM

The stagflation of the 1970s, which saw sluggish growth and rising unemployment and inflation, provided elites with the pretext for jettisoning the

ND/GS settlement. Keynesian theory entailed, it was argued, that inflation and unemployment could not coexist. Their simultaneous emergence was held to demonstrate not merely that Keynesianism was bad economics but that it was in fact the very cause of the hitherto unknown stagflation. But the welfare state could not be done away with overnight. It took the massive mobilization of the business class and a liberal Democratic president.

Jimmy Carter, elected in 1976 as a liberal president, promised a more progressive tax system. After his inauguration, a barrage of lobbying by newly mobilized business groups facilitated the passage of a decidedly non-progressive tax bill in 1978, while the flat and regressive Social Security tax saw a major increase (Ferguson and Rogers, 1987: 109). Though Democrats held huge majorities in Congress, they capitulated to and normalized the neoliberal agenda. A precedent was set for the later Reagan and Bush tax cuts (Hacker and Pierson, 2011: 132–4).

Carter rang all the neoliberal bells. "Government cannot solve our problems, it can't set our goals, it cannot define our vision. Government cannot eliminate poverty or provide a bountiful economy or reduce inflation or save our cities or cure illiteracy or provide energy" (Carter, 1978). He cut social spending and increased military spending (Ferguson and Rogers, 1987: 111). He was the first major postwar deregulator, removing regulations on airlines, oil, railroads and trucking. He ignored a major assault on unions in the mid-1970s (Burns, 2014: 45–58). Pentagon spending spiked. These reversions to neoliberal politics occurred when the Democratic Party was still nominally "liberal," supposedly sustaining ND/GS traditions. It was Bill Clinton who would finally transform the hearts and minds of Capitol Hill Democrats and turn the party into a solid bastion of Reaganite policy.

THE TENTH INTERVENTION: BILL CLINTON AND
THE REAGANIZATION OF THE DEMOCRATIC PARTY

Bill Clinton was to be the first real Reaganite. Reagan's attempt to undo the post-ND/GS settlement and make permanent a post-New-Deal, post-Great Society settlement rested upon two major objectives, to balance the federal budget and to abolish "welfare." The idea was to do away with as many federal social programs as he could get away with. He accomplished neither of these goals, ironically running up the greatest deficit in the nation's history. Clinton took up the gauntlet. He balanced the federal budget (thereby accelerating the transfer of the ineluctable deficit from the public to the private sector) and in 1996 did away with Aid to Families with Dependent Children (AFDC), "welfare as we know it." By abolishing AFDC, the new *Personal Responsibility* and Work Opportunity and Reconciliation Act (emphasis added) eliminated federal standards for welfare benefits and imposed a five-year lifetime limit and a two-year continuous limit on benefits, prohibited immigrants from receiving welfare, and cut $24 billion from the food stamp program. Clinton repealed part of the Social Security Act of 1935. The 1996 Act requires recipients to begin working after two years of receiving benefits, punishing those in special need during recessions when jobs are scarce. The "personal responsibility" language resurrects a core tenet of classical liberalism – that in a "free" society an individual's fortunes are always the result of one's personal choices, for which one bears sole responsibility. Neoliberalism blamed poor people by claiming that welfare recipients' personal failings, rather than systemic job-creation failure, were at the root of poverty. Clinton's "three strikes you're out" legislation inaugurated mass incarceration hitherto unknown in the U.S., creating the world's largest prison population.

Clinton's welfare-to-work scheme removed impoverished women from state welfare rolls with no corresponding policy to ensure that they would have access to even minimally sufficient jobs to make up for the lost income. Nor were measures taken to ensure that welfare recipients who could not find work would not be bounced from the rolls in recessions. Here again the lack of national economic management and the role assigned to the states, which imposed lifetime limits on benefits, took a heavy toll on the poor during recessions. *This is now the new normal.* It nullified the seventh factor (see Chapter 5, pp. 130–1) making for the unique economic robustness of the Golden Age, the welfare state. The combination of shrinking welfare rolls and inflexible lifetime limits resulted not in a higher level of employment but in more workers living in severe poverty (Abramsky, 2014: 45). Here was neoliberalism's creeping retreat to 1920s economic orthodoxy, which only entrenched the chronic American problem of persistent poverty. Prior to Clinton's abolition of AFDC, 4.43 million families were on the program. In 2010, two years after the financial meltdown, only 1.86 million families were on AFDC's successor program, Temporary Aid to Needy Families (TANF). Clinton's "reforms" had worsened the dire consequences of the crisis for America's most destitute families. According to the Census Bureau, by 2011 almost 50 million Americans were living at or below the federal poverty line (United States Bureau of the Census, 2012). The Great Society was on the way out.

In 1996, Clinton tried to cement "bipartisan" cooperation with Republicans, by declaring that "the era of big government is over" (Clinton, 1996). The following year he slashed billions from Medicare and Medicaid (Selfa, 2000: 7). By 1999 Medicare had its first spending decline since its inception; fees were higher and services reduced (ibid.: 11). Its 1997–98 home healthcare services declined by 45 percent; 600,000 fewer people received care (Pear, 2000; *The New York Times*, 2000). The 1997 Balanced Budget Agreement (BBA) further reduced the social-policy divisions between the parties by embracing the neoliberal policy of tax reduction for the wealthy. BBA gave a modest tax break to the middle quintile of families, a substantially bigger one to the top 20 percent and the biggest to the wealthiest 1 percent.

Austerity politics was now well under way. The Democratic Party thus abandoned millions of poor, elderly, sick and disabled Americans. The effects of Clinton's "reforms" were devastating: before 1996, 70 percent of poor Americans had guaranteed access to a lifeline; by 2009, fewer than a third did (Hartmann, 2013; Diamond, 2011). The number of families living on less than $2 per person a day more than doubled between 1996 and 2011, as did the number of extremely poor children (Edin and Shaefer, 2012). Edin and Shaefer (2015) trace the rise in "deep poverty" (families with income below half the poverty line) to Clinton's withdrawal of the cash-assistance safety net for poor families with children. *"Deficit reduction" (read: reducing social spending) is now a central goal of domestic economic policy for every administration, Republican and Democratic.* The majority of Americans do not support the reductions in Social Security, Medicare and Medicaid that have been successfully pushed by both parties since the Reagan administration. The Reaganization/neoliberalization of both parties marks yet another blow to democracy in America.

The historic significance of Clinton is that he did not merely organize the Democratic Party to embrace an otherwise despised ideology for pragmatic reasons, the way Nixon was able to carry off the establishment of diplomatic and economic relations with China without abandoning anti-communism. Clinton didn't merely rally his fellow Democrats to this or that Reaganite policy; he made the Democratic Party into a neoliberal institution (Levine, 2014). The U.S. political system no longer needs Republicans, except to disguise an effectively one-party system.

Clinton's most-cited defense of the success of his presidency is most telling. In 1999 he claimed that he had presided over "the longest period of peacetime economic expansion in American history" (Clinton, 1999). Clinton was able to maintain a sustained period of expansion even as inequality was growing faster than it had under George H. W. Bush and the median wage was continuing the decline it had begun in 1975 (Sottile, 2015; Lazonick, 2014). As noted in Chapter 5, the postwar situation was as it was in the 1920s: stagnant wages were given artificial purchasing power by a massive increase in household debt, far greater than the 1920s increase. During Clinton's tenure, the average American family experienced a 53 percent increase in credit-card debt, from $2,697 to $4,126; low-income families experienced a 184 percent rise in their debt; and even high-income families had 28 percent more credit-card debt in 2001 than they did in 1989 (Draut and Silva, 2003). Fittingly, the administration of the man who neoliberalized the Democratic Party underscored the dependence of austerity-laden "prosperity" on an unprecedented household-debt burden.

It speaks volumes about Democratic-Party "liberalism" that the party no longer makes an issue of poverty and unemployment in America. The subjects have become taboo. The 2016 Democratic presidential candidate campaigned as if Americans had never had it so good. Not a word about declining wages and the explosion of low-wage jobs. The transition from American "bastard Keynesianism" to the era of financialized neoliberal capitalism has, since Clinton, been spearheaded by Democrats. Barack Obama elicited more intense enthusiasm among the population than any president since Franklin Roosevelt. In both the primary contest and his first presidential try he received more FIRE (finance, insurance and real estate)-sector contributions than Hillary Clinton and John McCain. And he carried on the Clinton project of doing away with the legacy of the New Deal and the Great Society. Inequality grew faster under his two-term administration than it did under Bush or Bill Clinton (Sommeiller et al., 2016).

THE ERA OF SECULAR STAGNATION — THE CONDITION OF OVERRIPE CAPITALISM

We have seen that the U.S. economy was lifted from its default condition of low or declining living standards and great inequality during only two relatively brief periods of American history, the 1920s and the Golden Age. The end of the Golden Age saw elites mobilized to undo the ND/GS settlement and move the political economy back toward a 1920s configuration.

The outcome of this effort was predictable. Since the mid-1970s, the growth of wages has been severely arrested, and the gap between wages and productivity has continually widened (Economic Policy Institute, 2016). Thus, inequality has skyrocketed to record levels. All this mirrors the 1920s. Low wages combined with the curtailment of government spending, i.e. the lowering of the social wage, has, as we have seen, generated a significant slowdown of economic growth relative to the highly uncommon growth rates of the Golden Age. Growth rates depressing wages and employment have persisted to this day. Prominent economists have forecast that this may last "forever" (Summers, 2013a). Hence the revived discussion among economists, since Lawrence Summers' 2013 IMF speech, of secular stagnation.

Let us first look at the discussion of secular stagnation by three important commentators and then examine the financial and real-economic transformations characteristic of an economy suffering from long-term lethargy. Chief among these are securitization as a major source of financialized growth; the new financialized economy transfigured to generate profits relatively independent of production, employment and household purchasing power; the explosion of debt among firms and households; changes in the operations of the firm; the altered nature of profit maximization; the impact of these corporate metamorphoses on workers in the form of living standards, inequality and job polarization; and the ongoing expulsion of labor from both production and service industries. Because these developments are consequences of long-term stagnation, I shall begin with a more detailed discussion of post-Golden-Age stagnation.

SUMMERS, KRUGMAN AND SKIDELSKY ON SECULAR STAGNATION

The inevitability of secular stagnation has been the subject of widely discussed articles by the economic luminaries Lawrence Summers, Paul Krugman and Robert Skidelsky. Their combined observations underscore the features of mature capitalism which implicitly reveal the revolutionary possibilities identified by Marx and Keynes and unwittingly show these to be the only alternatives to perpetual slow-growth-cum-austerity. Skidelsky recalls that Keynes and his eminent American student Alvin Hansen forecast "that new inventions would require less capital than in the past. This has now come to pass … Kodak needed and built vastly more infrastructure than its digital successors Instagram and Facebook – and (of course) employed many more workers. The inventions of the future may well consume even less capital (and labor)" (Skidelsky, 2014.) Lawrence Summers has failed to note the conspicuous link between Skidelsky's disaccumulationist prediction and his own widely discussed concerns regarding the possibility of chronic secular stagnation. In his 2013 speech to the IMF, Summers noted that a series of bubbles has been necessary to avert stagnation since the 1980s. Yet even with the excessive stimulus that bubbles provide, Summers pointed out, the economy's growth and employment rates remain sluggish. And we never saw the mild-to-moderate real-economy inflation normal in times of robust growth. Most significantly, we did not see robust investment outside the tech bubble.

The dot.com bubble of the 1990s buoyed growth and employment from very low to low, well below peak rates, while inflation remained below target levels. Writing in the *Financial Times* about the housing bubble ("Why stagnation might prove to be the new normal"), Summers reminds us that "manifestly unsustainable bubbles and loosening of credit standards during the middle of the past decade, along with very easy money, were sufficient to drive only moderate economic growth" (Summers, 2013b). He concludes that "The implication of these thoughts is that the presumption that normal economic and policy conditions will return at some point cannot be maintained ... [T]he underlying problem – that is to say, a chronic demand shortfall, the need for bubbles to sustain such growth as there will be and secular stagnation – may be there *forever*" (emphasis added). The lesson, Summers maintains, is clear: central-bank support of admittedly unsustainable bubbles must become normal "policy support." And he alludes to the cheapening of capital goods as central to this dynamic: he avers that "Declines in the cost of durable goods, especially those associated with information technology, mean the same level of saving purchases more capital every year" (ibid.).

The New York Times's Paul Krugman, America's most widely read economist, puts it well in "On the Political Economy of Permanent Stagnation": "I worry that a more or less permanent depression could end up simply becoming accepted as the way things are, that we could suffer endless, gratuitous suffering, yet the political and policy elite would feel no need to change its ways" (Krugman, 2013a). Martin Wolf of *The Economist* is frank about the ruling-class consensus: "The elites of the high-income countries quite like this new world. The rest of their population like it vastly less. Get used to this. It will not change" (Wolf, 2012).

Let us now turn to the financial and real-economic transfigurations required by an economy characterized by long term real-economic stagnation and the rejection of social democracy.

SECURITIZATION: INVESTMENT AND PROFITS
WITHOUT PRODUCTION

The deregulation that began under Jimmy Carter and proceeded apace under successive administrations enabled an assortment of "non-bank" banks or finance houses that had emerged during the Great Boom to issue commercial paper, i.e. to make loans to businesses to meet short-term needs like meeting payrolls and stocking inventories. More and more of these finance houses – mortgage, loan, finance and insurance companies; check cashing and payday lenders; currency exchanges; securities and commodities firms; mutual funds; hedge funds; money-services businesses and credit-card systems – acted like commercial banks. Traditional banks were pushed out of issuing commercial paper and lending to households and firms (Hoogvelt, 2001: 86–7). On top of this the stagnant economy since the mid-1970s had increased the pressure on both non-financial corporations (NFCs) and banks to "innovate," to find new ways of doing business. For NFCs the "shareholder value" model came to predominate, and with it the growth of private equity (PE) firms and the widespread buying back of a company's stock issues. For financial firms, profit-making based on novel securities became standard procedure. I begin with the new strategy of financial firms based on securitization. I take up shareholder value, PE and buybacks in later sections.

"Securitization" or "loan selling," an innovation rooted in the finance sector, makes possible *a built-in financial activity independent of the fortunes of a real economy mired in long-term slow growth, i.e. secular stagnation* (*The Economist*, 1986: 8–12). Debt was turned into an income-earning asset. Debt payment or expected payments was packaged and sold as tradable paper, i.e. made available to firms for short-term needs such as meeting payroll or stocking inventories. The new security or bond thus functions as money. Because financial returns are more profitable than productive investment (see p. 167), influential economists and financial rentiers began to view securitization as a qualitative transition from productive to financialized or "weightless" capitalism, ushering in a stage of capitalist development in which production was irrelevant to profits. What they failed to note, as we shall see, are the potentially devastating effects of the link between securitization and increasing debt, both household and corporate. John Edmunds, in an influential article, baldly stated the new outlook:

Securitization – the issuance of high-quality bonds and stocks – has become the most powerful engine of wealth creation ... *financial instruments are the leading component of wealth today as well as its fastest-growing generator* ... Historically, manufacturing, exporting, and direct investment produced prosperity through income-creation ... Nowadays, wealth is created when the managers of a business enterprise give high priority to rewarding the shareholders and bondholders. The greater the rewards, the more the shares and bonds are likely to be worth in the financial markets ... An economic policy that [achieves] growth by wealth-creation therefore *does not attempt to increase the production of goods and services, except as a secondary objective.* (Edmunds, 1996: 118; emphasis added)

We are told that production is yesterday's wealth-creating process. Now, manufacturing, productive investment and the jobs and income generated by production are "secondary" and theoretically dispensable in wealth creation. This is the direction in which the ruling class is moving American capitalism.

Capitalism's defining credo is that the creation of exchange value is of foremost importance, no matter how it is created. Production relates only contingently to the expansion of exchange value. In the capitalists' ideal world, production is made unnecessary, and money is made by making money. Financialization in this sense represents the ideal form of capitalism. Karl Marx expressed this in *Capital*:

[E]xchange value, not use value, is the determining aim of this movement [from M to M']. ... [T]he form of circulation M...M', the initial and terminal form of which are real money, expresses most graphically the compelling motive of capitalist production – money-making. The process of production appears merely as an unavoidable intermediate link, as a necessary evil for the sake of money-making. (Marx, [1885] 1967b, 58)

After almost 50 years of declining living standards, slow growth and anemic NFC revenues, the recourse to finance had become a structurally mandated feature of capitalist development. The outcome has been, as we have seen, a dramatically rising increase in finance's share of total economic activity. During this process, employment, wages and economic security have declined, inequality has grown and the wealthiest have never had it so good. Facilitating the gigantic fortunes now possible in finance were the dot.com and housing bubbles and the related bailout of the big banks and consequent Federal Reserve policy of "quantitative easing" (QE). But we must first discuss how the new forms of financialization and their creation of bubbles are essentially dependent on debt.

THE NEW FINANCIALIZATION

As noted in Chapter 5, the financial sector's share of total corporate profits increased greatly after 1960. What eventually emerged during the dot.com and housing bubble years was a source of profit, namely unsustainable debt, divorced from production and therefore consistent with slow growth, high unemployment and declining wages. The persistence of unsustainable debt was essential for financialized profit-making in mature chronically stagnant capitalism. This would have been impossible without the new financialization.

Today's financialization differs from the 1920s shift from production to speculation. The latter was almost exclusively about the stock market and margin buying. Just as industrial capitalism tends to commodify everything it can, financialized capitalism tends to capitalize everything it can (Leyshon and Thrift, 2007: 97–115). Virtually any flow of income of any kind can be securitized and sold to a financial investor. *The Economist* painted a vivid picture: "Fancy investing in a security whose payoff depends on how much beer is sold in British pubs ... [Y]ou can purchase the rights to a slice of the revenues from old Italian films ... or the royalties earned by ... Rod Stewart. There is barely a[n actual or potential] cash flow anywhere ... that cannot be re-assembled into a bond-like security that the most conservative of investors might buy" (*The Economist*, 1998).

Since the 1990s, short-term UK and US financial speculation delivered far higher profits at much less immediate risk than did investment in new plants and equipment or designing new products in a long-stagnant economy (New Economics Foundation, 2011; Centre For Research on Socio-Cultural Change, 2009; Trades Union Congress, 2013). "[I]nvestment got dampened due to an increase in the opportunity cost for corporations because of high yielding financial assets" (Rohit, 2013: 145). The business press is replete with stories on the exceptionally low level of business investment. For the first time in decades, gross capital investment has fallen well below 20 percent of GDP (Cassidy, 2014). Underinvestment in the real economy emerges "because all those projects which fetch a lower rate of profit than a higher rate of return on financial assets will not be undertaken any more" (Rohit, 2013: 70). We have seen

George Soule's identification of the same phenomenon as the principal cause of the late 1920s turn to financial speculation in response to declining sales and revenues during that decade. Investment in property and less tangible assets was becoming the norm. By 2000, government bond interest rates and returns on shares were in many cases twice the profits returned by productive investment. Financial profits at these levels were unheard of before 1980 (Pettifor, 2006: 3–7). These profits became conspicuous in the fortunes made during the dot.com and housing bubbles. This kind of profit-making only exacerbates both corporate and household debt growth, fosters the formation of growing bubbles and makes large-scale NFC insolvency a genuine future possibility, as we shall see in our discussion of the buyback phenomenon.

FINANCIALIZATION AND THE GROWTH
OF LEVERAGED CORPORATE DEBT

Non-financial-corporation and financial-sector debt grew even faster than household and government debt and enabled outsized household debt. These firms were borrowing heavily beginning three decades before the housing bubble. The incentive to finance investments with debt or leverage is great, whether retained earnings are high or low. Leverage enables financial institutions to make great returns without substantial cash outlays. A financial institution that lays out 20 percent and borrows 80 percent has a debt-to-equity ratio, or leverage, of 4:1. If the value of the purchased asset increases by 20 percent, equity increases by 100 percent. But leverage magnifies losses as well as gains. If an asset's value falls by 20 percent, the entire equity is wiped out. Financial-sector borrowing suffered this outcome after the housing bubble burst (Leopold, 2009: 195).

Between 1980 and 2008 leverage had financed NFC acquisitions by larger NFCs and banks by bigger banks. Giant companies spent as much on buying other companies as on productive investment (Savage and Williams, 2008: 13). In the post-Golden Age, this was a means of buying, not earning, revenue that was unavailable through selling more output. Here was a signal strategy of financialized capitalism: *investment aimed at producing new value was replaced with outlays, largely debt-financed, aimed at purchasing assets already in place. This type of investment does nothing to generate employment or household purchasing power.* The aggressor company's assets increased, as if the company had made money in the traditional sense, by expansion in product markets. Its share price would go up and managers would reap a windfall.

The more recent borrowing surge was to purchase debts to be securitized and sold to investors. The variety and magnitude of these debts was so great that financial institutions themselves had to borrow in order to purchase these instruments. Financial-sector debt grew faster than that of any other sector, from about 20 percent of GDP in 1980 to over 117 percent by the end of 2007 and 119 percent on the eve of the 2008 crisis. Financial-sector debt was greater than household debt, a new and troublesome development (Magdoff and Yates, 2009: 68; Dumenil and Levy, 2011: 104–5). Absence of effective regulation enabled these institutions to borrow *serially* on a tiny capital cushion, with leverage ratios as high as 30:1. Such vast borrowing was both facilitated and made hugely destabilizing by borrowers' ability to use as collateral the dubious securities they already owned. The ability to borrow for speculative purposes was now virtually unlimited.

The total nominal value of these securitized products exceeded global GDP (Sayer, 2015: 202). The entire financial system had become highly vulnerable to serious debt-payment decline. The extent to which financial institutions' profit had come to hinge on both their own and household debt was the stuff of a ticking time bomb. That bomb was the twofold dot.com and housing bubble of the 1990s and the years up to 2008.

THE DOT.COM AND HOUSING BUBBLES

The founding and rapid growth of new computer and internet technology-oriented companies in the early 1990s led first to an investment boom in this sector which caused share prices to rise faster than the companies' revenue growth. Entrepreneurs borrowed heavily to invest in internet-related enterprises they believed to be the wave of the future. Dot.com start-ups exhibited "irrational exuberance": many with the highest price-to-earnings ratios had the lowest earnings (Steinberg, 2012). Thus, high share prices, the main motivator of hi-tech investments and generator of dot.com profits, were unrelated to the key criterion of success in the real economy, sales revenues and earnings.

Rising stock prices provided investment advisors with "evidence" of their reliability. By 2000, 97 percent of fiber-optic capacity lay idle, indicating a stock-price bubble and overproduction. (A bubble exists if the price of a given asset is grossly exaggerated relative to the present value of the asset or the expected payoffs.) The bubble inevitably burst in 2001 and shares plummeted. This pointed to the exceptional weakness of the long-sluggish real, productive economy, which had been slow-growing since the mid-1970s. One would expect that the sizeable dot.com bubble, with its explosion of demand for houses, consumer durables and luxury goods, would accelerate the growth rate.

Yet the expansion of the 1990s was the weakest of the entire postwar period, "the most sluggish recovery in modern times," as *Business Week* put it (cited in McNally, 1999). *Debt-driven bubbles seemed necessary to sustain even exceptionally sluggish growth rates*, a telling measure of the depth and intransigence of the stagnation that had plagued the economy since the mid-1970s (Summers, 2013a, b). The upcoming housing bubble confirmed this perception (Summers, 2013b, 2014a; Krugman, 2010, 2012a, 2013a, b, 2013c; Skidelsky, 2014; Turner, 2014a).

After the dot.com bubble burst, Alan Greenspan dramatically lowered interest rates to facilitate another surge in debt-fuelled spending, this time on houses. If bubbles were necessary to sustain even slow growth rates, then let the late tech bubble be succeeded by a new, more powerful one. Many asset-backed securities issuers took on enormous debt to purchase traditional mortgages, mortgage-backed securities, credit-card receivables, auto loans and student debt, betting that continually soaring housing prices would buoy household confidence – ensuring, the issuers imagined, that debtors would continue payments. It was the rapidly growing securitiza-tion of home mortgages that immediately precipitated the Great Recession. Mortgage debt grew faster than GDP, personal disposable income or household debt. In the mid-1990s mortgage debt was an increasingly large part of total household debt. The housing bubble was well under way before the dot.com bubble burst. With housing loans, the largest single activity of commercial banks, securitization permitted these institutions to lend to pro-spective buyers of homes with no apparent risk to the lending institutions. Mortgage issuers, who received handsome fees, bundled many mortgage loans into a single package, a mortgage-backed security (MBS), which was then sold to investors, including institutional investors like pension funds, in the U.S. and all over the world. Payments from the assembled loans were now directed to the investor.

Mortgage originators had exploited borrowers' financial naïvety, concealing the fact that the interest rate would shoot upward due to "adjustable-rate" financing. As *The New York Times* put it, financial insti-tutions were "lending money to nearly anyone who asked for it" (Goodman and Morgenson, 2008). Financial executives dubbed such ballooning loans "NINJA": no income, no job, no assets. Soaring demand for houses pushed home prices upward, leading homeowners to claim their homes as collateral for home-equity loans for home improvements, new flat-screen TVs and to meet additional decreasingly affordable healthcare, childcare and education costs. Many others borrowed to buy houses for speculative purposes, to resell or "flip" them when house prices continued to rise. A growing demand shortfall in the real economy was no obstacle to the amassing of financial profits. *Once again debt was doled out as a substitute for wage-driven purchasing power in an economy plagued by decades of sluggish growth and working-class underconsumption.*

MBSs were a species of collateralized debt obligation (CDO), which bundled and sliced into tranches credit-card, student and auto loans and more, including mortgage loans. These too were sold to investors worldwide. CDOs were themselves a type of derivative, the widest ranging type of security. Derivatives removed virtually all limits on the kind of entity that could be securitized. They are financial products or instruments, i.e. vehicles for financial investment, whose value derives from another financial product such as credit-card loan, mortgage loan, etc. Securitization almost infinitely broadened the range of what could be counted as a "financial instrument" and turned into a derivative. The derivatives market, almost nonexistent in 2000, grew steadily until 2004; it exploded to $17.3 trillion by the end of 2005, just before the housing bubble began to leak in 2006. By 2010, the derivatives market had skyrocketed to $1.2 quadrillion, far greater than the global GDP (Cohan, 2010).

The housing bubble was bound to be much larger than the dot.com bubble because of the burst of derivative trading made possible by Bill Clinton's 1999 repeal of the Glass–Steagall Act, which had forbidden the wholesale fusion of commercial and investment banks' activities. *Financialized capitalism could "produce" far more new "products" than was possible in the long-stagnant real economy.* To the extent that this is becoming the norm, long-term slow real-economy growth, serious unemployment and growing inequality will persist indefinitely.

The financial innovation industry tried to eliminate the risk they knew to be built into CDOs by insuring them. Credit default swaps (CDSs) are supposed to insure loans and bonds that speculate on ability to repay debt, largely mortgage debt. CDO sellers like Goldman Sachs sold MBSs they knew to be toxic, then bet against them by purchasing CDSs as insurance. The stage was set for disaster: by 2006 more than 40 percent of all mortgages were sold to NINJA borrowers. CDSs on MBSs were now eight times larger than the securities themselves (McNally, 2011: 105). When the mortgage market imploded, CDS issuers were unable to cover the losses they had insured. Toward the end of 2008, interest payments to investors were in irreversible decline. It had become evident that MBSs, CDOs and CDSs were virtually worthless, since no private investor would buy them. Credit markets froze. Interbank lending ceased, since no bank could trust the others' solvency. CDS trades unwound six months later in the September debacle. Stock markets around the world plunged, since the tainted securities had been peddled globally. U.S. retirement funds were reduced by 50 percent, institutional investors holding the savings of millions of workers took stunning losses, and investment banks holding billions in toxic instruments were rendered insolvent. This would so poison the body economic, we were told, that a massive government bailout was demanded by the masters of finance.

THE ELEVENTH INTERVENTION: THE BAILOUT AS DECLARATION OF FINANCE CAPITAL'S COMMAND OF THE STATE

Contrary to elite claims, the bailout was entirely unnecessary. The Obama administration could have revalued homes at non-bubble market prices, assessed each distressed household's financial situation, and reset affordable mortgage payments based on these assessments, allowing homeowners to stay in their homes. *Ten million* homeowners did not have to lose their homes. The fiscal conservatism of New Deal Roosevelt and neoliberal Obama led each to eschew policies that would have averted the austerity suffered by workers under each administration. Americans were told that the whole economic system would collapse were the banks not recapitalized. But government rescue was not needed to save American capitalism; it saved the financial wing of the capitalist class from suffering the losses resulting from its bad bets. The decisive political power of finance capital signaled that the effective privatization of the State was in full swing. The post-Golden-Age ruling class, finance capital, dominates the State so decisively that it is now immune to the consequences of present and future economic crises. And financial reform law was not meant to prevent future crises.

The Dodd–Frank financial reform law was drawn up in close consultation with bank lobbyists and is riddled with loopholes and exceptions that make enforcement near-impossible. Bank advocates lobby to underfund enforcement agencies, to defang policies that limit the power of capitalists – making regulation of financial institutions unworkable (Reich, 2015a: 72–3). An amendment written entirely by Citibank lawyers was added to the December 2014 budget bill that exempts large banks from crucial features of Dodd–Frank (Lindorff, 2015). Banks were freed from liability if commodity-based derivatives they bet on collapsed.

Then-president Obama's handling of the crisis underscored the hegemony of finance capital. Meeting with the big bankers, he said he would disregard popular anger and rescue the rentiers. One banker said, "The sense of everyone after the meeting was relief ... he mostly wanted to help us out, to quell the mob." Obama reassured the bankers: "My administration is the only thing between you and the pitchforks. You guys have an acute public relations problem that's turning into a political problem ... I'm not here to go after you ... I'm going to shield you" (cited in Suskind, 2012: 234). Nothing would be done to prevent the perpetuation of financial bubbles, and just about everything would be done to protect the bubble-blowers from retribution. Most significantly, we have seen that some of America's most distinguished economists anticipate that the perpetuation of bubble-driven sluggish economic growth and serial Great Recessions may be the most likely future of financialized neoliberal capitalism.

TARP AND QE AS EMBLEMS OF FINANCIAL HEGEMONY

The eventual "solutions," the Troubled Asset Relief Program (TARP) and the still-ongoing QE policy, the exchange of bad assets for good, have left the very richest richer than ever and done nothing to reverse the ongoing decline of the median wage or to halt foreclosures resulting from the crisis. The original TARP proposal proposed by George W. Bush's Treasury Secretary, Henry "Hank" Paulson, a former CEO of Goldman Sachs, was an explicit transfer of the banks' losses to the State: the Treasury would purchase the banks' "toxic assets" at highly inflated prices, "cash for trash." But because there was in fact no objective means for determining the greatly overpriced money value of these "distressed" assets, the Bush administration changed course and simply redirected $700 billion of capital injections into the banks. This was a tacit admission that the banks had suffered not a liquidity crisis but were in fact insolvent or bankrupt and needed recapitalization. Scott Alvarez, the Fed's general counsel, admitted that all along the plan, withheld from Congress and the public, was to inject equity into the banks (Smith, 2014). At Paulson's command, TARP stipulated that no conditions were to be placed on the banks, such as limiting executive compensation. Nor would bankruptcy judges rewrite the terms on mortgage debt, and there would be no future review or legal action. Finance capital's hold on the State was as tight as a noose.

This price had to be paid, Paulson warned, to avert economic collapse and "martial law." Public outrage was accompanied by almost unanimous support for the bailout among the political establishment and the news media. After the White House and national media warned of imminent global economic collapse if the legislation were not passed, Congress approved the $700 billion rescue package in early October 2008. The managers of the banks were not replaced and, with no effective limits on executive pay, some TARP funds took the form of large compensation payments or bonuses to executives.

In the words of Neil Barofsky, special inspector general in charge of oversight of TARP, "TARP was little more than a massive transfer of wealth from taxpayers to undeserving Wall Street executives" (Barofsky, 2012: 183). Because the "too big to fail" axiom was now official policy, the bondholders of the banks and other financial institutions were assured that they would be paid in full in the event of future losses (Moseley, 2013: 646). The biggest banks ended up 20 percent larger than they were before the crisis and "controlled a larger part of our economy than ever" (Barofsky, 2011). During the TARP debates, Democrat Senator Dick Durbin stated that "the banks, hard to believe in a time when we're facing a banking crisis that many of the banks created, are still the most powerful lobby on Capitol Hill. And they frankly own the place" (cited in Grim, 2011). The aggressively anti-democratic character of neoliberal capitalism was now in full view. Prior to overseeing TARP, Barofsky had been unaware that what former IMF Chief Economist Simon Johnson had called a "quiet coup" had been successfully effected: "I had no idea that the U.S. government had been captured by the banks and that those running the bailout program ... would come from the very same institutions that had both helped cause the crisis and then become the beneficiaries of the generous terms of their bailout" (Barofsky, 2012: 19).

The official story that TARP was to provide banks with the means to resume lending was senseless, since households were already up to their ears in unpayable debt and their credit-worthiness was at a postwar low. TARP recipients were disarmingly frank about their unwillingness to lend. Said a senior big bank official, "no one is going to lend a nickel until the economy turns ... Who are we going to lend money to? Only people who don't need it" (Sorkin, 2008).

The Fed's QE program was far more consequential than TARP, whose $700 billion gift to the banks merely provided them with sufficient operating capital to remain in business. The stated aim of QE, the chief policy instrument for engineering recovery since the meltdown, was to help businesses and households recover from the crisis. The Fed would pump more money into the economy by buying securities, in this case government bonds, from banks with electronic cash. Like the countercyclical policy of lowering interest rates to stimulate spending, QE was alleged to stimulate the economy by pushing long-term interest rates down, incentivizing new lending by banks. After nine years, QE has accomplished none of these aims. Banks would not lend to households whose incomes are at 60-year lows, many of whose members are unemployed or underemployed, whose debts are at 60-year highs and whose houses are worth less than their mortgage obligations. Nor would businesses expand capacity and hire more workers. What QE cash did accomplish was to pay huge bonuses to financial-sector executives, recapitalize insolvent banks and initiate a historic seven-year bull market rally.

QE is best explained as follows. First, aversion to fiscal policy reflects neoliberal preference that the private sector, not government, manage the economy. Second, Paulson and then-Chairman of the Federal Reserve Ben Bernanke recognized that the biggest banks were not merely illiquid but insolvent, and needed recapitalization. Finally, QE created conditions whereby the very wealthy could become wealthier through a prolonged stock-market boom even as the productive economy remained stagnant.

QE embodies entrenched neoliberalism and contains the seeds of the form economic "growth" will take under financialized capitalism. The "shareholder value" conception of the real-economy firm (see p. 179 and its signature strategy, debt-financed stock buybacks, are implicit in QE. In 2013, the Fed purchased $1 trillion of risky assets from banks that lend to corporations; those firms spent $500 billion in stock buybacks in the same year. Company managers who realize stock options benefit from options that are increasingly valuable by virtue of buybacks that keep share values on the rise. The stock market would now be the fastest-growing and most reliable source of profit, but not in the traditional fashion, wherein share prices rise because productive companies are growing and profitable. With tens of billions per month given to the banks and no corresponding lending by the banks, the liquidity remains in the financial system and is put to use in the stock market, funding corporate stock buybacks and threatening yet another bubble, this time in corporate leveraged debt.

QE funds were also used by financial firms to award bonuses to officers, to execute derivatives trading, to carry trade in bonds and to engage in other and sundry forms of speculation. The result has been windfall profits. This outcome was one of the Fed's primary motives in sustaining QE, in spite of years of evidence of its failure to achieve its disingenuously stated goals.

THE TWELFTH INTERVENTION: OCCUPY

In response to the bailout's rescue of the banks with no relief for the victims of the crisis, and, most importantly, to the ensuing awareness of the vast inequality characterizing American society, mass protests sprung up around the country. It began on September 17, 2011, two years after the alleged "recovery' began, with the occupation of Zuccotti Park near Wall Street. The peaceful action was met with police violence, as all mass actions have been throughout American history. Occupy was not an isolated and exclusively American phenomenon. It was partially inspired by the Arab Spring and the periodic protests across Europe, North Africa and West Asia in response to austerity policies. Many of these protests have been unfocused responses to austerity policies and political repression; others have aimed to unseat a head of state (Tunisia and Egypt). Occupy deliberately put forward no political agenda other than to register indignation at the ability of "the 1 percent" to immiserate "the 99 percent" with impunity. The idea was to introduce no political agenda that might generate disunity within the movement. There was certainly no general critical analysis of capitalism nor a call for a democratic socialist alternative.

For this reason the movement was seen by many on the Left as insufficiently focused to have a lasting effect. And some of the movement's tactics were politically immature. Picketing the banks, for example, betrays a naïvety regarding the workings of power in American capitalism. The banks in themselves have no power whatever – the enormous power they in fact wield is legislated, and there are virtually no limits to a sovereign government's ability to regulate banking activity. (Even banks' hours of operation are determined politically.) If picketing is appropriate, it is the legislators who should be harangued to proscribe bank practices contrary to the interests of working people. Picketing the banks implicitly denies the political roots of financial power.

None of this means that Occupy was not a historically significant movement. Occupy brought together, probably for the first time in American history, people with a range of different but importantly related issues: the unemployed, the underemployed, student debtors, credit-card debtors, people who had been evicted from their homes, those whose mortgages were underwater, i.e. whose homes were worth less than their mortgages, the homeless, and others who had suffered the manifold depredations of the dismantling of the welfare state and other neoliberal punishments. This diverse constituency was united by their awareness of the deep significance of the conflict of interest between "the 1 percent" and "the rest of us," phrases which were to become common parlance in U.S. culture, even occurring frequently in the mass media. Occupy made *inequality* more widely acknowledged and discussed than it had been since the Great Depression (Schram, 2015). Class injustice was brought to the fore, and with it the makings of a more developed class consciousness among Americans. That there will be comparable movements in the future is certain. Occupy's next round can build upon the odiousness of inequality in its theory and practice. With the link binding inequality and capitalism, and great wealth and political power, increasingly evident, an essential element upon which an anti-capitalist movement can be built is in place. But Occupy's successor will need to do what unions have traditionally done, and what the Chicago Teachers' Union recently did with great success (see Chapter 8), namely build a larger base by connecting to a larger constituency outside the choir.

DEBT AND THE TRANSFORMED NATURE OF THE FIRM AND
OF INVESTMENT UNDER FINANCIALIZED CAPITALISM: LBOS,
PRIVATE EQUITY AND THE SHAREHOLDER-VALUE MOVEMENT

Investment, LBOs and Private Equity

The developmental dynamics of financialized capitalism discussed above are recasting the nature of the non-financial corporation (NFC). The management practices and goals of productive firms have been transformed to prioritize making money with money and decreasing the role of production in generating profits. The concept of *investment* is thus transformed. The term has traditionally signified productive outlays to increase revenues by the sale of additional material output. It now increasingly refers to any outlay that generates a financial return, typically by means other than producing tangible output.

Mergers and acquisitions are one way for a firm to increase revenues and profits without necessarily producing additional output. The "leveraged buyout" (LBO) or hostile takeover, which gained momentum in the early 1980s, was *the financial successor of the industrial merger* and initiated the portfolio or financialized conception of the large NFC. Here a private equity (PE) company purchases the target firm, largely with borrowed money. The target firm is than saddled with the debt or leverage, thereby relieving the PE company of the burden of debt repayment. The bought-out company typically lacked the financial wherewithal to service the debt, and so "strips" or sells off much of its purportedly unprofitable physical assets and lays off workers, often raiding their pension funds in the process. In the process more jobs are destroyed than created (Davis et al., 2011). In the financialized and stagnant system, increasing *earnings* through *lowering costs* by buying a company and cutting its workforce replaced increasing *revenues* by *expanding sales* as a principal focus (Osenton, 2004: 171–3, 234–6).

Takeovers, layoffs and shedding of unprofitable units were seen as enhancing productivity, so the acquired firm's share price always spiked at acquisition. As *Newsweek* put it, "[T]he more people a company fires, the more Wall Street loves it, and the higher its stock price goes" (Sloan, 1996). The acquired company was then sold as a more productive enterprise at a higher price than its acquisition cost. The wave of corporate downsizings in the 1980s and 1990s was among the first widely publicized indication of PEs' LBOs (Sayer, 2015: 212). *The LBO and the PE buyout made the stock market a market not merely for shares in companies but for the control of whole companies.* The business press coined a new term: "the market for corporate control." Corporate performance shifted from long-term organizational and product innovation to enhanced market capitalization (stock price) of the company after takeover (Lazonick and O'Sullivan, 2000: 18). The firm's performance is now evaluated by reference to its earnings per share (EPS) of stock. (EPS is the ratio of earnings or after-tax profits to total shares of stock outstanding.) PE buyouts are a potential source of a future credit crash. From 2000 to 2008, PE firms did almost 3,200 buyouts at a $1.2 trillion cost, $1 trillion of which consists of debt/leverage (Kosman, 2009). This growing form of making profits underscores the debt-driven nature of contemporary American capitalism.

With cost-cutting and buyouts in full swing during the 1980s and 1990s, America's most profitable companies binged on shedding jobs, mainly in order to raise share prices. From the mid-1980s through the 1990s IBM laid off 60,000 workers, Sears-Roebuck 50,000, AT&T 40,000, Boeing 28,000, Digital Equipment 20,000 and General Motors 24,000 (Newsweek Staff, 1996). These were "structural layoffs" of workers and of jobs that would never come back (Smith, 2012: 57). *The withering of framework innovations, saturation of the biggest growth markets and increased global competition made healthy returns from widget sales less promising than massive returns from financial machinations.* The stock market was seen as the best source of wealth in a stagnant economy. This has been reflected in a corresponding transformation of the nature and function of the firm under financialized capitalism.

Shareholder Value: The Transformed Function
of the Large Firm and its Managers

What prevails now is the so-called "shareholder value" conception of the firm: as existing not to turn out innovative products but primarily to return the greatest amount of exchange value to shareholders. The aim of the company is to meet the need of absentee owners, i.e. shareholders, for greater wealth. This transformation of corporate objectives has been termed a shift from "retain and invest" to "downsize and distribute" (Lazonick, 2014, 2015). The flip side of this transformation of companies has been a corresponding transformation of the role of the stock market. *The stock market's primary function is no longer to fund companies; companies now fund the stock market.*

Pressure on managers to push share prices higher is unending. Top management internalized this when corporations made grants of company stock or stock options a major compensation. When stock prices rise, managers reap a windfall. Corporate market capitalization after LBO takeovers emerged as the exclusive measure of managerial effectiveness. By the late 1990s the largest management compensations were driven by stock prices. Exercised stock options averaged 63 percent of the top 100 CEOs' earnings (Crotty, 2005: 93).

FINANCIALIZED CAPITALISM'S DEPENDENCE
ON BURGEONING DEBT

The overriding goal to employ as much debt as possible to finance both household consumption and corporate acquisitions demonstrates the centrality of debt to financialized capitalism, and the liability of debt-driven capitalism to instability and crisis. With debt ubiquitous, managers of targetable firms tried to ward off takeover by loading their firms with debt-financed stock buybacks and cash dividends (Crotty, 2005: 90). We have seen that since the end of the Second World War it has taken increasing amounts of debt to generate one dollar of GDP. Lord Adair Turner has aptly termed this "debt addiction": "We seem to need credit growth faster than GDP growth to achieve an optimally growing economy, but that leads inevitably to crisis and post-crisis recession" (Turner, 2014b: 1; 2016).

Finance capital's extraction of income from the productive economy began with the draining of industry; the siphoning from the household awaited the housing bubble. In both cases, cash resources of NFCs and households were disgorged to manipulators whose objectives were strictly financial. Capitalism is a putatively beneficial system of *production* for profit. Profit is its fundamental objective, and must be acquired through production, with employment and wages as the means to the promised benefits. But finance is not *productive* of widgets; it is *extractive* of interest payments on debt. It is a parasite on both labor and industry (Hudson, 2015a). The bleeding of households and firms results in crisis in the productive economy. The creation of household debt that could not be paid caused the 2008 debacle. The next crisis might well be the explosion of the corporate-debt bubble. The triggering mechanism could be the practice of stock buybacks.

BUYBACKS AND THE DEBT-DRIVEN, PRIVATE-INVESTMENT-STARVED NEW NORMAL

No longer does the market allocate capital; it now *drains NFC resources*. The buyback binge could become a major factor in the next credit-bubble crisis. When both corporate managers and institutional investors demanded ever-climbing stock prices, corporations engineered price rises by buying back more shares than they issued. "The value of corporate stock buybacks exceeded new issues at an annual rate of $354 billion" (Economic Policy Institute, 1999). Since 2009 most of the money corporations have borrowed has been used to repurchase their own stock (Urie, 2014). From 2004 to 2015 companies spent about $7 trillion buying back their own stocks. *The Wall Street Journal* reported that "total buybacks since the beginning of 2005 [amounted] to $4.21 trillion – or nearly one-fifth of the total value of all U.S. stocks today" (Zweig, 2014). Since a firm's performance is now evaluated, as we have seen, by EPS, buybacks are billions from heaven, since they reduce the number of shares outstanding and thereby increase EPS. Executives' compensation is driven further upward and inequality is heightened.

Unlike during the LBO movement, the financial vampire need no longer find a promising object of acquisition from which to seek wealth. Buybacks permit companies to self-loot, i.e., to raid their own companies' revenue streams. Executives now saddle their own companies with debt in order to remunerate themselves with the enormous bonuses characteristic of this financial gambit. "The top 50 non-financial U.S. companies in terms of cumulative amounts spent on stock repurchases since 2000 are now often giving more money back to shareholders in buybacks and dividends than they make in profits – the first time that's happened outside of recessionary periods" (Brettell et al., 2015).

Profits, Buybacks, Declining Investment and Superfluous Cash

Executive compensation has come to replace investment as the final destination of profits. Between 2003 and 2012, 54 percent of the S&P 500 Index companies' profits came from buybacks alone (Sorkin, 2015). 99 percent of profits, amounting to $4.3 trillion, were distributed to shareholders. 41 percent went to cash dividends and 58 percent to stock buybacks (Lazonick, 2011a, 2011b). The new deployment of profits was startling; in 2008 alone the S&P 500 spent 108 percent of their net profits on buybacks (Lazonick, 2011a). Allocating profits to productive investment is no longer necessary for the firm to reap record profits – or, more precisely, for executives to reap record compensation. *This is what we might expect given secular stagnation and the long-term atrophy of net investment.*

Companies' now-standard practice of reducing costs by freezing and sometimes lowering wages, reducing or eliminating benefits, speeding up remaining workers and cutting back investment has, we have seen, left them with historic levels of cash fruitless for production in an economy also characterized by depressed household purchasing power and saturated growth markets (Murphy et al., 2013). As a *Washington Post* report put it in a revealing headline, "U.S. Companies Buy Back Stock in Droves as They Hold Record Levels of Cash" (Yang, 2010). Apple sits on more than $250 billion in idle cash (Mickle, 2017). In an economy in which private investment is (mistakenly) taken to be the animating source of good wages and high employment, the reduced need for large investment outlays to keep firms financially profitable is a key source of the surplus trillions sitting idly in corporate coffers, much of which is directed to financial rather than productive projects. Between 1980 and 2015, corporate cash holdings have rocketed to an astonishing 10 percent of GDP in the U.S. (Dobbs et al., 2015: 3). Total corporate cash surpluses are in excess of $15 trillion (Rasmus, 2015). Capital's tendency to overaccumulate is now magnified by a historic surfeit of *liquid* capital, a development appropriate to financialized capitalism.

In an article titled "Debt Gone Wild," Advisor Perspectives reported that S&P's 500 Index companies listed buybacks or dividends among the principal uses of otherwise productively superfluous proceeds (Roberts, Lance, 2015). A *Wall Street Journal* headline sums it up: "As Activism Rises, U.S. Firms Spend More on Buybacks Than Factories" (cited in Monga et al., 2015). The biggest firms have spent the largest percentage of net income on buybacks. Between 2006 and 2015, the five largest firms by income, ExxonMobil, Microsoft, IBM, Apple and Proctor & Gamble spent, respectively, 59.2 percent, 71.1 percent, 88.8 percent, 45.5 percent and 69.2 percent of their net income on buybacks. The top 50 firms spent 59.8 percent on buybacks (MacEwan, 2016). Between 2004 and the second quarter of 2017, many very large firms have spent more than $7 trillion on repurchasing their shares (Whitney, 2017: 9). In 2016, big banks distributed to shareholders 65 percent of their revenues in buybacks and dividends. In 2017, the *Wall Street Journal* reported large banks' projection that nearly 100 percent of the year's expected earnings would be distributed to shareholders (Hoffman and Tracy, 2017). As William Lazonick recently put it, "Given the importance of these corporations to the ... economy, ... the twenty-first-century industrial economy has become a 'buyback economy'" (Lazonick, 2016).

Buybacks and NFC Debt

The 2008 crisis displayed the hazards of burgeoning debt in the face of frozen wages and long-term stagnation. The chief economic strategist of the French bank Société Générale, Albert Edwards, has identified a major source of the next crisis: "We have seen massive credit expansion in the U.S. This is not for real economic activity; it is borrowing to finance share buybacks" (cited in Elliott, 2016). Bloomberg, a prominent source of business news and data analysis, is explicit on the use of debt to fuel the enrichment of the 0.1 percent: "It's official, using proceeds from debt sales to send cash to stockholders has never been more popular" (Renick, 2015). Between 2009 and 2015 corporations issued a dizzying $9.3 trillion in bonds not for productive purposes but to goose stock prices (Martens and Martens, 2015). Buybacks mark the latest stage in the remarkable growth of corporate debt discussed above, and the greatest threat of the bursting of the NFC-debt bubble.

Buybacks and the Next Financial Cataclysm

That corporations are repeating the history of households near the peak of their debt binge is hinted at by a Goldman Sachs study, which shows that corporate leverage is at its highest level since 2005 (Alloway and Weisenthal, 2015). Corporate mortgaging of imagined future cash flows have broken records. Hussman Funds reports that "Not only is the equity market at the second most overvalued point in U.S. history, it is also *more leveraged against probable long-term corporate cash flows than at any previous point in history*" (cited in Whitney, 2015; emphasis added). That the seemingly robust stock market rests on a bed of sand is reflected, in the judgment of Goldman Sachs's chief equity strategist, in "Corporate buybacks [being] the sole demand for corporate equities in this market" (Wang, 2016). There is good reason to predict that the next financial convulsion might originate in the NFC and not, like the last, among households and financial firms.

7

The Landscape of Austerity: Polarization, the Destruction of Jobs, and the Emerging Police State

The big function of the new technologies is to save labor costs. They do this by replacing expensive labor with cheap labor at a remote location. Or they do it – it amounts to the same thing – by replacing on-site labor with a machine.

James K. Galbraith, *The End of Normal* (1974), p.133

THE NEW EXPULSION OF LABOR:
AI, ROBOTIZATION AND DECLINING INVESTMENT COSTS

An extensive Associated Press (AP) study reports that:

Five years after the start of the Great Recession, the toll is terrifyingly clear: Millions of middle-class jobs have been lost ... the world over ... Most of the jobs will never return, and millions more are likely to vanish as well ... jobs are disappearing in the service sector, home to two-thirds of all workers. They're being obliterated by technology. (Condon and Wiseman, 2013)

Increasingly advanced scheduling software has reduced the number of office assistants and secretaries. The Department of Labor documents a loss of 1.1 million such jobs between 2000 and 2010. Similar technologies have reduced during the same period the number of bookkeepers by 26 percent, typists by 63 percent, travel agents by 46 percent and telephone operators by 64 percent (Zeiler, 2013).

This intervention reflects a new resource available to capital, IT-informed technologies, which intensifies qualitatively the neoliberal assault on labor and functions to approach asymptotically a zero-cost economy by continuously reducing the need for labor as an essential input to the accumulation process. That AI, automation and robotization are major threats to employment on a global scale is attested to by detailed private and government studies. Oxford researchers Carl Frey and Michael Osborne, investigating the probability of computerization for 702 occupations, concluded that 47 percent of U.S. jobs are likely to be automated by the early 2030s (Frey and Osborne, 2013). Two years later they worked with Citibank's researchers on a report announcing that 57 percent of the jobs in China, Germany, Japan, Korea and the U.S. are susceptible to automation (Frey and Osborne, 2015). A recent report from the Obama White House announced an 83-percent chance that workers earning $20 an hour or less could be replaced by robots by 2021 and a 31-percent chance that workers earning between $20 and $40 per hour could lose their jobs to machines (Lee, 2016). And the National Bureau of Economic Research found that each robot installed in an American factory reduces jobs in the local area by an average of 6.2 workers (Acemoglu and Restrepo, 2017). Researchers at the University of Chicago have estimated that from the turn of the millennium to 2015, half of the total job loss in the U.S. was the result of the replacement of workers by computers, software and robots (Thompson, 2015). Businessmen lick their chops. The robots never rest, take time out, ask for a raise, require health insurance, complain of unsafe working conditions or form a union.

The mechanization defining "the second machine age" is the latest instance of a tendency inherent in capitalist development (Brynjolfsson and McAfee, 2011a, 2014, 2015). Capitalists tend to invest relatively more in machinery than in labor. The accumulation process requires that output increase without end, and capitalism's legitimizing ideology requires that workers' standard of living rise equally endlessly. Productivity, then, must rise if capitalism is to deliver the goods. Innovative technologies can increase labor's efficiency until it is increasingly irrelevant to production. Marx's forecast that capital will invest less in labor and more in advanced technologies has been borne out.

The "digital revolution" greatly intensified investment in capital goods displacing labor. The ongoing digitalization has significantly cheapened capital goods so that capital-intensive investment requires notably smaller outlays in order to increase productivity (Roberts, 2015; Karabarbounis and Neiman, 2013; Keynes, 1964: 220; Summers, 2013b; Harding, 2013; Skidelsky, 2014; Livingston, 1994, 2011). The Frey/Osborne/Citibank study concludes that "digital innovation is much less capital absorbing" than investments in pre-digital technologies (Frey and Osborne, 2015: 73; see also Frey, 2015). The economist Marshall Steinbaum points out that the fact that "the price of capital inputs to production has been falling" is the primary explanation for "capital [having] gained national income at the expense of labor" (Steinbaum, 2017).

Furman and Orszag underscore the other side of the coin, that while the cost of capital has been low or even declining, the return on capital has been uncommonly high (Furman and Orszag, 2015). Historic inequality has resulted. Lawrence Summers comments that "the rate of profitability in the United States is at a near-record high level, as is the share of corporate revenue going to capital" (Summers, 2016). Simcha Barkai of the Stanford University Graduate School of Business notes that "Given that the cost of capital has declined substantially, replacing all the productive capital that currently exists in the economy would be relatively cheap" (Barkai, 2017). Even so, cheap capital and high profits have not induced more investment (Steinbaum, 2017; Furman and Orszag, 2015).

The Industrial Revolution created a new, non-human muscular system for capitalism with labor-displacing machine power. Digitalization and automation/robotization have done away with many of the remaining workers tending machines, and added a neural system to mechanized muscle power. The second machine age is distinguished from the first by digitalized machines' ability to perform more functions requiring not merely physical power but intelligence. The impact on employment and workers' compensation will be greater than that of the first Industrial Revolution.

Gas-station attendants are replaced by self-service pumps, bank tellers by ATMs, secretarial work by personal computers, travel agents by travel-marketing websites, grocery clerks by self-checkouts, and telephone customer service by voice menus and online FAQs. A 1980s office employing 40 people without computers required, by the 1990s, only four workers using four computers. Office productivity can be enhanced by replacing less powerful computers and software with more powerful ones. Thus, actual workers are replaced by computers and potential workers are kept out of the workplace by better computers.

Between 1990 and 2000, computers were developed that had the capacity to "talk to each other." Cognitive tasks became automated. Digitalization to perform mental tasks enables capitalists to expel labor both from production and from service industries. These technologies are, unlike earlier automation, unlimited. "Underneath the physical economy, with its physical people and physical tasks, lies a second economy that is automatic and neutrally intelligent, *with no upper limit to its buildout*" (Arthur, 2011; emphasis added). Brynjolfsson and McAfee demonstrate that robotic technology is increasingly efficient, as human labor is not, and provides a greater return on investment than does human labor. In 1952 the Nobel economist and father of input–output analysis, Wassily Leontief, forecasted in *Scientific American* that "Labor will become less and less important … More and more workers will be replaced by machines. I do not see that new industries can employ everybody who wants a job" (cited in Acemoglu and Restrepo, 2016). In the 1980s he anticipated the impending displacement of the *mental* requirements of work:

> Computers and robots replace humans in the exercise of mental functions in the same way as mechanical power replaced them in the performance of physical tasks … More and more complex mental functions will be performed by machines … powerful computers are now performing mental operations that could not possibly be accomplished by human minds. Any worker … can … be replaced by a machine … the role of humans as the most important factor of production is bound to diminish – in the same way that the role of horses in agricultural production was first diminished and then eliminated by the introduction of tractors. (Leontief, 1983)

It is the prospect of large-scale job loss that led two *New York Times* economics commentators to project a "vast remaking of [the] U.S. economy" (Goodman and Healy, 2009). What this threatens to look like is the subject of what follows.

Offshoring and Outsourcing as Weak Explanations

Offshoring of production and outsourcing of jobs have accounted for significant U.S. job loss (Roberts, 2013, 2014). But as Bill Clinton's Labor Secretary Robert Reich reports, "America has lost at least as many jobs to automated technology as it has to trade" (Reich, 2010: 53). Lawrence Summers has more recently echoed this conclusion: "Almost every economist who has studied the question believes that technology has had a greater impact on the wage structure and on employment than international trade" (Summers, 2017). The *Harvard Business Review* draws the obvious inference: "The more processes can be automated, the less it makes sense to outsource activities to countries where labor is less expensive" (Lewis, 2014). There is a key difference between sending work overseas and mechanization. Some outsourced jobs can be and in fact are being "re-shored" back to the U.S., because of rising wages abroad, declining wages in the U.S. and substantial transportation costs (Conerly, 2014; Sirkin, 2015; Cheng, 2015). But mechanized jobs do not come back. China is the world's leader in the production of industrial robots, and U.S. jobs can be sent there to be done by robots that have displaced Chinese labor (Javelosa, 2017). Jobs exported to China and done by robots will remain there (Miller, 2016). A *New York Times* analyst predicts that "[Robots] will replace most of the workers, though you will need a few people to manage the robots" (Rampell, 2012b; see also Barajas, 2014). *The Times* elaborates that "[W]hile many … jobs were lost to competition with low-wage countries, *even more* vanished because of computer-driven machinery that can do the work of 10, or in some cases, 100 workers … Those jobs are not coming back, but many believe that the industry's future … lies in training a new generation for highly skilled manufacturing … that requires people who know how to run the computer that runs the machine." (Davidson, 2012; emphasis added). But those who run computers are far fewer than the workers displaced by computerized machines. These writers describe *long-term net job loss*. A 2015 study of job loss in manufacturing, the most detailed work to date on the subject, found that the "employment" of robots and other forms of automation accounted for 88 percent of the 7 million factory jobs that have vanished in the U.S. since peak employment in 1979. Productivity growth, not outsourcing or offshoring, is the largest contributor to job loss over the past several decades (Hicks and Devaraj, 2017: 6–7).

Erik Brynjolfsson states that "People in a wide slew of industries are being replaced by digital labor and losing their jobs – not to mention their ability to find a new one." Comparing a tax consultant to TurboTax, he asks "How can a skilled worker compete with a $39 piece of software. She can't. People are racing against the machine, and many of them are losing that race" (May, 2013; see also Thibodeau, 2014). The Associated Press documents that "Technology – specifically powerful software that runs computers and an array of machines and devices – is eliminating the need for many jobs throughout companies and across industries" (Wiseman and Condon, 2013). Let us look at the range of tasks computers and robots can accomplish, and the extent to which mounting automation and robotization threaten the employment security of numerous Americans.

"Non-cognitive" Job Categories

Job loss in the welding trade is rampant, where robotic welding replaces manual welding. In one example, a company invested $135,000 in the robotic welding cell, and about $50,000–60,000 to develop the automated tooling and fixturing. Productivity improved more than 300 percent. (Robotic Industries Association, 2014). In line with this book's emphasis on the cheapening of capital goods as a key contributing factor in the decline of net investment, the fall in prices of industrial robots has been remarkable. In a study of 17 countries, the price of robots has fallen substantially, with an average drop of approximately 50 percent from 1990 to 2005, and a drop of more than 80 percent in 6 countries (Graetz and Michaels, 2015). Robots do the work, on average, in half the time of human workers (Robotic Industries Association, 2014). The typical robot doing heavy industrial work costs well below $400,000. *This magnitude of investment is far less than the outlay required for transformative stimulants, and is nowhere near capable of absorbing the enormous surpluses that companies are sitting on.* With costs of these technologies falling, net investment is either miniscule or nonexistent.

Robots greatly reduced computer-electronics production costs, doing most of the work in making the most valuable parts of computers: the motherboard, housing microprocessors and memory. Workers add batteries and the screen. The robots cost only $20,000–25,000. Robots attend assembly lines in the auto industry, where they cost $28,000–50,000, a fraction of the company's depreciation set-asides. There are 3.5 million professional truck drivers in the U.S., the most common job in 30 states (Santens, 2015). They drive all over the country, stopping regularly to eat, drink, rest and sleep. Entire businesses across the country, including restaurants and motels, serve their wants and needs. Millions of workers depend on the employment of truck drivers. But technology to operate self-driving trucks is now available. These vehicles will be able to drive at night, under any weather conditions and to safely caravan with only inches between them. (Kaplan, 2015: 141). Delivery will be quicker, providing a substantial incentive for their adoption. In May 2015, the first self-driving truck was used on the road in the state of Nevada. Morgan Stanley projects that the pace of current research indicates that complete autonomous capacity for trucks will be a reality by 2022 (Planes, 2014). While this type of projection is an estimate, it is not an ungrounded exaggeration. As of 2017, residents of Tempe, Arizona can hail Uber's self-driving Volvo (Hawkins, 2017).

Once, the warehouses of C&S, the country's largest grocery wholesaler, sprawled across half a million square feet. Shelves were loaded and unloaded by workers wearing headsets and driving forklifts and pallet jacks, directed by a computer speaking to them in four languages. Now the new system occupies only 30,000 square feet and is controlled by a handful of technicians. The work is now done by 168 robots directed by a central computer. A human forklift operator delivers the article to a truck for shipment (Gianchandani, 2012). This is a form of Taylorism, which reduces the number of workers, training time and knowledge that would be otherwise required of warehouse workers.

In 2015 Amazon had become the world's largest retailer. Its warehouses have been major employers, but warehouse work is moving to robotization. Robots have been developed to load and unload boxes from delivery trucks (Rapacki, 2013). Workers wear headsets by which a "synthetic intellect" that keeps track of all warehouse items directs them to ordered items more efficiently than a human could. Amazon has determined that de-skilled workers can be replaced with "forged laborers," i.e. robots. It bought, in 2012, the robotics company Kiva Systems. Amazon's CEO Jeff Bezos indicated he was "intent on displacing as much human labor from his warehouses as possible" (Markoff, 2015: 97, 206).

In mid-2017 Amazon bought the upscale grocery store and supermarket Whole Foods, where it will "utilize technology to minimize labor" (Kosman, 2017). Whole Foods would be run much as Amazon's supermarket-sized planned retail prototype operates, with as few as six workers during a given shift. Checkout workers would disappear, as IT technology would allow customers to pay with smartphones (Tierney, 2014; Soper and Giammona, 2017). Because labor costs are the single largest component of a supermarket's operating costs, Amazon estimates profit margins of 20–40 percent. The industry as a whole employs an average of 89 workers per store and averages a mere 1.7 percent profit margin. Supermarket real-estate costs would also be cut, with a two-storey design that would eliminate at least half of the aisles that account for a supermarket's sprawl.

In Seattle a smaller AmazonGo store is experimenting with these innovations. Customers use an app on their phones to track items they've picked for purchase and to record the items with the help of electronic sensors (Kosman, 2017; see also Kosman, 2016). Amazon also has working plans to employ drones to deliver packages and to provide snacks and sports paraphernalia to fans at event stadiums. Flying warehouses would supply the drones and be refuelled and replenished by blimp-like shuttles. In December 2016 Amazon staged a drone delivery, dropping off a TV and a bag of popcorn to a customer in Cambridge, England. Domino's, the popular American pizza chain, has begun delivering pizzas by drone.

In Flextronics' California solar-panel plant, where the assembly line runs 24/7, there are many more robots than human workers. Agriculture – among the first industries to automate – made comparably impressive advances in recent years. Robots can pick oranges and strawberries, and can tell when the berries are ripe for picking. The "work" can be done day and night. At Earthbound Farms in California, robot arms with suction cups deposit containers of organic lettuce into shipping boxes faster than the workers they replaced. Each robot has replaced two to five workers (Markoff, 2012).

The fast-food industry was once regarded as immune to automation, but Momentum Machines developed automata that shape burgers from freshly ground meat, not the inferior frozen patties customarily used in the industry. These machines make 350–400 burgers per hour, far more than a human worker could. The company's co-founder avers "Our device isn't meant to make employees more efficient. It's meant to completely obviate them" (Ford, 2015: 12-16). The range of automatable tasks is impressive: at the Mayo clinic, robots now deliver drugs from the pharmacy to the bedside (Walsh, 2013).

As for wages, robots easily outcompete humans. The minimum wage in the U.S. is almost everywhere $7.25 an hour; production robots "demand" around $4 an hour (ibid.). A minimum wage increase to $15 an hour, recently legislated in Washington state, may prove to be a Pyrrhic victory for workers. Legislation, in disaccumulationist capitalism, is ineffective for addressing hardship affecting working people due to structural changes inherent in mature capitalism.

Cognitive or White-Collar Job Categories

The professions too have reduced the need for labor in skilled jobs. In law, computers can do much of the discovery processing, and draw up commercial contracts. An estate plan that might otherwise cost $3,500–5,000, for several hours of work, can be completed by a computer in 15–30 minutes for less than $1,000. In medicine, computers are beginning to be used for diagnosis and are used for reading X-rays. In education, online courses are taught by fewer teachers, and student work is evaluated by relatively few instructors with the aid of computers for checking spelling, grammar and for plagiarism. (Kaplan, 2015: 145–51).

Artificial intelligence (AI) has made significant labor-displacing strides in translating from one human language to another. The translation services company Geofluent developed technology capable of translating online chat messages sent by Spanish and Chinese customers to English-speaking employees (Lionbridge, 2015). Insurance companies and Visa have policy payouts and credit-card bills done by IBM's Watson Supercomputer (Sottile, 2017). Coca-Cola will use AI bots to create ads, the same bots already "composing" commercial jingles (Marshall, 2017). *The Washington Post* used a computer to turn out stories on the 2016 Olympics and U.S.

election campaign (Keohane, 2017). Perhaps most remarkably, the Smart Tissue Autonomous Robot outperformed a surgeon in a test of the required skills (Sottile, 2017). Robots are expected to perform and assist in a range of surgical procedures in the near future (Templeton, 2017).

ONGOING JOB LOSS SINCE THE END OF THE WAR AND INTO THE FUTURE

While expert projections of job loss differ in some respects, the overall picture is the same: technological unemployment will increase substantially. Frey and Osborne's 2013 study predicts that among the jobs most likely to suffer loss from computerization are commercial pilots, machinists, typists, real-estate agents, technical writers, retail salespersons, accountants, auditors and telemarketers. An *MIT Technology Review* study indicates that, in addition to the more obviously endangered jobs in manufacturing and truck driving, among the most vulnerable jobs are butchers, secretaries and stenographers, payroll clerks, bank tellers, file clerks, cashiers, typists, pharmacists, bookkeepers and postal clerks (Rotman, 2013). The *Review* notes that *the percentage change in nonfarm employment has been in decline through the entire postwar period*. For the last seven decades, job growth per decade averaged 37.7 percent, 24.5 percent, 31.3 percent, 27.4 percent, 20.2 percent, 19.8 percent and finally -1 percent. Gartner, Inc., a leading technology research and advisory company, warned in 2015 that within ten years about one-third of existing jobs will replaced by software and robots (Gartner, Inc., 2015). McKinsey & Company's research suggests that about "45 percent of the activities individuals are paid to perform can be automated by adapting currently demonstrated technologies" (Chui et al., 2015; see also Arthur, 2017). Most recently, in a study of 15 economies accounting for approximately 65 percent of the world's total workforce, the World Economic Forum (WEF), in a report "The Future of Work," projects that job losses from the development of robotics, 3D printing, nanotechnology and biotechnology are expected in every industry (World Economic Forum, 2016). WEF concludes that two-thirds of the job losses will be due to "smart machines" taking over routine tasks. The study suggests that women will be the biggest losers, since they make up the majority of the workforce in the job categories most likely to be affected by technological displacement.

The Pew Research Center surveyed two thousand experts about the impact of the new technologies on employment and the direction in which these technologies are moving society as a whole. Pew reports that "Half of these experts (48 percent) envision a future in which robots and digital agents have displaced significant numbers of both blue- and white-collar workers – with many expressing concern that this will lead to vast increases in income inequality, masses of people who are effectively unemployable, and breakdowns in the social order" (Pew Research Center, 2014). The petering out of the dominant framework stimulants since the mid-1960s and the advance of IT and automation have been major factors in the slowdown of both the growth of GDP and creeping disaccumulationist unemployment.

Digitally driven unemployment imparts a distinct shape to the working population: it polarizes the labor force. There becomes a fast-growing increase in demand for highly paid skilled IT labor, a largest-growing (greater) increase in demand for unskilled low-paid labor, and a dramatic decline in demand for mid-skilled, mid-wage labor. (See below for the meaning of the crucial distinction between the categories of fastest-growing jobs and jobs with the largest growth.) While this tendency began well before the 2008 Great Downturn, it was conspicuous during the downturn. As *The Washington Post* put it, "The vast majority of job losses during the recession were in middle-income occupations, and they've largely been replaced by low-wage jobs since 2010: Mid-wage occupations ... made up about 60 percent of the job losses during the recession. But those mid-wage jobs have made up just 27 percent of the jobs gained during the recovery" (Plumer, 2013). This is the "hollowing out" or "polarization" of the labor force, the much-lamented "decline of the middle class" (Casselman, 2015). Here is a key element in the dynamics generating the current gradual but inexorable decline in working-class living standards implicit in secular stagnation, technological progress and burgeoning inequality.

The Decline of the Middle Class and the Growing Degradation of Work

The disappearance of median-skill-and-wage (MSW) jobs and the rapid growth of low-skill-and-wage (LSW) jobs has been conspicuous for more than 30 years. From 1985 to 1995 most new jobs were part-time, temporary and low wage, with fewer benefits, fewer hours and no security. By 1993, 46 million American workers were in what *The New York Times* called "jobs without hope" (cited in Sale, 1995: 227). The U.S. Bureau of Labor Statistics (BLS) projected in 1994 that the greatest job growth from 1994 to 2005 would be in four low-paying and frequently precarious occupations: cashiers, janitors and cleaners, retail sales clerks and waiters and waitresses

(*Wall Street Journal Almanac 1998*, 1997: 302). In 2010 the BLS confirmed these projections in its reports on the "Fastest Growing Occupations" and the "Occupations With the Largest Job Growth" (Lockard and Wolf, 2012a, b). Subsequent projections, issued every two years, exhibited the same patterns. In its press releases BLS tends to focus on the former category, the jobs projected to grow fastest. The two fastest-growing occupations, biomedical engineers and network systems and data communications analysts, require a college degree and offer better-paying jobs. The implication is that job prospects for current students are promising. But to gauge job prospects for working-class students accurately we must know the degree requirements of the total number of types of job listed in both categories, and most importantly the number of new jobs expected to materialize in each projection.

Of the total jobs listed in both the fastest-growing and largest-growth categories, only one in five requires a post-high-school degree. The fastest-growing occupation is biomedical engineers, projected to grow 72.02 percent, from 16,000 in 2008 to 27,600 in 2018. That's 11,600 new jobs. This percentage figure is high, but the actual number of new jobs is unimpressive. Compare that fastest-growing occupation with retail sales-persons, the fifth occupation on both the 2010 and 2014 Largest Growth lists. Retail sales workers will grow by a mere 8.35 percent. But that amounts to an increase from 4,489,000 jobs in 2008 to 4,863,000 jobs in 2018: a total of almost 375,000 new jobs. As is suggested by this comparison, the majority of new jobs are projected to be low-paying. The figures for 2017 are no less dire. Of the ten fastest-growing occupations, only one, nursing, pays more than $33,000 a year, well below the median income, and none of the other nine requires a college degree (Karlin, 2017; Buchheit, 2017: 46).

Similar research shows that these tendencies are in operation in Europe (Bowles, 2014; Pisani-Ferry, 2015). The effects of the new automation on the character of society include widespread and sustained austerity for a large segment of the working class. Each study cited above sees these developments as increasing inequality and tending to foment social disorder. As a leading businessman remarked, "[W]hen a large percentage of unemployed youths think they don't have a future, that usually leads to some form of civil instability" (McKinsey & Company, 2014). I return to this theme later on.

MANUFACTURING AND THE SOCIETY OF "ABUNDANCE"

The "decline of manufacturing" is a development intended to mark the decline of both the middle class and the U.S. economy as a whole. It is supposed to follow that "making our country great again" requires an increase in manufacturing output and a restoration of employment in America's factories. But there is no truth in these claims (Walsh, 2012).

In fact, domestic manufacturing output has continuously *increased* since 1947, and has further increased since the 1990s (Walsh, 2012; Federal Reserve Bank of St. Louis, 2012, 2016). The jobs picture is, however, very different. In domestic manufacturing, jobs increased in the 1960s, and, as productivity in the industry also increased, the number of jobs remained about the same while manufacturing output grew further. But in 2000, as output continued to increase right up to the September 2008 crisis, employment fell dramatically. These data cannot be explained by offshoring. The increase in automation and robotization since 2000 is the most plausible explanation. And this kind of development cannot be reformed or legislated away, as Obama himself averred: "government cannot prevent all the downsides of the technological change" (Obama, 2013). It is not government's business to determine companies' fixed investments. This lesson applies globally, because manufacturing's share of worldwide economic activity is declining, "even as manufacturing output continues to grow exponentially. Ever more is being done with ever less human labor ... the *industrial* proletariat is rapidly disappearing" (Walsh, 2013; emphasis added).

The decline in manufacturing jobs has been accompanied by a decline in the wages of the remaining workers. As part of the post-Golden-Age drive to increase earnings in the face of depressed revenues by driving labor costs down, more manufacturing workers have been hired through temporary staffing agencies (Jacobs et al., 2016). Since as early as 1989 there has been a steady increase, from 1 percent of all production workers to 9 percent in 2015, in the number of frontline production workers hired through these agencies (Ausick, 2016). "Temp" wages can be 33 percent lower than direct-employment wages, and half of all "temp" production workers receive government aid. In fact, most government aid goes to *working* households (ibid.).

When advanced technologies eliminate jobs, they displace workers from one sector to another. Historically, workers have migrated from agriculture to manufacturing and finally to services. Some commentators assume that current technological job reduction will exhibit the same pattern. But when technology displaced manufacturing workers in the past, many of those workers gained white-collar, higher-paying jobs. Now, the largest-growth occupations are low-paying, e.g. in retail, food service and personal care. And we shall see that the longstanding rise in long-term unemployment *after* recessions and the high unemployment rates since 2000 suggest chronic, structural problems. The course of job creation and the rapid growth of relatively new and unsavory job categories suggest a new employment pattern peculiar to the Age of Austerity.

No one urges job restoration in agriculture. The discussion of techno-logical unemployment in Chapters 3 and 7 and in Appendix B, together with what we saw above and will see in following sections, imply that job restoration in manufacturing is as undesirable as bringing workers back to the land. Obama's "number one priority" to "replace the [jobs] that we've lost in recent decades – jobs in manufacturing" (Obama, 2013) misses the *historic function* of productivity-increases-cum-automation. It is the ultimate historic task of capitalism to reduce necessary labor time and to increase leisure time and with it to realize latent possibilities for human flourishing. The false investment-driven conception of the accumulation process includes the notion that investment is job-creating. But investment does not necessarily create employment and in fact tends to reduce it under mature disaccumulationist capitalism. Retaining the investment thesis per-petuates slow growth in the real economy and generates growth through bubbles. *The only alternative to the secular-stagnation scenario of perpetual bubbles and their subsequent real-economic devastation is the allocation of the surplus to public, democratically determined investment and to higher wages. Private profit has no place in this picture.*

THE HOLLOWING OUT OF THE MIDDLE CLASS
AND JOB POLARIZATION

Since the early 1970s each successive decade has ended with a smaller share of adults in middle-income households than at the beginning of the decade (Pew Research Center, 2015a). Both extreme ends of the income spectrum have grown; the very lowest and the very highest income tiers have grown the fastest. The tendency of neoliberal financialized disaccumulation-ist capitalism has been to "hollow out" the middle class and to radically polarize the U.S. class structure and jobs market (Pew Research Center, 2015b). As a result, the middle class is no longer America's economic majority (O'Connor, 2015; Pew Research Center, 2015). These tendencies have been the subject of many empirical studies (Acemoglu, 1999; Autor et al., 2006; Autor, 2010; Goos and Manning, 2007; Goos et al., 2009). Jobless recoveries too have been acutely researched (Bernanke, 2003, 2009; Gordon and Baily, 1993; Groshen and Potter, 2003; Jaimovich and

Siu, 2012). The evidence is compelling: *job polarization accounts for jobless recoveries* (Jaimovich and Siu, 2012). The Associated Press (AP), in three extensive studies, analyzed employment data from 20 countries; followed hiring practices by industries, pay and task; tracked job losses and gains during business cycles and interviewed an impressive range of people, from CEOs to the unemployed, including robot manufacturers, software developers and other technology experts as well as economists (Condon and Wiseman, 2013; Wiseman et al., 2013; Wiseman and Condon, 2013). AP's conclusions dovetail with the work of the aforementioned authors.

Autor's 2010 study of job polarization identifies a 30-year trend of changes in the demand for worker of different skill and wage levels. The occupational categories studied were in the median-skill-and-wage (MSW) group; in the submedian, low-skill-and-wage (LSW) group and in the high-skill-and-wage (HSW) group. Comparing the 1980s, the 1990s and 1999–2007, polarization and the inequality it generates began in the 1990s and accelerated during 1999–2007. In the 1980s the LSW group declined as a share of total employment and the HSW group increased. Unmistakable evidence of continued polarization appeared in the 1990s, when LSW increased its share, HSW increased its share substantially and all MSW job categories exhibited a reduced share. From 1999 to 2007, LSW's share increased, HSW remained unchanged and MSW's share loss continued. In the bubble period of U.S. economic growth, beginning with the dot.com bubble and the increased use of AI-informed automation in both industrial and service workplaces, jobs at the extremes of the occupational-wage-and-skill spectrum increased their shares of total employment while mid-skill and mid-wage jobs suffered consistent losses (Canon and Marifian, 2013).

The fact of polarization does not tell us whether this is an empirical *trend*, possibly due to contingent features of a passing stage of capitalist development, or a *tendency* rooted in essential features of capitalism's developmental dynamic. Autor's analysis of job polarization supports the analysis of this book, that it is a tendency. He accounts for the declining demand for mid-skilled labor, the rising demand for high-skilled labor and the striking increase in demand for unskilled labor. The type of mid-skill labor in most rapid decline performs *routine tasks*, "procedural, rule-based activities" typical of a great portion of mid-skill occupations. Routine procedures characterize both productive and service occupations and are increasingly performed by computers, robots and other machines (Autor, 2010; Osborne, 2015; Brynjolfsson and McAfee, 2011b; Arthur, 2011; Wiseman et al., 2013; Wiseman and Condon, 2013; Canon and Marifian,

2013). Thus, *the automation process has increased the demand for unskilled labor, decreased the demand for routine labor and increased the demand for non-routine, higher-skilled, better-paid labor, increasingly complemented by "smart machines."* As extensive automation does away with mid-skilled and mid-wage work, it raises the demand for (fewer) high-skilled workers, many of whom tend, oversee and repair the automata.

Increasing mechanization of work under capitalism is necessary to sustain the requirement of ever-increasing productivity. Thus, computerized automation is the latest form of a general tendency of capitalist development. A structurally induced pressure to lower both capital and labor *costs* is part-and-parcel of this tendency. Automated capital goods must become cheaper. The widespread acknowledgement that capital goods both displace labor and have become cheaper over time is discussed in Appendix A. The largest-growth jobs as a share of total employment have been LSW jobs (*The Economist*, 2014). "Workers in many types of middle-rank positions – such as skilled production-line workers and people in clerical or adminis-trative jobs – have had to migrate into jobs as food-service workers, home health-care aides, child-care employees and security guards" (Autor, 2010). These are jobs that are among those least susceptible to automation.

The cheapening of capital goods in the digital age, the tendency for advances in productive capacity to incorporate digital technologies, and the fact that these advances displace labor point to three central conten-tions: that private net investment is both decreasingly relevant and inimical to the growth of wages and employment in contemporary capitalism, that wages and employment can be sustained only by public investment, and that both high wages and shorter work hours are essential to avert stagnation and to provide workers with a quality of life within post-mature capitalism's grasp.

JOBLESS RECOVERIES AND WAGE AND
EMPLOYMENT PATTERNS IN THE DIGITALIZED ECONOMY

Labor-market polarization manifests itself revealingly in the business cycle. The overall health of the economy is manifest in its ability to regain its strength after periods of weakness. That is, the economy's remaining strength as evidenced in the succession of recoveries after recessions is perhaps the most reliable indicator of its remaining productive power. Let us review the income and employment record of the six complete recoveries and recessions, and the seventh and current anemic expansion, beginning in 2009, which we are still in, and for which data are therefore incomplete. These six cycles and the current weak recovery are characteristic of the end of the Golden Age and the entrenchment of the austerity period. We examine first the behavior of income in these periods, and second the employment picture for the three occupational groups discussed above, i.e. LSW, MSW and HSW. These six cycles take place over the years of the long decline of the profit rate in the U.S., the withering of the framework stimulants fuelling the Great Boom, the beginning of the Age of Austerity and long-term stagnation, and the intensification of the economy's financialization. The income and employment pictures for this period reveal much about that stage of capitalist development displaying what Robert J. Gordon has argued is the exhaustion of capitalism's prosperity-generating productive potential (Gordon, 2012, 2014, 2016). It reveals that severe constraints on Americans' ability to make a living are an increasingly dismal feature of post-democratic capitalism. The first three of the six recessions are 1969–70, 1973–75 and 1981–82, and the most recent three are 1990–91, 2001 and 2007–09 (Jaimovich and Siu, 2012).

Austerity-Generating Income Behavior
in Post-Golden-Age Business Cycles

Most recessions after the Second World War exhibited a troubling pattern. With respect to income, in every expansion since the end of the war, the bottom 90 percent of households received a smaller and smaller share, and the top 10 percent a rising share, of increased economic growth (Tcherneva, 2015). Even as their share shrank, the majority of these households still captured the majority of economic growth until the 1970s, the end of the Golden Age and the beginning of the Age of Austerity. By the early 1980s, a growing majority of income growth was captured by the wealthiest 10 percent of families. This distribution has continued up to the present.

During the 2001–07 recovery, the bottom 90 percent of households experienced almost no income growth, and in the first five years of the latest expansion, 2009–13, all of the income gains have gone to the top 10 percent of families, while the income of the bottom 90 percent actually fell (Tcherneva, 2017). Comparing gains of the top 10 percent, the wealthiest 1 percent and the richest 0.01 percent in the 2001–07 and the incomplete 2009–13 expansions, the top 10 percent received 98 percent and 118 percent of the gains from growth in the two expansions. The top 1 percent appropriated 76 percent of growth in each expansion, while the wealthiest 0.01 percent captured 30 percent and 21 percent.

Thus, one-fifth to one-third of total income growth was garnered by a minute sliver of the best off (Tcherneva, 2015). This degree of inequality is unprecedented in U.S. history.

Austerity-Generating Employment Behavior in Post-Golden-Age Business Cycles: The Jobless Recovery

Downturns used to be followed quickly by an increase in new jobs, as companies hired to meet the new demand created by the resumption of consumer spending. But this changed during the last six recessions, where we find the historical novelty of the *jobless and wageless recovery* (Sum et al., 2011). Aggregate employment behavior changed markedly in the last three recessions. After the first three, total employment evidenced recovery within six months of the trough in production. This is considerably longer than the time it took for employment to recover in all the previous postwar cycles. The last three downturns exhibited an even darker picture. It was not until 18 months after the trough of the recession beginning in March 1991 that the employment upturn began. After the trough of the recession that began in March 2001, unemployment continued its fall for 23 months into the recovery, which began in November of that year and didn't return to pre-recession level before the Great Recession began in December 2007. That downturn ended in June 2009, but again it was 23 months before employment began its uptick.

The AP study referred to at the start of this chapter reported that 42 months after the Great Recession ended the U.S. had gained only 3.5 million jobs, only 47 percent of the 7.5 million jobs lost (Condon and Wiseman, 2013). The official unemployment rate did not fall to where it was at the start of the recession until the fourth quarter of 2015 and had not improved as of April 2016 (Center on Budget and Policy Priorities, 2016). The uniqueness of the most recent recovery is reflected in data closely related to what we have seen regarding job polarization and inequality. The growth in total wages and salaries compared with the growth in corporate profits for the first year of the eleven recoveries since the Second World War correlates to the data discussed. For the ten recoveries prior to the current one, the average ratio of profit to wage and salary growth was 3:1. In the current downturn, as of 2010, the ratio was 50:1 (Henwood, 2010). *A new phenomenon in American capitalism, the jobless recovery accompanied by unprecedented inequality, marks the emergence of a new epoch in the history of mature capitalism, persistent secular stagnation, increasingly insecure employment prospects and declining living standards as the system's "new normal."* This is evidenced most starkly in the employment record of the Obama presidency: of all the new jobs created during those eight years, 94 percent were part-time, low-paid jobs (Katz and Krueger, 2016). The share of the U.S. workforce engaged in "alternative work arrangements" (see below) grew from 10 percent in 2005 to 16 percent in 2015. During the same period the number of workers in traditional full-time jobs dropped by 400,000. James Galbraith saw the handwriting on the wall in 2009: "We are not in a temporary economic lull, an ordinary recession, from which we will emerge to return to business as usual. We are at the beginning of a long, profound, painful, and irreversible process of change. We need to start thinking and acting accordingly" (Galbraith, 2009).

The above employment data are essential for a full grasp of the declining job prospects for the labor force as a whole, the post-Golden-Age economy of austerity and the jobless recovery. But these data leave open the kinds of jobs the digitalized economy is generating, the skills likely to be required of workers, income distribution across the working population and the degree of security that existing jobs provide. Jaimovich and Siu illuminate these factors by sharpening the focus: they examine cyclical recoveries according to changes in employment recovery of LSW, MSW and HSW occupational groups.

What Work Will Look Like

Routine occupations, mid-skill-and-wage, account for most of the job loss in all six downturns. The hollowing out of these jobs has been going on since the 1990–91 recession (Jaimovich and Siu, 2012). After the first three recessions, employment recovery in routine occupations paralleled the recovery of non-routine jobs. In the last three downturns there was no recovery in routine occupations. During that period, after a temporary cessation of growth in LWS and HWS occupations, these eventually resumed their upward trend. MSW jobs in 1982–2012 made up more than half of all U.S. employment; their disappearance is the major cause of the uncommon weakness of recoveries during this time.

That disappearing routine occupations and their counterpart, job-market polarization, account for jobless recoveries was hinted at in the earlier, 1982 recession. While routine occupations accounted for the bulk of the job loss in each of the six recessions, the loss of mid-skill, mid-wage occupations was greater than the total employment loss in the 1982 recession, because employment in non-routine job categories was growing. The tendency for LSW and HSW jobs to grow over time is the correlative of the permanent disappearance of MSW routine work (Siu and Jaimovich, 2012). The most recent Pew Research Center study of job and wage polarization finds that mid-income households' income and share of total income continued to decline, as LSW and HSW households' shares have correspondingly grown (Pew Research Center, 2016).

Much of the decline in MSW employment and wages has been in manufacturing, and has turned formerly MSW production workers into LSW workers. Manufacturing wages are stabilizing at the level of fast-food chains and big-box retailers (Jacobs et al., 2016). A rising percentage of these workers have to depend on government aid – food stamps and Medicaid – to make ends meet. Here is a classic example of neoliberalism's heightened exploitation of workers even as their contribution to production increased: from 1997 to 2012, as manufacturing wages have declined, manufacturing labor productivity has grown at an average annual rate of 3.3 percent, one-third more than in the non-farm economy (Scott, 2015; Bivens and Mishel, 2015; see also Baker, 2007).

That *the impact of computerized technologies is likely to bring about the secular immiseration of the rapidly growing stratum of unskilled workers* has been argued by economists Jeffrey Sachs and Laurence Kotlikoff (Sachs and Kotlikoff, 2012). They show that machines complement a substantial percentage of HSW workers, whose skills must change in order to work with the machines. Thus, the hopes of potential LSW workers to join the HSW group requires them to invest in education and training furthering "their own skill acquisition and physical capital." But declining wages of young LSW workers are a formidable obstacle to their acquiring the training and education needed.

The declining percentage of the highly skilled in the total labor force will tend to drive down the wages of LSW aspirants. The outcome is clear: each generation is less likely to achieve HSW status than its predecessor. That each successive generation of LSW workers is more numerous and worse off than the previous generation is what growing inequality looks like. As Thomas Piketty points out, it tends to turn the most affluent into a stratum that is more affluent over time and functionally *dynastic* (Piketty, 2014). An increasing percentage of the most wealthy will have inherited their booty from their ruling-class parents. A small core group of families will rule America. The correlative of burgeoning economic inequality is declining political democracy.

All of the developments discussed above have brought about a permanent employment crisis. Traditional lifetime full-time jobs with benefits belong to a lost era. Let us look at the kind of work arrangement that will characterize the new normal.

BURGEONING UNSTABLE WORK AND THE EMERGING PRECARIAT

A 2016 study by Lawrence Katz and Alan Krueger demonstrated that 94 percent of U.S. net job growth from 2005 to 2015 came in "alternative work arrangements," defined as "temporary help agency workers, on-call workers, contract company workers, independent contractors or freelancers": jobs without a fixed paycheck and virtually no benefits (Katz and Krueger, 2016). No permanent full-time jobs with adequate benefits were offered. Such full-time jobs as were available were for temporary workers and independent contractors, through agencies or on call. Permanent full-time jobs belong to a past era and low-pay insecure work is "the new normal." This is an example of the "risk shift" entailed by the decline of the ND/GS settlement. The social and political individualism of the 1920s, when all workers were forced to bear the cost of social insurance themselves, is reinstated. This is the position of today's contingent workforce. Never provided with the government social insurance enjoyed in other advanced countries, American workers are in store for a severe regime under which they will have as little social support as elites can get away with providing (Johnson, 2014; Standing, 2014).

The workers described by Katz and Krueger do "contingent" work, and as of 2015 constitute 15.8 percent of the total workforce, 23.6 million workers, up from 10.7 percent (14.2 million) in 2005. Thus, almost one in six "full-time" workers were almost always without the job security, vacations, health benefits and paid time off typically available to workers during the Great Boom (Martin, 2016). Press reports mask underlying realities. The media reported that total employment rose by 9.1 million during this same period. Unmentioned is the decline between 2005 and 2015 by almost 400,00 in the number of conventional full-time positions.

Two closely related types of work are coming to define the employment prospects of the typical worker under austerity capitalism. *A drastic and growing change in the nature of employment is under way, with two major transformations in the labor market.* One is the refashioning of a growing number of workers into independent contractors. The other is the replacement of permanent, full-time work by what is misleadingly termed "steady jobs."

The Worker as Independent Contractor

For most of the nation's history the employer of record has been the corporation. This arrangement is undergoing radical transformation. In a feature article entitled "The End of Employees," *The Wall Street Journal* points out that "Never before have big employers tried so hard to hand over chunks of their business to contractors. From Google to Wal-Mart, the strategy prunes costs for firms and job security for millions of workers" (Weber, 2017). Now the employer is becoming the intermediary connecting the independent or contract worker, provided and allegedly employed by a contracting agency, with a job task at a hotel, retailer or hair salon (Weil, 2014). Our everyday perception of FedEx workers does not reveal that the company calls its drivers "independent contractors." FedEx requires FedEx Ground workers to pay for the trucks they drive, their uniforms, their scanners, fuel, general maintenance, insurance they are required to purchase, tires, oil changes, meals during work time, and workers' compensation insurance. When they are not working, either because of illness or vacation, they must hire their own replacements (Reich, 2015b). In a nod to "flexibility," the company does not specify the hours of work. Instead, it determines how many packages must be delivered on a given work day, and organizes the workload so that drivers end up working between 9.5 and 11 hours a day. In 2005 California FedEx workers resisted, successfully suing the company on the grounds that they are employees. In 2014, a federal appeals court agreed, awarding the workers overtime pay they had been denied and reimbursement for their expenditures a conventional employer would have covered.

Uber drivers are perhaps the paradigm case of this type of contract, part-time, on-demand work. Uber produces nothing, owns no cars and claims to have no employees, since its drivers are independent contractors. The company hires and fires its drivers, determines fares and appropriates 20 percent of their income. As with FedEx, Uber's drivers must pay for their cars, insurance, gas and repairs. Uber's contracts are non-negotiable, and the company abjures liability in case of driver, passenger or pedestrian injury. The company claims that a driver can make as much as $350–400 a day. But *Business Insider*'s study of the typical Uber driver's pay determined that most drivers have nothing resembling a living wage (Kosoff, 2014; Hill 2015). The company's wage claims take no account of daily fuel and maintenance costs, car payments, commercial insurance and registration. Price competition from newcomers Lyft, Curb and Sidecar forced Uber to cut its rates. Cutting its labor costs by turning its workers into independent contractors forced other companies entering the industry to do the same, and a race to the bottom set in. The resulting fall in drivers' income put more than a few on food stamps (ibid.). Uber drivers, like FedEx drivers, are challenging the company in California courts.

Computerized technology aids just-in-time employment. Software can identify last-minute staffing needs. This type of work arrangement – unregulated industry, and companies divesting, via subcontracting, from responsibility for "their" workers – makes it a paradigm case of post-ND/GS austerity capitalism. The following example of subcontracting shows how the new organization of work renders ineffective any constraints on companies' treatment of workers. A major hotel chain subcontracted to a general contractor to renovate guest rooms at some hotels. That contractor subcontracted to several other contractors, some of whom further subcontracted. More than a dozen subcontractors worked on the same project. A State-led investigation found that the subcontractors committed countless labor-law violations. With so many layers of contractors involved, it was impossible legally to determine responsibility for the violations. Three contractors were mildly sanctioned. The original general subcontractor denied wrongdoing and incurred no penalties (Lombos et al., 2014). That companies cannot be held accountable for these violations was averred by the regulators: "The issue of which entity was legally the employer and responsible ... was never resolved" (Massachusetts Employee Task Force on the Underground Economy and Employee Misclassification, 2013: 6).

"Steady Work" With Unsteady Income

The mainstream media and government agencies have adopted the misleadingly optimistic term "steady jobs" to describe what is claimed to be today's most desirable job category. The term does not connote work that pays a predictable, living wage with benefits. Since the 1970s, that kind of work has become increasingly difficult to find. In fact "steady jobs" refers to the part-time, low-paid work with no benefits and unpredictable, ever-changing schedules that has replaced it (Morduch and Schneider, 2017a,b). When both the number and scheduling of work hours are unpredictable, instability and insecurity become an abiding feature of life. Tentative shifts make it not unusual for training and work times to be changed on a few hours' notice. Just-in-time scheduling means that workers must carry cell phones at all times and be "on call." It is not uncommon for someone on the way to work to receive a text message cancelling the job. She won't be paid for the promised work, but she must pay the person who picks up her child from school and provides childcare.

Not only is the household's income unstable, but so are its expenses. At the core of precarity is the disconnect between a household's expenses and income, because each of these is subject to month-to-month change. A study of 250,000 households by the JPMorgan Chase Institute found that 80 percent of households lacked the cash buffer to manage the mismatch between income and expenses in a given month. And pervasive material insecurity is not confined to the poor. Only households that earn at least $105,000 a year, twice the median wage, are secure against this kind of volatility. A not-uncommon scenario might have a family covering the expense of replacing a terminally broken water heater by using funds earmarked for the utility bill. Next month, late fees and interest has the family paying the missed utility bill by letting the phone bill go unpaid. Anything from medical emergencies and auto repairs to bridal showers and Christmas gifts are among the many factors that can, when both income level and expenses are unpredictable, upset a household's balance sheet for a year or more (Cohen, 2017). This comes as no surprise when half of American jobs pay less than $18 an hour, about $37,000 a year – well below the median wage of $55,000 a year – *if* one works full time. Forty percent of jobs pay less than $15.50 an hour (Long, 2017).

The Extent and Fatal Toll of Precarity

The outcome of the austerity policies and changes in the labor market and wage levels described in this book is uncomfortably close to Marx's forecast that capitalist development results in the (slow-motion) immiseration of the working class. In fact, as of 2013, 76 percent of Americans are one or two paychecks away from the streets (Johnson, 2013). A 2016 Bankrate study found that 63 percent of Americans had no savings for contingencies such as a $1,000 emergency-room visit or a $500 car repair (Steiner, 2016). That same year the Federal Reserve found that 47 percent of respondents could not come up with $400 to cover an emergency (Gabler, 2016). A GoBankingRates study revealed that 34 percent of American adults have no savings at all (Huddleston, 2016). And The National Bureau of Economic Research disclosed that almost half of Americans die nearly broke (Williams, 2016). Nothing resembling these statistics characterized the period 1949–73. *The New York Times* alludes to the "weak growth in wages [as] an indicator of a new economic order in which working people are at the mercy of their employers. Unions have lost clout. Companies are relying on temporary and part-time workers while deploying robots and other forms of automation in ways that allow them to produce more without paying extra to human beings" (Goodman and Soble, 2017).

The young, who have experienced the most severe later stage of post-1975 capitalism, have experienced a dramatic deterioration of their life circumstances. The Pew Research Center reports that "It's becoming more common for young adults to live at home – and for longer stretches" (Fry, 2017). 19 percent of millennials aged 25 to 34 are still living with their parents, the highest proportion on record. The U.S. Census Bureau determined four longstanding criteria of American adulthood: moving out of the parents' house, getting married, getting a job and having a child. In 1975, 45 percent of Americans satisfied these criteria by the age of 34; that number fell to 24 percent by 2016. Increasingly, young Americans cannot afford to get married, have children or buy a house. In 1975, eight in ten Americans were married by age 30; today, eight in ten are married by age 45. And as the wage–productivity gap grew steadily since 1974, more women have taken to the labor force to shore up declining household income (Baker, 2007; Reich, 2010: 61–2). The percentage of women aged 25–34 who were out of the labor force to take care of their home and family declined from 43 percent in 1975 to 14 percent in 2016 (Vespa, 2017). While some of this is likely the result of progressive social trends, the evidence is nevertheless strong that more and more are delaying marriage, family and home ownership for financial reasons.

That the victims of austerity policies are trapped in their subordinate position is evidenced by their lack of socioeconomic mobility. A Pew Charitable Trust study compared social mobility among the OECD countries in the years 1984–2004 and found that the United States had the lowest share of low-income workers whose status improves from year to year (Acs and Zimmerman, 2008; see also Carr and Wiemers, 2016). The best predictor of an individual's socioeconomic status, in the U.S. and the UK, is the status of his or her parents (Irvin, 2008: 28). If you are born poor or lower-middle class you are most likely to die in the same status. If you are born rich, you will almost certainly die rich.

There is decisive evidence that contemporary precarity and its correlative, widening inequality, tend to generate uncommon rates of physical and mental health disorders (Wilkinson and Pickett, 2010; Ehrenreich, 2016: 40, 44–5, 47–8, 50, 155–62; Brenner, 1973, 1976, 1984; Galea, 2011). A Princeton study found that middle-aged non-Hispanic white Americans suffered a great increase in mortality between 1998 and 2013 (Case and Deaton, 2015). *This was the first such trend in American history*. The increase is *entirely* concentrated among persons with only a high-school degree or less, a reliable criterion of poverty. Among whites with any college experience, mortality rates have declined during this period. Disease is not the issue. The predominant causes of death are suicide, chronic alcohol abuse and drug overdoses. Paul Krugman has noted that these statistics mirror "the collapse in Russian life expectancy after the fall of communism" (Krugman, 2015). Case and Deaton label these mortalities "deaths of despair." It is noteworthy that among the population in question, wages have fallen by over 30 percent since 1969 (Cooper, 2015). In a detailed study of the health effects of austerity, based on data from the Great Depression, Asian countries during the 1990s Asian Financial Crisis and European countries suffering austerity policies after the 2008 crisis, the researchers found that the more austerity was practiced in a country, the more people became ill and the more people died (Stuckler and Basu, 2013). Most recently, David Ansell, a physician and social epidemiologist, has demonstrated in an exhaustive study that the acceleration of the growing inequality between high and low socioeconomic groups over the past three decades has resulted in higher mortality rates for the poorest strata of the working class. He concludes that "[I]nequality triggers so many causes of premature death that we need to treat inequality as a disease and eradicate it, just as we seek to halt any epidemic" (Ansell, 2017: vii). Capitalism, in its post-welfare-state form, kills.

THE AMERICAN WORKER BECOMES MARGINAL
TO THE U.S. ECONOMY

Consumption demand, the bulk of which consists in working-class household spending, has, since the 1920s, generated 66–72 percent of total demand, or GDP. One of the key criteria of the decline of the productive economy in overripe capitalism may be the increasing irrelevance of the American worker to the integrity of the economy. The latter term is far too general to function as an index of anyone's well-being, capitalist or worker. The very wealthy can do quite well, indeed superbly, even as "the (productive) economy" languishes and workers are immiserated.

We have seen one of the bases of this unsettling conclusion: when the opportunities for adequately remunerative investment in production evaporate, profits need not dwindle, since the surplus can be invested in financial instruments which bring greater returns than are possible from production. A second development, more directly related to the fate of the American worker/consumer, is the conviction among elites that while U.S. workers are becoming too penurious to sustain consumption demand at a level supportive of generous profits, overseas consumers are not.

Key elite figures have expressed this conviction. Two years before he was appointed head of The President's Council on Jobs and Competitiveness, Jeffrey Immelt, then CEO of General Electric, reminded the Detroit Economic Club that "We all know that the American consumer cannot lead our recovery. This economy must be driven by business investment and exports" (Immelt, 2009). We have seen why framework investment in the real economy is not a promising option. And America's becoming a leading exporter on the magnitude required would require price competition that would put further downward pressure on U.S. wages. Barack Obama's Secretary of Defense Ashton Carter described the outsourcing of consumption demand in a major 2015 speech on the economic dimension of the U.S. "rebalance to the Asia-Pacific":

> [The] Asia-Pacific is the defining region for our nation's future ... half of humanity will live there by 2050 ... more than half of the global middle class and its accompanying consumption will come from that region ... President Obama and I want to ensure that ... businesses can successfully compete for all of these customers ... over the next century, *no region will matter more for American prosperity*. (Carter, 2015a; emphasis added)

The U.S. working class has been written off as a source of economic vitality. Its dwindling middle class is to be replaced by the "global middle class." Its principal function, as the single largest component of the costs of production, will be to provide cheap and therefore debt-addicted labor.

THE DEVELOPMENT OF INEQUALITY

Like employment, in the figures shown above, inequality too has been building since shortly after the Second World War. It accelerated first during the first stage of the Age of Austerity and again after the crisis of 2008. During the upswing of 1949–53, most income growth went to the majority, the bottom 90 percent of the income distribution. After that, the 90 percent's share of income gains (not to be confused with the working majority's share of total income, which, as we have seen, grew for 40 years after the peak of the New Deal), shrank from one decade to the next, and the share of the top 10 percent rose (Tcherneva, 2014). By the 1980s, when the business counteroffensive was in full swing and finance capital began its ascendancy relative to industrial capital, the trend accelerated and, for the first time since the end of the war, the bottom 90 percent's share dropped dramatically, from 57 percent in 1970–73 to 20 percent in 1982–90.

During this same period, the 10 percent's share climbed from 42 percent to 80 percent. With each upturn after 1982, an ever-larger share of income growth went to the top. So predominant was the political-economic power of elites that during the first three years of Obama's economic "recovery," 2009–12, a whopping 116 percent of income growth was taken by the top 10 percent. This means that the real incomes of the 90 percent dropped by 16 percent. That the incomes of the bottom 90 percent actually fell during this "recovery" period was a historic first. *Median household income had never before fallen during an economic recovery.* By 2012, the elites' share of total national income had set records, with the top 10 percent of income recipients copping more than half the country's total income, while the top 1 percent took more than 20.1 percent of the income earned by Americans (Saez, 2015a; Gould, 2013). That record was beaten by the top 1 percent again in 2014, who increased their share of total income from 20.1 percent in 2013 to 21.2 percent in 2014 (Saez, 2015b). The epoch of neoliberal financialized capitalism featured the *redistribution* of income inherent in rising inequality, and the *extraction* of income from both industry and labor characteristic of the dominance of the rentier class.

According to the Economic Policy Institute (EPI), between 1979 and 2006, the year preceding the deflation of the housing bubble, the top 1 percent of earners in the U.S. more than doubled their share of national income, from 10 percent to 22.9 percent. The top 0.1 percent did even better, increasing their share by more than three times from 3.5 percent in 1979 to 11.6 percent in 2006. The wealthiest's record share of national output had no discernible impact on the growth rate (EPI study cited in Chang, 2011).

This was one of the highest levels of inequality on record since 1913, the year the government instituted an income tax. Since the "recovery" began in June 2009, the rich have become richer than ever, and inequality has broken records (Federal Reserve System, 2017; Saez, 2015b; Lowry, 2013; Greenhouse, 2011; Yadoo, 2017). Moreover, during the recession job losses at every wage level occurred throughout the economy, but during the recovery employment gains were concentrated in lower-wage occupations, which grew almost three times as fast as mid- and higher-wage occupations (Lowry, 2014). Inequality therefore accelerated (National Employment Law Project, 2012). It is important to keep in mind that the gross inequality figures of recent years are not merely the result of the current slump but are a continuation of tendencies in operation since the end of the Second World War, and have intensified since the early years of the Age of Austerity.

Since 1979, the top 1 percent have enjoyed an increasing share of national income and wealth (Bivens, 2014).

Astonishingly, the richest 20 Americans had by 2015 come to own more wealth than the bottom 50 percent of the population (Collins and Hoxie, 2015). By 2016, the richest 1 percent of families controlled a record high of about 39 percent of the nation's wealth, nearly twice as much as the bottom 90 percent, whose share continues to shrink. As for income, the top 1 percent took in a record high of 23.8 percent of the nation's earnings; the bottom 90 percent made less than half of total earnings. Blacks and Hispanics have fared even worse, holding on average about one-quarter of the income of white families (Federal Reserve System, 2017). Thomas Piketty described the outcome of this tendency starkly: "What primarily characterizes the United States at the moment is a record level of inequality of income from labor" (Piketty, 2014: 265). By 2017, the top 10 percent of Americans command 77 percent of all wealth. The top 1 percent increased its share of total wealth by 35.5 percent in 2013 to 38.5 percent in 2016. As of mid-2017, the bottom 75 percent of the population – about 240 million people – own less than 10 percent of all national wealth (Federal Reserve System, 2017).

Financialization of executive compensation is a major contributor to U.S. inequality. Sixty percent of America's most wealthy are the top business and Wall Street executives. These are the richest 0.1 percent, and stock options account for most of their wealth (Bakija et al., 2010). By 2000, "mega-option grants" of a million shares or more were standard; average compensation of top CEOs increased from $1.26 million in 1970 to $37.5 million in 1999. Inequality exploded: the ratio of CEO pay of the 100 largest corporations to that of the average worker "rose from 38 in 1970, to 101 in 1980, to 222 in 1990, and finally to the unbelievable level of 1,044 in 1999" (Crotty, 2005: 93–4). As of 2015, top CEOs make on average 300 times more than the typical worker (Mishel and Davis, 2015). This tendency has persisted in the wake of the "Great Recession." Profits as a share of national income stand at a postwar high, and wages' share at a postwar low (Ruccio, 2017). It is noteworthy that profits' rising share intensifies a tendency that has been in operation during the entire postwar period (ibid.). Robin Harding has noted that profits have become independent of investment: "Profits in the U.S. are at an all-time high but, perversely, [productive] investment is stagnant" (Harding, 2013). J. W. Mason identifies this as a long-term trend and identifies the post-Golden-Age use of what would otherwise be investment-directed funds: "[T]he strong empirical relationship of corporate cash flow and borrowing to productive corporate investment has disappeared in the last 30 years and has been replaced with corporate funds and shareholder payouts" (Mason, 2015).

Since 2008 and the emergence of the Occupy movement the general public has acquired an uncommon awareness of the inequality scandal (Hussey, 2014). President Obama saw fit openly to bemoan the situation, undoubtedly with the hope that the citizenry would infer from his crocodile tears that he intended to do something about it. He announced, in his January 28, 2014 State of the Union address that "corporate profits and stock prices have rarely been higher, and those at the top have never done better. But average wages have barely budged. Inequality has deepened ... [the] cold hard fact is that even in the midst of recovery, too many Americans are working more than ever just to get by — let alone get ahead" (Obama, 2014). This intonation was followed by neither policy recommendations nor legislation intended to address this world-historic state of affairs. In fact, income inequality grew faster under Democrat Obama than under Republican Bush (Stoller, 2012). Focusing on Obama's first term, since the beginning of the "recovery" in June 2009 through 2011, the average income of the top 1 percent grew by 11.2 percent, while the bottom 99 percent saw their incomes shrink by 0.4 percent. Thus, 121 percent of the gains in real income during the Obama "recovery" went to the top 1 percent (Saez, 2015a). Recoveries in the Age of Austerity are not merely jobless, they are "income-less" as well. The majority of new jobs during these recoveries were low-paying (Rampell, 2012a). The poorest quintile of households saw falling income while the top 20 percent regained losses incurred during the recession. As I have argued throughout this book, not only is wage growth necessary to achieve recovery in these times of austerity but it must also be a permanent feature of any industrially mature economy that would rule out long-term austerity (Onaran and Stockhammer, 2014). Four years into the recovery, 2.7 million more people were in poverty than at the beginning of the alleged expansion, and those eligible for food stamps rose by 14 million (*Investor's Business Daily*, 2013). By 2014, the evidence was strong that half of Americans were in or close to poverty (Buchheit, 2014). Austerity has become the default position of the working class. The term "recovery" has acquired a usage so bizarre as to have rendered it meaningless.

THE SHAPING OF AMERICAN "DEMOCRACY"

In mainstream thinking, a given country's level of political democracy is determined by factors such as regular elections, freedom of speech and association, and a universal franchise. But these factors are consistent with a political system in which genuine democracy is absent. Genuine democracy obtains when candidates running for national office meet the following criteria: they are, as candidates, not merely as ultimate victors, chosen by an informed electorate, their platforms are significantly different, some (at least one) run on platforms beneficial to the working population, no candidate is unduly influenced by the rich and powerful and, when elected, the victor governs in the interests of the working majority. In America, none of these conditions is met.

Citizens are woefully uninformed about major issues relating to domestic and foreign policy. The United States has the most fully developed system of propaganda or public-opinion management in the world. The organized effort to engineer public opinion was initially motivated by government's conviction that citizens' resistance to "their" government's commitment to war must be overcome. The context was the overwhelming antipathy of most Americans to the nation's participation in the First World War. Accordingly, Woodrow Wilson's presidential campaign for re-election rested on his promise to stay out of the war. Wilson was re-elected in 1916; in 1917 he committed the nation to the war. The public was angered and disillusioned. A week after declaring war, Wilson put together the Committee on Public Information, sometimes referred to as the Creel Commission, after its chairman George Creel, a newspaper publisher and writer. The Committee embarked upon a comprehensive national agenda, distributing tens of millions of pamphlets, training speakers to address civic groups, placing ads in newspapers and magazines across the country, ghostwriting newspaper and magazine stories and books nominally authored by government officials, and submitting ten news releases a day for the duration of the war (Gutstein, 2009: 62–3). The sole purpose was to promote patriotism and public support of government policies by influencing Americans to internalize beliefs and attitudes that would lead them to embrace the beliefs and attitudes propagated by government. In his book *How We Advertised America*, Creel attributed eventual public support of the war effort to the Committee's propaganda blitz (Creel, 1920). The psychological techniques of perception management deployed by the Commission remain in use to this day (Gutstein, 2009; Carey, 1996).

The strategies of political belief-shaping were soon extended from government to the private sector, so that the two giant and core institutions of any modern socioeconomic formation, business and the State, had at their disposal the means to shape public beliefs and feelings. It was Edward Bernays, a nephew of Sigmund Freud and a member of the Creel Commission, who further perfected the methods of psychological control.

He virtually invented "public relations" and substantially advanced the methods of advertising. (He coined the term "torches of freedom," cited in Chapter 3, to hawk cigarettes to potential female smokers.) In his 1928 book *Propaganda*, he described the shaping of the minds of "the masses" in modern "democratic" society:

> The conscious and intelligent manipulation of the organized habits and opinions of the masses is an important element in democratic society. Those who manipulate this unseen mechanism of society constitute an invisible government which is the true ruling power of our country. We are governed, our minds molded, our tastes formed, our ideas suggested, largely by men we have never heard of. This is the logical result of the way in which our democratic society is organized. (Bernays, [1928] 2005: 37)

With respect to the criteria of genuine democracy identified at the top of this section, Bernays was frank that candidates for national office are not selected by an informed electorate. "A presidential candidate may be 'drafted' in response to 'overwhelming popular demand,' but it is well known that his name may be decided upon by half a dozen men sitting around a table in a hotel room" (ibid.: 60). Powerful party institutions, typically backed by wealthy interests, choose candidates who will run for presidential office. Ken Silverstein has shown how the socioeconomic elite inside and outside the Democratic Party selected Barack Obama, as an appealing and pliant then-small-time political figure, to be brought into elite circles and groomed for national prominence (Silverstein, 2006).

During the 2016 Democratic National Convention, allegedly an event where elected delegates from around the country convene to determine the party's nominee for president, the Democratic National Committee openly sabotaged Sanders' campaign and brought it about that Hillary Clinton, a paradigm of neoliberal orthodoxy, would be the party's choice. The fact that numerous polls and surveys indicated that Sanders would surely beat Trump in the election mattered less to party officialdom than perpetuating neoliberal business as usual. Apropos, not long after the Creel Commission's research and Bernays' techniques were put into practice, one of America's leading public intellectuals and political commentators described the implications for democracy of scientific thought-control: "The manufacture of consent ... was supposed to have died out with the appearance of democracy ... But it has not died out. It has, in fact, improved enormously in technique ... Under the impact of propaganda, it is no longer possible ...

to believe in the original dogma of democracy," i.e. that it consists in rule by an informed citizenry (Lippman, 1932: 248–9).

Democracy can be looked at from two sides, since it requires both an informed citizenry and a political leadership responsive to the wishes of an enlightened citizenry. The science of propaganda is designed to preclude the first of these requirements. The second has recently been subject to the most rigorous empirical study to date of the responsiveness of the State managers to the preferences of the governed. In 2014, Martin Gilens of Princeton University and Benjamin Page of Northwestern University employed a comprehensive data set including measures of the key variables for 1,779 policy issues, from 1981 to 2002. The goal was to determine the responsiveness of policymakers to the expressed preferences of critical sectors of the electorate. Their findings were inconsistent with the claim that America is a political democracy:

[T]he preferences of the average American appear to have only a miniscule, near-zero, statistically non-significant impact upon public policy. [On the other hand] ... the preferences of economic elites (as measured by our proxy, the preferences of "affluent" citizens) have far more impact upon policy change than the preferences of average citizens do. To be sure, this does not mean that ordinary citizens always lose out; they fairly often get the policies they favor, but only because those policies happen also to be preferred by the economically-elite citizens who wield the actual influence ... the majority does *not* rule ... When a majority of citizens disagrees with economic elites of with organized interests, they generally lose ... even when fairly large majorities of Americans favor policy change, they generally do not get it. (Gilens and Page, 2014: 575)

Economic elites, who may not actually *govern*, in fact *rule*, because those who do govern do so in the interests of the elites. The authors conclude that "majorities of the American public actually have little influence over the policies our government adopts ... if policymaking is dominated by powerful business organizations and a small number of affluent Americans, then America's claims to being a democratic society are seriously threatened" (ibid.: 577; see also Bartels, 2008; Gilens, 2007, 2011, 2012; Page et al., 2013; Page, 2014).

Gilens and Page never explicitly state the essence of what they have demonstrated, that the United States is not only an oligarchy, it is a plutocracy. More ominously, there is a tendency for slow-growth economies with an increasing degree of wealth concentration to evolve into dynasties. Because slow demographic and economic growth and increasingly concentrated wealth are the key determinants of the relative growth of inherited wealth, and trend-based forecasts indicate that these conditions will persist in the United States, "inherited wealth will probably rebound as strongly [in America] as in Europe" (Piketty, 2014: 428). In fact, dynastic rule is approaching nineteenth-century dimensions on a global scale (ibid.: 378).

THE THIRTEENTH INTERVENTION:
THE BERNIE SANDERS MOVEMENT

Occupy was motivated principally by the financial crash and the State's rescue of the perpetrators and disregard for the victims. The growth of a substantial constituency supporting the presidential candidacy of the professed "socialist" Vermont Senator Bernie Sanders was a response to two longer-term realities of American life, much of it discussed above. The persistently declining living standards and job opportunities afflicting the majority and the capitulation of the Democratic Party to neoliberal policy led many Democrats and independents to question the political and economic institutional features of American society. That Sanders described himself as a "socialist" when in fact he was at best a European-style social democrat is less significant than the fact that Americans were prepared to countenance an economic alternative labeled "socialist." For decades this was unthinkable. Sanders was far more popular than the much-reviled Hillary Clinton, his rival for the presidential nomination. And surveys showed that he would be a sure winner against Trump. The Democratic National Committee was fully aware of this, yet did everything in its power to derail Sanders' campaign. To very many Democrats who associated the party with the ideals of the New Deal and the Great Society, the party's dismissal of a great portion of its membership in favor of one of the most mistrusted presidential candidates in U.S. history led to the greatest loss of confidence in the party in its history.

Hillary Clinton's presidential defeat by Donald Trump was in large part a response to her avowed aim to continue party (neoliberal) business as usual and her failure to acknowledge declining working-class living standards. A brutal indication of the Democrats' fall is found in a poll in July 2017 (seven months into Trump's presidency) showing Hillary Clinton to be more unpopular than the despised president Donald Trump (Camacho, 2017). The Democratic Party, once thought to be the sole political-institutional stronghold of working-class interests, is now considered by only 37 percent of the population to "stand for something" (Clement and Balz, 2017). And as of mid-2017, surveys show that Sanders remains the most popular politician in the country. There has never in living memory been a more propitious moment for raising workers' expectations for their own lives and underscoring that the existing escape routes are permanently blocked.

ANTICIPATING SOCIAL DISLOCATION: THE DECLINE OF DEMOCRACY AND THE EMERGENCE OF THE REPRESSIVE STATE

The gradual disappearance of the traditional middle class is a recipe for social dislocation. A most consequential function of the middle class in modern capitalist democracies is that it is an essential bulwark against class struggle and political instability. As the French economist and public-policy expert Jean Pisani-Ferry writes in "The End of Work As We Know It," "technology is in the process of completely transforming the global labor market ... As changes in the job market break down the middle class, a new era of class rivalry could be unleashed" (Pisani-Ferry, 2015). The impending crisis does not concern radical analysts exclusively. The founder and executive chairman of the World Economic Forum expressed concern in an essay "The Nature of Work":

> [T]he new on-demand economy, where providers of labor are no longer employees in the traditional sense but rather independent workers ... will it trigger the onset of an inexorable race to the bottom in a world of unregulated virtual sweatshops? ... a social class of workers who move from task to task ... while suffering a loss of labor rights, bargaining rights and job security – would this create a potent source of social unrest and political instability? (Schwab, 2016: 48–9)

The global increase of mass surveillance and militarization of society, especially in the U.S., are anticipations of the steps capitalist elites are prepared to take to suppress the resistance embodied in serious social dislocation (Ahmed, 2015). A coordinated corporate–military mobilization to suppress dissent and predictable social disorder attending austerity-as-normal portends fascism. Chapter 4 showed that there is historical precedent for a fascist response when capitalism threatens to immiserate the working majority. Alarming State repression is evident in the U.S., France and the UK. Rosa Luxemburg's alternative, "socialism or barbarism," is perhaps too general. Historical experience suggests "socialism or fascism."

In earlier periods of labor activism and union formation, private and government violence visited on strikers and labor activists was unequalled in any other capitalist country (see Chapter 2). In the Great Depression, local police forces had as much antipersonnel weaponry as the U.S. army. The response isn't likely to be different in these austere times. Fundamental constitutional protections have been suspended and the Executive claims powers characteristic of police states. Under the 2012 National Defense Authorization Act (NDAA), the U.S. military may seize and imprison any person anywhere in the world on "terror" allegations, without charges, evidence or trial. Such measures violate habeas corpus, which requires a fair trial before a court of law when a person may be imprisoned. One year before the passage of the NDAA, the Justice Department had drafted a white paper justifying the extrajudicial assassination of any U.S. citizen who allegedly "poses an imminent threat of violent attack against the United States" (United States Department of Justice, 2011). Every Tuesday morning Barack Obama met with advisors to determine additions to the White House's "kill list," permitting the president to extrajudicially assassinate any American citizen "suspected" of terrorism or aiding terrorist organizations. A citizen might be targeted if he is suspected of being an "operational leader of al-Qaida or an associated force." The terms "associated force" and "imminent threat" as used in the white paper are so vague and ambiguous as to permit virtually unrestricted implementation whenever the State so pleases. In the 1950s the use of "communist sympathizer" was equally promiscuous. The difference, as crucial as can be, is that what is licensed now is extrajudicial assassination or murder, a threat unimaginable under McCarthyism.

Indefinite detention of suspects of either terrorism or aiding terrorist organizations, with no access to a lawyer, no trial and no unambiguous charge, is now in effect. The State jettisoned habeas corpus, a Constitutional requirement. Posse comitatus, proscribing the deployment of the U.S. Army or its equipment against U.S. citizens, is a thing of the past. The U.S. Army may now be deployed against the citizenry across the nation, not merely in "hot spots" such as Ferguson, Missouri (Tighe and Brown, 2015). During the protests against the police killing of Michael Brown in Ferguson, local police patrolled the community driving armored military vehicles intended for war zones and brandishing military weaponry. The ongoing provision of military equipment to local police was noted with alarm by the American Civil Liberties Union (ACLU): "American policing has become unnecessarily and dangerously militarized ... through federal programs that have armed state and local law-enforcement agencies with the weapons and tactics of war, with almost no public discussion or oversight" (American Civil Liberties Union, 2014). In emails, Missouri National Guard officers referred to protesters as "enemy forces" and "adversaries" (Starr and Bruer, 2015). Thus, "protect and serve," the national motto of the local police, has in effect been replaced with "defeat and conquer." And police officers' use of force against unarmed and non-violent citizens has been virtually ignored, and sometimes effectively endorsed, by the Justice department (Apuzzo and Liptak, 2015). The widely publicized police brutalization, the shootings and killings of unarmed black men in 2015–16, are the latest incidences of a national tradition.

Militarized police forces operate in the streets and in Americans' homes. Special Weapons and Tactics (SWAT) teams were meant to address hostage situations and sometimes armed criminals. Since the 2008 crisis, "local police ... increasingly using them to execute search warrants and drug searches ... [this] has led to devastating consequences" (Smith, 2014; American Civil Liberties Union, 2014). In 2011–12, SWAT teams were heavily armed for drug searches and serving common search warrants. SWAT teams force their way into people's homes in the middle of the night deploying explosive devices like special grenades meant to temporarily blind and deafen residents, sometimes killing them. Drugs or weapons were found in 35 percent of these break-ins. This amounts to domestic terrorism, with neighborhoods as war zones. Its frequency has risen since 2008. The distinguished former *New York Times* foreign correspondent Stephen Kinzer has referred, in this connection, to the "slow-motion military coup" (Kinzer, 2017).

The record suggests that the continuous militarization of American society is motivated by elites' fear that prolonged austerity will erupt in social disorder – as demonstrations, strikes, workplace vandalism, riots in ghettoized districts, increased crime, mass shootings – which must be met by militarized State repression. Numerous studies and commentators warn that austerity increases the risk of violence, and of social and political instability. The Center For Economic and Policy Research has shown, in cross-country evidence from 1919 to 2008, that "austerity has tended to go hand in hand with politically motivated violence and social instability ... societies become unstable after budget cuts. The results show a clear correlation between fiscal retrenchment and instability" (Ponticelli and Voth, 2011).

The same warnings are voiced by prominent economists and business publications. Joseph Stiglitz (cited in Palast, 2001) coined the term "the IMF riot" to describe what Americans should fear in case of sustained austerity. Forbes reported that "Harvard's [economist Kenneth] Rogoff expects serious social unrest due to income disparities in the U.S." (Lenzer, 2011). The highest reaches of government are keen to the issue. The U.S. Army War College urged that the possibility of "unforeseen economic collapse" was likely to instigate "purposeful domestic resistance," which "would force the defense establishment to reorient priorities in extremis to defend basic domestic order and human security ... This might include use of military force against hostile groups inside the United States" (Freier, 2008). Accordingly, the U.S. Department of Defense commissioned university studies to prepare the State for large-scale civil "breakdown" (Ahmed, 2014). The universities have not given a thought to the agenda behind these studies.

Retired U.S. Army General Wesley Clark has called for the internment of anyone deemed "disloyal" to the U.S. government. In a 2015 interview Clark was asked, in connection with the mass shooting in Chattanooga, Tennessee, "How do we fix self-radicalized 'lone wolves?'" He replied: "We have got to identify the people who are most likely to be radicalized. We've got to cut this off at the beginning" (Clark, 2015). But he went on to comment on the threat posed by those "disloyal to the United States ... it's our right and obligation to segregate them from the normal community for the duration of the conflict [i.e. the 'war on terror']." This call for mass surveillance, already in full swing in the U.S., and mass incarceration, reflects strategies currently put in process by ruling elites.

What is happening is the *militarization of American society*, explicit in the routine and recorded behavior of the police in the recent history of wholesale police terrorization of black people. Common tactics deployed by police in the majority of recorded cases of police violence toward persons of any color include: brutalizing or shooting someone for refusing to provide the cops with an ID, for stepping back from an approaching police officer, for fleeing when a cop arbitrarily draws his or her gun, for taking a walk in a white neighborhood, for saying to a cop "You have no reason to approach me," and much more (Martinot, 2015). In fact, people are not required by law to produce an ID demanded by a police officer, and stepping away from a cop is not a crime. The police justification is patented: "The subject was uncooperative" or "I felt threatened." When cases of clearly wrongful police killings are brought to court, the courts almost always exonerate the cops.

These incidents display a frequent and uniform standard trained response (ibid.) The police do not have the right to demand automatic, unthinking compliance, a right possessed only by military officers. Citizens are not required by law to respond with unquestioning obedience to every police command. The above examples contain occasions when a citizen may legitimately deny compliance with police orders. Incidents like this show the universal assumption made by police that an officer "can play the role of a commanding officer, as if in a military institution, and the civilian on the street must respond with the obedience of a platoon member" (ibid.). On this false assumption, the cop sees his own words as equivalent to binding law, turning civil society, the realm of non-government private life, into a military institution. Thus, failure to "obey" the orders of a police officer becomes "disobedience" that can be punished on the spot. The police now have power without precedent and, by merely issuing an order, can turn a law-abiding citizen into a criminal.

Most cases of illegitimate police violence have been validated by legislatures and the courts. A blow to democracy has become commonplace: society itself has become militarized. The provision of military equipment to the police has little to do with the defense of the citizenry against criminals, and very much to do with imposing on society a military complexion, the atmosphere appropriate to a regimented citizenry. The preparations discussed above for the use of State and state violence to suppress dissent transform the police's function from law enforcement to *social control*. This is what suspension of democracy and repressive rule look like (Turse, 2009; Balko, 2013).

Distinguished mainstream commentators have expressed concern over the "decreasing ability of the broad swath of Americans who are below the highest income levels to afford what is typically seen as a middle-class lifestyle" (Judson, 2009: 116). Judson, whose book is titled *It Could Happen Here*, is on the faculty of the Yale School of Management and undoubtedly reflects the anxiety of those sectors of the elite who fear the delegitimizing effect of persistent austerity: "[I]f an overwhelming majority of us fails to benefit from [the] system or, worse, suffers misery and drastic reductions in our standard of living, how long will we continue to support it?" (ibid.: 113). Loss of legitimacy due to declining working-class living standards portends insurrectionary or perhaps revolutionary responses. "When people who believe themselves to be middle class are not able to meet their expectations for a middle-class lifestyle, discontent spreads like wildfire" (ibid.). Judson does not comment on the gruesome ruling-class preparations for the social eruptions that he anticipates.

THE SUPPRESSION OF DISSENT

Mass disaffection with the political-party duopoly and the press has incentivized many Americans to turn to alternative sources of reporting and analysis. Heterodox websites and magazines have attracted tens of millions of readers who correct the "fake news" of the corporate media and the White House Press Office with real-world takes on U.S. policy.

The political elite and corporate-owned social media have begun a concerted attempt to counter Americans' increasing access to critical analysis by controlling the content we can get online. The State has outsourced its censorship to corporations. Facebook is shutting down accounts and limiting their reach, based on past content that is alleged to be "Russia-based" (Shane and Goel, 2017). Much of the material that is categorized as such is Left analysis originating in the U.S. and re-posted by Russia or an alleged Russian-friendly entity. Google has installed new algorithms to lower the search engine's rankings and slow down the access speeds of widely hit Left sites (Winfield et al., 2016; Leight, 2017). The idea is that as it becomes harder and harder to gain access to critical analyses of mainstream reporting, readers will be herded into the orbit of easier-to-find, preauthorized, orthodox political-economic pabulum.

That the political elite is taking remarkable steps to utilize corporations to effect censorship, divert readers from critical analysis and undermine net neutrality was on display in October 2017, in the Senate Judiciary Committee's hearings unabashedly headed "Extremist Content and Russian Disinformation Online: Working With Tech To Find Solutions" (U.S. Senate, 2017). Facebook has responded to political pressure by creating a resource which purports to reveal to readers which alleged Russian propaganda outlets they have liked or followed. Google recently announced that it will conceal articles from Russia Today (RT) by dropping the news source from its top advertising tier (Fandos et al., 2017). And the U.S. Department of Justice has required RT to register as a "foreign agent" under the Foreign Agents Registration Act, a law established in 1938 to counter Nazi propaganda (Kramer, 2017).

Most significantly, Facebook is taking steps to censor news that challenges the prevailing orthodox rendering of U.S. and world events. In mid-January 2018, Facebook announced on its corporate blog that it intends to ensure that the news shown on its site comes from vetted, orthodox sources. It has hired thousands of "content moderators" to sniff out "fake news" (Wagner, 2017). The company seeks to quell the social discord and opposition that results when readers are informed of matters either occluded or omitted from the mainstream media. Numerous surveys show that public trust of the mainstream press is at an all-time low. Samidh Chakrabarti, Facebook's product manager for civic engagement, warns that "[social media] allows people to spread misinformation and corrode democracy" (cited in Fiegerman, 2018). This is the "downside" that social media has for "democracy." Thus, Facebook will take battle against "fake news" and "political polarization." Independent and accurate analyses of growing inequality, ongoing illegitimate wars, the increasing brutality and surveillance functions of the State and the growing precariat will be the target of Facebook's army of censors.

What counts as "fake news"? Mark Zuckerberg is an unabashed Democratic Party loyalist. So Hillary Clinton's characterization, soon after her loss to Donald Trump, of the release of the transcripts of her speeches to Goldman Sachs as "fake news" is a revealing indication of the political use of the term. Fake news embarrasses power. Clinton had reassured the Goldman executives that they should ignore her "public" criticisms of the banks' policies, because they are politically expedient and do not reflect her "private" convictions. The American public's reaction to Clinton's mendacity was not approving.

It was clear from the questions and demands of Committee members that what disturbs elites is the widespread social opposition evident across the nation and preceding the election of Trump. Russia has been selected as the scapegoat. Democratic Senator Diane Feinstein of California asserted that Russia "sought to sow discord and amplify racial and social divisions among American voters." Republican Senator Chuck Grassley of Iowa charged that Russia sought to instigate protests against the recent wave of police violence against black and brown people, especially in Ferguson, Baltimore and Chicago. He proclaimed that Russia "spread stories about abuse of black Americans by law enforcement. These ads are clearly intended to worsen racial tensions and possibly violence in those cities." Democratic Senator Mazie Hirono of Hawaii laid out the agenda behind the Committee's summoning of the tech bigwigs. She insisted that the tech companies be required to adopt a "mission statement" confirming their determination "to prevent the fomenting of discord" (U.S. Senate, 2017).

It is the social dislocation brought about by persistent austerity, the perfidy of the political parties and the perceived inaccessibility of the American Dream that unhinges the economic and political plutocracy. The Committee heard from the counter-terrorism "expert" Clint Watts, who spelled out the socially disruptive potential of dissident speech. "Civil wars don't start," he said, "with gunshots, they start with words. America's war with itself has already begun. We all must act now on the social media battlefield to quell information rebellions that can quickly lead to violent confrontations and easily transform us into the Divided States of America … Stopping the false information artillery barrage landing on social media users comes only when those outlets distributing bogus stories are silenced – silence the guns and the barrage will end" (ibid.).

The recommendation that news outlets that challenge the mainstream media, which in America is in fact a Ministry of Information, be censored met with *not a word of dissent* from Committee members. The tech representatives testified that they are currently hiring "thousands more" monitors with the intention of suppressing "misinformation." The corporations that provide access to the internet will be able to decide what we have access to and what shall be hidden from us. Already a number of the most prominent Left sites – alternet.org, consortiumnews.com, democracynow.org, wikileaks.org, truthout.org, counterpunch.org, wsws.org – have reported a drop in views from 20 to 70 percent since Google changed its algorithms (North, 2017). Controlling bodies by military means is not the only way to achieve the objectives of a police state. Changing the way people talk and think can contribute to undermining existing power structures. The social superordinates are determined to disallow this outcome.

WHERE THINGS STAND

The historical unfolding of capitalism has led to declining living standards for working people, the tendency for the working population to polarize with respect to both skills and wages, and for the middle class accordingly to decline. Debt has become essential to make ends meet, and both wages and secure employment have been on the decline for many decades. Very many working-class households see no prospect of improvement for their children. Hopelessness begins to take root. The prospect for social disruption tends to increase under these conditions, and the State has begun repressive measures in response. What is to be done?

8

Conclusion

Under overripe capitalism, secular stagnation and its attendant austerity threaten to persist "forever," as Lawrence Summers put it. The task facing egalitarian democrats is to address this issue in a way that benefits working people. The march of neoliberalism is to be reversed. The pathological state of overripe capitalism points to its own diagnosis and prescription. The remedy is the democratic and egalitarian deployment of capitalism's two essential resources, which now remain idle: investable capital and currently unemployed and under-employed labor. The only feasible and desirable alternatives are the appropriation of the private surplus by the organized working population commanding a genuinely democratic State, and its use to enhance social and private consumption; and the spreading of the labor force over the relatively few remaining jobs, with a greatly reduced work week and a healthy living wage for all workers. IT, automation and robotization enable the same work to be done by fewer workers and in less and less time. An ever-larger portion of the economic surplus is available to shorten the work week, raise wages and provide for expanded and improved social consumption, e.g. in education, healthcare and infrastructure. Economic growth in the future must be led by public investment and, most importantly, workers' wages (Lavoie and Stockhammer, 2013; Onaran and Stockhammer, 2014). Alas, these conditions cannot be met under capitalism. This is the strongest case for the democratization of both the political and the economic spheres, i.e. for democratic socialism. This is the sole desirable and feasible alternative to a future of working-class austerity enforced by a militarized, repressive State.

The evidence indicates that American capitalism, and, by implication, every industrially mature capitalist society, reaches a critical developmental stage. At that point the kind of real-economic growth that brings secure employment and living standards to the majority, much less to every working household, slows down. What comes to predominate is financialized growth, where such economic growth as there is is sustained by bubbles, which bring with them working-class austerity and precarity, social dislocation and a resulting repressive State. It is increasingly clear that *capitalism and democracy are incompatible*. There emerges the need for economic and political democracy. Economic democracy has never existed under capitalism and political democracy is in conspicuous decline. Some form of socialist democracy is the order of the epoch.

The transition from capitalism to thoroughgoing democracy will not happen automatically, no matter how obvious it may become that capitalism is constitutionally unable to "deliver the goods." What are the prospects for radical change? We must consider the consciousness of the working class, especially noteworthy changes in its self-conception and its attitude toward capitalism's legitimizing ideology, as well as actual tendencies that have formed in resistance to the established order.

THE CONSCIOUSNESS OF THE WORKING CLASS

A historic change in very many Americans' political consciousness has made it now possible, for the first time in American history, for a great many working people to discuss the merits of socialism. Americans' characteristic feelgood optimism and ardent nationalism have not prevented them from coming to the realization, albeit through a glass and darkly, that mainstream politics is not meant to promote the interests of working people. The emergence of both the Tea Party and the Green Party and, more significantly, the Bernie Sanders movement, attest to a good number of Americans' conviction that greater possibilities are desirable and possible and that the current party duopoly will not permit their realization. The Republican Party was defeated by Donald Trump; and the Reaganized Democrats, comparable to Tony Blair's "New Labour," no longer sustains the hopes of working people. The longstanding and increasing hardship burdening working people persisted under two terms of Obama's presidency, in spite of the dramatic promises – to end the Afghanistan war, to close Guantanamo Bay, to end torture as a political tactic, to make it possible for all workers to choose whether or not to join a union, to end the huge tax advantages of the rich, to restore the middle class – none of which were in fact kept. Disillusion is rampant. Most voters now identify as Independent, even those who vote for Democratic presidents as the lesser of two evils. Gallup polls conducted in 2007, 2013 and 2015 found that a majority of Americans "maintain [the] need for a major third party" (McCarthy, 2015). Could such a party be a socialist party?

The Sanders movement marked the near-universal demolition of perhaps the most powerfully reactionary of American conceits, that mere talk of socialism is "un-American." In the U.S. this notion has taken the form of a species of nationalism that draws on the signature notion that America is The City on the Hill, the greatest country in the world and, fittingly, the globe's sole superpower. America's pontifical status is alleged to be due to its exemplary display of "freedom and democracy." Freedom and democracy were largely defined against what was claimed to be their antithesis, socialism or communism. An American's identity was partially constituted by his enjoyment of freedom and democracy, i.e. by his *not* being a socialist or a communist. Thus was generated America's unique economic nationalism: to be American is to be anti-socialist/communist. Identification with capitalism came to be essential to being an American. Hence, during the anti-communist witch hunt of the McCarthy era the congressional agent of the hunt was the House Committee on *Un-American* Activities. In virtually no other country was being a socialist considered *unpatriotic*. In the U.S., rejecting capitalism was tantamount to rejecting America. American communists were held to be freedom-hating, un-American Americans. No wonder the stubbornness of anticommunism among Americans.

The Sanders phenomenon undid much of that. That the most popular politician in America now is a professed socialist would have been inconceivable a few years ago. A deep-seated American precedent has been broken: it is now possible to raise the question of socialism's superiority to capitalism without being considered a traitor or a crackpot. Sanders, probably unwittingly, latched onto a profound change in Americans' political consciousness. Decades of wily and mendacious political promises accompanied by steadily declining living standards has made the fabled American Dream seem increasingly fantastical. Many Americans are now capable of construing the economic system as a construction external to their selfhood and subject to change with no threat to their integrity as Americans. Americans' political identity is in the process of transformation. With this comes transformative social and political possibilities unknown since the 1930s. These possibilities are promising only in conjunction with effective popular education and militant organization. Left strategy is in this connection of the first importance.

ACTUALLY EXISTING TENDENCIES OF RESISTANCE

Since the turn of the millennium the world has seen a burst of mass uprisings. In early 2011 there were mass rebellions in Egypt, Tunisia and across North Africa and West Asia. Anti-austerity marches occur across Europe regularly. Mass actions brought about the fall of the Quebec government in 2012. Idle No More was the largest Canada-wide social action movement since the North American civil rights movement of the 1960s. Brazil saw Confederation Cup riots in 2013 and mass protests against FIFA World Cup spending and social inequality in 2014. In the U.S. demonstrations shut down the Wisconsin legislature in 2011, and in 2012 Chicago teachers, with the support of the majority of Chicagoans, successfully struck and marched to improve classroom conditions, prevent further teacher layoffs and restore essential services to challenged students. (More about this action on pp. 230–2.) And Occupy emerged in response to the financial crisis. Mass disaffection, the substrate of effective political organization, is not in short supply. But the raw material of active resistance lacks lasting significance if its form is politically ephemeral. Each of these movements set specific aims for itself; when these aims were achieved, or after the participants had made their goals clear, the movement went home. Even mass actions protesting about what are in fact long-term, possibly permanent, afflictions such as neoliberal capitalism, have targeted the suppression of specific outbreaks of the disease as their goal, thus rendering their efficacy temporary. A paradigmatic example is the 2005 mass protest in France against neoliberal austerity, in which 1.2 million workers in 150 cities and towns struck *for one day* and demonstrated against privatization. Once the privatization of France's water and utilities was perceived to have been defeated, the demonstrators disbanded.

What is required is a movement that addresses specific issues in the broader context of struggling to bring about a different *kind of society*. Organizing and fighting for government-funded healthcare for all, surely one of the issues an American movement would take on, in the name of defeating one of neoliberalism's sacred cows, is not enough. Neoliberalism is not a socioeconomic formation but rather an ideology, designed to legitimize financialized austerity capitalism: a material social-relational settlement that is the proper target of any tendency aiming to transform society. What is most likely to trip up any movement aiming to bring about democratic socialism is that such a movement's struggles will consist at a given time in directing its energies to some specific goal achievable in the short- or medium-term. The danger is that when that goal is achieved, the movement will return home. The only antidote to this politically perennial gaffe is that the movement define itself as aiming for economic and political democracy, i.e. socialism.

The key issue is democracy. Radical transformation must begin from the existing values of the American people and their lived experience of increasing hardship. Hardship is not democratically chosen. Decreasing social mobility and the loss of opportunities for fulfilling work would not be democratically chosen. Americans know this and thus implicitly know that their situation under austerity capitalism has been imposed upon them by others who are not similarly situated. The common reference to "the 1 percent" acknowledges not merely that the independently wealthy have more than the American worker has but also that the 1 percent can impose a settlement advantageous to themselves even as that same arrangement imposes afflictions upon the lives of working people. The popular response to the State's rescue of the big banks reflects at least the shoots of such an awareness. This was acknowledged by then-president Obama, when, in an April 2009 speech intended to soothe popular indignation at a bailout for the richest as tens of millions faced eviction and bankruptcy, he offered a response to "a lot of Americans [who are asking] 'Where's our bailout?'" (Obama, 2009b). Americans, disillusioned with both political parties, are less likely than ever to hold individual politicians responsible for policies baldly benefiting only elites. There is a sense of a rigged game. Awareness of *systemic* causality has been evident in various forms of resistance since the grand movements of the 1960s and early 1970s. Many of the cognitive and linguistic tools are currently available for formulating the notion of a *system*, a *kind of society*, whose nature precludes democracy. Many of the key conceptual building blocks are already available for constructing an understanding of capitalism as a system which stands against the working majority, in the same way that sexism and racism stand against women and people of color.

A going movement, like for example Occupy, might very well choose to educate along these lines after it has come into being as resistance around a single issue. But that is possible only if the movement define itself at its inception not merely as a single-issue response but also by reference to *some* objective that is not tied to the specifics of a current struggle, e.g. single-payer healthcare. The latter should be put forward as a particular instance, but not the entirety, of a larger and longer-term social objective, to create a different *kind of society*. That the kind of society that best empowers working people is democratic socialism will become evident only if the movement's membership includes socialist activists who contribute to the education of the membership by offering perspicuous diagnoses of *experienced* stagnation, declining living standards, vanishing social services and increasing under- and unemployment as *systemic* afflictions. These diagnoses should contain implicit pointers to the kind of society that serves us best. The experience of austerity and ongoing education would facilitate rendering the implicit explicit: the anti-democratic, stifling character of the political-economic system lies at the core of our deepest-seated afflictions. Radical democratization is what we seek.

Space does not permit a detailed discussion here of a second important development in the U.S.: the remarkable number of bottom-up endeavors in thousands of communities establishing various types of worker-owned cooperatives, common land trusts and other forms of worker-owned and -controlled enterprises. These provide the beginnings of a real-world picture of economic democracy in action (Alperovitz, 2006, 2013; Albert, 2004). In a detailed description of what he calls "workers' self-directed enterprises," Richard Wolff offers a carefully reasoned defense of the desirability and feasibility of economic democracy, and a realistic description of exactly how such an enterprise would be run and how such enterprises could successfully compete with capitalist firms (Wolff, 2012). Elements of Wolff's model can be among the demands made by workers willing to strike to achieve their goals. We have seen that no major gains have been made by working people without the strike. In America the labor movement is hopelessly tied to the Democratic Party, and its membership is at a postwar low. Moreover, in times of austerity workers are for the most part reluctant to strike. For the most part. But the 2012 Chicago teachers' strike demonstrates that the strike can even in these times be successful and be carried out in such a way as to open the door to social change beyond the immediate issue.

The 2012 strike by members of the Chicago Teachers Union teaches a critical lesson for the labor movement as a whole, but its example is also essential for any organized tendency aiming radically to transform political and economic institutions and relations. The union had voted to strike against the expansion of for-profit charter schools and standardized testing, and for pay raises based on years of service and educational skills, not merit defined in a way tied to students' performance on standardized tests; also a shorter school day, smaller class sizes, and additional hiring of social workers and counselors to help the most troubled students, among other issues. The strike's outcome featured important but limited gains for the teachers and students. Chicago's ultra-neoliberal mayor, former White House chief of staff Rahm Emanuel, who had placed ads opposing the strike in newspapers and on television, won a longer school day. The teachers won a pay raise based on service and educational skills and defeated Emanuel's effort to do away with tenure. But these gains and loses are perhaps the least significant features of the strike.

The union, under the uncommonly astute leadership of Karen Lewis, an African–American former high-school teacher, had learned an incalculably valuable lesson from the British Columbia Federation of teachers. For a large-scale and illegal strike to make progress, it must not act alone, with the support only of teachers and students, but must win vast outside support from as broad as possible a range of community constituencies. The new union leadership, elected in 2010, understood that any labor action must drive home the ways in which a successful strike will advance the interests not merely of teachers but also of students, parents and in fact of the community as a whole. In this way the union can communicate to the entire community that the realities at stake in this strike are not single-issue matters but relate to macro-political issues such as the corporate-backed urge to privatize and corporate domination of both private and public life. In the union's countless meetings with community groups it wove local and national concerns together, underscoring, for example, the nationwide elite campaign to demonize public schools and their teachers with a view towards advancing the interests of private, for-profit alternatives to public education. Chicagoans were reminded that even the widely distributed commercial film trashing public schools and lauding charter schools, *Won't Back Down*, strongly promoted by Bill Gates and other elite figures, had to concede that the record of charter schools with respect to their own professed standards was no better than that of the public-school system. What was at stake, the union argued, was not merely the fate of Chicago's teachers and students but the future of American education. The teachers' union alerted Chicagoans to the anti-worker agenda of neoliberalism in many of its forms.

The union attended to the political education of its mass base. Most meetings with community institutions began with a discussion of the role of banks in bankrupting many American communities and looting workers' pension funds. Racism too was on the agenda, because Emanuel had presided over the closing of tens of schools, mostly in poor and black neighborhoods. The idea was to relate the teachers' struggle to the security and the future of Chicago's – and the nation's – entire working class. When the strike began, the pattern was the same: every day the teachers would begin by picketing their schools and then proceed to downtown to march with as many community supporters as possible. On at least one day, 35,000 teachers and other Chicagoans marched through the heart of the city. Traffic was brought to a standstill and a good part of the city was in effect closed down. Still the teachers retained the support of the majority of the city's households. After the strike, several polls and surveys showed that the union had majority support of Chicagoans, with mayor Emanuel winning the support of less than 20 percent of the city's households. And the union was highly effective in contributing to the defeat of Emanuel in his bid for re-election. The strategies and tactics of the Chicago Teachers Union are not confined to unions. *Any organized political tendency, and I have in mind principally a party, can and must proceed along these lines if long-term transformative objectives are to be realized.*

That a movement around a specific issue can decisively strengthen other broad movements was best illustrated in the 1960s, when the civil rights movement and the anti-war movements were in full swing. These tendencies operated independently until Dr. Martin Luther King and Muhammad Ali denounced the war in Vietnam as emblematic of the system buttressing both racism and imperialism. By the fall of 1967 the civil rights and anti-war movements had effectively merged, generating some of the largest demonstrations of the postwar period. Any going movement has a multitude of pressing issue with which it can make common cause.

THE INDISPENSABILITY OF THE LEFT'S CONTRIBUTION TO TRANSCENDING CAPITALISM

I have argued that effective transformative organization must encompass a range of issues which those who would become active in the organization can see as closely related. The Chicago Teachers Union related its own grievances to issues around racism, privatization and neoliberalism in general. Ultimately, the movement must incorporate into its agenda the conviction that another kind of society is called for and feasible, namely democratic socialism. This is an alternative solution that goes beyond this or that combination of issues. It involves not merely pointing out "bad things" about the existing political-economic settlement and calling for their correction, but rather it paints a quite different picture of how social, economic and political life may be organized in order to preclude disastrous consequences. This cannot be done without education about how capitalism works and what a desirable and possible alternative would look like. And this education can be effected only by knowledgeable socialist activists prepared both to learn from and to educate working Americans. Such education would not of course consist in lectures on the implications of declining net investment and the need to socialize the surplus. But there are in fact matters that most workers are aware of now and which bear an intimate relationship to those issues. These include: the unprecedented impossibility of finding secure full-time work with substantial benefits; the reality of low wages and shrinking or non-existent benefits, speedup, increasing job-destroying automation and the rising cost of living since 1975, i.e. increasing immiseration; the increasing inaccessibility of adequate healthcare; the increasing inability to send one's kids to a traditional college or university and the dim future those kids face. The task of socialist education is to link these issues to a lack of democracy in that single arena with the greatest impact on mental and physical health and security the most, i.e. the political-economic arrangements of the current order. With Americans more convinced than ever that the political institutions are unresponsive to their most pressing needs, space is made for raising the question of whether we Americans have any longer a *political* democracy at all. Perhaps what is at the root is the absence of democracy in the *economy*, specifically in the workplace, where most Americans spend most of their lives. Richard Wolff's *Democracy At Work* is an indispensable resource in this connection.

James Baldwin once remarked that freedom cannot be given to one; freedom must be *taken*. From this it follows, Baldwin insists, that if Americans are not free, they do not want to be free. The profound kernel of truth in this remark is that the socialist Left cannot take pride in its not having mobilized and actively organized to participate in and contribute to the radicalization of unions and social movements. Nothing need prevent socialists from this kind of revolutionary commitment. My hope is that this book will aid in the realization of this end.

Appendix A

Economic Maturity and Disaccumulation – A Mildly Wonkish Summation

The income shift to profits and the turn to finance during the 1920s is bound up with a key criterion of industrial maturity, the expulsion of capital (measured by investment outlays) and labor from the process of production. The disproportionate share of profits in total income is a function of the ratios of capital to output, capital to labor and labor to output (Coontz, 1965: 153). P/O, the profit:output ratio, is the share of profits in total output or income. C/O, the capital:output ratio, is the share of (the value of) capital in total income. And L/O, the labor:output ratio, is the share of labor's income in total income. Thus, P/O is defined as:

$$P/O = 1 - (C/O + L/O)$$

For the period 1919–29, the capital:output ratio fell and the capital:labor ratio rose (Kuznets, 1961: 64, 209). A given amount of output (measured in 1929 dollars) was able to be produced with a smaller amount of capital (measured by investment outlays), and a given quantity of capital required a declining amount of labor. From this it follows that fewer inputs, of both capital and labor, were required to produce a given quantity of output. That is to say, *both capital and labor were expunged from the production process, i.e. investment in both equipment and labor declined, even as the volume of production increased dramatically*. The stage of disaccumulation had been reached and the economy had ripened to industrial maturity. As a result, the share of profits in national income tended during this period to grow larger, even as profit became increasingly unnecessary to finance investment in capital and labor. Towards the end of the decade, the bulk of surplus profits was increasingly channeled from production to the financial sector. This pattern is characteristic of mature, unregulated, weak-labor capitalism. The equilibrium level of employment will tend to decline, labor will tend to be increasingly otiose to production, wages will drift downward, and financial investment and profits will tend to become larger shares within their spheres. The disproportionate growth of finance leads to the formation of dangerous bubbles, which must in the end burst. The ensuing stock-market crash or asset deflation brings about a shock of awareness, but it is never the root malady. "Cause and effect run from the economy to the stock market, never the reverse" (Galbraith, 1954: 93). That is the story of the 1920s and of the post-Golden Age, from 1974 to the present. I return to this theme in the following chapters.

THE DYNAMICS OF INVESTMENT

Declining Net Investment, the Expulsion of Labor and Capital from Production, and the Necessity of Government Investment, Government Employment, Less Work and High Wages

Since the Great Depression and the unprecedented expansion of the Golden Age, epochal developmental transformations occurred which were reflected in major changes in twentieth-century capitalism's growth process. Less net investment in more advanced capital equipment has been necessary since the basic industrial structure of the economy was finally in place; the cost of capital goods has declined over the normal course of technological development. That is what we should expect. The capital-goods industry matured exactly as the consumer-goods industry would develop on its maturation during the 1920s: an increasing number of both kinds of good was produced with decreasing labor and less (net) investment. Productivity, that is, increased steadily in both sectors.

Investment has been misleadingly regarded as the Let There Be Light of capital accumulation and economic growth. It is represented, in Marxian economics, by the M in the circuit M-C-M'. But investment was the driving force of capitalism only during industrialization – up to 1911 (Livingston, 1994: 3–23, 84–122). Thereafter, net investment has atrophied and consumption has become the key propellant of economic growth. Investment or "capital formation" is money spent to bring "fixed capital" into being. Fixed capital is the non-human input to production: plant, equipment and, now, software. These non-human means of production are also referred to as "fixed assets." The capital stock is the sum total of society's fixed capital. I shall be concerned with fixed capital's worth or money value and its productive power.

Investment spending, which increases the nation's stock of capital, is distinguished from capital consumption or depreciation, the wearing out or diminution and/or obsolescence of (some portion of) the capital stock.

If worn-out capital is replaced with capital of the same kind, the way we replace a worn-out battery with a new one, then capital accumulation does not take place and the power or productivity of the existing capital stock is not increased. Standards of living and profits in this case can be increased only by workers laboring longer hours. But the system requires that profits must be increased without limit, and there are limits to the length of the work day. This is why ongoing productivity increases are necessary. So replacement of the means of production typically involves more than mere duplication; replacements tend to be more efficient than what they replace. Depreciated capital is replaced by advanced, more productive equipment. This is in fact the general rule of replacement. "Capital-widening" investment, which adds more of the same to the existing stock, is atypical of new investment and occurs when, for example, there is a surge in demand for a new product. Generally, replacement investment is "capital-deepening," enhancing the productive power of the capital stock.

Capital goods are costs of production, and capitalism requires constant efforts to reduce production costs, including the cost of capital goods. This was understood by the most prominent authentic Keynesians of the twentieth century. Anatol Murad pointed out that

> [I]f productivity has doubled in shoemaking, it is likely to have doubled also in machine making. Even as ... new invention resulted in a machine capable of turning out twice as many shoes with a given amount of labor, so it is likely to result in a machine capable of turning out twice as many shoe machines. (Murad, 1954: 238)

The result is a decline in the cost of the means of production. At issue here is the relation between private investment, productivity increases and economic growth. Let us review the key concepts essential to an understanding of the anatomy of investment, the qualitative change in the role of investment in the capitalist growth process, and the implications for the future of neoliberal financialized capitalism.

Murad's insight is illustrated by the relation between gross and net investment. Gross investment represents the total addition made to the capital stock in a given period, including the replacement of consumed capital. But it does not indicate the actual change in the economy's stock of productive assets, nor in the economy's productive power, during that period, because it does not account for depreciation of existing stock. If what gross investment adds to the capital stock is no greater than what is lost through depreciation, i.e. if replacement comes to mere substitution, then neither capital accumulation nor increased productivity has been achieved. Because capitalism requires endless accumulation and continuous increases in productivity or productive power, gross investment is an unreliable measure of the economy's *development*. We want to know the positive difference investment has made to the economy's productive potential. Accordingly, we must subtract depreciation or the consumption of existing stock from gross investment. We are left now with what counts, net investment.

Net investment represents the amount spent on capital assets (gross investment), less depreciation. *Very much is at stake if net investment has been in decline since the early twentieth century, and consumption and public investment have become the principal mature-industrial engines of growth.* The capitalist will have become an idle wheel in the production process and profit will have become decreasingly necessary to sustain and further economic growth. The economist Evsey Domar, co-originator of the widely acknowledged Harrod–Domar Model of economic growth, was perhaps the first to establish the declining net investment thesis in theoretical and empirical detail (Domar, 1953). He demonstrated that the replacement requirements of a growing economy are less than the depreciation charges, so that a portion of the resulting saving from depreciation can finance innovations that both expand capacity and reduce costs of production (ibid.: 3–13). Domar's summing up must transform our thinking about the relations between investment, growth and employment: "in a growing society replacement falls far short of depreciation. Hence, investment net of depreciation cannot be identified with investment net of replacement" (ibid.: 2). Domar showed that depreciated equipment can be replaced with more productive capital for less than the cost of replacing the old facilities. In other words, *net investment is made obsolete by technological progress*. The implications for political economy are momentous.

Replacement is financed out of depreciation reserves, which are not counted as part of profits, and replacement investment has become a growing share of total investment. This insight was picked up and developed by such economic luminaries as Robert A. Gordon and Simon Kuznets. Two years after Domar's contribution, Gordon wrote:

> the larger the ratio of capital consumption to gross investment, the larger the fraction of the latter which is financed automatically out of depreciation charges. Such investment requires no net saving by either business firms or individuals … the larger replacement expenditures, with continuing technological change, the greater the possibility of having a

steady increase in output with no net investment at all … [A]s Kuznets has pointed out, "mere 'replacement' may signify increase in production capacity," and "a rise in the ratio of capital consumption to total output means, other conditions being equal, a declining need for net additions to capital stock." (Gordon, R. A., 1955: 293–4. The Kuznets citation can be found in Kuznets, 1952: 161)

The upshot is that while we are accustomed to the notion that technological progress tends to expel labor from the process of production, we have not noted that this same tendency brings about the expulsion of both of the factors of production, with capital displaced from production along with labor. Gordon wrote:

[A] fairly constant secular relation between gross investment and GNP has been accompanied by a long-run decline in the ratio of net investment to national income …. industries may be able to maintain their share of gradually expanding total output with little new net investment … the process of replacement combined with continuing technological change means that the capital stock does not have to grow in proportion to the rise in output. (ibid.: 293, 300)

Net investment, then, is not merely a declining proportion of gross investment. It is also a vanishing component of GDP. It takes less and less additional investment to keep capitalism going. Growth and continuous technological innovation may proceed even as the capital:output ratio declines. What follows from this upsets the conventional thinking of both orthodox and heterodox theorists. Should net investment drop to zero, so that gross investment comes to no more than capital consumption, i.e. the value of gross investment equals the value of depreciation funds, the capital stock and its productive power can still grow. All that is required is that the lost capital is replaced at the same or lower cost by more advanced capital. Indeed, were net investment to be negative, such that capital consumption exceeds gross investment, the capital stock and its productive power might still increase (Livingston, 2011: 217). A key upshot of this outcome of normal capitalist maturation is that *as net private investment has become absorbed into gross investment, the additional expenditures necessary for economic growth become public investment and rising household-consumption expenditures, not private investment.*

The empirical work of a number of scholars – Harold Vatter, John Walker, Gar Alperovitz, Karl Beitel, James Livingston and Steve Roth

(Vatter, 1975, 1982; Vatter and Walker, 1990, 1992; Vatter et al., 1995; Beitel, 2009; Livingston, 2011: 45–51; Roth and Livingston, 2011) – has shown that net investment has continually atrophied in the U.S. since 1911. Indeed, Simon Kuznets shows that during the 1920s net investment was zero (1952, 1961).

A relatively recent development in the capital-goods sector, namely the tendency of technological improvements to reflect digitalization and IT, intensifies the atrophy of net investment. Computerized automation is, then, the latest form of a general tendency of capitalist development. And there is also the structurally induced pressure endemic to the system of private profit to lower the costs of production. We should expect, then, that automated capital goods should become cheaper over time. In the relevant literature we find repeated confirmation of this expectation. Here are some representative citations from current studies: "machines or computers, goods for which prices have fallen substantially" (Canon and Marifian, 2013), "the cost of information [having] gone down" (Wiseman and Condon, 2013), "machines that keep getting more powerful, cheaper and easier to use" (Wiseman et al., 2013) and "advances in technology reduce the costs of automation" (Brynjolfsson and McAfee, 2011a). Lawrence Summers, in "Why stagnation might prove to be the new normal," avers that "Declines in the cost of durable goods, especially those associated with information technology, mean the same level of saving purchases more capital every year" (Summers, 2013b). Technical change in these times, remarks Summers, increasingly takes the form of "capital that effectively substitutes for labor" (cited in *The Economist*, 2014). James Galbraith draws the obvious implication of this development: the labor-saving nature of cheaper automated technology entails that "the result will be a permanent move toward lower rates of employment in the private, for-profit sector" (Galbraith, 2014: 142).

Capital saving can be traced to 1915, when an oil refinery absorbed four times more investment capital and produced one-third the output of the same physical plant in 1925 (Livingston, 2011.: 54). The story of the atrophy of net investment began at the dusk of the period of industrialization, between 1909 and 1911, when the growth of real GDP began a significant slowdown, and the ratio of net investment to national output exhibited secular decline (Vatter et al., 1995: 591–2, 596–7; Romer, 1989: 1–37; Balke and Gordon, 1989: 84–5). I have argued that this long-term tendency points to the need for the principal driver of economic growth to shift from investment to consumption.

Both the growth rate of investment spending and the ratio of business investment to total output fell from 1911 through the 1920s, and continued after the Second World War (Vatter et al., 1995: 596–7). The relation between saving and investment displayed Keynesian tendencies from the very beginning of the twentieth century: "from 1900 to 1930 the percentage of national income being saved each year tended to increase [while] the portion invested in real physical equipment declined" (Cochran, 1957: 25). And Karl Beitel has noted the tendency of greater output to require less capital since the mid-1940s: from the end of the Second World War to 2007 "the rise in the nominal output-to-capital ratio is entirely due to the cheapening of the price of capital-goods relative to the price composite of goods and services that enter directly into GDP" (Beitel, 2009: 78). Capital drives not only labor but also itself from production. Capital does away with the need for capital. The conclusion to which this analysis leads is monumental, and underscores capital's systemic tendency to generate the need to transcend itself.

The research of James Livingston and Steve Roth has identified the major trends in fixed business capital from the 1930s to the immediate aftermath of the 2008 crisis. They have compiled data from the Bureau of Economic Analysis (BEA)'s National Income and Product Accounts to trace the relation between fixed investment, especially business, non-residential investment, and the economy as a whole, i.e. GDP (Roth and Livingston, 2011: 211–29). Most economists expect that when the economy is proceeding normally, fixed business investment should grow along with GDP. This expectation is historically unfounded. We have seen that during the years 1922–6, when virtually all that decade's fixed capital was installed, and the decade's growth rate was highest, net investment stood at zero. Production, productivity and profits soared, driven entirely by consumption demand or wages. The Depression and Second-World-War years should not be expected to exhibit a representative picture of either GDP growth or private business investment in a capitalist economy not skewed by abnormal crisis conditions. Thus, our attention is drawn to the private-investment–GDP relation during the postwar years, the 60 years from the 1950s to the present (ibid.: 218–29, especially 221).

During this period, capital consumption exceeded net investment. The productive power of the nation's capital base grew steadily. This is why the change in the capital stock from one year to the next does not equal net investment. Were net investment merely capital-widening, replacing worn-out stock with more of the same, the addition to the capital base would be reflected in net investment. But typical capital replacement is capital-deepening, i.e. the consumed capital is replaced with more productive capital at the same or lower prices. Hence, economists at the BEA re-estimate the value of the total capital every year, taking this feature of replacement investment into account (ibid.: 217). This is called the "revaluation" of the capital stock. With this more accurate measure, it is possible, as noted above, for the capital stock to grow in productive capacity with no increase in net investment. A corollary of this tendency of capital is that outlays for productivity-enhancing investments continuously both decline as a percentage of GDP and increase as a percentage of gross investment. This is what Domar was calling attention to in the citations on p. 237 above. Over the period in question, revaluation has tended to account for a greater share of changes in the capital base than net investment (ibid.: 229).

If we look at the years after the Depression and the war, more indicative of the "normal" condition of the economy, we find that capital consumption exceeds net investment in every decade beginning with 1950 and through the 2000s (ibid.: 218–19). Under these circumstances we should expect government to compensate for the decline in net investment as a percentage of GDP. That this was indeed the case during the Depression and the war is not remarkable. What is telling regarding the economic role of government in uncommonly prosperous times is that during the Great Boom, 1948–73, purchases by all levels of government grew at a rate of 4.2 percent, outpacing the real GNP growth rate of 3.67 percent. Especially significant in the light of what we have seen in the preceding sections regarding private-sector employment is that during the Boom years government employment grew at 3.62 percent, while civilian employment grew at a mere 1.57 percent (Walker and Vatter, 1997: 80). Because of the secular decline of net investment, government spending on a large scale is essential for prosperity under capitalism.

With the beginning of the neoliberal period and its persistent reduction in government civilian spending, after 1973 and up to the early 1990s the growth rate of government purchases and employment fell sharply to 1.8 percent, the real GNP growth rate to 2.4 percent and the private-sector labor-force growth rate to 2.0 percent (Wray, 2008). Thus, the relatively robust growth rates of the Golden Age was in large part induced by government's growing faster than the economy, while the slower economic growth of the post-Golden-Age period was induced in great part by the even slower growth of government. This is consistent with the now widely discussed claim that the private economy has for some time been mired in secular stagnation. I discuss the secular-stagnation thesis further in Chapter 6.

In sum, the tendency of capitalist development is to render private-sector work decreasingly necessary to providing the population with a just and comfortable standard of living. The tendency of computerized technological progress is to reduce the time it takes workers to produce the value of the wage and to render the wage bill a decreasing portion, and profits an increasing portion, of net revenues. As the *Financial Times* reports, "profits in the U.S. are at an all-time high, but, perversely, investment is stagnant" (Harding, 2013). With net productive investment in atrophy, the surplus has tended to shift from production to finance, with its extractive appropriation of interest payments and tendency to create unsustainable bubbles and therefore real-economy instability.

The unprecedented cheapening of capital goods in the digital age, the tendency for advances in productive capacity to incorporate digital technologies and the fact that these technologies displace labor, point to three central conclusions: that private net investment is decreasingly relevant and is inimical to the growth of output, wages and employment in the real, productive economy; that wages and employment can be sustained only by public investment; and that both high wages and shorter work hours are essential to avert stagnation and destructive financial bubbles, and to provide workers with a quality of life well within overripe capitalism's grasp.

Karl Marx, and John Maynard Keynes, in *Economic Possibilities For Our Grandchildren*, had the last word on this matter. I develop their views in Chapter 4 and Appendix B.

Appendix B

What Keynes Really Prescribed

There is no clear evidence from experience that the investment policy which is socially advantageous coincides with that which is most profitable.

John Maynard Keynes, *The General Theory of Employment, Interest and Money* [1936] (1964), p.157

The outstanding faults of the economic society in which we live are its failure to provide for full employment and its arbitrary and inequitable distribution of wealth and income.

Ibid., p.372

[W]e should be aiming at a steady long-period trend towards the reduction in the scale of net investment and an increase in the scale of consumption (or, alternatively, of leisure).

John Maynard Keynes, *The Long-Term Problem of Full Employment* [1943] (1980c), p.324

In 1933, the trough year of the Depression, Keynes wrote, "The decadent international but individualistic capitalism, in the hands of which we found ourselves after the war, is not a success. It is not intelligent, it is not beautiful, it is not just, it is not virtuous – and it doesn't deliver the goods. In short, we dislike it, and we are beginning to despise it" (Keynes, [1933] 1982a: 239). The president and his advisors were deriving policy prescriptions working from an economic theory inappropriate to the realities of contemporary capitalism. Keynes begins *The General Theory of Employment, Interest and Money* with a fundamental critique of that orthodoxy.

NEOCLASSICAL ECONOMIC THEORY

Orthodox theory claims to demonstrate that capitalism is immune to severe, sustained crisis. The system naturally tends to equilibrium. That is, there could be no persistent condition in which the supply of goods would either fall short of or exceed the demand for goods. No plant would remain idle and no worker willing and able to work would be unemployed. Only forces external to the system, such as a change in consumer preferences, could upset this equilibrium. Temporary oversupply in one market is offset by undersupply in another market. The imbalance is corrected by the price mechanism, which attracts labor and capital from oversupplied markets to undersupplied markets. The economy thus tends toward a state of "static equilibrium" at full employment.

One of Keynes's signal contributions is to have shown that a capitalist economy can reach equilibrium at *any* level of employment. There is no reason why the supply of and demand for both products and labor cannot be equal over an indefinite period of time with a high percentage of the labor force unemployed. *The possibility of secular stagnation was placed squarely on the historical agenda.* Keynes considered neoclassical theory (which he referred to as "classical") to be a secularized version of Divine providence. It fails to describe the real world: "[T]he characteristics ... assumed by the classical theory happen not to be those of the economic society in which we actually live, with the result that its teaching is misleading and disastrous if we attempt to apply it to the facts of experience" (Keynes, [1936] 1964: 3).

The implications for the employment of labor, which Keynes saw as the principal concern during both the Depression and, as we shall see, during periods of prosperity, are momentous. If the full-employment assumption were accurate, there could be no involuntary unemployment. Unemployment could occur only because labor was priced too high: workers would be choosing to demand wages that employers were unwilling to pay. They could choose to be employed simply by lowering their wage demands. And if they did not, the market would cure their obstinacy. Wages would be driven down to the level at which all workers willing and able to work would be hired. This mainstream position was put forward by the distinguished British economist A. C. Pigou just three years before the appearance of *The General Theory* (Pigou, 1933). Many orthodox economists and even more employers took this position in the 1920s and 1930s. On this conception of how capitalism works, protracted depressions are impossible. But the Great Depression and its protracted involuntary unemployment were incompatible with accepted theory. Another theory of capitalism was called for. Keynes thought he had provided it. It started with the problematic nature of Say's Law of Markets.

Say's Law, a proposition of the early nineteenth-century French economist Jean Baptiste Say, putatively justified static equilibrium theory.

It stated that production creates a corresponding demand. Everything produced – consumer goods and capital goods – will be sold, either to consumers or to businesses, because workers either spend all of their income or they save some of it. If every worker spends her entire income, then there is no gap between consumption and income. Total purchasing power would be continually passing from hand to hand. This "circular flow" of income and output through the economy would maintain equilibrium, clear markets and make depressions a theoretical impossibility. But what happens, Keynes asked, when workers spend only a portion of their income and save the rest? There is now a gap between income and consumption; some portion of total output will not be sold (consumed). Unless the gap is somehow closed, equilibrium will be upset and overproduction, excess capacity and unemployment will appear. In an exclusively private economy, only business investment can close the gap created by savings and restore equilibrium. Orthodox theory assures us that investment must and will perform this function.

Savings represent a "leakage" from the circular flow, bringing about a shortfall of consumption relative to output, and therefore a decline in profits, wages, employment and prices in the consumer-goods industries. Enter investment (which, along with consumption, constitutes the entirety of private spending). The income saved increases the supply of money available to lend, and so decreases the cost of borrowing, i.e. the rate of interest. This stimulates businessmen to borrow to invest: to purchase capital goods. The providence of the market then works its wonders: the unemployed in the shrinking consumer-goods sector now find employment in the expanding capital-goods sector. Thus the circular flow of income and output is maintained; economic contractions and unemployment of workers willing and able to work remain impossible. Any overproduction or shortages will be self-correcting. The lovely equipoise of income and consumption, supply and demand, will reassert itself.

Mainstream theory assumes that savings equals investment. If households spend less than their income, businessmen must spend *that much* more. Two key assumptions of orthodox theory are at work here. First, consumers will reduce their consumption in order to save only because the rate of interest on saving, the banks' payment to households for the use of their money, is rising. Second, the rate of interest on savings will rise because investors are demanding funds. Consumption and investment are claimed to be reciprocally motivated: consumption declines because saving and investment rise to the same degree. Keynes saw that this neoclassical conception of the relation between consumption and investment, and savings and investment, was deeply flawed.

KEYNES'S CRITIQUE OF NEOCLASSICAL THEORY:
THE GENERAL THEORY OF EMPLOYMENT, INTEREST AND MONEY

What motivates households' decision to save is not the same as what motivates capitalists' decision to invest. Households' saving is determined not by the rate of interest but by changes in their level of income. In the case of rising income, the "marginal propensity to consume," i.e. the portion of rising income that is consumed or turned into effective demand rather than saved, tends to decline (Keynes, [1936] 1964: 31, 97, 126). Households tend to save rather than consume an increasing portion of rising income; the "marginal propensity to save" tends to increase with rising income. As we saw in Chapter 4, Keynes believed that there is a level at which households' consumption demand is sated (ibid.: 376). Once a reasonably comfortable standard of living is attained, households will pledge larger percentages of increased income to savings – to provide for retirement, to finance their children's future education, and for similar considerations (ibid.: 97). For the very rich, the propensity to save is very high, and higher the richer they become. Since (a) even a constant savings rate will produce an increase in the absolute amount of savings, (b) consumption patterns are largely stable, and (c) savings must be put by private business in the service of investment, *the volume of investment must be constantly increased in order to maintain the full employment level of income and avert severe downturns.* Keynes had stressed this point in his communication with Roosevelt (see Chapter 4, p. 118). If the system equalizes saving and investment, investment opportunities will arise in step with rising savings. However, neoclassical theory provides no reason to believe that remunerative investment outlets will emerge corresponding to the increasing availability of an investment-seeking surplus.

Keynes argued that a mismatch between savings and investment upsets the reciprocity or equilibrium assumed by orthodoxy. The habit of saving is relatively stable: households set aside roughly the same percentage, *but a larger amount*, of their rising income year after year. Historically, annual statistics show a fairly constant savings rate over extended periods of time. But businessmen's decisions to invest are not correspondingly stable: they do not depend on the amount of savings households make available for borrowing. (I set aside for the moment the fact that Keynes seemed unaware that as early as the 1920s large industrial corporations were able to finance investment out of retained earnings.) The investment decision depends on investors' estimations of the "marginal efficiency of capital," the expected additional profit from an additional investment (ibid.:136). Anticipations of future profit do not exhibit the dependability of household-saving decisions; they vary widely from time to time, and are always subject to ineradicable uncertainty. Every market must at some point become saturated, bound to contract. That is, at some point, replacement demand must become an increasingly large share of total demand. Think of the demand for railroads, automobiles, radios and iPhones. There is no guarantee that comparably robust markets will providentially materialize in response; economic downturns do not automatically self-correct. Framework stimulants especially are few and far between. That no innovation replaced the automobile was a key factor in the demise of the 1920s boom. Keynes's conclusion was that money tends not to be invested as rapidly as it is saved. Corporate savings, representing potential production, tend to exceed opportunities for remunerative investment; potential production tends to exceed actual production. Excess capacity and idle investment funds become chronic problems. Keynes would draw the appropriate conclusion in *The General Theory*: "the richer the community the wider will tend to be the gap between its actual and its potential production … not only is the marginal propensity to consume weaker in wealthier communities, but owing to its accumulation of capital being already larger, the opportunities for further investment are less attractive" (ibid.: 31). This is to be expected in a ripened, industrially mature economy.

For Keynes, the weakness of investment was a crucial factor accounting for the Great Depression. There is an important ambiguity in this claim. Investment did indeed fall more precipitously after 1929 – by 70 percent – than production, productivity or employment. But it does not follow that a very low level of investment was the *precipitating cause* of the protracted downturn. We have seen that it was the fundamental weaknesses of the economy of the 1920s that made for the crisis of the 1930s. Chief among these was stagnant wages and the consequent failure of consumption to rise with production, profits and, most importantly, productivity gains. When signs of market saturation became evident in 1926, business did not conclude that the surplus needed to be shifted from profits to consumption, nor did government heavily tax business to finance massive public investment. Capitalists continued to treat their profits as investment-seeking and government persisted in laissez-faire. Businessmen imagined that a shift of investment capital from industry to finance would keep the cash flowing with no disruption to the productive economy. This tactic was, as we have seen in Chapter 3, counterproductive. *With insufficient household spending power,* investment *in production* during the 1920s was excessive. Hence the extraordinary investment plunge of the early 1930s. But it does not follow that the Great Depression was rooted in a dramatic decline in investment. The latter was the outcome of declining *consumption* expenditures resulting in large part from households' eventual inability to take on additional debt to buttress low wages.

Keynes is generally thought to have assumed that the growth process under mature capitalism was investment-driven, as it was during the period of industrialization. It is just as generally overlooked that Keynes understood that in both capital- and consumer-goods production, a point would be reached at which the marginal efficiency of capital, the additional profit to be expected from an additional investment, would fall off precipitously. Capitalist development tends "to make capital-goods so abundant that the marginal efficiency of capital is zero" (ibid.: 221). Capital goods would become abundant *relative to the existing level of effective household consumption demand.* Investment depends on capitalists' expectations of future profits from effective consumption demand. But we have seen that Keynes had observed that household demand (in the British pre-consumer*ism* society of his time) eventually levels off, due to relative satiety. It is limited *consumption* demand that stifles would-be-unlimited investment demand. Because investment demand depends on expectations of robust consumption demand, it is ultimately consumption that drives economic growth and the accumulation of capital.

Hence, Keynes's insistence that insufficient demand is the ultimate source of economic retardation is to be understood as referring to an insufficiency of *private consumption* and, as we shall see, *public investment* demand, as Keynes made clear in his communication to Franklin Roosevelt. And we have seen that these same factors remain a central policy concern during periods of prosperity. I will approach this matter by considering what Keynes took to be the paramount economic issue raised by the 1929 collapse and its aftermath.

It is insufficient consumer purchasing power that brings about the divergence between aggregate saving and aggregate investment that can generate an equilibrium well below the level of full employment. Keynes understood that the solution was to channel chronically superabundant savings into higher wages and a permanent and extensive program of public investment financed by government expenditures in excess of tax revenues, i.e. by deficit spending. He did not understand that this cannot be accomplished under capitalism.

KEYNES, SECULAR STAGNATION AND THE TRANSITION
FROM PRODUCTIVE TO FINANCIAL INVESTMENT

The demands on capital are historically great. A capitalist economy must continue investing to close the ever-widening gaps between consumption and income and between actual and potential production. As we have seen, because the economy tends to expand over historical time and wealthy households account for much of society's saving, *investment will have to increase at an increasing rate relative to income* in order for savings to equal investment. Because consumption demand accounts for most of the GDP, the inducement to invest depends in the final analysis on capitalists' expectations of future *consumption* growth (Solow, 2008: 105). But if investors know that consumption tends to decline as a proportion of rising income – and Keynes assumed that they do know this – then both the inducement to invest in productive enterprise and the level of employment will tend to decline precisely when the greatest amounts of savings are available. *The absolute magnitude of private production-seeking investment must rise, if full employment is to be maintained.* Businessmen will not maintain a constant rate of investment *in production* unless they expect household income to rise at a greater rate.

For Keynes, this portended secular stagnation, a chronic affliction of mature capitalism. While postwar economists had for more than half a century dismissed secular stagnation as an issue of a bygone era, the current crisis has revived the discussion, with major economists now forecasting secular stagnation "forever." (Summers, 2013a,b; Davies, 2013; Krugman, 2010, 2012, 2013a,b,c; Skidelsky, 2014). However, this revived discussion misses the roots of long-term economic retardation and austerity because it misidentifies investment as the driver of economic growth under mature capitalism. It forgets that gaps between national income and aggregate consumption, and between actual and potential production, can only be closed by substantial increases in consumption (financed through either direct employment or public investment providing jobs to the unemployed), the new engine of growth after the achievement of industrialization. The mainstream, however, continued to see the capitalist and hence the private investor as the animating force of the system.

Keynes did not believe that private investment would close the gaps. We have seen that Keynes took human wants to be limited and that he expected increases in productivity to lead to increased preference for leisure – apparent today when European workers demand shorter work hours when productivity increases. He did not construe the typical worker as imbued with the culture of consumer*ism*, leading workers to demand higher levels of consumption as a reward for increased productivity. As for the capital-goods sector, investment would tend to stagnate once basic industrialization was accomplished. In both capital- and consumer-goods production, a point would be reached at which the marginal efficiency of capital, the additional profit to be expected from an additional investment, would fall off precipitously. Capitalist development tends "to make capital-goods so abundant that the marginal efficiency of capital is zero" (Keynes, [1936] 1964: 221).

John Stuart Mill was the first political economist explicitly to recognize a tendency for capital to become, as economies develop, so plentiful as to threaten the extinction of profits (Mill, [1848] 1909: 318–20). Keynes put it this way: "The situation, which I am indicating as typical, is one in which capital is so abundant that the community as a whole has no reasonable use for any more, but where investment is being made in conditions which are unstable and cannot endure, because it [i.e. investment] is prompted by expectations which are destined to disappointment" (Keynes, [1936] 1964: 321). The settlement to which Keynes points is the possibility that net investment may become unnecessary and that capitalists may come to see non-productive kinds of outlay, e.g. financial investment, as the wave of the future. In his Galton lecture (delivered before the Eugenics Society in 1937) Keynes reminds us that "Many modern inventions are directed towards finding ways of reducing the amount of capital investment necessary to produce a given result" (Keynes, [1937] 1973: 127). *It is a central contention of this book that the long-run tendency of capitalist development has in fact been to reduce the amount of investment funds necessary to produce more efficient equipment.* At the same time, capitalism has generated a stream of "inventions which enable a unit of capital to yield a unit of product with the aid of less labor than before ... [These] improvements will proceed in the future as in the recent past and ... that they will proceed in the near future up to the best standard that we have ever experienced in any previous decade; and I calculate that inventions falling under this head are not likely to absorb much more than half of our savings" (Keynes, [1937] 1973: 130).

These outcomes have come to pass (see Chapters 3 and 7) as precipitants of both the Great Depression and of the current Great Recession. In a 1945 letter to T. S. Eliot, Keynes points to a possible outcome of these developments, one which this book defends in Chapter 7: "A full employment policy by means of investment is only one particular application of an intellectual theorem. *You can produce the result just as well by consuming more or working less*" (Keynes, [1945] 1980d: 384; emphasis added). Indeed, I argue that the implication of Keynes's reasoning is that it has now become possible and necessary that those whose income does not afford a comfortable standard of living be enabled to consume more *and* that *all* work less.

Keynes was led to his line of reasoning by historical considerations almost entirely absent from the analyses of contemporary *soi-disant* "Keynesians." In the Galton Lecture he had argued that the extraordinary growth of the U.S. economy from the mid-nineteenth century through 1910 was due to momentous investment opportunities exogenous to the economy as conceived in orthodox theory. Population growth was for Keynes perhaps the decisive factor, but the opening of the frontier and the building of the railroad system also figured as major propellants of growth. These have in common the features of what I have termed framework stimulants. In order to ensure continuous economic growth and uninterrupted full employment, stimulants of this kind must be reliably generated on an ongoing basis. Keynes thought this to be highly unlikely. Large-scale *private* investment opportunities would not materialize in step with the growth of investible savings. The result would be chronic or secular stagnation. A different sort of exogenous stimulant was called for. The source of such a stimulant would depend on the *point* of the economic system, the social goals to which any "civilized" (a favorite adjective of Keynes's in writing about an optimal economic system) set of economic arrangements should aspire.

An essential purpose of any defensible economic system should be to improve people's lives. For Keynes this meant not merely increased material security and a rising standard of living but also the ability to pursue activities more civilized and commensurate with humans' higher cultural capacities than those associated with the accumulation of wealth. As shall be seen later in this appendix, this included the cultivation of human capacities requiring time otherwise taken by working to "make a living." Keynes's views in this connection strikingly resemble those developed by the young Marx.

We saw in Chapters 1 and 3 that the historical evolution of more efficient means of production has reduced the need for productive labor in both the capital-goods and consumer-goods sectors. The possibilities for humans' cultural maturation are thus created by the historical maturation of capital. In order that these possibilities be realized, society's resources must be mobilized and put to use, i.e. invested, for social purposes antithetical to the accumulation of wealth as an end in itself. Investing for social purposes requires "a somewhat comprehensive socialization of investment," removing many investment decisions from private hands

(Keynes, [1936] 1964: 378). The State becomes the increasingly prominent agent of investment. Where Keynes and Marx diverged was in their conceptions of who would be in positions of State power. Keynes, like Hegel, imagined the agents of a rational State to be a class of enlightened civil servants, educated, public-minded persons whose highest priority was the public good. Unsurprisingly, these turn out to be people much like Hegel and Keynes. I do not romanticize Keynes. He shudders at the thought of the "boorish proletariat" rising to positions of political power (Keynes, [1925] 1972: 258). But he did understand that an agency or "National Investment Board" dissociated from the profit motive and concerned with the public interest must be responsible for the investment decisions of large enterprises (Keynes, [1945] 1980e: 408). The same Board, as we shall see, would limit profit levels and the income of "entrepreneurs."

Keynes's considered theory and the policy recommendations it generates are to be found not merely in *The General Theory* but in companion writings fleshing out the 1936 analysis. I draw upon both *The General Theory* and these writings in the following sections. Keynes offered not merely what he took to be practical means to immediate recovery from the Depression but also a bigger picture of a very different kind of society, a vision implicit in *The General Theory* itself. Keynes envisaged a kind of society much closer to democratic socialism than the social democracy common in Europe before neoliberalism. Its leadership would be steadfastly committed to the public interest. What distinguishes this arrangement from genuine socialism is that socialism entertains no notion of the "public" or common interest unless the class of citizens is coextensive with the class of workers. As long as class division persists, there is no *common* interest. The socioeconomic transformation envisioned by Keynes was no mere utopian possibility, a mere "better idea." Failure to put in place the institutional changes Keynes urged would, he argued, fail to address capitalism's tendency to underconsumption and overproduction. Financial and real-economy crisis would follow upon adherence to the status quo.

I describe below what Keynes took to be the "immediately practical" policies feasible within the sclerotic ideological confines limiting Roosevelt's policy choices. This is what has come to be misleadingly called "demand management": fiscal and/or monetary policy intended to stimulate production and employment. We shall see that Keynes regarded monetary policy in a downturn as comparable to "pushing on a string" And fiscal policy as commonly understood was quite marginal to Keynes's prescription. In the final section I discuss the alternative long-term policy Keynes imagined, and the kind of society appropriate to it.

Let us see now what Keynes thought to be essential to "putting people to work" *within the framework of the present system*. I shall argue that it is not at all clear that Keynes's recommendations, however technically workable they may be, are realistic within a capitalist framework.*

FULL EMPLOYMENT MEANS *FULL* EMPLOYMENT:
WHY AGGREGATE DEMAND POLICY IS MISGUIDED

Soi-disant Keynesians propose *aggregate demand management* (ADM), or "pump priming," which was explicitly rejected by Keynes as "too late" to revive an economy in deep slump and provide full employment (Keynes, [1937] 1982c: 394). ADM aims to close the "output gap," the difference between what the economy is actually turning out and what the economy could produce were it employing all available "factors of production" (capital and labor). Keynes enjoined instead the stimulation of *effective* demand. Government was to transfer purchasing power directly to workers via employment in public works programs. He regarded as necessary and permanent what the New Deal enacted hesitatingly and temporarily.

The idea for Keynes was to close the *labor–demand gap*. ADM would try to boost "the economy" in general with the hope that increased purchasing power will eventually trickle down to the unemployed. Seven decades of pretend Keynesianism has in fact not produced the full employment Keynes claimed was possible. Full employment can be attained only by government's direct *targeting* of demand to those in need of employment (Tcherneva, 2009, 2011c). He considered literally *full* employment to be possible with feasible government policy. "[T]he real problem fundamental yet essentially simple … [is] to provide employment for *everyone*." (Keynes, [1942] 1980a: 267).

Keynes's measure of the output gap that needed to be closed was identified with the number of unemployed that needed to be hired in order to produce full employment (Keynes, [1942] 1980b: 280–303). Keynes wrote not of fiscal policy but of "public works." Policy must *target* first and foremost the unemployed by directly providing wages, through public works programs, to those in need of work, as Roosevelt had done in the

---

* What follows draws upon the original work of Pavlina R. Tcherneva, especially "Keynes's Approach to Full Employment: Aggregate or Targeted Demand?" Working Paper No. 542, *Levy Economics Institute of Bard College* (2008) and "Permanent On-The-Spot Job Creation – The Missing Keynes Plan for Full Employment and Economic Transformation," *Review of Social Economy*. Vol. LXX, No. 1, March (2012).

WPA. Wages must be the direct object of employment policy. Keynes's approach to the problem of unemployment is not production-centered, it is *labor-centered*: "I sympathize, therefore, with the pre-classical doctrine that everything is produced by labor ... It is preferable to regard labor, including, of course, the personal services of the entrepreneur and his assistants, as the sole factor of production" (Keynes, [1936] 1964: 213–14).

Keynes thought the private sector unsuitable to tackle the problem of joblessness, since the private sector itself is the structural source of the inherent tendency towards unemployment. Under capitalism "[T]he evidence indicates that full, or even approximately full, employment is a rare and short-lived occurrence" (Keynes, [1936] 1964: 250). Employers may be paying wages insufficient to contribute to a full-employment level of spending and/or may have gloomy profit expectations, dampening their incentive to hire and produce. Hence, it is not the responsibility of the private sector to provide all job-seekers with work "any more than it is their business to provide for the unemployed by private charity" (Keynes, [1933] 1982b: 151). In the system of private ownership of productive facilities, it is a utopian pipe dream to talk of the "social responsibility" of business unless it is, as Milton Friedman had it, "to increase its profits" (Friedman, 1970). Either government provides *ongoing* (see pp. 256, 257, 258–9) employment opportunities or we shall have to learn to live with chronic and growing long-term unemployment.

There are two problems with the private-sector approach to addressing unemployment. The first concerns the *economic* disconnect between boosting aggregate demand and raising employment. The remedy for this is to establish the connection *politically*, by a government policy of directly employing the jobless. The second problem is that ADM's distributional effects are inequitable. This can be avoided by turning policymakers' attention to closing the *employment* gap directly by government hiring the unemployed for public purposes.

THE DISCONNECT BETWEEN STIMULATING
PRIVATE DEMAND AND REDUCING UNEMPLOYMENT

"Aggregate demand" is too general a notion to generate the specific types of demand required for specific occupations, in different regions of the nation, and for highly specific purposes. Employment is in fact a function of *effective* demand, because the private factors determining aggregate spending are subject to inherent uncertainty: there is no way to guarantee that aggregate demand will in fact rise to the level required to provide employment for those ready, able and willing to work. Hence a thoroughly private economy cannot deliver the most important public good – jobs to all who need them. Neoliberal politics dismisses this warning. In his jobs summit speech, then-president Obama affirmed that any politically acceptable remedy for intractable joblessness must be market-based: "Now, the true engine of job creation in this country will always be America's businesses, but government can create the conditions necessary for businesses to expand and hire more workers" (Obama, 2009a). Keynes regarded this as a recipe for chronic unemployment. History has proven him right. The "conditions necessary" have since the Great Recession been lower taxes and interest rates, neither of which had had any impact on employment.

Employment is indeed a function of aggregate demand, but private demand alone has not, because it cannot, produced full employment. Seventy years of pseudo-Keynesian policy, amounting to one form or another of aggregate demand management, has failed to maintain full employment. This is due to ADM's dependence upon three conditions inherently uncertain and immune to government correction: the incentive of households to consume (rather than save) out of current income; the rate of interest; and capitalists' expected return on investment, the estimated prospects for future profits. Since 2008 U.S. government policy has been powerless to affect the first and third of these, which is why the second, e.g. the Fed's lowering of interest rates, amounts to, in Keynes's words, "pushing on a string." Interest, for Keynes, is merely a payment for the use of money, a carrot to discourage hoarding money. The rate of interest, then, is determined by the demand for money and the supply of money in circulation. Manipulating interest rates in order to increase the level of demand, then, reverses the actual causal relation between the demand for money and the interest rate.

Interest is in fact a leakage from the income stream that performs no effective economic function. Interest is not a "reward for saving," as some economists have claimed, nor is it determined by the supply and demand for savings and investment, or supply and demand in goods markets. "[I]nterest rates are determined by the demand and supply for money, not by the demand and supply for durable goods" (Keynes, [1932] 1979: 81; cited in Parrini and Sklar, 1983: 570). Keynes takes this to follow from the fact that capitalists are motivated to invest in order to accumulate more money, not in order to consume more goods. He cites Marx's M-C-M' schematism and notes that "the nature of production in the actual world is not, as economists seem to suppose, a case of C-M-C', i.e. of exchanging commodity (or effort) for money in order to obtain another commodity (or effort). That may be the standpoint of the private consumer. But it is not the attitude of business, which is a case of M-C-M', i.e. of parting with money for commodity (or effort) in order to obtain more money" (ibid.). It is therefore pointless to try to create jobs by lowering interest rates.

Nothing illustrates this better than the current crisis. In a severe slump, capitalists correctly see low wages, under- and unemployment and declining sales revenues as portending low profits. Keynes avers that government tax and interest-rate incentives might indeed induce capitalists to invest and perhaps increase profits. His point is that *these inducements cannot guarantee that investors will use those profits to hire labor*. The increased surplus may be held, or used to acquire other companies or invested in financial assets or paid to corporate executives as bonuses or used for stock buybacks. Consumption expenditures too are subject to uncertainty. Government cannot determine whether tax cuts will be saved, spent or pledged to creditors. A good number of the currently unemployed are homeowners with mortgage payments outstanding. Will unemployment transfers be used to feed the family, pay medical bills, service credit-card or student debt, or reduce mortgages? No one, including government, can say.

The only sure way to employ the unemployed, argued Keynes, is to *target* those workers and regions suffering unemployment and directly offer them jobs. Only government can do this. The failures of the Obama administration illustrated perfectly that lowering taxes or making it easier to borrow are fools' errands in a major downturn. Hyman Minsky put it simply: the only guarantee of full employment is *to change the way income is earned* (Minsky, 1968). The persistence and severity of capitalist crises forces upon us the notion that workers are owed an income from society as a whole, as represented by government, and not from private profit-seekers.

Keynes's prescriptions applied not merely to the Great Depression. He believed that his arguments about effective unemployment policy were applicable to any severe recession and depression at any time, *and* to periods of relative prosperity. The limitations imposed by private control of investment decisions, a market in labor power and profit-driven investment decisions are sufficient to warrant large-scale public employment as the sole remedy for less-than-full employment. The problem, then, was not this or that contraction, but capitalism as such. Keynes saw the broad socialization of investment as a necessary condition of capitalism's viability (Keynes, [1936] 1964: 378). In fact, he saw evidence for the centrality of public investment in the "liquidity trap," the very feature of today's hobbled economy that foiled Obama/Bernanke's policy of quantitative easing. In the liquidity trap, as Keynes described it, money has become "a bottomless sink of purchasing power ... there is no value of it at which demand [for money] is diverted ... into a demand for other things" (ibid.: 231). Whoever sets the price of money, in our case the Fed, cannot know whether reducing the cost of borrowing will bolster investors' anticipations of adequate remuneration (nor whether households will consume potential supplements to their purchasing power). Capitalists size up the market and form expectations regarding the adequacy of future returns on the basis of considerations beyond the influence of current government policy. Regarding this scenario Keynes wrote: "I am now somewhat skeptical of the success of a merely monetary policy ... I expect to see the State ... taking an ever-greater responsibility for directly organizing investments" (ibid.: 164). "If *two-thirds or three-quarters of total investment* is carried out or can be influenced *by public or semipublic bodies*, a long-term program of a stable character should be capable of reducing the potential range of fluctuation" (Keynes, [1943] 1980c: 322; emphasis added).

Keynes's promotion of the large-scale socialization of investment presumed a rational State bureaucracy determined to advance the fundamental interests of working people. His political naïvety is remarkable. It was beyond Keynes's sense of proud bourgeois identity to imagine working people as constituting the personnel of the State. "[T]he *class* war," he wrote, "will find me on the side of the educated *bourgeoisie*" (Keynes, [1925] 1972b: 297).

THE INEQUITABLE DISTRIBUTIONAL EFFECTS
OF CONVENTIONAL PUMP PRIMING

Two important consequences followed from Keynes's conception of effective employment policy. The need for targeted demand management means that the *distribution* of demand is more relevant to addressing unemployment than is the size of the government stimulus, since mainstream policy maldistributes whatever benefits it manages to muster. And the economy is in need of employment-generating public works projects at every stage of the business cycle, not merely in downturns.

That closing the employment gap, i.e. the labor–demand gap, requires the direct boosting of effective demand sharpens the policy objective. The unemployed are unevenly distributed across the country, and not all regions are distressed in the same way. To be sure, desperation is evident across the board, but many of the illnesses are site-specific. Keynes recommended *specific* stimulus where it is needed. Jobs are needed for this specific infrastructure project, in this region, requiring workers with these skills and equipment of this kind.

ADM leaves the distribution of the stimulus undetermined. In fact, pump priming has had an effect similar to the effects of affirmative action programs: the principal beneficiaries have been the already better educated and better paid. When fiscal and monetary stimuli have induced recovery during the postwar period, the upswing is led by home construction and consumer durables. These spenders do not include the long-term unemployed or the very poor. The sole guarantor that those in greatest need will benefit is for government to directly employ targeted workers in public works projects. There is minimal guesswork involved. "Anything we can actually do we can afford. Once done it is *there*. Nothing can take it away from us" (Keynes, [1942] 1980a: 270). As the economist Pavlina Tcherneva puts it, "[N]o country is a finished proposition ... [Countries] face new challenges and develop new kinds of needs. The public sector can stand ready through a program of direct job creation to provide jobs for all who wish to work in projects that satisfy those needs" (Tcherneva, 2011a: 22). The repair and maintenance of public property of all kinds could and should be an ongoing project with permanently available employment during contractions *and* expansions. Keynes contrasted this approach to unemployment insurance, for which "we have nothing to show ... except more men on the dole" (cited in Tcherneva, 2012: 66). The dole, unemployment insurance, does an injustice to workers, because "Every working person is worth more than the dole he gets" (cited in Tcherneva, 2012: 66).

THE FAILURE OF AGGREGATE-DEMAND-MANAGEMENT
KEYNESIANISM AND THE CURRENT EMPLOYMENT CRISIS

Authentic Keynesian policy repudiates trickle-down economics. On the contrary, as Minsky noted, "instead of the demand for low-wage workers trickling down from the demand for high-wage workers, such a policy should result in increments of demand for present high-wage workers 'bubbling up' from the demand for low-wage workers" (Minsky, 1968: 338).

Keynes regarded government stimulus to be ongoing and permanent. The considerations elaborated above are not specific to periods of slump. Joblessness in fact persists through the expansion. Paul Krugman's characterization of Keynesianism as "depression economics" misses the mark (Krugman, 2009). The Golden-Age habit of defining full employment as unemployment of no more than around 3.5–4 percent has no basis in Keynes, who insisted that the "real problem, fundamental yet essentially simple [is] to provide employment for everyone" (Keynes, [1942], 1980a: 267).

Since truly effective policies designed to eliminate unemployment have never been adopted in the U.S., we should expect that the pattern of jobless-ness since the end of the Second World War displays a worsening trend of the kind symptomatic of deeply rooted structural contradiction. Two current trends are a good measure of the depth of industrially mature capitalism's faux Keynesianism. We are seeing both the mass destruction of full-time jobs, many of which will never return, and record levels of long-term unemployment (unemployed for 15 weeks or longer). Most revealing is that long-term unemployment has been rising since the late 1960s, well before the triumph of neoliberalism. The short-term unemployed have been a shrinking percentage of all unemployed throughout the entire postwar period. Looking at the business cycle over the last 40 years, an ominous trend emerges: in each business-cyclical *expansion*, the long-term unemployment rate remains either at or above the level of the previous expansion. In a word, for more than 40 years the short-term unemployed have been a declining, and the long-term unemployed an increasing, percentage of all unemployed (Tcherneva, 2011b). By Keynes's own standards, pretend-Keynesian fiscal policy has been a 70-year bust. At the current historical juncture, liberal, left-liberal and social-democratic politics are beside the point. What then is Left?

THE PRESENT AGE OF ABUNDANCE AND
THE WITHERING AWAY OF NECESSARY LABOR

Keynes took his analysis to have deeper and more far-reaching consequences than were detailed in *The General Theory*. He imagined an evolutionary – not revolutionary – social reorganization of capitalism which would finally rid the system of its ugliest manifestations by addressing "[t]he outstanding faults of the economic society in which we live," which "are its failure to provide for full employment and arbitrary and inequitable distribution of wealth and income" (Keynes, [1936] 1964: 372).

He spelled out the unprecedented possibilities created by the maturation of capitalism most boldly in *Economic Possibilities For Our Grandchildren*

(Keynes, [1930] 1972c). Keynes saw what are taken to be essential features of capitalism as tied to the historical circumstances under which they were once, but are no longer, necessary. In "Am I a Liberal?" he wrote "[T]here is now no place ... for those whose hearts are set on old-fashioned individualism and laissez-faire in all their rigor – greatly though these contributed to the success of the nineteenth century. I say this, not because I think that these doctrines were wrong in the conditions which gave birth to them ... but because they have ceased to be applicable to modern conditions" (Keynes, [1925] 1972b: 300–1).

Fierce acquisitiveness, the unbridled love of money, greed and the accompanying gross inequality, are undesirable but practically necessary evils under the historically specific circumstances of nineteenth-century industrialization, when the nation as a whole is dedicated to overcoming the scarcity of capital. With the lion's share of aggregate income directed to accumulation, income not aimed at investment must be kept relatively low. This required a low level of consumption demand, i.e. low wages. But once that task is accomplished, and capital is abundant, i.e. no longer scarce, acquisitiveness, inequality and the disfigurement of human motive that goes along with them will have performed their historic function and can then be repudiated as useless fossils. Keynes put it this way in *Economic Possibilities*: "All kinds of social customs and practices, affecting the distribution of wealth and of economic rewards and penalties, which we now maintain at all costs, however distasteful and unjust they may be in themselves, because they are tremendously useful in promoting the accumulation of capital, we shall then be free, at last, to discard" (Keynes, [1930] 1972c: 329).

> *When the accumulation of wealth is no longer of high social importance,* there will be great changes in the code of morals. We shall be able to rid ourselves of many of the pseudo-moral principles ... by which we have exalted some of the most distasteful of human qualities into the position of the highest virtues ... The love of money as a possession – as distinguished from the love of money as a means to the enjoyments and realities of life – will be recognized for what it is, a somewhat disgusting morbidity, one of those semi-criminal, semi-pathological propensities which one hands over with a shudder to the specialists in mental disease ... I see us as free, therefore, to return to some of the most sure and certain principles of religion and traditional virtue – that avarice is a vice, that the exaction of usury is a misdemeanor, and the love of money is detestable. (Ibid.: 329, 330–1; emphasis added)

Summary of Keynes's Full Political Economy

The tendency of capitalist development to create productive wealth in excess of remunerative investment outlets, and the correlative development that we become capable of "finding ways of reducing the amount of capital investment necessary to produce a given result" have made profound transformations in our way of life both possible and necessary (Keynes, [1937] 1973: 127). Keynes argued that the failure to realize capital's self-transcending potential will exacerbate the system's core endemic liabilities: excess capacity, low levels of working-class consumption, financial crisis and destabilizing inequality. *It is a central contention of this book that the long-run tendency of capitalist development has in fact been to reduce the amount of investment funds and labor power necessary to produce more efficient equipment.* At the same time, capital-displacing innovations have generated a stream of "inventions which enable a unit of capital to yield a unit of product with the aid of less labor than before … [These] improvements will proceed in the future as in the recent past and … that they will proceed in the near future up to the best standard that we have ever experienced in any previous decade" (Keynes, [1937] 1973: 130). Both capital and labor are displaced on an ongoing basis from production over the course of capitalist development.

When highly productive capital is no longer scarce and the economy is "'properly run' so that full employment is achieved, the marginal efficiency of capital [expected profits from additional investments] can be expected to fall to 'approximately zero within a single generation'" (Keynes, [1936] 1964: 220–1). Profits under maturity and *in the absence of consumerism* will asymptotically approach zero. With the development of society's means of production having been advanced such as to provide full employment and a comfortable standard of living for all, the surplus created in production must take the form not of profits for owners but of investment in public works and higher wages.

Keynes's Adumbration of Institutional Socialism

The Hoover Commission had noted the tendency of technological improvements to be labor-saving (see Chapter 3, pp. 77–8). Keynes unpacked the unprecedented possibilities thereby generated. He spelled out the remarkable consequences in *Economic Possibilities*: "In quite a few years – in our own lifetimes I mean – we may be able to perform all the operations of agriculture, mining, and manufacture with a quarter of the human effort to which we have been accustomed" (Keynes, [1930] 1972c: 325). *Keynes concluded, we shall see, that we would be able to reduce the work week to 15 hours at most, and with no reduction, in fact an increase, in workers' wages.* Continuous productivity increases in both the capital- and consumer-goods sectors and the ongoing expulsion of labor from the production process created serious imbalances in the 1920s and 1930s and persist, as we shall see, as paramount problems today. "The increase in technical efficiency has been taking place faster than we can deal with the problem of labour absorption" (ibid.: 321). This creates *"technological unemployment* ... due to our discovery of means of economising the use of labour outrunning the pace at which we can find new uses for labour" (ibid.: 325). We are presented with two possible alternatives: either a shortening of necessary labor time or chronic unemployment and persistent stagnation.

This book argues that Keynes's bold circumvention of technological unemployment is in fact the only approach consistent with democracy and the universal provision of a just living wage. This option is anathema to orthodoxy. "[W]e shall endeavor to spread the bread thin on the butter – to make what work there is still to be done to be as widely shared as possible. Three-hour shifts or a fifteen-hour week may put off the problem for a great while. For three hours a day is quite enough to satisfy ... most of us!" (ibid.: 329). Thus, the "greatest change" towards which Keynes points is *"that mankind is solving its economic problem* ... [namely] the struggle for subsistence, [which] always has been hitherto the primary, most pressing problem of the human race" (ibid.: 325, 326–7; emphasis in original).

Prior to capitalism, humans faced the problem of *scarcity*, the insufficiency of the means of producing what they need to subsist. *Economic Possibilities* makes clear that by "subsistence" Keynes does not mean the mere ability to stay alive but rather the requirements of a decent, rewarding standard of living. "Think of this in terms of material things – houses, transport, and the like" (ibid.: 325). When this becomes possible, society has reached the stage of "abundance" (ibid.: 304, 306). While Keynes believed that this stage had not yet been fully reached, he predicted "that the standard of life in progressive countries one hundred years hence [the years from 1930 to 2030] will be between four and eight times as high as it is today ... I draw the conclusion that ... the *economic problem* may be solved, or be at least within sight of solution, within a hundred years" (ibid.: 325–6, emphasis in original).

What makes this "greatest change which has ever occurred in the material environment of life for human beings" is that scarcity is regarded by orthodox economic theory as an ineradicable feature of human life

(Keynes, [1930] 1972c: 331). Every economics textbook begins with the standard definition of "scarcity", which consists of two assertions: that human desires are unlimited and that the resources needed to satisfy these desires are limited. From this it is inferred that scarcity is endemic to the human condition. Keynes rejected the metaphysical notion that human desires are boundless and substituted a notion of scarcity more in line with ordinary usage. With scarcity conceived as the historically contingent inability to produce and distribute all the material requisites of a good life, capitalism's ability to create a superabundance of highly efficient means of production "means that the economic problem is not – if we look into the future – *the permanent problem of the human race*" (ibid.: 326; emphasis in original).

Keynes's conception of what Marx called the "historic mission" of capital (Marx, [1894] 1967b: 259) is remarkably close to the vision outlined by Marx in his early writings. The unparalleled productivity increases brought about by industrial capital create a species of freedom unachievable prior to capital's maturation. Humankind is now able to enjoy both a desirable standard of living and the time to develop a range of capacities, available only to the human animal, that must remain unexercised as long as humans are compelled to spend most of their lives "making a living," i.e. working, preparing for work, travelling to work, returning from work and recuperating from work. It is odd indeed that a certain form of society would be the first in history that "makes it possible for me to do one thing today and another tomorrow, to hunt in the morning, fish in the afternoon, rear cattle in the evening, criticize after dinner, just as I have a mind, without ever becoming hunter, fisherman, herdsman or critic" (Marx, [1932] 1969: 22) and *at the same time prevents the realization of this possibility*. Keynes wrote similarly that "a point may soon be reached, much sooner perhaps than we all of us are aware of, when those needs are satisfied in the sense that we prefer to devote our further energies to non-economic purposes" (Keynes, [1930] 1972c: 326). He makes it clear that this actualization of a distinctly human potential that has lain dormant during all of humankind's history will create a "problem" of a different kind: how will people use this newfound freedom to "cultivate ... the art of life itself ... and not sell themselves for the means of life" (ibid.: 328). The desirability of a society of abundance was an ongoing concern of Keynes's. He alluded to the idea in a number of writings more than ten years after he wrote *Economic Possibilities*. "The natural evolution should be towards a decent level of consumption for everyone; and, when that is high enough, towards the occupation of our energies in the non-economic interests of our lives. Thus we need to be slowly reconstructing our social system with these ends in view" (Keynes, [1937] 1982c: 393).

The following passage from a 1934 BBC radio address exhibits Keynes's understanding that attention to underconsumption was the path to capitalist restoration: "When the rate of interest has fallen to a very low figure and has remained there sufficiently long to show that there is no further capital construction worth doing even at that low rate, then I should agree that the facts point to the necessity of drastic social changes directed towards increasing consumption. For it would be clear that we already had as great a stock of capital as we could usefully employ" (Keynes, 1934: 86). *Keynes here describes America's current condition: low interest rates, low levels of investment due to a surfeit of productive capital, and the need for higher levels of consumption.*

HOW WELL HAS KEYNES'S FORECAST OF AN ECONOMY OF ABUNDANCE HELD UP?

Keynes posed this question: "What can we reasonably expect the level of our economic life to be a hundred years hence? What are the economic possibilities for our grandchildren?" (Keynes, [1930] 1972c: 322). Two features of mature capitalism identified by Keynes place this question on the agenda. Capitalism will continue to grow output over the long run, and the productivity of both labor and capital will also grow (ibid.: 325). Since the costs of net additions to capital stock can be expected to decline (see Chapters 3, 7 and Appendix A), a number of novel possibilities are open for the first time in human history. With the superabundance of capital goods having made it subject to diminishing returns, *private investment would need to be replaced by public investment and by private and public consumption as the principal drivers of economic activity.*

The dramatic change in the *kind of society* that "the age of leisure and abundance" will bring about is so different from the way we have been living that we look forward to it with "a dread" (ibid.: 328). "For we have been trained for too long to strive and not to enjoy ... It is a fearful problem for the ordinary person, with no special talents, to occupy himself" (ibid.). The society of abundance and leisure requires of us *a different way of life* corresponding to a very different kind of society.

There is no reason to take this new way of being to be unattainable or unthinkable. Many people already identify skills they would like to develop, or activities they would care to pursue more fully, if only they "had the time." Glimmerings of a new species of freedom are discernible in existing popular dreams. Working people will develop a culture of their own, in contrast to what is imposed by advertising and the capitalist ethos, which includes celebrity culture and its images of excess. "[W]e shall use the new-found bounty of nature quite differently from the way in which the rich use it today, and will map out for ourselves a plan of life quite otherwise than theirs." (ibid.)

But is Keynes's vision realistic? Does it present us today with challenges we must take seriously? These are the questions taken up by 18 distinguished economists in *Revisiting Keynes*, devoted entirely to an assessment of *Economic Possibilities For Our Grandchildren* (Pecchi and Piga, 2010). The contributors unwittingly attest to a central contradiction in contemporary liberal thinking about the opportunities presented by the historical development of mature capitalism.

There is general agreement among the economists that Keynes's forecast that "the standard of life in progressive countries one hundred years hence [from 1930 to 2030] will be between four and eight times as high as it is today" is not only confirmed but has in fact been *overachieved*. Keynes's forecast implies an annual growth rate as high as 2.1 percent. In fact, the actual growth rate for the relevant grouping of countries between 1950 and 2000 was 2.9 percent; per capita GDP increased four times between 1950 and 2000, half the time forecast by Keynes. Projecting 2.9 percent over one century, we find a seventeen-fold increase in standards of living, "more than double Keynes's upper bound" (ibid.: 28). The overachievement of Keynes's growth forecast is, the economists concur, counterbalanced by the failure of his prediction of increased leisure time and a shorter work week to come to pass. Keynes was right that economic growth creates emancipatory possibilities, but wrong in thinking that these would be actualized.

This mainstream's obvious *Schadenfreude* is misconceived. That production and productivity must over the long run rise under capitalism is a structural requirement of the system. But whether or not the alternatives thereby made possible are seized is not an economic-structural outcome. It is a matter of political struggle. Keynes never fully acknowledged the realities of class power and effective class conflict, i.e. class struggle. He imagined that if a given alternative was "rational" and "civilized" and in the interests of most, then either members of the capitalist class would do the rational thing, or, if they resisted, they could be persuaded to do so by the gentle cajoling of enlightened, civic-minded State managers. But why would capitalists resign themselves to an arrangement whereby workers spent virtually all of their much-shortened work time producing what they need for a comfortable life and practically no time creating profit for capitalists? Confronted with a situation "in which capital [and profit] is so abundant that the community as a whole has no reasonable use for any more," capitalists have found uses for further investment funds which contribute not to making available to all what is necessary for a secure and satisfying life but to increasing the financial assets and consumption levels of the wealthy.

The uses to which advances in production and productivity will be put depends upon who *owns and controls* society's means of production and the surplus it generates, and the *kind of society* created by the mode of disposition of the surplus. The desire to maintain an egalitarian society will rest upon a number of foundational commitments, among which will surely be the imperative that *society will choose to produce luxuries, defined as goods and services beyond what is necessary for a comfortable and secure living, only after the necessities have become available to all.* By this principle, American society is currently able to provide both abundance, as Keynes understood it, along with a pleasing budget of luxuries to its entire population. An MIT study found that, as of 2000, "An average worker needs to work a mere 11 hours per week to produce as much as one working 40 hours per week in 1950 … [A] worker should be able to earn the same standard of living as a 1950 worker in only 11 hours per week … [T]he average worker could have a 29-hour work week if he were satisfied with producing as much as a 40-hour worker as recently as 1990" (Rauch, 2000). Were these figures adjusted to subtract from production the output required to support the rising superfluous luxury consumption of the very wealthy, the resulting work week would be notably shorter still. That a "just living wage" is not provided is explained by the contributors to *Revisiting Keynes* in ways which reveal more than the authors intend.

Lorenzo Pecchi and Gustavo Piga assert that "it is hard to believe that there will come a moment when people feel that the economic problem is solved and capital accumulation comes to an end. The aspiration for improvement is always there, no matter what level of living standard has been achieved, and with it the need to save, accumulate and work" (Pecci and Piga, 2010: 12). The key term here is "improvement," which to the authors means increased consumption. This reflects the "unlimited wants" component of the neoclassical scarcity thesis. But human improvement surely encompasses more than material consumption. The authors cite John Stuart Mill as another political economist who affirmed the desirability of the "stationary state" and the specific kinds of improvement it would make generally available. In remarking on how "striking" (ibid.: 15) the similarity is between *Economic Possibilities* and Mill's stationary state, they note that for Mill "a stationary condition of capital and population does not imply a stationary state of human improvements." Indeed not, but this is because the improvements Mill had in mind were quite different from the economists' and more in line with Marx's and Keynes's. As Mill put it in *Principles of Political Economy with Some of their Applications to Social Philosophy*, "There will be as much scope as ever for all kinds of mental culture, and moral and social progress; as much room for improving the Art of Living, and much more likelihood of its being improved, when minds cease to be engrossed by the art of getting on … Even the industrial arts might be cultivated, with the sole difference, that instead of serving no purpose but the increase of wealth, industrial improvements would produce their legitimate effect, that of abridging labor" (Mill, [1848] 1909: 339–40). Mill seems to be suggesting, by characterizing these possibilities as the "legitimate effect" of "industrial improvements," that the very point of technological advance is to reduce necessary labor time and thus create the possibility of cultural progress for working people.

ABUNDANCE, LEISURE AND CONSUMERISM

The most common justificatory explanation offered by the contributors to *Revisiting Keynes* of why Keynes's forecast of less work and greater leisure has not been met is that increases in production and productivity have instead led to increased consumption. Bradford DeLong expresses the most widely propagated critique of Keynes's thesis, that he underestimated the magnitude of our desires for "more of the necessities, conveniences, and luxuries of life … We know that we want hip replacements and heart transplants and fertility treatment and cheap air travel and central heating and broadband Internet and exclusive beachfront access" (DeLong, 2013).

It is peculiar to include advances in healthcare and "exclusive beachfront access" in a list of "our" current preferences. We shall surely want to distinguish preferences whose principle contribution to human well-being is to increase profits and/or luxury consumption from those which any reasonable person would see as contributing to human welfare under any political-economic arrangements. Joseph Stiglitz notes that among the former preferences are desires most of which would not exist

> but for advertising and marketing efforts by business and which are unnecessary if the priority is to provide a decent standard of living for all … [A]dvertising and marketing help shape preferences – and firms have

been as inventive in creating new demands as they have been in creating new products. ... Preferences are, at least in part, socially determined ... we are "taught" to consume by others, especially by firms ... There are biases in market forces: there are stronger incentives to "distort" preferences in certain directions, and these market forces have played a relatively larger role in America than elsewhere. (Pecchi and Piga, 2010: 56–7, 53)

What Stiglitz would regard as unmanipulated desires are what is reasonably thought to be a component of a comfortable life *given what the economy is capable of delivering*: the standard of living corresponding to a "just living wage." Anything beyond this level of consumption is considered wasteful *under circumstances of abundance and inequality*. These circumstances include the volume of output currently physically possible, what we have determined constitutes the highest standard of living available to all, given existing resources, and the prevailing distribution of income and wealth. In sum, the fact that much of current consumption and resource allocation is wasteful must be taken into account in determining whether we can "afford" shorter work hours at higher wages.

If society's resources are such that employment at a just living wage, education and healthcare can be provided to all with no sacrifice of anything equally or more valuable, then that society is to that extent a society of abundance. If some in that society are, through no fault of their own, deprived of these benefits while others enjoy superfluities of consumption, then we do not live in the kind of society that provides what we are entitled to.

Since much consumption is stimulated by false or misleading claims about alleged benefits, coming to see these claims as false can change certain patterns of consumption. There is no reason to doubt that consumers might come to regard certain habits of consumption as not only bad for themselves but productive of the kind of society they do not want to live in, and on that basis change their consumption habits. Stiglitz provides an example: cigarettes are now known to have been manufactured to make them *more* addictive after their addictive character had been demonstrated, much as advertising boomed in the 1920s once it had been established that ads boosted sales. Consumption patterns are after all habitual, and addiction is a species of habit. Consumers became aware of the addictive nature of nicotine and on the basis of their new understandings stopped smoking. "[I]ndividuals preferred not to have their preferences deformed in this way" (ibid.: 60–1). Persons stopped doing what they would not have done in the first place had they been better informed. A combination of existing ecological awareness and the painful realization by many debtors that their consumption patterns are uncomfortably close to addictive can lead to a comparable reassessment of consumption in general.

PRODUCTIVITY GROWTH: ABUNDANCE AND LEISURE OR SUPERPROFITS AND INEQUALITY

Because fewer inputs, of both capital *and* labor, are required to produce a given quantity of output, the share of profits in national income tends to grow larger. As Robert Solow points out in *Revisiting Keynes*, "The distribution of income and output between wages and profits depends on the ease with which capital can be substituted for labor" (ibid.: 92). Since production has, under ripened capitalism, become increasingly capital-intensive, and technological unemployment has been supplemented by speedup and outsourcing, capital's share of total income has never been higher than it is today.

Keynes imagined that rational legislation and a Board of National Investment given substantial planning powers could redistribute income on the required scale. I emphasize that the redistributional imperative urged by democratic egalitarians is especially urgent since it goes against powerful structural tendencies generated by mature capitalism. Robert Solow recognizes that the settlement described in *Economic Possibilities* puts this issue squarely on the table; if minimal requirements of distributive justice are to be met, property relations in the means of production will have to be radicalized. Solow's analysis is remarkable, coming as it does from one of America's most prominent MIT economists:

> If this kind of substitution [of capital for labor] is relatively easy ... profits will come over time to absorb an ever-increasing share of aggregate income ... That seems like a plausible outcome in Keynes's imagined world where technical progress and capital accumulation have "solved the economic problem." (The extreme case of this is the common scare about universal robots: labor is no longer needed at all. How will we live then?) The answer seems pretty clear. For the grandchildren ... to have a viable world, the ownership of capital will have to be democratized. If capital is the only source of income that matters, then everyone who matters – in other words, everyone – will need an adequate claim of income from capital ... Not much thought has been given to this problem. (Ibid.: 92–3)

Keynes thought it entirely possible that the determination of the incomes of both workers and "entrepreneurs" be established by the State. This would politicize the distribution of income to labor and to capital. The chronic deficiency of effective consumption demand, the failure of remunerative investment opportunities to materialize in step with increases in profits, and the superabundance of capital converge on the same vector – the need for an enlargement of the scope of democratic State activities to include what was once the province of the class of private investors. This includes the redistribution of income and increased household consumption. The "somewhat comprehensive socialization of investment" supervised by a Board of National Investment recommended by Keynes would be required of a society in which there is no longer a scarcity of capital, and therefore no longer the remuneration required to provide capitalists with an incentive to invest (Keynes, [1936] 1964: 378). "The remedy would lie in various measures designed to increase the propensity to consume by the redistribution of income or otherwise; so that a given level of employment would require a smaller volume of current investment to support it" (ibid.: 324).

A FINAL WORD ON THE INDISPENSABILITY, UNDER CAPITALISM, OF SUBSTANTIAL DEFICITS — PUBLIC OR PRIVATE

Government spending under the permanent condition of insufficient private demand must be in excess of tax receipts, because these represent a portion of already insufficient private demand. Since the gap between actual and potential output grows with an ever-growing economy, the magnitude of the government spending deficit must be substantial. Keynes's analysis logically implies that a persistent government deficit is essential if severe economic downturn is to be averted. During the 1920s and, as we saw in Chapter 5 during the postwar period, a growing deficit was required to support the largest portion of total demand (66–72 percent), household consumption spending. The seven historical U.S. attempts to balance the budget and reduce the national debt have been most revealing: each has resulted in depression or recession. The first six of the seven attempts to balance the budget and reduce the national debt (1817–21, 1823–36, 1852–7, 1867–73, 1880–93 and 1920–30) were quickly followed by depressions (Thayer, 1996). The seventh, Clinton's 1998–9 surplus, was followed by a crash eight years later. The delay was effected by a historic boost to demand provided by the unprecedented household credit explosion of the late 1990s up to the crash of September 2008.

Note that deficits averted economic downturn in America before the Keynesian era and the Roosevelt administration. Many severe recessions and depressions characterized the period of industrialization. During the 1920s, when wages barely moved while production and especially productivity soared, an underconsumption/overinvestment crisis was avoided by a mounting *private sector deficit*, i.e. growing consumer debt. Deficits are indispensable to mature capitalism because, as Keynes showed, the private market by itself cannot generate sufficient spending to maintain production, profits, employment and wages. Thus, spending over and above what the market makes possible must materialize. In the short run it makes no difference whether the spending over current income originates in the private or the public sector. But the long run is another story. The "magic of compound interest" and the pressures to keep labor costs low contribute to a tendency to make long-term private debt finally unpayable (Hudson, 2017: 44–5, 60–3, 72, 311–21). This is illustrated for the 1920s and the postwar period in Chapters 3, 6 and 7. Federal government deficits, on the other hand, are not bound to end in crisis or default.

We may conclude that the normal state of the U.S. economy is severe recession or depression if the economy is left to the dynamics of the unfettered market. Government deficit spending is necessary if economic crisis is to be averted.

Bibliography

Abramsky, Sasha (2014). *The American Way of Poverty: How the Other Half Still Lives*. New York: Nation Books.

Acemoglu, Daron (1999). "Changes in Employment and Wage Inequality: An Alternative Theory and Some Evidence," *American Economic Review*. Vol. 89, No. 5.

Acemoglu, Daron and Restrepo, Pascual (2016). "The Race Between Machine and Man: Implications of Technology For Growth, Factor Shares and Employment", *National Bureau of Economic Research*. Working Paper No. 22252, May. www.nber.org/papers/w22252

Acemoglu, Daron and Restrepo, Pascual (2017). "Robots and Jobs: Evidence From U.S. Labor Markets," *National Bureau of Economic Research*. Working Paper No. 23285, March. www.nber.org/papers/w23285

Ackerman, Frank and MacEwan, Arthur (1972). "Inflation, Recession and Crisis, Or, Would You Buy a New Car From This Man," *The Review of Radical Political Economics*. Summer.

Acs, Gregory and Zimmerman, Seth (2008). "U.S. Intergenerational Economic Mobility From 1984 to 2004: Trends and Implications," *The Pew Charitable Trust*.

Ahmed, Nafeez (2014). "Pentagon preparing for mass civil breakdown," *The Guardian*. June 12. www.theguardian.com/environment/earth-insight/2014/jun/12/pentagon-mass-civil-breakdown

Ahmed, Nafeez (2015). "The Pentagon's secret pre-crime program to know your thoughts, predict your future," *Insurgent Intelligence*. February 1. https://medium.com/insurge-intelligence/the-pentagon-s-secret-pre-crime-program-c7d281eca440#.ue4qzvow7

Albert, Michael (2004). *Parecon: Life After Capitalism*. London: Verso.

Albritton, Robert et al. (2002). *Phases of Capitalist Development: Booms, Crises and Globalizations*. New York: Palgrave Macmillan.

Alloway, Tracy and Weisenthal, Jason (2015). "Goldman Sachs Says Corporate America Has Quietly Re-levered," *Bloomberg*. November 23. www.bloomberg.com/professional/blog/goldman-sachs-says-corporate-america-has-quietly-re-levered/

Alperovitz, Gar (2006). *America Beyond Capitalism: Reclaiming Our Wealth, Our Liberty, and Our Democracy*. Hoboken, New Jersey: John Wiley & Sons.

Alperovitz, Gar (2013). *What Then Must We Do?: Straight Talk About the Next American Revolution*. Vermont: Chelsea Green Publishing.

Altschuler, Glenn and Blumin, Stuart (2009). *The G.I. Bill: The New Deal For Veterans*. New York: Oxford University Press.

American Civil Liberties Union (2014). *War Comes Home at America's Expense: The Excessive Militarization of American Policing*. June. www.aclu.org/sites/default/files/assets/jus14-warcomeshome-report-web-rel1.pdf

American Social History Project (1992). *Who Built America? Volume Two*. New York: Pantheon Books.

Ansell, David (2017) *The Death Gap: How Inequality Kills*. Chicago: The University of Chicago Press.

Apuzzo, Matt and Liptak, Adam (2015). "At Supreme Court, Eric Holder's Justice Dept. Routinely Backs Officers' Use of Force," *The New York Times*. April 21. www.nytimes.

com/2015/04/22/us/at-supreme-court-holders-justice-dept-routinely-backs-officers-use-of-force.html

Archer, Jules (2007). *The Plot to Seize the White House*. New York: Hawthorn Books.

Arndt, H. W. (1972). *The Economic Lessons of the Nineteen-Thirties*. London: Frank Cass and Company Ltd.

Arthur, W. Brian (2011). "The Second Economy," *McKinsey Quarterly*. October. www.mckinsey.com/insights/strategy/the_second_economy?p=1

Arthur, W. Brian (2017). "Where is Technology Taking the Economy?" *McKinsey Quarterly*. October. https://www.mckinsey.com/business-functions/mckinsey-analytics/our-insights/where-is-technology-taking-the-economy

Atack, Jeremy (1979). "Fact in Fiction? The Relative Costs of Steam and Water Power: A Simulation Approach," *Explorations in Economic History*. Vol. 16: 409–37.

Atack, Jeremy and Passell, Peter (1994). *A New Economic View of American History*. New York: W.W. Norton & Co.

Auerbach, Jerold S. (1966). *Labor and Liberty: The La Follette Committee and the New Deal*. New York: Bobbs-Merrill.

Ausick, Paul (2016). "Berkeley: 1 in 3 US Manufacturing Workers Get Public Aid," *24/7 Wall Street*. May 10. http://247wallst.com/jobs/2016/05/10/berkeley-1-in-3-us-manufacturing-workers-get-public-aid/

Autor, David H. et al. (2006). The Polarization of the U.S. Labor Market," *American Economic Review*. Vol. 96, No. 2.

Autor, David (2010). The Polarization of Job Opportunities in the U.S. Labor Market," *The Hamilton Project* and *The Center for American Progress*. April. http://economics.mit.edu/files/5554

Badger, Anthony J. (1989). *The New Deal: The Depression Years, 1933–40*. London: Macmillan.

Baker, Dean (2007). "The Productivity to Wages Gap: What the Data Show," *Center For Economic and Policy Research*. http://www.cepr.net/documents/publications/growth_failure_2007_04.pdf

Bakija, Jon et al. (2010). "Jobs and Income Growth of Top Earners and the Causes of Changing Income Inequality: Evidence From U.S. Tax Return Data," School of Public and Environmental Affairs, Indiana University. November. www.indiana.edu/~spea/faculty/pdf/heim_JobsIncomeGrowthTopEarners.pdf

Balke, Nathan and Gordon, Robert S. (1989). "Estimation of Prewar Gross National Product: Methodology and New Evidence," *Journal of Political Economy*. February.

Balko, Radley (2013). *Rise of the Warrior Cop: The Militarization of America's Police Forces*. New York: Public Affairs.

Barajas, Joshua (2014). "Smart robots will take over a third of jobs by 2025, Gartner says," *PBS Newshour*. October 7. www.pbs.org/newshour/rundown/smart-robots-will-take-third-jobs-2025-gartner-says/

Baran, Paul and Sweezy, Paul (1966). *Monopoly Capital*. New York: Monthly Review Press.

Barber, William J. (1996). *Designs Within Disorder: Franklin D. Roosevelt, the Economists, and the Shaping of American Economic Policy, 1933–1935*. New York: Cambridge University Press.

Barkai, Simcha (2017). "Declining Labor and Capital Shares," *Graduate School of Business, Stanford University*. www.gsb.stanford.edu/sites/gsb/files/jmp_simcha-barkai.pdf

Barnet, Richard J. and Muller, Ronald E. (1974). "Companies Go Abroad, and Jobs Go Along," *The New York Times*. December 22.

Barofsky, Neil (2011). "Where the Bailout Went Wrong," *The New York Times*. March 29. www.nytimes.com/2011/03/30/opinion/30barofsky.html

Barofsky, Neil (2012). *Bailout: An Inside Account of How Washington Abandoned Main Street While Rescuing Wall Street*. New York: The Free Press.

Bartels, Larry M. (2008). *Unequal Democracy: The Political Economy of the New Gilded Age*. New York: Russell Sage Foundation and Princeton University Press.

Beitel, Karl (2009). "The Rate of Profit and the Problem of Stagnant Investment: A Structural Analysis of Barriers to Accumulation and the Spectre of Protracted Crisis," *Historical Materialism*. Vol. 17.

Bennett, Michael J. (1999). *When Dreams Come True: The G.I. Bill and the Making of Modern America*. Dulles, Virginia: Potomac Books Inc.

Bernanke, B. S. (2003). "The Jobless Recovery," *Federal Reserve System*. http://www.federalreserve.gov/boarddoc/speeches/2003/200311062/default.htm

Bernanke, B. S. (2009). "On the Outlook For the Economy and Policy," *Federal Reserve System*. www.federalreserve.gov/newsevents/speech/bernanke20091116a.htm

Bernays, Edward [1928] (2005). *Propaganda*. New York: IG Publishing.

Beynon, Huw (1973). *Working For Ford*. London: Allen Lane.

Bivens, Josh (2014). "The Top 1 percent's Share of Income From Wealth Has Been Rising For Decades," *Economic Policy Institute*. Economic Snapshot. April 23. www.epi.org/publication/top-1-percents-share-income-wealth-rising/

Bivens, Josh and Mishel, Lawrence (2015). "Understanding the Historic Divergence Between Productivity and a Typical Worker's Pay: Why It Matters and Why It's Real," *Economic Policy Institute*. September 2.

Blair, John M. (1974). "Market Power and Inflation: A Short-Run Target Return Model," *Journal of Economic Issues*. June 8: 453–78.

Block, Fred (1984). "The Myth of Reindustrialization," *Socialist Review*. Vol. 14, No. 1.

Bluestone, Barry and Harrison, Bennett (1982). *The Deindustrialization of America*. New York: Basic Books.

Blyth, Mark (2002). *Great Transformations: Economic Ideas and Institutional Change in the Twentieth Century*. Cambridge: Cambridge University Press.

Boddy, Raford and Crotty, James (1974). "Class Conflict, Keynesian Policies, and the Business Cycle," *Monthly Review*. October.

Boddy, Raford and Crotty, James (1975). "Class Conflict and Macro-Policy: The Political Business Cycle," *The Review of Radical Political Economics*. Spring.

Bolch, Ben et al. (1971). "Housing Surplus in the 1920s?" *Explorations in Economic History*. Vol. 8.

Bowles, Jeremy (2014). "The Computerization of European Jobs," Breugel. http://bruegel.org/2014/07/the-computerisation-of-european-jobs/

Bowles, Samuel et al. (1984). *Beyond the Wasteland*. New York: Doubleday.

Bradford, John Hamilton (2010). *Systems, Social Order, and the Global Debt Crisis*. PhD dissertation, University of Tennessee. http://trace.tennessee.edu/utk_graddiss/778

Braverman, Harry (1974). *Labor and Monopoly Capitalism*. New York: Monthly Review Press.

Brecher, Jeremy (1972). *Strike!*. Boston: South End Press.

Brenner, Harvey (1973). *Mental Illness and the Economy*. Cambridge, MA.: Harvard University Press.

Brenner, Harvey (1976). *Estimating the Social Costs of National Economic Policy: Implications for Mental and Physical Health, and Criminal Aggression*. Ann Arbor: University of Michigan Library.

Brenner, Harvey (1984). *Estimating the Effects of Economic Change on National Health and Social Well-Being*. Ann Arbor: University of Michigan Library.

Brenner, Robert (1999). *Turbulence in the World Economy*. London: Verso.

Brenner, Robert (2006). *The Economics of Global Turbulence: The Advanced Capitalist Economies From Long Boom to Long Downturn, 1945–2005*. London: Verso.

Brettell, Karen et al. (2015). "The Cannibalized Company," *Reuters*. November 16. www.reuters.com/investigates/special-report/usa-buybacks-cannibalized/

Brinkley, Alan (1996). *The End of Reform: New Deal Liberalism in Recession and War*. New York: Vintage.

Bromwich, David (2015) "Are We 'Exceptionally Rapacious Primates'?" *The New York Review of Books*. November 5. www.nybooks.com/articles/2015/11/05/are-we-exceptionally-rapacious-primates/

Bruner, Robert F. and Carr, Sean D. (2007). *The Panic of 1907: Lessons Learned From the Market's Perfect Storm*. Hoboken: John Wiley & Sons.

Bruno, Michael and Sachs, Jeffrey (1985). *Economics of Worldwide Stagflation*. Cambridge, MA: Harvard University Press.

Brynjolfsson, Erik and McAfee, Andrew (2011a). *Race Against the Machine*. Lexington, MA: Digital Frontier Press.

Brynjolfsson, Erik and McAfee, Andrew (2011b). "The Workers Are Losing the War Against Machines," *The Atlantic*. October 26. www.theatlantic.com/business/archive/2011/10/why-workers-are-losing-the-war-against-machines/247278/

Brynjolfsson, Erik and McAfee, Andrew (2014). *The Second Machine Age*. New York: W.W. Norton and Co.

Brynjolfsson, Erik and McAfee, Andrew (2015). "Will Humans Go the Way of Horses? Labor in the Second Machine Age," Foreign Affairs. Vol. 94, No. 4. www.foreignaffairs.com/system/files/pdf/articles/2015/94402.pdf

Buchheit, Paul (2014). "Overwhelming Evidence That Half of America is In or Near Poverty," Alternet. March 23. www.alternet.org/economy/overwhelming-evidence-half-america-or-near-poverty

Buchheit, Paul (2017). *Disposable Americans: Extreme Capitalism and the Case For a Guaranteed Income*. New York: Routledge.

Bureau of Labor Statistics (1973). "Work Stoppages in the United States," Handbook of Labor Statistics. Washington, DC: Government Printing Office.

Burger, Albert (1973). "Relative Movements in Wages and Profits," *Federal Reserve Bank of St. Louis Review 55*, February.

Burns, Joe (2011). *Reviving the Strike: How Working People Can Regain Power and Transform America*. Brooklyn, NY: IG Press.

Burns, Joe (2014). *Strike Back: Using the Militant Tactics of Labor's Past to Reignite Public Sector Unionism Today*. Brooklyn, NY: IG Press.

Business Week (1974a). "Did Controls Flunk Their First Peacetime Test?" April 27.

Business Week (1974b). *Special Issue: The Debt Economy*. October 12.

Business Week (1985). Editorial, September 16.

Butler, Smedley Darlington (1935). *War Is a Racket*. New York: Round Table Press, Inc.

Cain, Louis P. and Paterson, Donald G. (1986). "Biased Technical Change, Scale, and Factor Substitution in American Industry, 1850–1919," *Journal of Economic History*. Vol. 46, No. 1: 153–64.

Calkins, Clinch (1937). *Spy Overhead: The Story of Industrial Espionage*. New York: Harcourt, Brace and Co.

Camacho, Daniel José (2017). "Hillary Clinton is More Unpopular Than Donald Trump: Let That Sink In," *The Guardian*. July 19. www.theguardian.com/commentisfree/2017/jul/19/hillary-clinton-donald-trump-unpopular-polling

Canon, Maria and Marifian, Elise (2013). "Job Polarization Leaves Middle-Skilled Workers Out in the Cold." The Federal Reserve Bank of St. Louis. *Regional Economist,*

January. www.stlouisfed.org/Publications/Regional-Economist/January-2013/Job-Polarization-Leaves-MiddleSkilled-Workers-Out-in-the-Cold

Capie, Forrest and Wood, Geoffrey (1997). "Great Depression of 1873–1896," in David Glasner and Thomas F. Cooley, *Business Cycles and Depressions: An Encyclopedia*. New York: Garland Publishing.

Carey, Alex (1996). *Taking the Risk Out of Democracy*. Champagne-Urbana: University of Illinois Press.

Carr, Michael D. and Wiemers, Emily D. (2016). "The Decline in Lifetime Earnings Mobility in the U.S.: Evidence From Survey-Linked Administrative data," *Washington Center For Equitable Growth*. September 7. https://tinyurl.com/gwbfd4s

Carter, Ashton (2015a). "Secretary of Defense Speech: Remarks on the Next Phase of the U.S. Rebalance to the Asia-Pacific," *U.S. Department of Defense*. April 6. www.defense.gov/News/Speeches/Speech-View/Article/606660

Carter, Jimmy (1978). *State of the Union Address*. www.presidency.ucsb.edu/ws/?pid=30856

Case, Anne and Deaton, Angus (2015). "Rising morbidity and mortality in midlife among white non-Hispanic Americans in the 21st century," *Proceedings of the National Academy of Sciences of the United States*. September 17. www.pnas.org/content/112/49/15078.full.pdf

Casselman, Ben (2015). "Most Americans Aren't Middle Class Anymore," *FiveThirtyEight*. December 9. http://fivethirtyeight.com/features/most-americans-arent-middle-class-anymore/

Cassidy, John (2014). "Is America an Oligarchy?" *The New Yorker*. April 18. www.newyorker.com/news/john-cassidy/is-america-an-oligarchy

Center on Budget and Policy Priorities (2016). "Chart Book: The Legacy of the Great Recession." May 10. http://www.cbpp.org/research/economy/chart-book-the-legacy-of-the-great-recession

Chafe, William H. (2009). *The Rise and Fall of the American Century: United States from 1890–2009*. New York: Oxford University Press.

Chandler, Alfred D., Jr. (1965). *The Railroads: The Nation's First Big Business*. New York: Harcourt, Brace.

Chandler, Alfred D., Jr. (1967). "The Large Industrial Corporation and the Making of the Modern American Economy," in Stephen E. Ambrose (ed.), *Institutions in Modern America: Innovation in Structure and Process*. Baltimore: The Johns Hopkins University Press.

Chandler, Alfred D., Jr. (1977). *The Visible Hand: The Managerial Revolution in American Business*. Cambridge, MA: The Belknap Press.

Chang, Ha-Joon (2011). "Five False Premises About Economic Recovery," *The Wall Street Journal*. August 7.

Cheng, Andria (2015). "Record number of manufacturing jobs returning to America," *Marketwatch*. May 1. www.marketwatch.com/story/us-flips-the-script-on-jobs-reshoring-finally-outpaced-offshoring-in-2014-2015-05-01

Chernow, Ron (2010). *The House of Morgan: An American Banking Dynasty and the Rise of Modern Finance*. New York: The Grove Press.

Chui, Michael et al. (2015). "Four Fundamentals of Workplace Automation," *McKinsey Quarterly*. November. www.mckinsey.com/business-functions/business-technology/our-insights/four-fundamentals-of-workplace-automation

Clark, General Wesley (2015). Interview on MSNBC. July 17. www.youtube.com/watch?v=eaPwqokBn9M

Clement, Scott and Balz, Dan (2017). "Poll Finds Trump's Standing Weakened Since Springtime," *The Washington Post*. July 16. https://tinyurl.com/yasz8gkj

Clews, Henry (1908). *Fifty Years On Wall Street*. New York: Irving Publishing Co.

Clinton, Bill (1996). *State of the Union Address*. January 27. http://clinton2.nara.gov/WH/New/other/sotu.html

Clinton, Bill (1999). "The Longest Period of Peacetime Economic Expansion in American History," *The White House*. January 8. https://clinton2.nara.gov/WH/Work/010899.html

Cochran, Thomas C. (1957). *The American Business System*. Cambridge: Harvard University Press.

Cogan, John F. (1993). "Federal Budget." *The Concise Encyclopedia of Economics*. Library of Economics and Liberty. www.econlib.org/library/Enc1/FederalBudget.html

Cohen, Patricia (2017). "Steady Jobs, With Pay and Hours That Are Anything But," *The New York Times*. May 31. www.nytimes.com/2017/05/31/business/economy/volatile-income-economy-jobs.html?_r=0

Cohan, Peter (2010). "Big Risk: $1.2 Quadrillion Derivatives Market Dwarfs World GDP," *Daily Finance*. June 9. www.dailyfinance.com/2010/06/09/risk-quadrillion-derivatives-market-gdp/

Collins, Chuck and Hoxie, Josh (2015). "Billionaire Bonanza: The Forbes 400 and the Rest of Us," *Institute For Policy Studies*. December 1. http://www.ips-dc.org/billionaire-bonanza/

Condon, Bernard and Weissman, Paul (2013). "Recession, Tech Kill Middle-Class Jobs," Associated Press Yahoo!News," March 23. www.yahoo.com/news/ap-impact-recession-tech-kill-middle-class-jobs-051306434--finance.html?ref=gs

Conerly, Bill (2014). "Reshoring Or Offshoring: U.S. Manufacturing Forecast 2015–2016," *Forbes*. September 2. www.forbes.com/sites/billconerly/2014/09/02/reshoring-or-offshoring-u-s-manufacturing-forecast-2015-2016/#2f9b3ba67419

Coontz, Sidney (1965). *Productive Labor and Effective Demand*. New York: Routledge & Kegan Paul.

Cooper, Jerry (1980). *The Army and Civil Disorder: Federal Military Intervention in Labor Disputes, 1877–1900*. Westport, CN: Greenwood Publishing Group.

Cooper, Ryan (2015). "Why Poor White Americans Are Dying of Despair," *The Hill*. November 6. http://theweek.com/articles/587242/why-poor-white-americans-are-dying-despair

Corbett, Jenny and Jenkinson, Tim (1996). "The Financing of Industry, 1970–1989: An International Comparison," *Journal of the Japanese and the International Economies*, Vol. 10.

Corbett, Jenny and Jenkinson, Tim (1997). "How Is Investment Financed? A Study of Germany, Japan, the United Kingdom and the United States," *Papers in Money, Macroeconomics and Finance. The Manchester School Supplement XLV*.

Corey, Lewis (1934). *The Decline of American Capitalism*. New York: Covici-Friede.

Council of Economic Advisors (1948). *Economic Report of the President*. New York: Reynal & Hitchcock.

Council of Economic Advisors (2000). *Economic Report of the President*. Table 30. Various years. Washington, DC: U.S. Government Printing Office.

Creamer, Daniel (1954). *Capital and Output Trends in Manufacturing Industries, 1880–1948*. Occasional Paper No. 41. New York: National Bureau of Economic Research.

Creel, George (1920). *How We Advertised America*. New York: Macmillan.

Crotty, James (2002a). "Why Do Global Markets Suffer From Chronic Excess Capacity? Insights from Keynes, Schumpeter and Marx." The University of Massachusetts. http://people.umass.edu/crotty/Challenge-drft-Jn18-02.pdf

Crotty, James (2002b). "Why Is There Chronic Excess Capacity?" *Challenge*. November–December.

Crotty, James (2005). "The Neoliberal Paradox: The Impact of Destructive Product Market Competition and 'Modern' Financial Markets on Nonfinancial Corporation Performance in the Neoliberal Era," in Epstein, G. (ed.), *Financialization and the World Economy*. Northampton, MA: Edward Elgar.

Davidson, Adam (2012). ""Skills Don't Pay the Bills," *The New York Times*. November 20. www.nytimes.com/2012/11/25/magazine/skills-dont-pay-the-bills.html

Davies, Gavyn (2013). "The Implications of Secular Stagnation," *Financial Times*. November 17.

Davis, Steven J. et al. (2011). "Private Equity and Employment," *National Bureau of Economic Research*. Working Paper 17399. www.nber.org/papers/w17399

DeLong, J. Bradford (2013). "Inequality on the Horizon of Need," *Project Syndicate*, May 30. www.project-syndicate.org/commentary/a-long-run-economic-destiny-of-mounting-inequality-by-j--bradford-delong

Denton, Sally (2012). *The Plots Against the President: FDR, A Nation in Crisis, and the Rise of the American Right*. New York: Bloomsbury Press.

Diamond, Marie (2011). "On the 15th Anniversary of 'Welfare Reform,' Aid Is Not Getting To Those Who Need It Most," *Think Progress*. August 22. http://thinkprogress.org/economy/2011/08/22/301231/tanf-15-anniversary/

Dobbs, Richard et al. (2015). "Playing To Win: The New Global Competition for Corporate Profits," *McKinsey Global Institute*. September. MGI Global Competition_Full Report_Sep 2015.pdf

Domar, Evsey (1953). "Depreciation, Replacement and Growth," *Economic Journal*. Vol. 63 : 1–33.

Domar, Evsey (1957). "Depreciation, Replacement and Growth – and Fluctuations," *Economic Journal*. Vol. 67, No. 268.

Draut, Tamara and Silva, Javier (2003). "Borrowing To Make Ends Meet: The Growth of Credit Card Debt in the '90s," *Demos*. www.demos.org/sites/default/files/publications/borrowing_to_make_ends_meet.pdf

Drucker, Peter F. (1949). *The New Society*. New York: Harper and Brothers.

DuBoff, Richard B. (1989). *Accumulation and Power*. Armonck, NY: M.E. Sharpe, Inc.

Dubofsky, Melvyn et al. (1978). *The United States in the Twentieth Century*. Englewood Cliffs, NJ: Prentice-Hall.

Dubofsky, Melvyn (1996). *Industrialism and the American Worker 1865–1920*. Wheeling, IL: Harlan Davidson, Inc.

Dumenil, Gerard et al. (1992). "Stages in the Development of U.S. Capitalism: Trends in Profitability and Technology Since the Civil War," in Moseley, Fred and Wolff, Edward (eds), *International Perspectives on Profitability and Accumulation*. Aldershot: Edward Elgar.

Dumenil, Gerard and Levy, Dominique (2011). *The Crisis of Neoliberalism*. Cambridge, MA: Harvard University Press.

Duncan, Richard (2012). *The New Depression*. Singapore: John Wiley & Sons.

Dunn, Bill (2014). *The Political Economy of Global Capitalism and Crisis*. New York: Routledge.

Eccles, Marriner (1951). *Beckoning Frontiers: Public and Personal Reflections*. New York: Alfred A. Knopf.

Economic Intelligence Service (1938). *World Economic Survey, Seventh Year, 1937–38*. Geneva: League of Nations.

Economic Policy Institute (1999). "Income Distribution and Wall Street," Economic Snapshots. http://www.epinet.org/webfeatures/snapshots/archive/120199/snapshots120199.htm

Economic Policy Institute (2016). "The Productivity–Pay Gap." August. https://tinyurl.
    com/y963dbwd
Economic Report of the President (1985, 1992, 1989, 1999). Washington, DC: Bibliogov.
The Economist (1986). "Corporate Finance." June 8.
The Economist (1998). "Bonds That Rock and Roll." May 7.
The Economist (2012). "Non-Bank Finance: Filling the Bank-Shaped Hole." December 15.
The Economist (2014). "The Future of Jobs: The Onrushing Wave." January 18. www.
    economist.com/node/21594264/print
Edin, Kathryn and Shaefer, H. Luke (2012). "Extreme Poverty in the United States, 1996–
    2011," *Policy Brief*, National Poverty Center. February.
Edin, Kathryn and Shaefer, H. Luke (2015). *$2.00 a Day: Living on Almost Nothing in
    America*. New York: Houghton Mifflin.
Edmunds, John C. (1996). "Securities: The New World Wealth Machine," *Foreign Policy*.
    Fall.
Edwards, P. K. (1981). *Strikes in the United States, 1881–1974*. New York: Palgrave
    Macmillan.
Edwards, Richard (1979). *Contested Terrain: The Transformation of the Workplace in the
    Twentieth Century*. New York: Basic Books.
Ehrenreich, John (2016). *Third Wave Capitalism*. Ithaca: Cornell University Press.
Elliott, Larry (2016). "Beware the great 2016 financial crisis, warns leading City pessimist,"
    The Guardian. https://tinyurl.com/yakhlxpq
Epstein, Abraham (1936). *Insecurity, a Challenge to America: A Study of Social Insurance in
    the United States and Abroad*. New York: Harrison Smith and Robert Haas.
Epstein, Ralph C. (1934). *Industrial Profits in the United States*. New York: National Bureau
    of Economic Research.
Fabricant, Solomon (1940). *The Output of Manufacturing Industries, 1899–1937*. New York:
    National Bureau of Economic Research.
Falkner, Harold U. (1959). *Politics, Reform and Expansion: 1890–1900*. New York: Harper
    & Row.
Fandos, Nicholas et al. (2017). "House Intelligence Committee Releases Incendiary Russia
    Social Media Ads," *The New York Times*. November 1. www.nytimes.com/2017/11/01/
    us/politics/russia-technology-facebook.html?_r=0
Faux, Jeff (2012). *The Servant Economy*. New York: John Wiley & Sons, Inc.
Fearon, Peter (1979). *Origins and Nature of the Great Slump, 1929–1932*. Atlantic Highlands,
    NJ: Humanities Press.
Federal Reserve Bank of St. Louis (2012, 2016). "All Employees: Manufacturing." https://
    research.stlouisfed.org/fred2/series/MANEMP
Federal Reserve System (2006). *Flow of Funds Accounts of the United States*. Credit Market
    Debt Outstanding. March 9. www.federalreserve.gov/releases/z1/20060309/Coded/
    coded-4.pdf, and www.federalreserve.gov/releases/z1/20061207/z1r-4.pdf
Federal Reserve System (2011). *Flow of Funds Accounts of the United States*, second quarter
    2011. www.federalreserve.gov/releases/z1/20110916/z1r-1.pdf
Federal Reserve System (2017). *Survey of Consumer Finances*. September 27. www.
    federalreserve.gov/econres/scfindex.htm
Fels, Rendigs (1949). "The Long-Wave Depression, 1873–97," *The Review of Economics
    and Statistics*, Vol. 31, No. 1: 69–73.
Ferguson, Thomas and Rogers, Joel (1987). *Right Turn: The Decline of the Democrats and
    the Future of American Politics*. New York: Hill and Wang.
Fiegerman, Seth (2018). "Facebook Admits that Social Media can 'corrode democracy',"
    CNN tech. January 22. http://money.cnn.com/2018/01/22/technology/facebook-
    democracy-social-media/index.html

Field, Alexander (2012). *A Great Leap Forward: 1930s Depression and U.S. Economic Growth*. New Haven: Yale University Press.

Finamore, Carl (2009). "Save Us From Those Who Would Save Us," *CounterPunch*. March 6–8. www.counterpunch.org/2009/03/06/save-us-from-those-who-would-save-us/

Forbath, William E. (1991). *Law and the Shaping of the American Labor Movement*. Cambridge, MA: Harvard University Press.

Ford, Martin (2015). *Rise of the Robots*. New York: Basic Books.

Fortune (1973). "The Clouded Prospects For Corporate Profits." May.

Foster, John Bellamy and Magdoff, Fred (2009). *The Great Financial Crisis: Causes and Consequences*. New York: Monthly Review Press.

Frank, Thomas (2016). "Swat Team – The Media's Extermination of Bernie Sanders, and Real Reform," *Harpers*. November.

Frederick, George (1928). "Is Progressive Obsolescence the Path Toward Increased Consumption?" *Advertising and Selling*, September 5.

Freier, Nathan P. (2008). "Known Unknowns: Unconventional 'Strategic Shocks' in Defense Strategy Development," *The U.S. Army War College*. Strategic Studies Institute. November 4. www.strategicstudiesinstitute.army.mil/pubs/display.cfm?pubID=890

Frey, Carl Benedikt (2015). "How to Prevent the End of Economic Growth," *Scientific American*. January 1. www.scientificamerican.com/article/how-to-prevent-the-end-of-economic-growth/

Frey, Carl Benedikt and Osborne, Michael A. (2013). "The Future of Employment: How Susceptible Are Jobs To Computerization?" Oxford University Engineering Sciences Department and the Oxford Martin Programme on the Impacts of Future Technology. September 17. www.oxfordmartin.ox.ac.uk/downloads/academic/The_Future_of_Employment.pdf

Frey, Carl Benedikt and Osborne, Michael A. (2015). "Technology at Work: The Future of Innovation and Employment," *Citi GPS*. February. www.oxfordmartin.ox.ac.uk/downloads/reports/Citi_GPS_Technology_Work.pdf

Friedman, Milton (1970). "The Social Responsibility of Business is to Increase its Profits," *The New York Times Magazine*, September 13.

Fry, Richard (2017). "It's becoming more common for young adults to live at home – and for longer stretches," *Pew Research Center*. May 5. www.pewresearch.org/fact-tank/2017/05/05/its-becoming-more-common-for-young-adults-to-live-at-home-and-for-longer-stretches/

Furman, Jason and Orszag, Peter (2015). "A Firm-Level Perspective on the Role of Rents in the Rise of Inequality," *The White House*. October 16. https://obamawhitehouse.archives.gov/sites/default/files/page/files/20151016_firm_level_perspective_on_role_of_rents_in_inequality.pdf

Gabler, Neal (2016). "The Secret Shame of Middle Class Americans," *The Atlantic*. May. www.theatlantic.com/magazine/archive/2016/05/my-secret-shame/476415/

Galbraith, James K. (2009). "A 'People First' Strategy: Credit Cannot Flow Where There Are No Creditworthy Borrowers or Profitable Projects," *The Levy Economics Institute*, Strategic Analysis. April.

Galbraith, James K. (2014). *The End of Normal*. New York: Simon & Schuster.

Galbraith, John Kenneth (1954). *The Great Crash of 1929*. Boston: Houghton Mifflin.

Galbraith, John Kenneth (1956). *American Capitalism*. New York: Houghton Mifflin.

Galea, Sandro (2011). "How Many U.S. Deaths are Caused by Poverty, Lack of Education, and Other Social Factors?" Columbia University, Mailman School of Public Health. July 5. www.mailman.columbia.edu/public-health-now/news/how-many-us-deaths-are-caused-poverty-lack-education-and-other-social-factors

Garraty, John A. (1971). *The American Nation: A History of the United States*. New York: Harper & Row.

Gengarelly, W. Anthony (1996). *Distinguished Dissenters and Opposition to the 1919–1920 Red Scare*. Lewiston, New York: Edwin Mellen Press.

Gianchandani, Erwin (2012). "Robotics and Automation: The Future of Manufacturing," Community Computing Consortium. August 19. www.cccblog.org/2012/08/19/robotics-and-automation-the-future-of-manufacturing/

Gilens, Martin (2007). "Inequality and Democratic Responsiveness in the United States," Politics Department, Princeton University. www.princeton.edu/~piirs/events/PU%20Comparative%20Conf%20May%202007%20Gilens.pdf

Gilens, Martin (2011). "Policy Consequences of Representational Inequality," in *Who Gets Represented?*, Enns, Peter K. and Wlezein, Christopher (eds). New York: Russell Sage.

Gilens, Martin (2012). "Under the Influence," *Boston Review*. July 1. http://bostonreview.net/comment/reply/3117

Gilens, Martin and Page, Benjamin (2014). "Testing Theories of American Politics: Elites, Interest Groups, and Average Citizens," *Perspectives on Politics*. Vol. 12, Issue 3: 564–81.

Glyn, A. et al. (1990). "The Rise and Fall of the Golden Age," in Marglin, Stephen A. and Schor, Juliet B. (eds.) *The Golden Age of Capitalism: Reinterpreting the Postwar Experience*. New York: Oxford University Press.

Goldfield, Michael (1989). "Worker Insurgency, Radical Organization and New Deal Labor Legislation," *American Political Science Review*. Vol. 83.

Goldstein, Robert J. (1978). *Political Repression in Modern America From 1870 to the Present*. Cambridge, MA: Schenkman Publishing Co.

Goodman, Peter S. and Gretchen Morgenson (2008). "Saying Yes, WaMu Built Empire on Shaky Loans," *The New York Times*. December 27.

Goodman, Peter S. and Healy, Jack (2009). "Job Losses Hint at Vast Remaking of U.S. Economy," *The New York Times*. March 6. www.nytimes.com/2009/03/07/business/economy/07jobs.html?pagewanted=all&_r=0

Goodman, Peter S. and Soble, Jonathan (2017). "Global Economy's Stubborn Reality: Plenty of Work; Not Enough Pay," *The New York Times*. October 7. www.nytimes.com/2017/10/07/business/unemployment-wages-economy.html?_r=0

Goos, M. and Manning, A. (2007). "Lousy and Lovely Jobs: The Rising Polarization of Work in Britain," *Review of Economics and Statistics*. Vol. 89, No. 1.

Goos, M. et al. (2009). "Job Polarization in Europe," *American Economic Review*. Vol. 99, No. 2.

Gordon, R. A. (1955). "Investment Opportunities in the United States Before and After World War II," in Erik Lundberg (ed.), *The Business Cycle in the Post-War World*. New York: St. Martin's Press.

Gordon, Robert A. (1974). *Economic Instability & Growth: The American Record*. New York: Harper & Row.

Gordon, R. J. and Baily, M. N. (1993). "The Jobless Recovery: Does It Signal a New Era of Productivity-Led Growth?" *Brookings Papers on Economic Activity*. No. 1.

Gordon, Robert J. (2012). "Is US Economic Growth Over? Faltering Innovation Confronts the Six Headwinds," Center For Economic Policy Research, *Policy Insight*. No. 63. September. www.nber.org/papers/w18315.pdf

Gordon, Robert J. (2014). "The Demise of U.S. Economic Growth: Restatement, Rebuttal, and Reflections," National Bureau of Economic Research. Working Paper 19895 www.nber.org/papers/w19895

Gordon, Robert J. (2016) *The Rise and Fall of American Growth*. Princeton, NJ: Princeton University Press.

Gould, Elise (2013). "The Top One Percent Take Home 20 Percent of America's Income," *Economic Policy Institute*. Economic Snapshot. July 18. www.epi.org/publication/top-1-earners-home-20-americas-income/

Graetz, George and Michaels, Guy (2015). "Robots at Work," London School of Economics, Centre For Economic Performance. Discussion Paper No. 1335. March. http://cep.lse.ac.uk/pubs/download/dp1335.pdf

Greenhouse, Steven (2011). "The Wageless, Profitable Recovery," Economix, *The New York Times*. June 30. http://economix.blogs.nytimes.com/2011/06/30/the-wageless-profitable-recovery/?_r=0

Grim, Ryan (2011). "Dick Durbin: Banks 'Frankly Own the Place'," *Huffington Post*. May 25. www.huffingtonpost.com/2009/04/29/dick-durbin-banks-frankly_n_193010.html

Groshen, E. L. and Potter, S. (2003). "Has Structural Change Contributed to a Jobless Recovery?" Federal Reserve Bank of New York, *Current Issues in Economics and Finance*. Vol. 9, No. 8: 1–7. www.ny.frb.org/research/current_issues/ci9-8.pdf

Gutstein, Donald (2009). *Not a Conspiracy Theory*. Toronto: Key Porter Books.

Hacker, Jacob (2006). *The Great Risk Shift*. New York: Oxford University Press.

Hacker, Jacob and Pierson, Paul (2011). *Winner-Take All Politics: How Washington Made the Rich Richer and Turned its Back on the Middle Class*. New York: Simon & Schuster.

Hansen, Alvin (1939). "Economic Progress and Declining Population Growth," *American Economic Review*. Vol. 29, March.

Hansen, Alvin (1941). *Fiscal Policy And Business Cycles*. New York: Allen & Unwin.

Harding, Robin (2013). "Corporate Investment: A Mysterious Divergence," *Financial Times*. July 24. www.ft.com/intl/cms/s/0/8177af34-eb21-11e2-bfdb-00144feabdco.html#axzz3sMPWqPJg

Hardt, Michael (2007). "Jefferson and Democracy," *American Quarterly*. Vol. 59, No.1: 41–78.

Harrington, Michael (1962). *The Other America: Poverty in America*. New York: Macmillan.

Hartmann, Thom (2013). *The Crash of 2016: The Plot to Destroy America – and What We Can Do to Stop It*. New York: Twelve (Hatchette Book Group).

Hawkins, Andrew J. (2017). "Uber's Self-Driving Cars Are Now Picking Up Passengers In Arizona," *The Verge*. February 21. www.theverge.com/2017/2/21/14687346/uber-self-driving-car-arizona-pilot-ducey-california

Heilbroner, Robert and Singer, Aaron (1994). *The Economic Transformation of America: 1600 to the Present*. New York: Harcourt Brace.

Heilbroner, Robert and Milberg, William (1996). *The Crisis of Vision in Modern Economic Thought*. Cambridge: Cambridge University Press.

Heilbroner, Robert and Milberg, William (1998). *The Making of Economic Society*. Englewood Cliffs, NJ: Prentice Hall.

Henle, Peter (1972). "Exploring the Distribution of Earned Income," *Monthly Labor Review Reader*, Issue 1868. Washington, DC: United States Bureau of Labor Statistics.

Henwood, Doug (2010). "What a Damn Mess," *Left Business Observer*. No. 130, November. www.leftbusinessobserver.com/DamnMess.html

Hicks, Michael J. and Devaraj, Srikant (2017). "The Myth and the Reality of Manufacturing in America," Center For Business And Economic Research, Ball State University. April. http://conexus.cberdata.org/files/MfgReality.pdf

Hill, Steven (2015). "The Future of Work in the Uber Economy," *Boston Review*. July 22. http://bostonreview.net/us/steven-hill-uber-economy-individual-security-accounts

Hoffman, Liz and Tracy, Ryan (2017). "Fed 'Stress Tests' Clear All Banks to Issue Payouts to Shareholders," *The Wall Street Journal*. June 28. www.wsj.com/articles/feds-stress-tests-all-banks-cleared-on-payouts-to-shareholders-1498681800

Hofstadter, Richard (1960). *The Age of Reform*. New York: Vintage.

Holt, Charles (1977). "Who Benefited From the Prosperity of the Twenties?" *Explorations in Economic History*. Vol. 14.

Hoogvelt, Ankie (2001). *Globalization and the Postcolonial World*. Second edition. Baltimore: The Johns Hopkins University Press.

Hoover, Herbert (ed.) (1929). *Recent Economic Changes in the United States: Report of the Committee on Recent Economic Changes*. New York: McGraw-Hill.

Hoover, Herbert (ed.) (1933). *Recent Social Trends in the United States: Report of the Committee on Recent Economic Changes. Vols. I and II*. New York: McGraw-Hill.

House of Representatives (1934). *Investigation of Nazi Propaganda Activities and Investigations of Certain Other Propaganda Activities*. Seventy Third Congress, Second Session, Washington, DC. December 29.

Huddleston, Cameron (2016). "69% of Americans Have Less Than $1,000 in Savings," *GoBankingRates*. September 19. www.gobankingrates.com/personal-finance/data-americans-savings/

Hudson, Michael (2015a). *Killing the Host*. Dresden: Islet.

Hudson, Michael (2015b). "Playing the Pension Funds," *Michael Hudson.org*. January 5. http://michael-hudson.com/2015/01/playing-the-pension-funds/

Hudson, Michael (2017). *J is For Junk Economics*. Dresden: Islet.

Humes, Edward (2006). *Over Here: How the GI Bill Transformed the American Dream*. New York: Harcourt Brace.

Hussey, Andrew (2014). "Occupy Was Right: Capitalism Has Failed the World," *The Guardian*. April 13.

Huston, James L. (1993). "The American Revolutionaries, the Political Economy of Aristocracy, and the American Concept of the Distribution of Wealth," *American Historical Review*. October.

Immelt, Jeffrey (2009). "An American Renewal." www.reliableplant.com/Read/18494/american-renewal-immelt-addresses-detroit-econ-club

Investor's Business Daily (2013). Editorial: "Obama Calls Income Gap 'Wrong' – After Widening It." July 30.

Irvin, George (2008). *Super Rich: The Rise of Inequality in Britain and the United States*. Cambridge: Polity Press.

Jackson, Kenneth T. (1987). *Crabgrass Frontier: The Suburbanization of the United States*. New York: Oxford University Press.

Jaimovich, Nir and Siu, Henry (2012). "The Trend is the Cycle: Job Polarization and Jobless Recoveries," National Bureau of Economic Research. Working Paper No. 18334, August 2012. www.nber.org/papers/w18334

Jacobs, Ken et al. (2016). "Producing Poverty: The Public Cost of Low-Wage Production Jobs in Manufacturing," UC Berkeley Center for Labor Research and Education. May. http://laborcenter.berkeley.edu/pdf/2016/Producing-Poverty.pdf

Javelosa, June (2017). "Robo Revolution: A Factory Cut Labor Costs in Half, Thanks to Tiny Robots," *Futurism*. April 22. https://futurism.com/3-tiny-robots-help-cut-chinese-warehouse-labor-costs-by-half-kelsey/

Jerome, Harry (1934). *Mechanization in Industry*. New York: National Bureau of Economic Research.

Johnson, Angela (2013). "76% of Americans are Living Paycheck-to-Paycheck," *CNN Money*. June 24. http://money.cnn.com/2013/06/24/pf/emergency-savings/

Johnson, Lyndon B. (1964). *State of the Union Address*. In Schlesinger, Arthur M. and Israel, Fred (1966). *The State of the Union Messages of the Presidents, 1790–1966*. 3 vols., pp.3156–61. New York: Chelsea House.

Johnson, Matthew (ed.) (2014). *Precariat: Labour, Work and Politics*. New York: Routledge.

Johnson, Simon (2009). "The Silent Coup." *The Atlantic.* May. http://www.theatlantic. com/magazine/archive/2009/05/the-quiet-coup/307364/

Johnson, Simon and Kwak, James (2011). *13 Bankers: The Wall Street Takeover and the Next Financial Meltdown.* New York: Vintage.

Judson, Bruce (2009). *It Could Happen Here: America on the Brink.* New York: Harper.

Kaplan, Jerry (2015). *Humans Need Not Apply.* New Haven: Yale University Press.

Karabarbounis, Loukas and Neiman, Brent (2013). "The Global Decline of the Labor Share," *The National Bureau of Economic Research.* Working Paper No. 19136, June. www.nber.org/papers/w19136

Karlin, Mark (2017). "Extreme Capitalism and the Case For a Guaranteed Income," *Truthout.* Interview with Paul Buchheit, June 25. www.truth-out.org/opinion/ item/41041-extreme-capitalism-and-the-case-for-a-guaranteed-income

Katz, Lawrence F. and Krueger, Alan B. (2016). "The Rise and Nature of Alternative Work Arrangements in the United States, 1995–2015," *Princeton University and NBER.* March 29. http://scholar.harvard.edu/files/lkatz/files/katz_krueger_cws_v3.pdf?m=1459369766

Katznelson, Ira (2013). *Fear Itself: The New Deal and the Origins of Our Times.* New York: Liveright Publishing Corporation.

Keohane, Joe (2017). "What News-Writing Bots Mean for the Future of Journalism," *Wired.* February 16. www.wired.com/2017/02/robots-wrote-this-story

Keynes, John Maynard [1925]. *A Short View of Russia.* (1972a): Donald Moggridge (ed.) *Collected Writings, Vol. IX, Essays in Persuasion,* 253–71. New York: Macmillan.

Keynes, John Maynard [1925]. *Am I a Liberal?* (1972b): Donald Moggridge (ed.) *Collected Writings, Vol. IX, Essays in Persuasion,* 295–306. New York: Macmillan.

Keynes, John Maynard (1930). *A Treatise On Money.* New York: Harcourt Brace.

Keynes, John Maynard [1930]. *Economic Possibilities For Our Grandchildren.* (1972c): Donald Moggridge (ed.) *Collected Writings, Vol. IX, Essays in Persuasion,* 321–34. New York: Macmillan.

Keynes, John Maynard [1931]. *Economy.* (1972d): Donald Moggridge (ed.) *Collected Writings, Vol. IX, Essays in Persuasion,* 135–49. New York: Macmillan.

Keynes, John Maynard [1932]. *Towards the General Theory.* (1979): Donald Moggridge (ed.) *Collected Writings, Vol. XXIX, The General Theory and After: A Supplement,* 35–160. New York: Macmillan.

Keynes, John Maynard [1933]. *National Self-Sufficiency.* (1982a): Donald Moggridge (ed.) *Collected Writings, Vol. XXI, Activities 1931–1939. World Crises and Policies in Britain and America,* 233–46. New York: Macmillan.

Keynes, John Maynard [1933]. *Spending and Saving.* (1982b): Donald Moggridge (ed.) *Collected Writings, Vol. XXI, Activities 1931–1939. World Crises and Policies in Britain and America,* 145–54. New York: Macmillan.

Keynes, John Maynard (1934). "Is the Economic System Self-Adjusting?" BBC radio address, reprinted in *The New Republic,* 1985, 85–7.

Keynes, John Maynard [1936] (1964). *The General Theory of Employment, Interest, and Money.* New York: Harcourt, Brace & World, Inc.

Keynes, John Maynard [1937]. *The Galton Lecture: Some Economic Consequences of a Declining Population.* (1973): Donald Moggridge (ed.) *Collected Writings, Vol. XIV, The General Theory and After. Part II: Defence and Development,* 124–33. New York: Macmillan.

Keynes, John Maynard [1937]. *How to Avoid a Slump.* (1982c): Donald Moggridge (ed.) *Collected Writings, Vol. XXI, Activities 1931–1939. World Crises and Policies in Britain and America,* 384–96. New York: Macmillan.

Keynes, John Maynard [1942]. *How Much Does Finance Matter?* (1980a): Donald Moggridge (ed.) *Collected Writings, Vol. XXVII, Activities 1940–1946. Shaping the Post-War World: Employment and Commodities*, 264–71. New York: Macmillan.

Keynes, John Maynard [1942]. *National Income and Expenditure After the War.* (1980b): Donald Moggridge (ed.) *Collected Writings, Vol. XXVII, Activities 1940–1946. Shaping the Post-War World: Employment and Commodities*, 280–303. New York: Macmillan.

Keynes, John Maynard [1943]. *The Long-Term Problem of Full Employment.* (1980c): Donald Moggridge (ed.) *Collected Writings, Vol. XXVII, Activities 1940–1946. Shaping the Post-War World: Employment and Commodities*, 320–5. New York: Macmillan.

Keynes, John Maynard [1945]. *Letter to T.S. Eliot.* (1980d): Donald Moggridge (ed.) *Collected Writings, Vol. XXVII, Activities 1940–1946. Shaping the Post-War World: Employment and Commodities*, 383–4. New York: Macmillan.

Keynes, John Maynard [1945]. *National Debt Enquiry: Summary by Lord Keynes of His Proposals.* (1980e): Donald Moggridge (ed.) *Collected Writings, Vol. XXVII, Activities 1940–46. Shaping the Post-War World: Employment and Commodities*, 396–412. New York: Macmillan.

Keyserling, Leon H. (1948). "Inflation: Dangers and Remedies," Council of Economic Advisors. Washington, DC: United States Government Printing Office.

Khatiwada, S. (2010). "Did the Financial Sector Profit at the Expense of the Rest of the Economy? Evidence From the United States." Discussion Paper 206. Geneva: International Labor Organization.

Kinzer, Stephen (2017). "America's Slow-Motion Military Coup," *The Boston Globe.* September 16. www.bostonglobe.com/opinion/2017/09/16/america-slow-motion-military-coup/WgzYW9MPBIbsegCwd4IpJN/story.html

Kohler, Thomas C. and Getman, Julius G. (2006). "The Story of NLRB v. Mackay Radio & Telegraph Co.: The High Cost of Solidarity," *Digital Commons @ Boston College Law School.* August. https://tinyurl.com/jxheupz

Kolko, Gabriel (1965). *Railroads and Regulation.* Princeton: Princeton University Press.

Kolko, Gabriel (1967). *The Triumph of Conservatism.* Chicago: Quadrangle Books.

Kosman, Josh (2009). *The Buyout of America.* New York: Portfolio Hardcover.

Kosman, Josh (2016). "Amazon Introduces Next Major Job Killer To Face Americans," *New York Post.* December 5. http://nypost.com/2016/12/05/amazon-introduces-next-major-job-killer-to-face-americans/

Kosman, Josh (2017). "Inside Amazon's Robot-Run Supermarket That Needs Just 3 Human Workers," *New York Post.* February 5. http://nypost.com/2017/02/05/inside-amazons-robot-run-supermarket-that-needs-just-3-human-workers/

Kosoff, Maya (2014). "Uber Drivers Speak Out: We're Making a Lot Less Money Than Uber Is Telling People," *Business Insider.* October 29. www.businessinsider.com/uber-drivers-say-theyre-making-less-than-minimum-wage-2014-10

Kotz, David (1978). *Bank Control of Large Corporations in the United States.* Berkeley: University of California Press.

Kramer, Andrew E. (2017). "Russia May Make All Outside News Media Register As 'Foreign Agents'," *The New York Times.* November 15. www.nytimes.com/2017/11/15/world/europe/russia-news-media-foreign-agents.html

Krippner, Greta (2005). "The Financialization of the American Economy," *Socio-Economic Review.* May.

Krugman, Paul (2009). *The Return of Depression Economics.* New York: W.W. Norton.

Krugman, Paul (2010). "The Third Depression," *The New York Times.* June 27. www.nytimes.com/2010/06/28/opinion/28krugman.html

Krugman, Paul (2012). "Rise of the Robots," *The New York Times.* December 8. https://krugman.blogs.nytimes.com/2012/12/08/rise-of-the-robots/

Krugman, Paul (2013a). "On the Political Economy of Permanent Stagnation," *The New York Times* blog, July 5. https://krugman.blogs.nytimes.com/2013/07/05/on-the-political-economy-of-permanent-stagnation/

Krugman, Paul (2013b). "Secular Stagnation, Coalmines, Bubbles, and Larry Summers," *The New York Times*. November 16. https://krugman.blogs.nytimes.com/2013/11/16/secular-stagnation-coalmines-bubbles-and-larry-summers/

Krugman, Paul (2013c). "A Permanent Slump?" *The New York Times*. November 17. www.nytimes.com/2013/11/18/opinion/krugman-a-permanent-slump.html

Krugman, Paul (2015). "Heartland of Darkness," *The New York Times*. November 4. https://tinyurl.com/ydx85e5a

Kuznets, Simon (1952). "Long-Term Changes in the National Income of the United States of America Since 1870," *Review of Income and Wealth*, Vol. 2: 29–241.

Kuznets, Simon (1961). *Capital in the American Economy*. Princeton: Princeton University Press.

Lamoreaux, Naomi R. (1985). *The Great Merger Movement in American Business, 1895–1904*. New York: Cambridge University Press.

Lapavitsas, Costas (2013). *Profiting Without Production*. London: Verso.

Lasch, Christopher (1972). *The World of Nations*. New York: Vintage.

Lavoie, Marc and Stockhammer, Engelbert (2013). *Wage-led Growth: An Equitable Strategy for Economic Recovery*. New York: Palgrave Macmillan.

Lazonick, William (2011a). "From Innovation to Financialization: How Shareholder Value Ideology is Destroying the US Economy," *The Roosevelt Institute*. June. http://rooseveltinstitute.org/wp-content/uploads/2011/07/innovation-and-financialization.pdf

Lazonick, William (2011b). "How Maximizing Value For Shareholders Robs Workers And Taxpayers," *The Roosevelt Institute*. July. http://rooseveltinstitute.org/how-maximizing-value-shareholders-robs-workers-and-taxpayers/

Lazonick, William (2014). "Profits Without Prosperity," *Harvard Business Review*. September. https://hbr.org/2014/09/profits-without-prosperity

Lazonick, William (2015). "The Myth of Maximizing Shareholder Value," *Institute For New Economic Thinking*. November 18. http://ineteconomics.org/ideas-papers/interviews-talks/the-myth-of-maximizing-shareholder-value

Lazonick, William (2016). "How Stock Buybacks Make Americans Vulnerable to Globalization," *AIR Working Paper #16-0301*. March. www.theairnet.org/v3/backbone/uploads/2016/03/Lazonick.BuybacksAndGlobalization_AIR-WP16-0301.pdf

Lee, Kristen (2016). "Artificial Intelligence, Automation, and the Economy," *The White House*. December 20. https://obamawhitehouse.archives.gov/blog/2016/12/20/artificial-intelligence-automation-and-economy

Leff, Mark H. (1983). "Taxing the 'Forgotten Man': The Politics of Social Security Finance in the New Deal," *The Journal of Economic History*, Vol. 70, No. 2.

Legal Information Institute (no date). 10 U.S. Code 12406, "National Guard in Federal Service," Cornell University Law School. www.law.cornell.edu/uscode/text/10/12406

Leight, Elias (2017). "Google Cracked Down on 340 Fake News Sites Last Year," *Rolling Stone*. January 25. www.rollingstone.com/politics/news/google-cracked-down-on-340-fake-news-sites-in-2016-w462939

Lenzer, Robert (2011). "Harvard's Rogoff Expects Serious Social Unrest Due to Income Disparities in the U.S." *Forbes*. February 10. www.forbes.com/sites/robertlenzner/2011/02/10/expect-serious-social-unrest-due-to-income-disparities-in-the-u-s/#4c c82cae3d8f

Leontief, Wassily (1983). "National Perspective: The Definition of Prospects and Opportunities," *The Long-Term Impact of Technology on Employment and Unemployment, A National Academy of Engineering Symposium*. Washington DC: National Academy Press.

Leopold, Les (2009). *The Looting of America*. Vermont: Chelsea Green Publishing.

Leuchtenburg, William E. (1963). *Franklin D. Roosevelt and the New Deal: 1932–1940*. New York: Harper Torchbooks.

Leven, Maurice et al. (1934). *America's Capacity to Consume*. Washington, DC: The Brookings Institution.

Levine, Andrew (2014). "What Is Clintonism?" *CounterPunch*. July 25–27. www.counterpunch.org/2014/07/25/what-is-clintonism/

Levine, Rhonda (1988). *Class Struggle and the New Deal*. Lawrence: University Press of Kansas.

Lewis, Colin (2014). "Robots Are Starting to Make Offshoring Less Attractive," *Harvard Business Review*. May. https://tinyurl.com/y7dnnhem

Leyshon, Andrew and Thrift, Nigel (2007). "The Capitalization of Almost Everything," *Theory, Culture & Society*. Vol. 24, Nos. 7–8: 97–115.

Licht, Walter (1995). *Industrializing America*. Baltimore: The Johns Hopkins University Press.

Lichtenstein, Nelson (2013). *State of the Union: A Century of American Labor*. Princeton: Princeton University Press.

Lindorff, Dave (2015). "Cold-War-Style Propaganda Posing as News," *CounterPunch*. January 1. www.counterpunch.org/2015/01/01/cold-war-style-propaganda-posing-as-news/

Lionbridge (2015). "Lionbridge Integrates GeoFluent® Machine Translation with Zendesk Customer Service Platform to Deliver Real-time Multilingual Online Support." www.lionbridge.com/lionbridge-integrates-geofluent-machine-translation-with-zendesk-customer-service-platform-2/

Lippman, Walter (1932). *Public Opinion*. London: Allen & Unwin.

Livingston, James (1986). *Origins of the Federal Reserve System: Money, Class, and Corporate Capitalism, 1890–1913*. Ithaca: Cornell University Press.

Livingston, James (1987). "The Social Analysis of Economic History and Theory: Conjectures on Late Nineteenth-Century American Development," *The American Historical Review*. Vol. 92, No. 1.

Livingston, James (1994). *Pragmatism and the Political Economy of Cultural Revolution, 1850–1940*. Chapel Hill: The University of North Carolina Press.

Livingston, James (2009). "Their Great Depression and Ours," *Challenge*. Vol. 52, No. 3.

Livingston, James (2011). *Against Thrift*. New York: Basic Books.

Lockard, C. Brett and Wolf, Michael (2012a). "Employment outlook: 2010–2020. Occupational employment projections to 2020," Bureau of Labor Statistics. *Monthly Labor Review*. January. www.bls.gov/opub/mlr/2012/01/art5full.pdf

Lockard, C. Brett and Wolf, Michael (2012b). "The 2010–20 Job Outlook in Brief," Bureau of Labor Statistics. *Occupational Outlook Quarterly*. Spring. www.bls.gov/careeroutlook/2012/spring/spring2012ooq.pdf

Lombos, Darlene et al. (2014). "The Shell Game of Contingent Employment," *Political Research Associates*. September 1. www.politicalresearch.org/2014/09/01/the-shell-game-of-contingent-employment/#sthash.OQMXcYfI.dpbs

Long, Heather (2017). "Half the Jobs in America Pay Less Than $18 an Hour. Can Trump Help?" *The Washington Post*. August 24. https://tinyurl.com/yb2xjsvs

Lorant, John H. (1975). *The Role of Capital-Improving Innovations in American Manufacturing During the 1920s*. San Francisco: Arno Press.

Lowrey, Annie (2013). "The Rich Get Richer Through the Recovery," *The New York Times*, Economix. September 23. https://tinyurl.com/y7lky79m

Lowrey, Annie (2014). "Recovery Has Created Far More Low-Wage Jobs Than Better-Paid Ones," *The New York Times*. April 27. www.nytimes.com/2014/04/28/business/economy/recovery-has-created-far-more-low-wage-jobs-than-better-paid-ones.html?_r=0

Lynd, Robert and Lynd, Helen (1959). *Middletown: A Study in Modern American Culture*. New York: Harcourt Brace Javanovich.

MacEwan, Arthur (2014). "Why the Shift From Production to Speculation?" *Dollars & Sense*. May/June.

MacEwan, Arthur (2016). "Stock Buybacks: Any Positive Outcome?" *Dollars & Sense*. November/December.

Maddison, Angus (1995). *Explaining the Economic Performance of Nations*. Brookfield, VT: Edward Elgar.

Magdoff, Harry and Sweezy, Paul (1987). *Stagnation and the Financial Explosion*. New York: Monthly Review Press.

Magdoff, Fred and Yates, Michael (2009). *The ABCs of the Economic Crisis*. New York: Monthly Review Press.

Marglin, Stephen A. (1990). "Lessons of the Golden Age: An Overview," in Marglin, Stephen A. and Schor, Juliet B. (eds.) *The Golden Age of Capitalism: Reinterpreting the Postwar Experience*. New York: Oxford University Press.

Markoff, John (2012). "Skilled Work, Without the Worker," *The New York Times*. August 18. www.nytimes.com/2012/08/19/business/new-wave-of-adept-robots-is-changing-global-industry.html?pagewanted=all&_r=0

Markoff, John (2015). *Machines of Loving Grace*. New York: HarperCollins Publishers.

Marshall, Alex (2017). "From Jingles to Pop Hits, A.I. Is Music to Some Ears," *The New York Times*. January 22. www.nytimes.com/2017/01/22/arts/music/jukedeck-artificial-intelligence-songwriting.html

Marshall, Alfred (1961). *Principles of Economics, Vol. I*. London: MacMillan and Co. For the Royal Economics Society.

Martens, Pam and Martens, Russ (2015). "Keep Your Eye on Junk Bonds: They're Starting To Behave Like '08," *Wall Street on Parade*. August 18. http://wallstreetonparade.com/2015/08/keep-your-eye-on-junk-bonds-theyre-starting-to-behave-like-08/

Martin, Patrick (2016). "Economic Inequality Soars in U.S.," *World Socialist Web Site*. July 2. www.wsws.org/en/articles/2016/07/02/rich-j02.html?view=print

Martinot, Steve (2015). "Police Torture and the Real Militarization of Society," *CounterPunch*. November 11. www.counterpunch.org/2015/11/11/police-torture-and-the-real-militarization-of-society/

Marx, Karl [1885] (1967a). *Capital*. Vol. II. New York: International Publishers.

Marx, Karl [1894] (1967b). *Capital*. Vol. III. New York: International Publishers.

Marx, Karl [1932] (1969). *The German Ideology*. New York: International Publishers.

Mason, J. W. (2015). "Disgorge the Cash: The Disconnect Between Corporate Borrowing and Investment," *The Roosevelt Institute*. February 25. http://rooseveltinstitute.org/wp-content/uploads/2015/09/Disgorge-the-Cash.pdf

Massachusetts Employee Task Force on the Underground Economy and Employee Misclassification (2013). *2013 Annual Report*. www.mass.gov/lwd/eolwd/jtf/annual-report-2013.pdf

May, Kate Torgovnick (2013). "Race With the Machines: Erik Brynjolfsson at TED2013," *TED*. February 26. www.ted.com/talks/erik_brynjolfsson_the_key_to_growth_race_em_with_em_the_machines

McCarthy, Justin (2015). "Majority in U.S. Maintain Need for Third Major Party," Gallup. September 25. www.gallup.com/poll/185891/majority-maintain-need-third-major-party.aspx?version=print

McKinsey & Company (2014). "Automation, jobs, and the future of work," McKinsey Global Institute Interview. December. www.mckinsey.com/global-themes/employment-and-growth/automation-jobs-and-the-future-of-work

McNally, David (1999). "The Present as History: Thoughts on Capitalism at the Millennium," *Monthly Review*. Vol. 51, No. 3. https://archive.monthlyreview.org/index.php/mr/article/view/MR-051-03-1999-07_9

McNally, David (2011). *Global Slump*. Oakland, CA: PM Press.

Meckfessel, Shon (2016). *Nonviolence Ain't What It Used To Be: Unarmed Insurrection and the Rhetoric of Resistance*. Oakland: AK Press.

Medawar, Peter (1973). *The Hope of Progress: A Scientist Looks at Problems in Philosophy, Literature and Science*. New York: Anchor Press.

Meyer, Stephen (1981). *The Five-Dollar Day: Labor, Management and Social Control in the Ford Motor Company, 1908–1921*. Albany: SUNY Press.

Mettler, Suzanne (2007). *Soldiers to Citizens: The G.I. Bill and the Making of the Greatest Generation*. New York: Oxford University Press.

Mickle, Tripp (2017). "Apple's Cash Hoard Set to Top $250 Billion," *The Wall Street Journal*. April 30.

Milberg, William and Winkler, Deborah (2010). "Financialization and the Dynamics of Offshoring in the USA," *Cambridge Journal of Economics*. Vol. 34.

Mill John Stuart [1848] (1909). *Principles of Political Economy With Some of Their Applications to Social Philosophy*. *Vol. II*. New York: D. Appleton and Co.

Miller, Claire Cain (2016). "Robot Revolution: The Long-Term Jobs Killer is Not China. It's Automation," *The New York Times*. December 21. www.nytimes.com/2016/12/21/upshot/the-long-term-jobs-killer-is-not-china-its-automation.html?_r=0

Mills, Frederick C. (1932). *Economic Tendencies in the United States: Aspects of Pre-War and Post-War Changes*. Cambridge, MA: National Bureau of Economic Research.

Minsky, Hyman (1968). "Effects of Shifts in Aggregate Demand on Income Distribution," *American Journal of Agricultural Economics*. Vol. 50, No. 2.

Mishel, Lawrence and Davis, Alyssa (2015). "Top CEOs Make 300 Times More Than Typical Workers: Pay Growth Surpasses Stock Gains and Wage Growth of Top 0.1 Percent," *Economic Policy Institute*. Issue Brief #399, June 21. www.epi.org/publication/top-ceos-make-300-times-more-than-workers-pay-growth-surpasses-market-gains-and-the-rest-of-the-0-1-percent/

Mitchell, Broadus (1947). *Depression Decade: From New Era Through New Deal: 1920–1941*. New York: Rinehart and Co.

Monga, Vipal et al. (2015). "As Activism Rises, U.S. Firms Spend More on Buybacks Than Factories," *The Wall Street Journal*. May 26. www.wsj.com/articles/companies-send-more-cash-back-to-shareholders-1432693805

Morduch, Jonathan and Schneider, Rachel (2017a). "The Power of Predictable Paychecks," *The Atlantic*. May 24. www.theatlantic.com/business/archive/2017/05/financial-diaries-predictable-paychecks/527100/

Morduch, Jonathan and Schneider, Rachel (2017b). *The Financial Diaries: How American Families Cope in a World of Uncertainty*. Princeton: Princeton University Press.

Moseley, Fred (2013). "The Bailout of the 'Too-Big-To-Fail' Banks: Never Again," in Wolfson, Martin H. and Epstein, Gerald A. (eds), *The Handbook of the Political Economy of Financial Crises*. New York: Oxford University Press.

Murad, Anatol (1954). "Net Investment and Industrial Progress," in Kenneth K. Kurihara (ed.) *Post-Keynesian Economics*. New Brunswick, NJ: Rutgers University Press.

Murphy, Maxwell et al. (2013). "Corporate Results Expose Lack of Confidence," *The Wall Street Journal*. November 18. http://blogs.wsj.com/cfo/2013/11/19/corporate-results-expose-lack-of-confidence/

Murray, Robert K. (1964). *Red Scare: A Study of National Hysteria, 1919–1920*. New York: McGraw Hill.

Nasser, Alan (1976). "The Twilight of Capitalism: Contours of the Emerging Epoch," *Critical Sociology*. Vol. 6, January.

Nasser, Alan (2014). "The Case Against Labor-Market Individualism," *CounterPunch*. October 30. www.counterpunch.org/2014/10/30/the-case-against-labor-market-individualism

National Employment Law Project (2012). *The Low-Wage Recovery and Growing Inequality*. Data Brief. August. www.nelp.org/publication/4050/

Nell, Edward (1988). *Prosperity and Public Spending: Transformational Growth and the Role of Government*. Boston: Unwin Hyman.

Nell, Edward (2005). *The General Theory of Transformational Growth: Keynes After Sraffa*. Cambridge: Cambridge University Press.

New Economics Foundation (NEF) (2011). *Response to Independent Commission on Banking Issues Paper*. December 3. https://tinyurl.com/yaj6c233

The New York Times (2000). "The Plunge in Home Health Care," Editorial. April 25.

Nicholson, Philip Yale (2004). *Labor's Story in the United States*. Philadelphia: Temple University Press.

Nordhaus, W. D. (1972), "The Worldwide Wage Explosion," *Brookings Papers on Economic Activity*. Washington, DC: The Brookings Institution.

Obama, Barack (2006). *The Audacity of Hope*. New York: Three Rivers Press.

Obama, Barack (2009a). *State of the Union Address*. http://www.cnn.com/2010/politics/01/27/sotu.transcript/index.html

Obama, Barack (2009b). *Remarks on the Economy*. www.nytimes.com/2009/04/14/us/politics/14obama-text.html

Obama, Barack (2013). "Remarks by the President on Economic Mobility," White House Press Office. December 4. www.whitehouse.gov/the-press-office/2013/12/04/remarks-president-economic-mobility

Obama, Barack (2014). *State of the Union Address*. The White House, Office of the Press Secretary. www.whitehouse.gov/the-press-office/2014/01/28/president-barack-obamas-state-union-address

O'Connor, Lydia (2015). "The Middle Class Is No Longer America's Economic Majority," *Huffington Post*. December 9. www.huffingtonpost.com/entry/middle-class-not-majority_5668b75be4b0f290e521f31e?ncid=newsltushpmg00000003

Okun, A. and Perry, G. (eds) (1974). *Brookings Papers on Economic Activity*. No. 1.

Onaran, Ozlem and Stockhammer, Engelbert (2014). "Why the Recovery Needs Wage Growth," *Social Europe*. May 21. www.socialeurope.eu/2014/05/recovery-needs-wage-growth/

Osborne, Michael A. (2015) "What Impact Does the Digital Revolution Have on Work and Inequality?" *Social Europe*. July 24. www.socialeurope.eu/2015/07/impact-digital-revolution-work-inequality/

Osenton, Tom (2004). *The Death of Demand*. New York: Prentice Hall.

Page, Benjamin et al. (2013). "Democracy and the Policy Preferences of Wealthy Americans," *Perspectives on Politics*. Vol. 11, No. 1: 51–73.

Page, Benjamin (2014). "The Majority Does Not Rule in US Democracy," *Social Europe*. May 6. www.socialeurope.eu/us-democracy

Palast, Greg (2001). "The Globalizer Who Came in from the Cold." October 10. www.gregpalast.com/the-globalizer-who-came-in-from-the-cold/

Panitch, Leo and Gindin, Sam (2009). "The Current Crisis: A Socialist Perspective," *Studies in Political Economy*. Vol. 83, Issue 1.

Panitch, Leo and Gindin, Sam (2013). *The Making of Global Capitalism: The Political Economy of American Empire*. London: Verso.

Parrini, Carl P. and Sklar, Martin J. (1983). "New Thinking About the Market, 1896–1904: Some American Economists on Investment and the Theory of Surplus Capital," *The Journal of Economic History*. Vol. XLIII, No. 3.

Pear, Robert (2000). "Health Providers and Elderly Clash on Medicare Funds," *The New York Times*. May 15. www.nytimes.com/2000/05/15/us/health-providers-and-elderly-clash-on-medicare-funds.html

Pecchi, Lorenzo and Piga, Gustavo (2010). *Revisiting Keynes*. Cambridge, MA: The MIT Press.

Perelman, Michael (1996). *The End of Economics*. New York: Routledge.

Perelman, Michael (2006). *Railroading Economics*. New York: Monthly Review Press.

Peterson, Wallace C. (1994). *Silent Depression*. New York: Norton and Company.

Pettifor, Ann (2006). *The Coming First-World Debt Crisis*. New York: Palgrave Macmillan.

Pew Research Center (2014). "AI, Robotics, and the Future of Jobs." August. www.pewinternet.org/2014/08/06/future-of-jobs/

Pew Research Center (2015a). "The American Middle Class Is Losing Ground: No Longer the Majority and Falling Behind Financially." December 9. www.pewsocialtrends.org/2015/12/09/the-american-middle-class-is-losing-ground/

Pew Research Center (2015b). "The Hollowing of the American Middle Class." December 9. www.pewsocialtrends.org/2015/12/09/1-the-hollowing-of-the-american-middle-class/

Pew Research Center (2016). "America's Shrinking Middle Class: A Close Look at Changes Within Metropolitan Areas." May 11. www.pewsocialtrends.org/2016/05/11/americas-shrinking-middle-class-a-close-look-at-changes-within-metropolitan-areas/

Pigou, A. C. (1933). *The Theory of Unemployment*. London: Macmillan.

Piketty, Thomas and Saez, Emmanuel (2006). "The Evolution of Top Incomes: A Historical and International Perspective," *American Economic Association: Papers and Proceedings*, Vol. 96, No.2.

Piketty, Thomas (2014). *Capital in the Twenty-First Century*. Cambridge, MA: Harvard University Press.

Pisani-Ferry, Jean (2015). "The End of Work As We Know It," *Project Syndicate*. July 1. www.project-syndicate.org/commentary/uber-automation-labor-markets-by-jean-pisani-ferry-2015-07?barrier=true

Piven, Frances Fox and Cloward, Richard (1978). *Poor People's Movements: Why They Succeed, When They Fail*. New York: Vintage.

Planes, Alex (2014). "Morgan Stanley's 'Utopian Society' Will Be Built By Tesla Motors Inc. Is It Time To Call A Top?" *Aol.Finance*. February 25. www.aol.com/article/2014/02/25/morgan-stanleys-utopian-society-will-be-built-by-t/20837892/

Plumer, Brad (2013). "How the Recession Turned Middle-Wage Jobs Into Low-Wage Jobs," *The Washington Post*. February 28.

Ponticelli, Jacopo and Voth, Hans-Joachim (2011). "Austerity and Anarchy: Budget Cuts and Social Unrest in Europe, 1919–2008," *Center For Economic Policy Research*. August. http://cepr.org/active/publications/discussion_papers/dp.php?dpno=8513

Porter, Glenn (2006). *The Rise of Big Business: 1860–1920*. Wheeling, IL: Harlan Davidson, Inc.

Powell, Lewis F. (1971). "Confidential Memorandum: Attack on American Free Enterprise System." Washington and Lee University. Powell Archives. http://law2.wlu.edu/deptimages/Powell%20Archives/PowellMemorandumPrinted.pdf

Preis, A. A. (1972). *Labor's Giant Step: The First Twenty Years of the CIO: 1936–55*. New York: Pathfinder Press.

Radice, E. A. and Hugh-Jones, E. M. (1936). *An American Experiment*. London: Oxford University Press.

Rampell, Catherine (2012a). "Majority of New Jobs Pay Low Wages, Study Finds," *The New York Times*. August 30. www.nytimes.com/2012/08/31/business/majority-of-new-jobs-pay-low-wages-study-finds.html?_r=0

Rampell, Catherine (2012b). "When Cheap Foreign Labor Gets Less Cheap," *The New York Times*. December 7. http://economix.blogs.nytimes.com/2012/12/07/when-cheap-foreign-labor-gets-less-cheap/?_r=0

Rapacki, Erin (2013). "Startup Spotlight: Industrial Perception Building 3D Vision Guided Robots," *Spectrum*. January 21. http://spectrum.ieee.org/automaton/robotics/robotics-hardware/startup-spotlight-industrial-perception

Rasmus, Jack (2015). "Corporate Cash Piles Exceed $15 Trillion," *Kyklos Productions*. October 15. www.kyklosproductions.com/posts/index.php?p=283

Rauch, E. (2000). "Productivity and the Workweek," *MIT Computer Science and Artificial Intelligence Laboratory*. Cambridge, MA.

Rauchway, Eric (2008a). *The Great Depression and the New Deal: A Very Short Introduction*. New York: Oxford University Press.

Ray, Gerda (1995). "'We Can Stay Until Hell Freezes Over': Strike Control and the State Police in New York, 1919–1923," *Labor History*. Vol. 36, Issue 3, Summer.

Reich, Robert (2010). *Aftershock: The Next Economy and America's Future*. New York: Alfred A. Knopf.

Reich, Robert (2015a). "Labor Day 2028," *Social Europe*. September 3. www.socialeurope.eu/2015/09/labor-day-2028/

Reich, Robert (2015b). "Why We're All Becoming Independent Contractors," *Social Europe*. February 24. www.socialeurope.eu/2015/02/independent-contractors/

Renshaw, Patrick (1999). "Was There a Keynesian Economy in the USA Between 1933 and 1945?" *Journal of Contemporary History*. Vol. 34, No. 3: 343–4.

Roberts, Paul Craig (2013). *The Failure of Laissez Faire Capitalism*. Atlanta, GA: Clarity Press.

Roberts, Paul Craig (2014). *How America Was Lost*. Atlanta, GA: Clarity Press.

Roberts, Paul Craig (2015). "The Collapsing U.S. Economy," *CounterPunch*. August 11. www.counterpunch.org/2015/08/11/the-collapsing-us-economy/

Robertson, James Oliver (1985). *America's Business*. New York: Hill and Wang.

Robotic Industries Association (2014). "Calculating Your ROI for Robotic Automation: Cost vs. Cash Flow," *Robotics Online*. Editorials. https://tinyurl.com/ya565vvn

Roediger, David (1985–6). "'Not Only the Ruling Classes to Overcome, But Also the So-Called Mob': Class, Skill and Community in the St. Louis General Strike of 1877," *Journal of Social History*. Vol. 19.

Rohit (2013). *It's Not Over: Structural Drivers of the Global Economic Crisis*. New Delhi: Oxford University Press.

Romer, Christina (1989). "The Prewar Business Cycle Reconsidered: New Estimates of Gross National Product, 1869–1908," *Journal of Political Economy*. February.

Roosevelt, Franklin D. (1934). "Address To Advisory Council of the Committee on Economic Security on The Problems of Economic and Social Security." November 14. www.ssa.gov/history/fdrstmts.html

Rosenberg, Nathan (1969). "The Direction of Technological Change: Inducement Mechanisms and Focusing Devices," *Economic Development and Cultural Change*. Vol. 18, No. 1, Part I.

Rosenof, Theodor (1975). *Dogma, Depression and the New Deal: The Debate of Political Leaders Over Economic Recovery*. New York: Associated Faculty Press, Inc.

Roth, Steve and Livingston, James (2011). *Asymptosis*. Spreadsheet, data for Appendix to Livingston, *Against Thrift* (2011). www.asymptosis.com/?s=against+thrift

Rothschild, Emma (1973). *Paradise Lost: The Decline of the Auto Industrial Age*. New York: Vintage.

Rotman, David (2013). "How Technology Is Destroying Jobs." *MIT Technology Review*. June 12. www.technologyreview.com/featuredstory/515926/how-technology-is-destroying-jobs/

Ruccio, David (2017). "Class and Trumponomics," *Real World Economics Review*. Issue No. 78, March 22: 62–85. www.paecon.net/PAEReview/issue78/Ruccio78.pdf

Sachs, Jeffrey D. and Kotlikoff, Laurence J. (2012). "Smart Machines and Long Term Misery," NBER Working Paper No. 18629, December. www.nber.org/papers/w18629.pdf

Saez, Emmanuel (2015a). "Striking it Richer: The Evolution of Top Incomes in the United States. (Updated with 2013 preliminary estimates)." January 23. http://eml.berkeley.edu//~saez/saez-UStopincomes-2013.pdf

Saez, Emmanuel (2015b). "Striking it Richer: The Evolution of Top Incomes in the United States (Updated with 2014 preliminary estimates)." June 25. http://eml.berkeley.edu/~saez/saez-UStopincomes-2014.pdf

Sale, Kirkpatrick (1995). *Rebels Against the Future*. Boston: Addison-Wesley.

Santens, Scott (2015). "Self-Driving Trucks Are Going to Hit Us Like a Human-Driven Truck," *Basic Income*. May 14. https://medium.com/basic-income/self-driving-trucks-are-going-to-hit-us-like-a-human-driven-truck-b8507d9c5961#.fo81xl8ey

Savage, M. and Williams, K. (2008). *Remembering Elites*. Oxford: Blackwell.

Sayer, Andrew (2015). *Why We Can't Afford the Rich*. Bristol: Policy Press.

Schlesinger, Arthur M. (1957). *The Age of Roosevelt: the Crisis of the Old Order: 1919–1933*. Boston: Houghton Mifflin Co.

Schlesinger, Arthur M. and Israel, Fred (1966). *The State of the Union Messages of the Presidents, 1790–1966*. 3 vols. New York: Chelsea House.

Schram, Sanford F. (2015). *The Return of Ordinary Capitalism*. New York: Oxford University Press.

Schwab, Klaus (2016). *The Fourth Industrial Revolution*. Geneva: World Economic Forum.

Scott, Robert E. (2015). "The Manufacturing Footprint and the Importance of U.S. Manufacturing Jobs," *Economic Policy Institute*. January 22. www.epi.org/publication/the-manufacturing-footprint-and-the-importance-of-u-s-manufacturing-jobs/

Selfa, Lance (2000). "Eight Years of Clinton-Gore: The Price of Lesser-Evilism," *International Socialist Review*. Issue 13, August–September: 7–15. https://isreview.org/issues/13/clinton-gore.shtml

Shane, Scott and Goel, Vindu (2017). "Fake Russian Facebook Accounts Bought $100,000 in Political Ads," *The New York Times*. September 6. www.nytimes.com/2017/09/06/technology/facebook-russian-political-ads.html?_r=0

Silk, Leonard (1973). "Profits are Carrots, Juices and Rewards," *The New York Times*. February 11.

Silverstein, Ken (2006). "Barack Obama Inc.: The Birth of a Washington Machine," *Harpers*. November. https://harpers.org/archive/2006/11/barack-obama-inc/

Sirkin, Harold (2015). "Reshoring Is More Than a Buzzword," *Forbes*. July 25. www.forbes.com/sites/haroldsirkin/2015/07/25/reshoring-is-more-than-a-buzzword/#46fbd861f631

Siu, Henry and Jaimovich, Nir (2012). "Jobless Recoveries and the Disappearance of Routine Occupations," VOX, *Center for Economic Policy Research*. www.voxeu.org/article/jobless-recoveries-and-disappearance-routine-occupations

Skidelsky, Robert (2014). "Secular Stagnation and the Road to Full Investment," *Social Europe*. May 22. www.socialeurope.eu/2014/05/secular-stagnation/

Sklar, Martin J. (1992). *The United States as a Developing Country: Studies in U.S. History in the Progressive Era and the 1920s*. New York: Cambridge University Press.

Skocpol, Theda (1995). *Social Policy In The United States*. Princeton: Princeton University Press.

Sloan, Allan (1996). "The Hit Men," *Newsweek*. February 26. www.highbeam.com/doc/1G1-18020688.html

Smith, Allan (2014). "America's SWAT teams are more Dangerous Than Ever," *Business Insider*. June 25. www.businessinsider.com/swat-teams-strayed-from-original-purpose-2014-6

Smith, Hedrick (2012). *Who Stole the American Dream?* New York: Random House.

Smith, Sharon (2006). *Subterranean Fire*. Chicago: Haymarket Books.

Smith, Yves (2014). "AIG Bailout Trial Bombshell III: Paulson Lied to Congress About TARP," *Naked Capitalism*. October 14. www.nakedcapitalism.com/2014/10/aig-bailout-trial-bombshell-iii-paulson-lied-to-congress-about-tarp.html

Solomon, Steven Davidoff (2012). "Profits in G.M.A.C. Bailout To Benefit Financiers, Not U.S.," *The New York Times*. August 21.

Solow, Robert (2008). "Whose Grandchildren?" in Lorenzo Pecchi and Gustavo Piga, *Revisiting Keynes*, 87–93. Cambridge, MA: The MIT Press.

Sommeiller, Estelle et al. (2016). "Income Inequality in the U.S. by State, Metropolitan area, and County," *Economic Policy Institute*. June 16. www.epi.org/publication/income-inequality-in-the-us/

Soper, Spencer and Giammona, Craig (2017). "Amazon Plans to Shed Whole Foods' Pricey Image," *Bloomberg.com News*. https://tinyurl.com/ya5n59bo

Sorkin, Andrew Ross (2008). "One Day Doesn't Make a Trend," *The New York Times*. October 20. www.nytimes.com/2008/10/21/business/21sorkin.html?_r=0

Sorkin, Andrew Ross (2015). "Stock Buybacks Draw Scrutiny From Politicians," *The New York Times*. August 10. www.nytimes.com/2015/08/11/business/stock-buybacks-draw-scrutiny-from-politicians.html?_r=0

Sottile, J. P. (2015). "How the US Set Sail on a Sea of Red Ink," *Truthout*. September 9. www.truth-out.org/news/item/32700-how-the-us-set-sail-on-a-sea-of-red-ink

Sottile, J. P. (2017). "The Robot Economy: Ready or Not, Here It Comes," *Truthout*. May 7. www.truth-out.org/news/item/40495-the-robot-economy-ready-or-not-here-it-comes

Soule, George (1947). *Prosperity Decade: From War to Depression, 1917–1929*. New York: Harper & Row.

Standing, Guy (2014). *The Precariat: The New Dangerous Class*. London: Bloomsbury Academic.

Starr, Barbara and Bruer, Wesley (2015). "Missouri National Guard's Term for Protesters: 'Enemy Forces'," *CNN*. April 17. www.cnn.com/2015/04/17/politics/missouri-national-guard-ferguson-protesters/

Stein, Ben (2006). "In Class Warfare, Guess Which Class is Winning," *The New York Times*. November 26. www.nytimes.com/2006/11/26/business/yourmoney/26every.html?_r=1&

Steinbaum, Marshall (2017). "Why Are Economists Giving Piketty the Cold Shoulder?" *Boston Review*. May 12. http://bostonreview.net/class-inequality/marshall-steinbaum-why-are-economists-giving-piketty-cold-shoulder

Steinberg, Jacob (2012). "The Tech Bubble is Back: It's 1999 All Over Again," *Seeking Alpha*. March 5. http://seekingalpha.com/article/411031-the-tech-bubble-is-back-its-1999-all-over-again

Steiner, Sheyna (2016). "Survey: How Americans Contend With Unexpected Expenses," *Bankrate.com*. January 6. www.bankrate.com/banking/savings/survey-how-americans-contend-with-unexpected-expenses/

Steiner, William Howard (1934). *Money and Banking*. New York: Henry Z. Walck.

Stockhammer, E. (2010). "Financialization and the Global Economy," Political Economy Research Institute. Working Paper No. 240.

Stockhammer, Engelbert and Onaran, Ozlem (2012). "Wage-led Growth: Theory, Evidence, Policy," Political Economy Research Institute. Working Paper No. 300. November 13.

Stoller, Matt (2012). "Growth of Income Inequality is Worse Under Obama Than Bush," *Nakedcapitalism.com*. April. www.nakedcapitalism.com/2012/04/growth-of-income-inequality-is-worse-under-obama-than-bush.html

Stuckler, David and Basu, Sanjay (2013). *The Body Economic: Why Austerity Kills*. New York: Basic Books.

Sum, Andrew et al. (2011). "The 'Jobless and Wageless' Recovery from the Great Recession of 2007–2009: The Magnitude and Sources of Economic Growth Through 2011 I and Their Impacts on Workers, Profits, and Stock Values," Center For Labor Market Studies, Northeastern University. May.

Summers, Lawrence (2013a). Speech at the International Monetary Fund Economic Forum, November 8. https://m.facebook.com/notes/randy-fellmy/transcript-of-larry-summers-speech-at-the-imf-economic-forum-nov-8-2013/585630634864563

Summers, Lawrence (2013b). "Why stagnation might prove to be the new normal," *Financial Times*. December 15. https://next.ft.com/content/87cb15ea-5d1a-11e3-a558-00144feabdco

Summers, Lawrence (2016). "Corporate Profits Are Near Record Highs. Here's Why That's A Problem," *Social Europe*. March 31. www.socialeurope.eu/2016/03/corporate-profits-near-record-highs-heres-thats-problem/

Summers, Lawrence (2017). "The Robots Are Coming, Whether Trump's Treasury Secretary Admits It Or Not," *Social Europe*. May 12. www.socialeurope.eu/2017/05/48469/

Suskind, Ron (2012). *Confidence Men*. New York: Harper Perennial.

Tcherneva, Pavlina R. (2008). "Keynes's Approach to Full Employment: Aggregate or Targeted Demand?" Levy Economics Institute of Bard College. Working Paper No. 542.

Tcherneva, Pavlina R. (2009). "A Message to President Obama: Stop Priming the Pump, Hire the Unemployed," *New Economic Perspectives*. http://neweconomicperspectives.org/2009/07/message-to-president-obama-stop-priming.html

Tcherneva, Pavlina R. (2011a). "Fiscal Policy Effectiveness: Lessons From the Great Recession," Levy Economics Institute of Bard College. Working Paper No. 649.

Tcherneva, Pavlina R. (2011b). "Beyond Pump Priming," One-Pager No. 16, Levy Economics Institute of Bard College.

Tcherneva, Pavlina R. (2011c). "The Case for Labor Demand Targeting," *Journal of Economic Issues*. Vol. XLV, No. 2.

Tcherneva, Pavlina R. (2012). "Permanent On-The-Spot Job Creation – The Missing Keynes Plan for Full Employment and Economic Transformation," *Review of Social Economy*. Vol. LXX, No. 1.

Tcherneva, Pavlina R. (2014). "Growth For Whom?" Levy Economics Institute of Bard College. October 6.

Tcherneva, Pavlina (2015). "When a Rising Tide Sinks Most Boats," *Jacobin*. April 13. www.jacobinmag.com/2015/04/income-inequality-99-1-percent/

Tcherneva, Pavlina (2017). "Inequality Update: Who Gains When Income Grows?" Levy Economics Institute. April. www.levyinstitute.org/publications/inequality-update-who-gains-when-income-grows

Templeton, Graham (2017). "Here Are the Surgeries You Could Soon Get From a Robot," *Inverse*. March 15. www.inverse.com/article/29056-robot-surgeons-medical-surgery-ai-autonomous-doctor

Thayer, Frederick C. (1996). "Balanced Budgets and Depressions," *American Journal of Economics and Sociology*. April. www.questia.com/read/1G1-18262055/balanced-budgets-and-depressions

Thibodeau, Patrick (2014). "One in three jobs will be taken by software or robots by 2025," *Computerworld*. October 6. www.computerworld.com/article/2691607/one-in-three-jobs-will-be-taken-by-software-or-robots-by-2025.html

Thompson, Derek (2015). "A World Without Work," *The Atlantic*. July/August. www.theatlantic.com/magazine/archive/2015/07/world-without-work/395294/

Tighe, Scott and Brown, William (2015). "The Militarization of Law Enforcement: Bypassing the Posse Comitatus Act," *Justice Policy Journal*. Fall. www.cjcj.org/uploads/cjcj/documents/jpj_militarization_of_law_enforcement_-_fall_2015.pdf

Trachtenberg, Alan (2007). *The Incorporation of America*. New York: Hill and Wang.

Trades Union Congress (2013). "How to Boost the Wage Share," Touchstone Pamphlets. www.tuc.org.uk/publications/how-boost-wage-share-0

Tugwell, Rexford C. (1933). "Design For Government," *Political Science Quarterly*, September.

Turner, Adair (2014a). "Do We Face Secular Stagnation?" Panel discussion, Oxford University, February 10. http://podcasts.ox.ac.uk/do-we-face-secular-stagnation-panel-discussion

Turner, Adair (2014b). "Escaping the Debt Addiction: Monetary and Macro-Prudential Policy in the Post Crisis World," *Center For Financial Studies*. February 10. https://tinyurl.com/y7ozsd4p

Turner, Adair (2016). *Between Debt and the Devil: Money, Credit, and Fixing Global Finance*. Princeton: Princeton University Press.

Turse, Nick (2009). *The Complex: How the Military Invades Our Everyday Lives*. New York: Metropolitan Books.

United States Bureau of the Census (1975). *Historical Statistics of the United States, Colonial Times to 1970*. Washington, DC: U.S. Department of Commerce.

United States Bureau of the Census (2012). "Poverty: 2010 and 2011," American Community Survey Briefs. September. www.census.gov/prod/2012pubs/acsbr11-01.pdf

United States Congress (1934). *Public Hearings Report of House Un-American Activities Committee, Investigation of Nazi Propaganda Activities and Investigation of Certain Other Propaganda Activities*, 73rd Congress, 2nd Session, December 24.

United States Congress, Senate Report (1937a). *Violations of Free Speech and Right of Labor*. Committee on Education and Labor, Report on Industrial Espionage. Washington, DC: Government Printing Office.

United States Congress, Senate Report (1937b). *Violations of Free Speech and Right of Labor*. Committee on Education and Labor. Washington, DC: Government Printing Office.

Urie, Rob (2014). "QE, Debt and the Myth of a Liberal Left," *CounterPunch*. October 31. www.counterpunch.org/2014/10/31/qe-debt-and-the-myth-of-a-liberal-left/

U.S. Senate (2017). *Extremist Content and Russian Disinformation Online: Working With Tech To Find Solutions*. Committee on the Judiciary. October 31. www.judiciary.senate.gov/meetings/extremist-content-and-russian-disinformation-online-working-with-tech-to-find-solutions

Vatter, Harold G. (1975). *The Drive to Industrial Maturity*. London: Greenwood Press.

Vatter, Harold G. (1982). "The Atrophy of Net Investment and Some Consequences For the U.S. Mixed Economy," *Journal of Economic Issues*. March: 237–53.

Vatter, Harold G. and Walker, John F. (1990). *The Inevitability of Government Growth*. New York: Columbia University Press.

Vatter, Harold G. and Walker, John F. (1992). "Stagnation and Government Purchases," *Challenge*. November–December.

Vatter, Harold G, Walker, John F. and Alperovitz, Gar (1995). "The Onset and Persistence of Secular Stagnation in the U.S. Economy: 1910–1990," *Journal of Economic Issues*. Vol. XXIX, No. 2, June.

Vespa, Jonathan (2017). "The Changing Economics and Demographics of Young Adulthood: 1975–2016," *United States Bureau of the Census*. Current Population Reports www.census.gov/content/dam/Census/library/publications/2017/demo/p20-579. pdf

Vogel, David (1989). *Fluctuating Fortunes: The Political Power of Business in America*. New York: Basic Books.

Walker, John F. and Vatter, Harold G. (1997). *The Rise of Big Government in the United States*. Armonck, NY: M.E. Sharpe.

Wall Street Journal Almanac 1998. (1997). New York.

Walsh, John V. (2012). "The Myth of U.S. Manufacturing Decline," CounterPunch. October 15. www.counterpunch.org/2012/10/15/the-myth-of-u-s-manufacturing-decline/

Walsh, John V. (2013). "A Quest for New Jobs Where None Exists," *Dissident Voice*. February 25. http://dissidentvoice.org/2013/02/a-quest-for-new-jobs-where-none-exists/

Walton, Gary M., and Ruckoff, Hugh (1990). *History of the American Economy*. New York: Harcourt, Brace and Jovanovich.

Wagner, Kurt (2017). "Facebook is Hiring Another 3,000 People to Pull Down Violent and Inappropriate Content," Recode. May 3. www.recode.net/2017/5/3/15531478/ facebook-hiring-3000-people-violent-inappropriate-video-content-post

Wang, Lu (2016). "There's Only One Buyer Keeping S&P 500's Bull Market Alive," *Bloomberg*. March 13. www.bloomberg.com/news/articles/2016-03-14/there-s-only-one-buyer-keeping-the-s-p-500-s-bull-market-alive

Watkins, John P. (2009). "Staring into the Abyss: The Current Economic Crisis," Gore School of Business Newsletter.

Weber, Lauren (2017). "The End of Employees," *The Wall Street Journal*. February 2. www. wsj.com/articles/the-end-of-employees-1486050443

Weber, Nicholas Fox (2007). *The Clarks of Cooperstown*. New York: Alfred A. Knopf.

Weil, David (2014). *The Fissured Workplace: Why Work Became So Bad For So Many and What Can be Done to Improve It*. Cambridge, MA: Harvard University Press.

Weinberg, Meyer (2003). *A Short History of American Capitalism*. Amherst, MA: New History Press.

Weisenthal, Joe (2012). "The Untold Story Of How Clinton's Budget Destroyed The American Economy," *Business Insider*. September 5. www.businessinsider.com/how-bill-clintons-balanced-budget-destroyed-the-economy-2012-9

Whadcock, Ian (2014). "Technology Isn't Working," *The Economist*. October 4. www. economist.com/news/special-report/21621237-digital-revolution-has-yet-fulfil-its-promise-higher-productivity-and-better

White, Richard (2012). *Railroaded: The Transcontinentals and the Making of Modern America*. New York: W.W. Norton & Co.

Whitney, Mike (2015). "Wall Street Panic," *CounterPunch*. August 14. www.counterpunch. org/2015/08/24/stock-selloff-panic-time-or-a-blip-on-the-radar/

Whitney, Mike (2017). "Let the Buybacks Begin," *CounterPunch* magazine. Vol. 24, No. 4.

Wiebe, Robert H. (1995). *Self-Rule: A Cultural History of American Democracy.* Chicago: University of Chicago Press.

Wilentz, Sean (1984). "Against Exceptionalism: Class Consciousness and the American Labor Movement, 1790–1920," *International Labor and Working Class History.* No. 29, Fall.

Wilkinson, Richard and Pickett, Kate (2010). *The Spirit Level.* New York: Bloomsbury Press.

Williams, Sean (2016). "Nearly 7 in 10 Americans Have Less Than $1,000.00 in Savings," *USA Today.* October 9. www.usatoday.com/story/money/personalfinance/2016/10/09/savings-study/91083712/

Wilson, Thomas (1941). *Fluctuations in Income and Employment.* London: Pitmann & Sons.

Winfield, Nick et al. (2016). "Google and Facebook Take Aim at Fake News Sites," *The New York Times.* November 14. www.nytimes.com/2016/11/15/technology/google-will-ban-websites-that-host-fake-news-from-using-its-ad-service.html

Wiseman, Paul and Condon, Bernard (2013). "Will Smart Machines Create a World Without Work?" Associated Press Yahoo!Finance. http://finance.yahoo.com/news/smart-machines-create-world-without-051025381--finance.html

Wiseman, Paul et al. (2013). "Practically Human: Can Smart Machines Do Your Job," Associated Press *Yahoo!News.* January 25. www.yahoo.com/news/practically-human-smart-machines-job-052642993--finance.html?ref=gs

Wolf, Martin (2012). "Is Unlimited Growth a Thing of the Past?" *Financial Times.* October 2. www.ft.com/intl/cms/s/0/78e883fa-0bef-11e2-8032-00144feabdco.html#axzz3hFmA5NfX

Wolff, Richard D. (2012) *Democracy at Work.* Chicago: Haymarket Books.

Wolman, Leo (1938). *Hours of Work in American Industry.* National Bureau of Economic Research. Bulletin 71, New York: Nov. 27: 1–20. www.nber.org/books/wolm38-1

World Economic Forum (2016). "The Future of Jobs Employment, Skills and Workforce Strategy for the Fourth Industrial Revolution," January. Davos, Switzerland. www.weforum.org/reports/the-future-of-jobs

Wray, L. Randall (2008). "Demand Constraints and Big Government," *Journal of Economic Issues.* Vol. XLII, No. 1, March.

Wray, L. Randall (2017). "Trumponomics: Causes and Prospects," *Real World Economics Review.* Issue No. 78, March. www.paecon.net/PAEReview/issue78/Wray78.pdf

Yadoo, Jordan (2017). "Rich Americans Are Changing What It Means to Be Average," *Bloomberg News.* September 13. www.bloomberg.com/news/articles/2017-09-13/rich-americans-are-changing-what-it-means-to-be-average

Yang, Jia Lynn (2010). "U.S. Companies Buy Back Stock in Droves as They Hold Record Levels of Cash," *The Washington Post.* October 7. www.washingtonpost.com/wp-dyn/content/article/2010/10/06/AR2010100606772.html

Zeiler, David G. (2013). "Robots Taking Jobs From Every Sector of the Economy," *Money Morning.* February 4. https://moneymorning.com/2013/02/04/robots-taking-jobs-from-every-sector-of-the-economy/

Zweig, Jason (2014). "Will Stock Buybacks Bite Back?" *The Wall Street Journal.* March 21. http://blogs.wsj.com/moneybeat/2014/03/21/will-stock-buybacks-bite-back/

INDEX

occupations
  fastest growing, 194
  greatest job loss in middle income, 193
  largest growing, 194
Occupy movement, 6, 176–7, 229
  heightened awareness of inequality, 177
  unites a diverse constituency, 176
offshoring and outsourcing, as weak
    explanations of job loss, 187–8
oligopoly, rules out destructive price
    competition, 31
oligopoly capitalism, formation of, 26–32
organized labor, defeat of by business after
    World War One, 54–5
overinvestment, 21–5
overproduction, 21–5

Page, Benjamin, study of democracy in
    America, 215–16
Panitch, Leo, misconception of nineteenth-
    century U.S. capitalism, 19–20
polarization of the labor force, 193–4,
    196–8, a structural tendency, not an
    empirical trend, 197
political capitalism, 32
poverty, most households in, during the
    1920s, 74
Powell memo, 153–5, business mobilization
    in response to, 155–7
precariat, 203–8
price leadership, 30–2
prices, in the 1920s, 66–8
private equity buyouts (PE), 177–8
production, growth of during 1920s, 61–2,
    66–8
productivity growth
  1920s, 69–70
  always means cutting down on labor, 41
  contribution to emergence of the Great
      Depression, 69
  during the 1920s, 62–5, 67–8
  enables higher wages, 41
  in capital goods industries, 62–5, 235,
      236
  in consumer goods industries and
      distribution of the surplus between
      capital and labor in the
profits
  channeled to finance, 234
  in the 1920s, 66–8
  unnecessary to finance investment, 234

proletarianization, early Americans'
    resistance to, 37–9
propaganda, development of in America,
    213–14
prosperity, and debt, people's, 11
public employment, Keynes on, 9, 253
"public works," essential to maintain
    adequate wages, 253
public investment, 2, 9, 97, 115, 121, 134,
    137, 143, 198, 225, 237
  ongoing, urged by Keynes as necessary
      to avoid depression, 99
  predominance of, as necessary condition
      for averting austerity, 48, 97
Public Works Administration (PWA),
    95–6

quantitative easing, 1, 174–5

railroad, as framework stimulant, 16–17,
    end of expansion of, 49–50
Reaganization of Democratic Party,
    159–62
red scare, after First World War, 55
  after Second World war, 139–40
regulation, 7–8
  initiated by business in early twentieth
      century, 32–4
  reasons for rejection of by business after
      industrialization, 153
regulatory capture, 33–4
Reich, Robert, on automation as great
    source of job loss, 187
Resistance
  actually existing, 227–32
  popular, to corporate combination, 28
robotic technology more efficient than
    human labor, 186
robotization, 11, as creating job loss,
    184–92
Rockefeller, John D., 27
Roosevelt, Franklin Delano
  as fiscal conservative, 9, 92
  as reluctant New Dealer, 92–4
  attacks Hoover from the right, 90
  opposition to "relief," 110–12
  plot to overthrow his administration,
      102–6
  rejects Bonus demands, 91

Sanders, Bernie, 6, 216–17, 226